THE SPIRITUAL VERNACULAR OF THE EARLY OTTOMAN FRONTIER

Edinburgh Studies on the Ottoman Empire
Series Editor: Kent F. Schull

Published and forthcoming titles

Migrating Texts: Circulating Translations around the Ottoman Mediterranean
Edited by Marilyn Booth

Ottoman Sunnism: New Perspectives
Edited by Vefa Erginbaş

Jews and Palestinians in the Late Ottoman Era, 1908–1914: Claiming the Homeland
Louis A. Fishman

The Spiritual Vernacular of the Early Ottoman Frontier: The Yazıcıoğlu Family
Carlos Grenier

Armenians in the Late Ottoman Empire: Migration, Mobility Control and Sovereignty, 1885–1915
David Gutman

The Kizilbash-Alevis in Ottoman Anatolia: Sufism, Politics and Community
Ayfer Karakaya- Stump

Çemberlitaş Hamamı in Istanbul: The Biographical Memoir of a Turkish Bath
Nina Macaraig

Nineteenth-century Local Governance in Ottoman Bulgaria: Politics in Provincial Councils
Safa Saraçoğlu

Prisons in the Late Ottoman Empire: Microcosms of Modernity
Kent F. Schull

Ruler Visibility and Popular Belonging in the Ottoman Empire
Darin Stephanov

Children and Childhood in the Ottoman Empire: From the 14th to the 20th Centuries
Edited by Gulay Yilma and Fruma Zachs

edinburghuniversitypress.com/series/esoe

THE SPIRITUAL VERNACULAR OF THE EARLY OTTOMAN FRONTIER

THE YAZICIOĞLU FAMILY

Carlos Grenier

EDINBURGH
University Press

To the memory of my grandmother,
Nélida Méndez Grenier (1921–2017)

Edinburgh University Press is one of the leading university presses in the UK. We publish academic books and journals in our selected subject areas across the humanities and social sciences, combining cutting-edge scholarship with high editorial and production values to produce academic works of lasting importance. For more information visit our website: edinburghuniversitypress.com

Edinburgh University Press Ltd
The Tun – Holyrood Road
12 (2f) Jackson's Entry
Edinburgh EH8 8PJ

First published in hardback by Edinburgh University Press 2021

Typeset in Jaghbuni by
Servis Filmsetting Ltd, Stockport, Cheshire

A CIP record for this book is available from the British Library

ISBN 978 1 4744 6227 3 (hardback)
ISBN 978 1 4744 6228 0 (paperback)
ISBN 978 1 4744 6230 3 (webready PDF)
ISBN 978 1 4744 6229 7 (epub)

Contents

Notes on Transliteration vii
Acknowledgements ix

Introduction 1
Who Were the Yazıcıoğlus? 3
The International Context 9
Sources 11

1. The Scribe and his Sons 29
Themes 32
Yazıcı Ṣāliḥ and the *Ġāzīs* of Rumelia 33
Meḥmed and Aḥmed, Sons of the Scribe 43
Summary 61

2. The Textual Genealogies of Ottoman Popular Islam 73
Narrative Sources 77
Ḥadīth and *Tafsīr* Sources 81
Miscellaneous Sources 86
Notes on Compositional Method 88
Patterns 90

3. Religion on the Frontier 100
The Nature of the Borderland 103
'To Know the Bond of Islam': From Sacred Knowledge to Communal Identity 114
Conclusion 129

4. The Yazıcıoğlus within Islam 137
The Meaning of the Ibn ʻArabī Tradition 138
Sufi Lineage and Community 151
The Shīʻī–Sunnī Question 155
Apocalypticism 161
Conclusion 171

5. Wonder and Cosmos at the Edge of the World 180
Wonder and Ethics in the *ʻAcāibü'l-Maḫlūqāt* 183
The *Rūḥu'l-Ervāḥ* and the Microcosm 191
Malḥama and Esoteric Revelation 196

Conclusion 206

Appendix 212
Bibliography 214
Index 234

Notes on Transliteration

Arabic: I have used the *International Journal of Middle Eastern Studies* (*IJMES*) system for Arabic and Persian. ال is written as al-, regardless of the vowel or consonant to follow. Diacritics are preserved in all personal names and titles of books and articles. Diacritics are not used in common toponyms.

***Persian*:** *IJMES* is also the basis for Persian transcription. However, the Persian final ه, when representing a vowel, is rendered as *e* rather than *ih*, *eh*, or *ah*, and for Persian words *v* is used instead of *w* to represent و when appropriate. Diacritics are likewise preserved in personal names and titles of books and articles. Diacritics are not used in common toponyms (for example, Khurasan).

Ottoman Turkish: Ottoman Turkish transliteration also follows the *IJMES* scheme in its main points. Long vowel marks are written only in elements that are of Arabic or Persian origin, while consonants are always given full diacritics. However, here I depart from *IJMES* in its use of *q* for ق, *ḫ* for خ and *ġ* for غ. Personal names and titles of books and treatises, when put together from Arabic grammatical constructions but appearing within an Ottoman context, are rendered using Ottoman conventions as follows: Şeyḫ Bedre'd-dīn, *Envārü'l-'Āşıqīn* (rather than Shaykh Badr al-dīn, *Anwār al-'Āshiqīn*, or Şeyḫ Bedr el-Dīn, *Envār el-'Āşıqīn*). For instance, the name of al-Qazwīnī's Arabic geography is written as *'Ajā'ib al-Makhlūqāt*, while Aḥmed Bīcān's Ottoman Turkish version of this text is written as *'Acāibü'l-Maḫlūqāt*. Anatolian and Rumelian place names, unless otherwise noted, are rendered as in modern Turkish (for instance, Konya, not Qonya). Greek names aim to comply with the Library of Congress guidelines, using k for κ and ch for χ.

Distinguishing Arabic, Persian and Ottoman Turkish contexts from each other calls for arbitrary decisions. For Anatolians living prior to the fourteenth century, the Arabic system described above is used, while for those living in the fourteenth century and later the Ottoman system has been applied. For instance, Ṣadr al-dīn Qūnawī [d. 673/1274] is based on the *IJMES* Arabic system, while Cemālu'd-dīn Aqsarāyī [d. 791/1388–89] is based on the Ottoman Turkish system. Individuals migrating between regions in which different languages dominated are usually denoted according to the language of their place of origin and education. The titles of works are always written using the scheme corresponding to the language of their contents.

Acknowledgements

Like all ephemera, this text is written in a script that erases itself. It speaks only to its moment. But even as it passes, it leaves behind countless friendships and relationships that endure. I can only begin to list them all here.

First, I must thank Ayla and Hamid Algar, who long ago introduced me to Turkish and to the study of Islam. Their generosity, ten years ago in Berkeley, continues to be a wellspring that nourishes my professional development. I am also immensely grateful to Baki Tezcan and Munis Faruqui for my first lessons in the historian's craft.

This project started life as a dissertation at the University of Chicago. I owe endless gratitude to Cornell Fleischer, my teacher and friend, who helped me surpass roadblocks both personal and academic, and whose trust in my potential sustained this project. If this study has any insight and depth, it is because of this trust. I thank John Woods, for teaching me how to read and understand the history of the Middle East and the world, and even more for helping me plot a steady course through my studies. And I am indebted to Hakan Karateke, who with patient rigor taught me the art of reading Ottoman Turkish, not just for its meaning, but for its *laṭāʾif*. I must also give thanks to Holly Shissler, Fred Donner, Frank Lewis and Paul Walker for their help.

I relied on the steady support of several institutions: the University of Chicago's Regenstein Library, Chicago's Department of History, the Center for Middle Eastern Studies and the Fulbright Commission in Turkey, which enabled me to conduct research in Istanbul. I owe the final stages of writing, as well as the beginning of a career, to Florida International University in Miami, my home. Without Erik Larson and the rest of the Department of Religious Studies, this study could not have been finished. I cannot express the gratitude I feel to each member of this community. I am also honoured to participate in FIU's Mohsin and Fauzia

Jaffer Center for Muslim World Studies, and I am especially thankful for the guidance of Mohiaddin Mesbahi, whose wisdom and vision nourishes the entire community of Islamic Studies scholars in Miami. Finally, I am grateful for the integrity, kindness and energy of my colleague and friend Iqbal Akhtar, as well as to Zafreen Jaffery. I am extremely grateful for the many ways in which my life has become connected to theirs. I owe them more than I can ever repay.

I must extend a special word of appreciation to Abdullah Uğur of Marmara University. It is thanks to his rigorous scholarship and collaborative spirit that our work on the Yazıcıoğlus has become a fruitful cooperation. His forthcoming study on Aḥmed Bīcān and the *Envārü'l-'Āşıqīn* will, I hope, complement my own study on the family.

I feel gratitude for the compassion, conversation and companionship of my dear friends and colleagues, some of whom include: Óscar Aguirre Mandujano, Nikolay Antov, Toygun Altıntaş, Abdurrahman and Zahit Atçıl, Mohamad Ballan, Mick Bechtel, Nicole Beckmann Tessel, Theo Beers, Evrim Binbaş, Andrea Brown, Tolga Cora, Andrew DeRouin, Madeleine Elfenbein, Annie Greene, Samuel Hodgkin, Nazlı İpek Hüner-Cora, Fatih Kurşun, Molly Laas, Gosia Labno, Liv Leader, Emin Lelic, Christopher Markiewicz, Austin O'Malley, Salma Nassar, Michael Polczynski, Maryam Sabbaghi, Basil Salem, Nir Shafir, Kaya Şahin, Tunç Şen, Pars Tarighy, Ahmet Taşcı, Corey Tazzara, Bill Walsh and Erin Weston. I thank Burcu Yavuz for all that she has given. And I thank Sasha Shirazi for her patience and support, and for being who she is.

Ultimately this book emanates not from my person, but from my family: from my parents, Stephanie and Guillermo Grenier, my sister Sasha and my grandmother Nélida Méndez Grenier (1921–2017). I dedicate this to her memory.

Introduction

By the early fifteenth century, the Ottoman conquests had brought Islamicate culture across the Dardanelles into new lands on the northern shores of the Mediterranean and on the Balkans. Turkish-speaking communities, led by *begs* and *paşas*, but ultimately held together by loyalty to the Ottoman sultan, occupied the quarters of cities such as Edirne, Salonica and Gelibolu. Campaigns and raids by land extended the range of these settlements to the rest of the Southern Balkans and by sea to other shores of the Aegean, everywhere encountering and bringing together complex populations of primarily Greek- and Slavic-speaking Christians. Although these lands were new to Muslims, the society developping there was still imagined as an extension of the Islamic world and of the Turkish-speaking Muslim society of Anatolia whence most of these settlers came. It was still subject to the social, political, intellectual and religious transformations that characterised the *Ḥijrī* ninth century. Scholars, Sufis, soldiers and bureaucrats – with all their ideas and ways of life – moved to the Ottoman frontier lands from Central Anatolia, Syria, Egypt and Iran. Armies like that of Tīmūr, who defeated Sultan Bāyezīd I in 1402, disrupted the region's political ententes; yet, they also stimulated artistic, literary and religious innovations that continued to form part of Ottoman culture and identity long thereafter. In a way, the Muslims of the new Ottoman state balanced between two worlds, between the Balkan and Mediterranean frontier (and the future that these represented), on one hand, and the Islamic faith and cultural norms that sustained their ethical outlook and bound them to a wider intellectual ecumene (and the history that these represented), on the other. From this balance, a new Ottoman Islam was born.

These abstractions are only real insofar as they affect individual human beings – the minds, habits, relationships and religious approaches of each inhabitant of the Ottoman frontier. From the sultan to the farmer, the

Muslims of Rumelia developped an understanding of their place in a society that was in many respects brandnew. It was a country of converts and Christians, speakers of Turkish and Greek, with a politics animated by a changing rhetoric on war, the sultanate and the meaning of Islam. To organise this world for themselves, all Ottoman Muslims had to form novel concepts around the history they had inherited, new notions concerning their social roles as members of a new society and new attitudes towards other Islamic societies and towards the future. At the centre of all these conceptual concerns stood a new understanding of God within the framework of Islam. Thus, both the frontier and the Islamicate ecumene contributed to the subjectivities of each frontier Ottoman. Although we have accounts of relatively few of those who lived and worked within this territory, we are fortunate to know and read the works of one particular family of Ottoman Muslims who reflected these tensions and forged a synthesis expressing, in religious terms, the character of this place and moment. And they did so in a way that was deeply influential and successful, far beyond what they could have imagined during their lifetimes.

This study explores the lives and works of an important family of writers active in the town of Gelibolu (Gallipoli), situated on the crossroads between fifteenth-century intellectual ferment and the experience of the frontier; from this position, they were able to profoundly shape the epistemic contours of nascent Ottoman intellectual life. The Yazıcıoğlus, represented by 'Yazıcı' Ṣāliḥ and his two sons Meḥmed (d. 1451) and Aḥmed (d. ~1466), wrote on cosmology, mysticism and religious instruction, and with each work they contributed to the Ottoman world of ideas as it would develop in later years – despite the fact that they spent their lives in a provincial port-city without any definite connection to the patronage networks of the Ottoman courts in Bursa and Edirne.

In 826/1423, while employed as a scribe, Ṣāliḥ wrote the *Şemsiyye* ('Solar [Poem]'), a Turkish composition on the planets and stars that was read at least until the seventeenth century. Meḥmed, the older son, composed an Arabic religious treatise entitled *Maghārib al-Zamān* ('The Setting-Places of Destiny'), which he in 853/1449 rendered into Turkish verse as *Kitāb-i Muḥammediyye* ('The Muhammedan Volume') – a work reaching such an enormous readership that it would rank as one of the most popular books ever to be produced in Ottoman Turkish, almost venerated as scripture in the provincial cities of the Ottoman Empire and beyond. Equally noteworthy is the *Envārü'l-'Āşıqīn* ('The Lights of the Lovers') by Meḥmed's younger brother Aḥmed (known to posterity as Aḥmed Bīcān, 'the Lifeless', for his ascetic dedication), a book of Turkish prose based on his brother's works. The numerous manuscripts of both texts which are preserved in archives across the Ottoman lands and elsewhere demonstrate their endruing place in *medrese* and domestic religious curricula.

The success of the Yazıcıoğlu family's other works is similarly remarkable. Meḥmed Yazıcıoğlu, prompted by conversations spanning the breadth of the Islamic world at the time, composed a commentary in Arabic on a central Sufi text, the *Fuṣūṣ al-Ḥikam* of Ibn al-ʿArabī. Aḥmed Bīcān, working closely from the *ʿAjā'ib al-Makhlūqāt* ('The Wonders of Creation') by the thirteenth-century Persian geographer Abū Zakariyā Qazvīnī, authored a *Maḫlūqāt* of his own, describing the characteristics of the world's seven climes. In 1453, Aḥmed finished the first edition of his *Kitābü'l-Müntehā* ('The Epilogue'), a translation and drastic expansion of his own brother's commentary on the *Fuṣūṣ*, completing another version of this text in 1465. The *Müntehā* is the most diverse of the brothers' texts. Around that date, Aḥmed also adapted a very old genre of natural-philosophical writing on jewels and precious stones into a short Turkish *Cevhernāme* ('Jewel-book'), authored a brief introduction to the principles of macrocosmic mysticism, titled the *Rūḥu'l-Ervāḥ* ('Spirit of Spirits') and then, shortly before his death, composed the *Bostānü'l-Haqāiq* ('The Garden of Realities'), a prose edition of his father's *Şemsiyye.*

The incredible variety of the writings of the Yazıcıoğlu family – which encompasses tracts on basic religious instruction, popular summaries of natural-philosophical traditions, arguments on apocalypse and piety, as well as learned commentaries on theoretical Sufism – is one of the most interesting and innovative characteristics of this corpus. In a single body of work, a world-encompassing epistemological panorama was thus presented. Considering the immense popularity of almost all these works as well as the fact that many of them were among the first Turkish-language works within their genres, it is perhaps no exaggeration to call the Yazıcıoğlus true creators of Ottoman popular Islam and pioneers of an Ottoman approach to various other intellectual and literary traditions. They expressed, for the first time with such comprehensiveness, the Ottoman spiritual vernacular.

Who Were the Yazıcıoğlus?

While these facts present a compelling argument for the important place that the Yazıcıoğlu family holds within Ottoman and Islamic intellectual history, this kind of description identifying the Yazıcıoğlus with their works and their works with them threatens to conflate the family's story with the history of Ottoman and Turkish genres and literary forms. Rather than proceeding in this direction, this study hopes to engage with these figures as individuals who wrote based on certain motivations, specific sources and ideas, for a specific fifteenth-century audience. Their innovations grew out of the geography of Gelibolu, from their intellectual genealogy and guided by the demands of their peers. In their lives, their concerns and their responses to these concerns, the members of the Yazıcıoğlu family are emblems of their time, because they themselves attempted to summarise their era, to illuminate its complexities and to create value from its contradictions. Any efforts to historicise the Yazıcıoğlus as individuals, then, is rewarded with a deeper understanding of their works.

In the closing chapters of *Kitābü'l-Müntehā*, Aḥmed Bīcān's spiritual manual written in the year of Constantinople's conquest, we read about the events of the Last Day of Judgement. After the righteous are distinguished from the sinners and unbelievers at the end of time, they are to assemble in the heavenly sanctuary before God as his absolute individualised self. God will greet the collected believers and say, 'I am your God whom you worshipped without seeing. Behold, I am your God.' He welcomes them in direct speech:

> O my servants, welcome! [. . .] You are the believers who held on to faith, and I am God, the Caring, the Protector, the king [. . .] You are my friends and intimates and visitants and the people of my affection [. . .] May peace be upon you, my servants. You are submitters/Muslims (*müslümanlarsıñız*), and I am the king of peace, and my abode is the abode of peace [. . .] from now on I am your familiar, sitting with you, and I have forever absolved you of the material world (*mülk-i kebir*), and the blessings and graces you deserve from me are many. Take pleasure and embrace your wives. And eat of many types of food and drink of many drinks! And enter your palaces and spend time in your gardens, diversely decorated.[1]

Aḥmed Bīcān relayed this divine promise to a crowd of new Muslims, sailors, soldiers and humble townsmen of Gelibolu, the focal point of the fifteenth-century Ottoman naval frontier. Above the cave-cell near the Dardanelles, where legend claims Aḥmed wrote these words, was an open-air mosque constructed from marble; this structure served as a mustering-place for soldiers bound for distant Balkan fronts and sailors who manned the galleys that fought Venetian ships in those waters. Its *miḥrāb* faces the straits, just north of the harbour neighbourhoods where in 1402 the Castilian ambassador refused to disembark, as the city was then ravaged by bubonic plague. There, too, in 1420 a Byzantine general and an Ottoman pretender negotiated for control of the town in mutual fear of the Ottoman Sultan Meḥmed I; it remained this kind of frontier for the following decades as the Yazıcıoğlu brothers lived there. Because of its strategic centrality Gelibolu was never securely within the *dār al-islām*. This anxiety was heightened even further for Aḥmed's audience, due to their commitment to Islam, a faith very new to the Rumelian lands – a commitment that for some entailed cutting ties to their past and their family and orienting their hearts towards an abstract future. They served a God they could not see, a God of whose absence they were continually reminded. Thus, Aḥmed's vision of heaven, where the 'king of peace' reigned alone, was juxtaposed against the violence and suffering of the frontier as its negation. To his flock of converts and soldiers, piety was salvation in the literal sense of a rescue from the world, a dream of being 'forever absolved' of all that was in it. The core of the faith that Aḥmed Bīcān strove to describe was a piety that could overcome the world, by transmuting war and hardship into the eternal peace of divine presence: 'I am your familiar, sitting with you'.

For Aḥmed Bīcān's audience, this ray of piety illuminated the chaos of the early Ottoman borderlands and connected them to the heart of Islamicate civilisation. The Ottoman borderlands were interwoven with the rest of the Islamic world thanks to the movement of ideas and texts. In this regard, the words of Aḥmed Bīcān and his brother Meḥmed gave testimony to the long historical process of Islamic religious knowledge being integrated into the intellectual culture of Muslim Anatolia and Rumelia. In his devotional poem *Muḥammediyye*, Meḥmed Yazıcıoğlu thanked a few of his teachers: the local dervish Bāyezīd, the late Egyptian *ḥadīth* scholar Zayn al-'Arab and, lastly, one Ḥaydar-i Khvāfī. This Ḥaydar, better known as Haravī due to his origin in Herat, was an established scholar of *ḥadīth* and Qur'an; he travelled to the Rumelian marches with credentials from the renowned schools of Ḥanafī jurisprudence in Timurid Samarqand. He was part of the first generation of international *'ulamā* to make for himself a career in the schools of the Ottoman capitals and, as such, an apt emblem for the metropolitanisation of Ottoman intellectual culture. We see Meḥmed and his brother quote and interpret texts from this environment, translating them into the idiom of their Turcophone public. In fact, this directive – to translate and popularise – was central to the Yazıcıoğlus' mission. Aḥmed wrote:

> These books are in the Arabic language, and some are in the Persian language. Not everyone can read them and be graced by their meaning. Few people know their expressions. I, this poor one, desired to create a book in Turkish out of this esoteric and exoteric knowledge, so that our people of this land may make use of this knowledge and may thus become knowledgeable and wise, and so that they hold law and truth in their hearts and their convictions and know the bond of Islam . . .

Hence, by and large, their writings can be characterised as lively Turkish anthologies of canonical Arabic writings.

The Yazıcıoğlus' approached the Islamic canon that they had inherited in a discriminating manner. They chose to transmit a select group of writings which they could adapt to the demands of frontier piety and thus had to adopt distinct positions within the polemical landscape of fifteenth-century Islamicate intellectual culture. The Yazıcıoğlus were particularly drawn towards ecumenical expressions that effaced the differences between the schisms and schools of thought of Islam, presenting a uniform and harmonious model of a single 'community of Muḥammad' (*ümmet-i Muḥammed*), distinct from the Christian and syncretistic communities around them. They also showed an inclination towards a broadly uncontroversial Sufism characteristic of their time and place. The primary personal relationship that they chose to celebrate in their writings was the one to the Sufi leader Ḥācı Bayram Velī, whose community in Ankara constituted their ethical anchor point in their later lives. Through the Bayramīs, the Yazıcıoğlu brothers accessed the theosophical vocabulary of the Andalusian mystic Ibn 'Arabī (d. 1240) and, thereby, entered a wider conversation on its meaning and acceptability, a conversation that simultaneously played out in the Timurid and Turkmen lands to the east. Adapting Ibn 'Arabī's message to a more accessible sacred-historical framework, they contributed one more voice to the eventual Ottoman consensus on Akbarian[2] Sunnī mysticism.

Meḥmed and Aḥmed Yazıcıoğlu were active during the last years of Murad II's reign and the first years of the reign of Meḥmed II, a crucial inflection point in the development of the Ottoman state. During the eventful years of the 1440s and 1450s when – thanks to the victories at Varna (1444), Kosovo (1448), Karaman (1451) and the Morea (1452) – the Ottoman state finally extended its dominion to the other major city on the straits, Constantinople, Aḥmed Bīcān alluded to the conquest without hyperbole. It is doubtful that Aḥmed had ever been to the city, since he did not describe its grandeur, as did other contemporaries; instead, he saw the conquest as one attribute of the world-historical personality of Meḥmed II, the *pādişāh* of an empire. Equally important to his political imagination was the 1444 Crusade of Varna. The King of Hungary venturing deep into Ottoman lands at the head of an international Catholic army evoked, for Aḥmed Bīcān, the apocalypse of the Blond People who would push the Muslims back to Syria in the prelude to the End Times; that people's defeat, mentioned in the *Müntehā*, was proof of the cosmic justice of the Ottomans' extension towards the Balkan frontiers in fulfillment of their own eschatological role. But despite this conscious enthusiasm for the

Ottoman political experiment, Aḥmed and Meḥmed appeared uninterested in, or at least several degrees distant from, the state itself. Although geographically central to the empire, Gelibolu was less of a stronghold upholding the state than a fortress at its edges, a '*dāru'l-cihād*' during the Yazıcıoğlus' lifetimes.

The idea of this moving frontier and Gelibolu's place at its centre was crucial to the Yazıcıoğlu brothers' self-understanding. Making constant reference to their city as the 'abode of holy war', the brothers even claimed to have participated in *ġazā* themselves, although in a spiritual capacity. 'Praise god that we perform *ġazā* [. . .] sometimes the unbelievers come to us, and sometimes we come to the unbelievers,' Aḥmed wrote, in reference not only to the Venetian ships that attempted to take the town, but also to the more general mentality of spiritual combat between the two faiths taking place between believers in the region. A consequence of the Orthodox Christian political and social presence in the Yazıcıoğlus' homeland was that philosophical conversations between members of the two confessional communities were inevitable. In fact, there survive many records of inter-confessional dialogues on religious subjects occurring in and around Gelibolu throughout the Yazıcıoğlus' lifetimes. Some of these dialogues expressed the conviction that the two religious systems of Islam and Christianity were compatible and the lines between them unclear. Specifically, both Muslims and Christians felt a confusion as to the relative positions of Jesus and Muḥammad in the hierarchy of prophets. In Latifi's *Tezkire*, for instance, we read of a preacher in Bursa's largest mosque who advocated the superiority of Jesus over Muḥammad.[3] The Yazıcıoğlus wrote their texts in part as a response to these sentiments favouring religious union: They aimed to differentiate Islam from Christianity, defining the former's identity for their frontier congregation, eradicating the confusion of the borderlands and fashioning a conflict between two distinct pious visions.

Aḥmed and Meḥmed Yazıcıoğlu were born into the second generation of Ottoman Muslim settlers in Rumelia. Their father, Ṣāliḥ, typified the first generation. A scribe by profession, he had arrived in Thrace during the last quarter of the fourteenth century, settling in Malkara and Gelibolu in the employ of the frontier warlord Qaṣṣāboğlu 'Alī. After the latter's death, Ṣāliḥ composed his only surviving text, an astrological compendium in honour of his next employer, a Gelibolu notable. The *Şemsiyye* is one of the first astrological texts in Turkish, and as such it prefigures the works of Ṣāliḥ's sons in two ways. First, it is self-conscious in its use of the Turkish language, approaching the Arabic and Persian textual heritage as ancient lore that must be translated into the local vernacular. All of

Meḥmed and Aḥmed's Turkish works would share this approach. Second, in terms of content Ṣāliḥ dealt with matters that would continue to pique the interest of his sons – specifically, the intersection of natural philosophy and piety. Aḥmed would return to this intersection in his own adaptation of his father's work, the *Bustānu'l-Haqāiq*.

Ṣāliḥ's two sons grew up in the orbit of Qaṣṣāboğlu's household and remained in the service of the next generation of Gelibolu notables, a cohort more closely linked to the Ottoman state. It seems that the brothers only twice ventured out of their Thracian homeland. It was in nearby Edirne that Ṣāliḥ's older son Meḥmed learned religious sciences from Ḥanafī teachers, and in Ankara that both Meḥmed and Aḥmed forged an enduring devotional bond with the spiritual leader Ḥācı Bayram Velī, becoming a part of his Sufi community. By the 1440s, both brothers, now probably middle-aged, had permanently settled in Gelibolu; professing awareness of their homeland's spiritual needs, they set out to compose their works.

The first of the brothers' known works is Meḥmed's *Maghārib al-Zamān*. Of all the family's major texts, this work will receive the least amount of attention in this study, partly because it is in Arabic and thus was far less widely read among its plebeian Turcophone audience. More importantly, its entire content is repeated in Aḥmed Bīcān's *Envārü'l-'Āşıqīn*, its Turkish translation. Aḥmed begun this translation, a wide-ranging masterpiece of catechistics and dogmatics, in the year of the Varna Crusade, in 1444; accordingly, its content exhibits a sharp consciousness of confessional distinction with respect to Christianity. The *Envār* is a single narrative of Islam from Creation to Resurrection, encompassing the stories of the prophets from Adam to Muḥammad, as well as information on the requirements of belief, piety and (to a lesser extent) ritual. Simultaneously, Meḥmed wrote the work for which the family is perhaps most famous, the *Muḥammediyye*, a *mes̱nevī* composed from the same material.

Meḥmed Yazıcıoğlu died in 1451. By the time of Aḥmed's next work, one detects a subtle change in the younger brother's attitude, a vague turn away from dogmatics in an inter-confessional setting and towards a more distant mystical piety. The first artifact of this new attitude was his *'Acāibü'l-Maḫlūqāt*, which departs from its original geographical text by Qazwīnī in its concern for moral lessons and its even more explicitly Sufi basis. In 857/1453, Aḥmed translated his brother's Arabic commentary on Ibn 'Arabī's *Fusūs*, expanding it into the first version of his *Müntehā* to which he added discussions of a wide array of pious and mystical topics. After a gap in his output, Aḥmed produced another version of the *Müntehā* in 870/1465, a version that featured a heightened eschatological intensity and a lengthy dedication to the reigning sultan. It is possible to assess this final *Müntehā* as the fulfillment of its title, 'The Utmost' – the capstone of Aḥmed Bīcān's career. From around this time, three more works written in Aḥmed Bīcān's name survive. The *Rūḥu'l-Ervāḥ*, related to some of the *Müntehā*'s content, introduces the reader to macrocosmic cosmology. The *Cevhernāme* discusses jewels, and the *Bustānu'l-Ḥaqāiq* transforms his father's *Şemsiyye* into prose. The circle of the Yazıcıoğlus' writings is thus neatly closed, with their last work reprising their first: The *Maghārib-Envār-Muḥammediyye* cluster of the brothers' jointly composed dogmatic texts was written just before Meḥmed's death, and the *Acāib*, *Müntehā*, *Cevhernāme* and *Bustān* comprised Aḥmed's independent works of a more speculative nature.

The International Context

The Yazıcıoğlus represent a moment in the evolution of an Ottoman religiosity that was to produce an enduring pious form. They united international currents with frontier demands, fused Sufism with law and other religious sciences, and consciously aimed to synthesise a faith for the Ottoman Muslim masses. In the wider Islamic world, three scenes of intellectual activity exerted influence on the Yazıcıoğlus' environment. The first consisted of the scholars of western Anatolia and the Ottoman Balkans, who were at that precise moment coalescing into the Ottoman scholarly hierarchies based in Bursa, Edirne and, later, Istanbul. During the Yazıcıoğlus' lifetime, the figures at the head of this community consisted of Molla Şemse'd-dīn Fenarī and his lineage, who ranked high in prestige among native-born *'ulema*. Clustered around the Fenarīs were migrant scholars from other parts of the Islamic world, populating the teaching posts of the *medrese*s recently established by the Ottoman state. These scholars received a ready welcome in the Ottoman capitals, since in the early and middle decades of the fifteenth century the local scholarly community laboured in the shadow of the more established centres of intellectual life in Timurid Khurasan and Transoxania. Under the lavish patronage of Tīmūr and his son Shāhrukh, a true flowering of Ḥanafī religious sciences took place in Samarqand and Herat, headed by Sa'd al-dīn Taftazānī and Sayyid Sharif Jurjānī; their students formed the core of the community of Ottoman migrants.

A third nucleus of activity, with a less direct relationship to the Yazıcıoğlus' context, was located in Mamluk Egypt and Syria. Aleppo, Damascus and Cairo were the world centres of Shāfi'ī jurisprudence, and some of the products of this milieu found their way to the Ottoman lands. Cairo was also one of the symbolic centres of a fifteenth-century intellectual avant-garde that spanned from Transoxania to the Balkans. İlker Evrim Binbaş[4] and İhsan Fazlıoglu[5] have discussed this network of elite intellectuals, sometimes known as the 'neo' *Ikhwān al-Ṣafā*. These individuals and those connected with them linked several notable radical ideologies and social movements, including the movement of Sayyid Nūrbakhsh; the Hurūfī movement of Fażlullāh Astarābādī; the movement of one of the *Ikhwān*'s intellectual pillars, Sa'īn al-dīn Turka; the rebellion of Şeyḫ Bedre'd-dīn; and the latent political command that inhered in Shāh Ni'matullāh, an important Sufi leader of Timurid Iran.

The Yazıcıoğlu brothers do not appear to have directly participated in these networks. The most proximate texts through which these networks can be reconstructed, such as 'Abdu'r-rahmān Bisṭāmī's *Durar Tāj al-Rasā'il* and the *Menāqibnāme* of Şeyḫ Bedre'd-dīn by his grandson Ḥāfiẓ Ḫalīl, make not even a single mention of the Yazıcıoğlu family. The Yazıcıoğlus' writings also show little evidence of the kind of experimentation that occupied these elite luminaries. Yet, they were not entirely disconnected from these dynamics. A prosopography of the Yazıcıoğlu brothers reveals two second-order connections to the *Ikhwān*: first, through the mystagogue who introduced them to Sufi esotericism, Ḥācı Bayram Velī, whose own teacher Ṣomuncu Baba had been involved with members of this group; and, secondly, through Meḥmed's instructor in the exoteric, Ḥaydar Haravī, whose position in Edirne's schools placed him in hostile opposition to Şeyḫ Bedre'd-dīn himself. Thus, the Yazıcıoğlus do indeed echo the Islamic 'republic of letters', and they may have assimilated their concerns, if not their answers. Neither experimentation nor systematisation was their purpose, even as their writings reveal the same preoccupations that nurtured the international avant-garde.

It is impossible to underestimate the centrality of another 'intellectual network' in the Yazıcıoğlus' lives – that is, the complex personal and institutional bonds that make up the social body of Sufism. The brothers' teacher Ḥācı Bayram linked them, across time and space, to the lineage of the Ṣafavī *shaykh*s who commanded the loyalty of a large community in eastern Anatolia and Azerbaijan. Through this link, the Yazıcıoğlus' social world extended to the Sufi community of Ankara and thence to the Bayramīs' sister *ṭarīqa*, the Ḫalvetīs, a strong presence in the *khānqāh*s of Azerbaijan and Shirvan that would become politically influential in the Ottoman lands during the reign of Bāyezīd II. These *ṭarīqa* connections, elaborated in internal Sufi histories, were certainly undercut and bridged by personal ones across *ṭarīqa* lines. For instance, a persistent tradition links Eşrefoğlu Rumī, a Qādirī Sufi and poet, to the circle of Ḥācı Bayram. What these fifteenth-century communities all held in common, beyond their mystical approach to piety, was that they each grappled with the legacy of the influential theosophy of the thirteenth-century mystic and philosophy Ibn al-ʿArabī.

Biancamaria Amoretti,[6] John Woods,[7] Cornell Fleischer, İhsan Fazlıoğlu, Hüseyin Yılmaz,[8] Christopher Markiewicz and others have noted the remarkable ideas that emerged during the fourteenth- and fifteenth-century post-Mongol crisis of authority, stimulated by new discussions about prophecy, caliphate, rulership, reason and revelation, phenomenal nature and the epistemological roles of text and intellect. These issues, which gave rise to Islamicate early modernity, await more extensive scholarly study and synthesis. Regrettably, these great issues of the age were not ones with which the Yazıcıoğlu brothers engaged. At the margins of more than one globe-spanning republic of letters, aware of much of it, but ignorant of even more, the Yazıcıoğlu brothers were concerned with a very immediate question – namely, the nature of faith. Rather than being concerned with questions of orthodoxy or heterodoxy, they worried about defining Islam through narrative and instruction. They expressed the broad boundaries of a fideistic normative religion, a circle wide enough to embrace the variety of Ottoman Islam, but narrow enough to remain meaningful as a vehicle of communal commitment.

Sources

This study is centred around the works of the Yazıcıoğlu family. I have attempted to use the oldest and most complete manuscript of each of these works, with occasional references to later manuscripts where necessary. I have not, however, compared each manuscript of a given work closely to other manuscripts, nor attempted to create any sort of manuscript genealogy. The works utilised are the following:

a. Yazıcı Ṣāliḥ's *Şemsiyye*, written during or shortly after 811/1409. This astrological almanac in Turkish exists in one copy (Süleymaniye Kütüphanesi, Pertevniyal 766; henceforth *Ş*) completed in early Muḥarram 861 / December 1456, situating it as the earliest dated manuscripts of any of the family members' literary output. A second, incomplete and slightly divergent manuscript preserved in Leiden (Leiden 1448) served to resolve discrepancies.

b. Meḥmed's *Maghārib al-Zaman*, written in Arabic, was accessed in a manuscript copy dated to early Shaʿbān 1225 / September 1810 (Süleymaniye Kütüphanesi, Nuruosmaniye 2596; henceforth *MZ*).

c. Meḥmed's *Muḥammediyye*, written in Turkish verse, was accessed in two ways. First, I was able to access what is alleged to be Meḥmed's own autograph copy of this poem (Vakıflar Müdürlüğü 431-A). More often, however, I utilised Amil Celebioglu's critical edition, which relies on this same copy.[9]

d. For the *Envārü'l-'Aşıqīn*, Aḥmed Bīcān's prose compendium of dogmatics and prophetic narrative, I have used the earliest known manuscript, copied in the middle of Rabīʿ al-Awwal 918 / June 1512 (Süleymaniye Kütüphanesi, Pertev Paşa 229-M; henceforth *EA*). Abdullah Uğur has discovered an earlier manuscript,[10] which, however, was not accessible to me; this is the basis of his own critical edition of the text.[11]

e. Aḥmed's *'Acāibü'l-Maḫlūqāt*, his Turkish abridgment of Qazwīnī's Arabic work of the same name, was accessed through an undated, but most likely sixteenth-century copy (Süleymaniye Kütüphanesi, Ali Nihat Tarlan 100; henceforth *AM*).

f. Meḥmed's Arabic *Sharḥ Fuṣūṣ al-Ḥikam* was read in a complete copy written in a much later hand (Süleymaniye Kütüphanesi, Pertev Paşa 293; henceforth *ShF*).

g. The 857/1453 *Kitābü'l-Müntehā* was read in a manuscript completed by one Meḥmed el-Sinobī on 26 Jumādā al-Ākhir 1003 / 28 February 1595 (Süleymaniye Kütüphanesi, Kılıç Ali Paşa 630; henceforth *KM857*). This was also the manuscript used by Ayşe Beyazit in her transliterated edition, which I equally consulted.[12]

h. I used two manuscripts of Aḥmed's 1465 *Kitābü'l-Müntehā*. The oldest and most interesting, Süleymaniye Kütüphanesi Hacı Mahmud Efendi 1657 (henceforth *KM870B*), is in a very rough hand, preserves archaic vocalisation and may date to a period soon after its composition. For convenience, however, a later, cleaner manuscript was also used (Süleymaniye Kütüphanesi, Yazma Bağışlar 7585; henceforth *KM870A*).

i. The *Rūḥu'l-Ervāḥ*, previously believed to exist only in a single manuscript in Vienna (Staatsbibliothek Cod. N. F. 202, 204, Historische Sammelhandschrift), was supplemented by another copy found in Istanbul (Atatürk Kitaplığı, Nadir Eserler, OE Yazmalar 1744; henceforth *RA*). There exists now a published transliteration by Siyabend Ebem, who has brought to light several further copies.[13] The Atatürk Kütüphanesi copy will be used here.

j. The copy of the *Bostānu'l-Ḥaqāiq* used here is Millet Kütüphanesi, A. E. Şerire 561 (henceforth *BH*), which is missing its last page. A more complete copy is known to exist in the Topkapı Palace Library, but this could not be consulted in the context of the present study.

k. *Cevhernāme*, a short poem attributed to Aḥmed Bīcān, was read in Fatma Kutlar's published edition, based on Süleymaniye Kütüphanesi, Ayasofya 3452.[14]

A range of other manuscripts and published sources of the period were also utilised for the purposes of this study. Beyond the oeuvre of the family, other works present in the Yazıcıoğlus environment assisted in building a framework. *Taḥrīr* registers and *vaqf* records have helped to contextualise their lives and careers within the human environment of Gelibolu and Thrace. The writings of some of the Yazıcıoğlus' acquaintances and peers, such as Aqşemse'd-dīn, Ḥācı Bayram Velī and Ḥaydar Haravī, were consulted in order to establish intellectual and personal relationships. Testimonies from travellers and other visitors to Gelibolu, including observers writing in Greek, Latin, Castilian and Catalan, proved necessary to describe the atmosphere in which the brothers lived and worked. And, as in most studies of the Ottoman centuries, the Ottoman biographical dictionary and chronicle traditions proved indispensable.

One work that will *not* be discussed as one of the Yazıcıoğlus' writings is perhaps the most famous of all the texts to which the family name is attached. The *Dürr-i Meknūn* ('The Hidden Pearl'), an encyclopedic volume on subjects closely related to the Yazıcıoğlus' concerns, has been attributed to Aḥmed Bīcān since at least the seventeenth century. With the exception of the much more popular *Muḥammediyye*, the *Dürr-i Meknūn* may be the one work that has attracted the greatest scholarly attention, especially in the West, in part due to the range of its content, the vivid quality of its narratives and its critical attitude towards its own social setting. I have argued elsewhere that the attribution is mistaken.[15] For this reason alone, this study sharply departs from other assessments of the Yazıcıoğlus, which strive to integrate the *Dürr-i Meknūn* into the rest of the corpus. My argument against Aḥmed Bīcān's authorship of the *Dürr-i Meknūn* is laid out more fully in another publication, but its argument will be briefly summarised here.

The attribution of the *Dürr-i Meknūn* to Aḥmed Bīcān appears to originate with the seventeenth-century scholar Kātib Çelebi, who stated in his famous bibliographical work *Kashf al-Ẓunūn*: 'The *Dürr-i Meknūn*, in Turkish, comprising eighteen chapters on some characteristics of the [Prophetic] birth and [religious] basics and their wonders, is by Aḥmad ibn al-Kātib, known as Bīcān'.[16] This identification appears to have been followed by all subsequent scholars. Indeed, at first glance it makes sense to attribute this text to Aḥmed Bīcān. The subject-matter of the *Dürr-i Meknūn*, ranging from cosmology over eschatology to prophetic lore, resembles the same subjects treated by Aḥmed Bīcān in his various known writings. What is more, the phrase '*dürr-i meknūn*', with its lexical meaning of 'hidden pearl', appears in his *Envārü'l-'Aşıqīn*, perhaps confusing matters for later bibliographers.[17] Nevertheless, the attribution of the *Dürr-i Meknūn* to Aḥmed Bīcān appears untenable for several reasons.

First, all of Aḥmed's known works bear clear textual signatures that are absent from the *Dürr-i Meknūn*. Aḥmed's writings all mention his own name. Not only did he advertise his authorship in each work, but he also tended to mention his hometown of Gelibolu and to discuss his Sufi training with Ḥācı Bayram, in each of these cases using formulaic phrases that recur from his first to his last work.[18] By contrast, the *Dürr-i Meknūn* is deliberately anonymous, concealing the social context from which it emerges. It also exhibits none of Bīcān's typical language, omitting the customary phrases of praise for Ḥācı Bayram, his home-town and his brother, which are present in Aḥmed's other writings. While it is true that apocalyptic texts from the early Ottoman period are often deliberately unsigned, the *Dürr-i Meknūn* is in fact no more preoccupied with the End Times than are Bīcān's *Envārü'l-'Āşıqīn* and *Kitābü'l-Müntehā*, which are signed. Just as significant as the absence of Bīcān's textual signatures is the way in which the *Dürr-i Meknūn* and Aḥmed Bīcān's works made use of an entirely distinct array of sources and textual influences. Aḥmed Bīcān's signed works, as Chapter 2 of the present monograph will demonstrate, are drawn from a set of canonical *medrese* texts, alongside a number of widely circulated Sufi writings. Aḥmed Bīcān's constant references to the writings of al-Ghazālī, Ibn 'Arabī, Fakhr al-Dīn Rāzī and other central figures of late medieval Islamic thought tell of his own intellectual upbringing in the developing *zaviye* and *medrese* systems. Yet, none of these sources are cited in the *Dürr-i Meknūn*; in fact, the author pointedly criticised the very institutions centred around these curricula, institutions which the Yazıcıoğlus clearly held dear. Moreover, the author also made use of an array of sources of which there is no trace in Bīcān's writings, such as the prognosticatory writings of 'Abdu'r-raḥmān Bisṭāmī, as well as the distinctive body of local lore synthesised with classical geographies, as traced by Stéphane Yerasimos.[19]

Any reader of the two texts will also notice a profound difference in tone and message. The *Dürr*'s author adopted a strident, apocalyptic rhetorical posture, decrying the moral hypocrisy of his community and warning against decadence. His veiled criticism of Ottoman political consolidation, expressed through the stories of Solomon and Nebuchadnezzar, finds no equivalent in Aḥmed Bīcān's signed writings, which pay little attention to the state and, on the rare occasions when they do, praise it. The author of the *Dürr-i Meknūn* also oriented the text around unique philosophical concerns, using, for instance, the Alexander Romance to meditate on the merciless movement of history. The author reproduced an inscription from an ancient ruin that Alexander had discovered during his travels: 'We did not know that the Hereafter followed right behind us and that kingship would not remain faithful. So, look at us and make a lesson of it: Do not rely upon the world and do not take pride in your lives'. Aḥmed's message, even while deploying similar narrative frames, is both Sufi in tenor and conventionally pious; the mission of Bīcān's Alexander is not to warn or lament but to act as exemplar of pious striving. While Bīcān in his *Envār* and *'Acāib* was animated by prophetic history as a guide to prophetic faith, taking the reader across a living landscape of Muslim scholars and Sufi practitioners who show the way to inner truth in an uncertain world, the author of the *Dürr-i Meknūn* put the reader on a path across distant geographies and through fantastic stories, drawing from each lessons on history and political power.

If the *Dürr-i Meknūn* is not by Aḥmed Bīcān, then it is most likely by another Anatolian or Rumelian author living around the same time.[20] For this reason, earlier analyses of the *Dürr-i Meknūn* – most prominently those by Stéphane Yerasimos,[21] Laban Kaptein[22] and Kaya Şahin[23] – retain their insights regardless of the identity of the text's author. It is only our biography of the real Aḥmed Bīcān that suffers for its absence, having been shorn of what otherwise would have been considered one of the Yazicioglus' masterpieces, a text unique in its critical attitude towards fifteenth-century Ottoman state and society. The real Aḥmed Bīcān was a far less defiant figure: Like his brother, he was a Sufi of Rumelia, conventional in outlook, rooted in his local community and dedicated to the institutions in which he was raised.

This study inherits an array of secondary literature that is unwieldy for the very simple reason that all scholarship until now has treated the *Dürr-i Meknūn* as a work of Aḥmed Bīcān. From an early date on, this misattribution has affected the way in which the Yazıcıoğlus have attracted scholarly attention, especially in the West. In 1753, the French diplomat Joseph Brue translated passages from the *Dürr-i Meknūn*. However, it was Joseph von Hammer-Purgstall who first made these texts widely known in Europe, by translating portions of the *Muḥammediyye* and the *Dürr-i Meknūn*; in 1834, he remarked that the latter contained 'more recondite learning, more entertaining history, more beautiful specimens of poetry than I ever saw collected in a simple volume'.[24] In his anthology of Ottoman poetry, E. J. W. Gibb published a fuller, although somewhat dismissive, treatment of the family's signed verse works. Regarding the *Muḥammediyye*, he said: 'The subjects of the book – the legends concerning the beginning and the end of all things and the mission of the Prophet – might, in the hands of a great poet, a Dante or Milton, be moulded into some splendid epic [. . .] But [Meḥmed's] aim was neither artistry nor poetry, but simply to convey instruction in a pleasant way . . .'[25] He added that the book was popular 'particularly with old ladies'.[26] However, as the object of much of this early interest was the *Dürr-i Meknūn*, these discussions fail to cohere into an accurate picture of the family's intellectual trajectory.

This same concern applies to most subsequent studies of the family. Franz Taeschner, in his work on Ottoman geography, located Aḥmed in first place with his *ᶜAjā'ib al-Makhlūqāt* and, predictably, the *Dürr-i Meknūn*. Edith Ambros and Victor Ménage then contributed short encyclopedia articles on Ṣāliḥ and Aḥmed;[27] Fahir İz published portions of the *Dürr-i Meknūn*; and the *Envārü'l-'Āşıqīn* was modernised by Ahmet Kahraman and released serially by the Turkish daily *Tercüman* in 1973.[28] In 1986, Âmil Çelebioğlu and Kemal Eraslan, in an important contribution written for the *İslam Ansiklopedisi*, tried to enumerate the works of all three men and attempted a biography that, while brief, was still more detailed than any other that had come before.[29] Çelebioğlu greatly advanced the field with his published critical edition of the *Muḥammediyye* (which will be used here), adding a detailed biographical exposition and comments on the work's literary qualities.[30] He also published an article including some excerpts of the hitherto-unknown *Şemsiyye*.[31] More recently, Fatma Kutlar uncovered the *Cevhernāme*,[32] and Ayşe Beyazit, demonstrating the rising popular interest in the legacy of Ibn 'Arabī in contemporary Turkey, produced a transscribed edition of the *Müntehā*.[33] The first attempt to go beyond the bibliographical was by Stéphane Yerasimos in 1990.[34] Yerasimos' *Légendes d'empire: La Fondation de Constantinople et de Sainte-Sophie dans les traditions turques* stated that the *Dürr-i Meknūn* offered the first of the 'anti-imperial histories' in Turkish. In doing so, he put Aḥmed Bīcān on the map as an object of serious literary and historical study. The depth and detail of his reading of the *Dürr* has not been matched by any other piece of modern scholarship, and the work certainly ranks as one of the finest on Ottoman intellectual history in recent decades. Yet, because of questions of the *Dürr*'s authorship, the Yazıcıoğlus' place among the Ottoman critics of empire is not as clear as Yerasimos had hoped; therefore, his work, while illuminating, is of limited relevance to a study on the family's thought world.

The scholar most closely identified with the study of the Yazıcızoğlus at this time is Laban Kaptein, whose critical edition and German translation of the *Dürr-i Meknūn* present a most useful resource.[35] His other major contribution, *The Apocalypse and the Antichrist Dajjal in Islam*,[36] consists of a meticulous analysis of the apocalyptic chapters of the *Dürr-i Meknūn* in view of the long tradition of Islamic apocalyptic literature based on Qur'an and *ḥadīth*. Parts of this text operate as a useful biography of Aḥmed Bīcān. Yet, Kaptein has remained focused on the text's apocalyptic character, continually advancing the viewpoint that Aḥmed Bīcān's work displays 'eschatological images straight from the traditional Islamic stock'[37] and that apocalyptic or messianic qualities ascribed to sultans like Meḥmed II and Süleymān were 'not tailor-made to suit a unique situation or personage'.[38] More recently, Kaya Şahin has disputed this interpretation. Attention to the prognosticatory elements of Aḥmed Bīcān's authentic *Müntehā*, a text used by neither Kaptein nor Yerasimos, has allowed Aḥmed's apocalypticism to be read in a new light, as an argument for the Ottoman state as the unique beneficiary of God's grace at the end of time ushered in by the 1453 conquest. Şahin has thus defended the views of Cornell Fleischer, Barbara Flemming and others, while rejecting Yerasimos' assertion that apocalyptic writing necessarily constitutes a form of social criticism. Yet, Yerasimos, Kaptein and Şahin have mainly concerned themselves with the contents of the *Dürr-i Meknūn* (whose attribution to Aḥmed is dubious) and, chiefly, with its legend of Constantinople's foundation and its apocalyptic sections. Meḥmed and Ṣāliḥ have been excluded. Thus, a contextualisation of the Yazıcıoğlus' writing as a body that *excludes* the *Dürr-i Meknūn* – considering how each remaining component relates to each other and to the lives and experiences of their authors – riemains yet to be attempted.

Tobias Heinzelmann has recently published a study on the uses of the Yazıcıoğlus' texts as part of Ottoman book culture in the centuries after its completion.[39] Heinzelmann has charted the diverse uses of the Yazıcıoğlus' major writings, comparing them to the fate of the writings of Yūnus Emre during those same centuries. This study differs from Heinzelmann's project in its close attention to the contemporary context of the Yazıcıoğlus themselves. Here I deliberately avoid considering the later fate and usage of the Yazıcıoğlus' writings, opting to interpret them as part of the fourteenth- and fifteenth-century world.

Finally, a new chapter in the study of the Yazıcıoğlus has now opened up, thanks to the work of Abdullah Uğur who has completed a thorough critical edition of Aḥmed Bīcān's *Envārü'l-'Āşıqīn*.[40] Based on his meticulous reading of early manuscripts of the text and careful analysis of their contents, Uğur has proposed his own reconstruction of the life of Aḥmed Bīcān; this reconstruction is in agreement with most major points presented here. The present study hopes to complement Uğur's important contribution, in the hopes that future scholars of the Yazıcıoğlus may enjoy a greater range of scholarly resources from which to draw.

This wider world of the Yazıcıoğlus – that is, the world of Islamic religious thought of the fifteenth century – is only beginning to be understood. Prior to the last decade, scholars of this time-period ventured with trepidation into a disorienting wilderness, but by now some paths have been cleared. Shahzad Bashir's work on the Nūrbakhshīs,[41] as well as his later outline of the Ḥurūfī movement of Fażlullah Astarābādī,[42] have become vital reading; recently, the study of Ḥurūfism has been greatly enhanced by Fatih Usluer[43] and Orkhan Mir-Kasimov.[44] Two works of the last few years have revolutionised our knowledge of the intellectual concerns of cosmopolitan fifteenth-century elites: Matthew Melvin-Koushki's study of the Timurid intellectual Sa'īn al-dīn Turka,[45] and İlker Evrim Binbaş's work on Timurid intellectual networks from the point of view of one of its key players, Sharaf al-dīn 'Alī Yazdī.[46] Christopher Markiewicz's work on Idrīs Bidlīsī and other Persian emigrés to the Ottoman lands has revealed many discrete regional scholarly networks through which various political and religious ideas were expressed and communicated during the late fifteenth and early sixteenth centuries.[47] An ambitious recent monograph by Hüseyin Yılmaz has mapped Ottoman political writing throughout the fifteenth and sixteenth centuries, observing that the concept of the caliphate – and political authority in general – became increasingly imbued with ideas adapted from Sufism.[48] Our understanding of political and religious thought during the long century between the death of Tīmūr and the accession of Sultan Süleymān thus continues to grow and develop.

The diversity of Ottoman piety of the fifteenth century has also remained understudied. Since its modern beginnings in the work of Fuat Köprülü[49] and Abdulbaki Gölpınarlı,[50] and despite the important studies by Irène Mélikoff[51] and many others, the field has at times been constrained by the contemporary Turkish political landscape. The study of Ottoman Sufism of the early period has only recently moved beyond an overtly politicised preoccupation with orthodoxy and its enemies, notably in the works of

Ahmet Karamustafa[52] and Ahmet Yaşar Ocak, whose monograph on Ottoman heresies reframed the study of heterodoxy in the empire.[53] Dina Le Gall has described the Ottoman Naqshbandis,[54] and Hasan Karataş and John Curry have reconstructed the complex history of the Ḫalvetiyye.[55] Zeynep Oktay Uslu has examined the works of the Sufi poets Yunus Emre and Kaygusuz Abdal with an eye towards the formation of vernacular Sufi Turkish literary culture.[56] Scholastic Sunnī piety has also been approached anew. Abdurrahman Atçıl's recent monograph, building on classic works by Richard Repp[57] and İsmail Hakki Uzunçarşılı,[58] has provided the first general picture of the fifteenth-century Ottoman scholarly hierarchies, with an eye towards their own ideologies and that of the state.[59]

Especially important for this study are the works by Derin Terzioğlu and Tijana Krstić. Both Krstić and Terzioğlu have examined the Ottoman Empire through the lens of 'confessionalisation'. This term, transferred from post-Reformation historiography, has come to denote a process, usually located in the sixteenth century, whereby the state encouraged and enforced a uniform religious outlook among its subjects – in the case of the Ottoman Empire, a normative Ḥanafī Sunnism. Terzioğlu has identified catechistic manuals, much like earlier ones produced by the Yazıcıoğlus, as important vectors for spreading a common Ottoman piety.[60] Krstić has seen in the evolving stories of Ottoman converts to Islam a way of understanding the Ottoman confessionalisation process as well, and in describing this trajectory, she has laid out a framework for conceptualising early Ottoman inter-confessional relations, a framework to which this study is deeply indebted.[61] While the Yazıcıoğlus of the fifteenth century predate the height of the Ottoman 'age of confessionalisation', the idea remains a useful one, insofar as the success of their populist but 'orthodox' writings can be seen as marking the early stage of this important process.

Looking to the fourteenth and early fifteenth centuries, scholars have once again begun to turn to the topic treated here, the formation of religious discourse in Anatolia and Rumelia during the pre-Ottoman and early Ottoman period. Of special note is the work of Sara Nur Yıldız whose recent studies on Anatolian scholars and their writings furnishes illuminating comparisons to this book's subjects.[62] In several important edited volumes,[63] Yıldız and A. C. S. Peacock have collected scholarship on pre- and early Ottoman Anatolian religious and intellectual dynamics; these volumes have now become essential starting points for any future research on the subject.

A new development offers useful resources to future historians of Ottoman intellectual history. *Treasures of Knowledge: An Inventory of the Ottoman Palace Library (1502/3–1503/4)*, edited by Gülru Necipoğlu,

Cemal Kafadar and Cornell Fleischer, consists of a collaborative exploration and detailed analysis of the inventory of the palace library of Sultan Bāyezīd II, as it was drawn up by his librarian Khayr al-dīn al-ʻAtūfī.[64] While al-ʻAtūfī's register post-dates the most active phase of the Yazıcıoğlus' careers by fifty years, it shows an intellectual world not too distant from it, where many of the texts and schools of thought revered by the Sufis of Gelibolu are not only present but prominent.

In a recent monograph, A. C. S Peacock has approached the problematic of Anatolian religious life from a new perspective.[65] Peacock has searched for the development of the characteristic features of Anatolian Islam in the late thirteenth and fourteenth centuries – the period in which the Mongols exerted political hegemony over most of the peninsula. While scholars have often tended to interpret the early Ottoman world of the Yazıcıoğlus and their contemporaries as the germinal phase of an imperial Ottoman society, Peacock has emphasised this period's continuity with a Seljuq, Mongol, Eretnid and *beġlik* culture which by the fifteenth century was already well-established. Indeed, many of the elements discussed in this study find their precursors in the Persian and Turkish literature of Mongol Rum. For instance, Anatolian writers on religious topics in the Mongol period focused on the problem of confessional diversity as articulated through ideas of religious warfare and conversion in a manner very similar to the Yazıcıoğlus, as shown in Chapter 3; however, the Yazıcıoğlus did not seem to be overly concerned with defining Sunnī Islam as distinguished from Shīʻism – a feature of Anatolian discourse that Peacock has identified in some pre-Ottoman writings.[66] Nor is the Yazıcıoğlus' deep attachment to institutional Sufism something new to their moment, but rather a more enduring feature of Anatolian Islam, which had been highly visible throughout Anatolia since the time of Jalālu'd-dīn Rūmī in the thirteenth century. Even the Anatolian Turkish deployed by the Yazıcıoğlus was first crafted into a literary language in the cities of Konya, Kırşehir, Aydın and Sivas in the early fourteenth century.[67] Although this study does not dwell on the continuities that link the Yazıcıoğlus to the pre-Ottoman societies of Mongol and *beglik* Anatolia, it is important to keep in mind that their lives and careers were shaped by this inheritance and not simply defined by the dramatic historical moment in which they found themselves – that is, the conquest of Rumelia and the transformation of the Ottoman *beglik* into a fledgling empire.

* * *

In attempting to examine the mentalities of the Yazıcıoğlu brothers, this study hopes to balance the large scale of their intellectual world with the much narrower scope of their personal horizons, preoccupied as they were with their own home-town of Gelibolu. Here the 'international' is represented by their texts' content – their sources in the canon of the Arabic religious sciences, as well as the Ibn 'Arabī-derived elements of their Sufism. Their local setting is represented by the structures that emerge from these sources – the Islam they represent, its themes and images, and its presentation in Turkish. They were local architects building with imported timber. This relationship between the local and the supra-local is a major feature, not only of this study's subjects, but of the Islamic world in the late medieval and early modern period in general, united by what Marshall Hodgson has called the 'common Islamicate social pattern', a sense of communal identity coloured but not fractured by the requirements of individual political situations, each of which grew to be defined by early modern empires as the Islamic Middle Period progressed. The Yazıcıoğlus' spiritual vernacular can be considered a perfect exemplar of the localisation of an Islamic discursive tradition.

The Yazıcıoğlus can also help the scholar access something very elusive in the study of the intellectual culture of the Islamic world: a non-elite perspective. Never close to the seat of power and apparently not well-travelled, the Yazıcıoğlus were provincial in the true sense of the word. Although their work was drawn from standard material, it was in its form and preoccupations nevertheless 'popular'. This non-elite perspective does not, however, extend to a distrust of the Ottoman state. Although they depended not on the first rank of Ottoman functionaries but on local *beg*s for their livelihood, in their dogmatic elaborations they do seem to have acquired a sense of legitimacy from the expansion of the Ottoman enterprise on the Balkans and in the Mediterranean. They epitomise a class of provincial writers attached to the Ottoman idea, but several degrees removed from the state itself.

Before continuing, one concept needs further clarification. Writing in vernacular Turkish and aiming for a general Turcophone audience, the Yazıcıoğlus expressed a broad civic faith. This raises the natural question of whether one can apply the term 'popular religion' to the religious system they expressed. The term must be used carefully. In contrast to a 'high' faith developped by elite *medrese* professors, the Yazıcıoğlus were expressing a 'popular religion' – their vision of Islam was, indeed, very popular, aiming to satisfy the religious needs of ordinary Muslims. However, this was in no respect a 'heterodox' form of Islam, and it was completely unconnected to other ideas that may be evoked by the term 'popular religion': There is nothing drawn from folk magic traditions, no syncretism and very little that could be considered 'heterodox' by readers at that time or by most Sunnī Muslims afterwards. Their vernacular piety is a popularisation of a standard Sunnism, not a 'folk' or iconoclastic or antinomian form of Islam. The system of the Yazıcıoğlus builds its emotional weight from the standard stories of sacred history, presenting through these sequential narratives a variety of emotional effects and ideological statements related to their many concerns – faith, worship, mysticism, death and politics. What made this piety 'popular' was not a departure from urbane norms, but rather its relative de-emphasis on doctrinal and legalistic nuance, and its appropriately frontier-oriented embrace of a simple Muslim identity. It was, in their words, for the 'unlettered' (*ummī*) believer, and it was designed to help them believe in the right things.

This book will express the Yazıcıoğlus' alternately local and supra-local horizons and constraints by means of its chapter structure. Chapter 1 will attempt to create a biography of the Yazıcıoğlu family, rooted in the turbulent social ecology of Thrace from the 1370s to the 1460s. Although the careers of Aḥmed, Meḥmed and their father Ṣāliḥ took place in an era scarcely lit by documentary evidence, by reading clues scattered throughout their works and in archival sources such as endowment deeds and tax registers, it becomes possible to add significant detail to the biographical sketch worked out by Âmil Çelebioğlu and to discern the patterns of a local patronage network centred on the naval frontier city of Gelibolu during the decades before the Conquest of Constantinople. While Ṣāliḥ, as part of a very early wave of Turkish Muslim settlement in Europe, followed the households of warlords who autonomously fought on the Balkan frontiers, his two sons found themselves attached to various Ottoman notables and military men from Gelibolu. Thus, the 'Ottoman' character of this network evolved over time, as the Yazıcıoğlus' patrons transformed from a self-sufficient clique of warlords into men who by 1450 held distinct Ottoman pedigrees.

Chapter 2 integrates the Yazıcıoğlus with the wider world by exposing how their own library and intellectual heritage represent the spread of scholarship from distant parts of the Islamic world. Using the methodology of source criticism, I will identify and analyse the works that comprised the Yazıcıoğlus' essentially anthological output, in the hope of representing the library available to the provincial scholars of a frontier state that would soon become a world empire. I found that most of their sources derived from a relatively narrow and highly canonical set of writings which had been carried into Ottoman lands by established scholars from Timurid Iran. In the Yazıcıoğlus' library, one could find Qur'an commentaries, collections of prophetic traditions, legal compendia and mystical treatises that correspond to the curriculum of a mid-level student of orthodox Ḥanafī orientation, just as that tradition began to dominate instruction in Ottoman *medreses*. Hence, the most popular expositors of Ottoman vernacular Sunnism composed their works by using a conventional set of sources that in a straightforward manner reflected their middling educational attainment.

Having established the biographies of the members of the Yazıcıoğlu family and the boundaries of their literary horizons, Chapter 3 returns to Gelibolu, rehistoricising them in the town where they spent their entire lives. I will show that the atmosphere of this contested city fostered a cluster of intense debates, described in Ottoman, Byzantine and Western European sources, between local Christians and Muslims on the nature of the difference between Islam and Christianity. From this time and place there survive testimonies, for instance, of a captive Greek archbishop engaged in inconclusive debates with Muslims in the Ottoman camp, of a preacher in an Ottoman mosque who denied the superiority of Muḥammad over Jesus and of a circle of Ottoman religious scholars who speculated that Christians and Muslims were equal in God's sight. It is the ambiguities created by these dialogues that the Yazıcıoğlus attempted to counter with their vernacular catechisms which reinforced confessional boundaries. Although embedded in classicising forms, the Yazıcıoğlus' writings spoke directly to the uneducated new Muslims, the converts, soldiers and sailors who constituted their audience. They endeavoured to clarify confessional boundaries and affirm the religio-political identity of Muslims on this fluid frontier. Their influential form of Ottoman vernacular religiosity was, in this sense, a product not of the heartland, but of the borderland.

Chapter 4 turns abroad once again, attempting to describe the form of normative Islam in which the Yazıcıoğlu brothers were raised – the doctrinal content of their popular Ottoman Sunnism. I will examine the positions advanced in their writings with respect to several long-term ideological frictions within Islamic intellectual history: between Sunnism and forms of Shī'ism, between mystical teachings and legalist conceptions of faith, and between various philosophical stances on the origins of religious knowledge. Here it has proven crucial to contextualise the brothers and their circle within the dogmatic structures of contemporary Sufi mysticism. I will show that the Yazıcızoğlu brothers and the populist Islam they represented were largely unconcerned with distinguishing between Sunnism and Shī'ism and that they believed in the compatibility of mysticism with legalist orthodoxy. However, this synthesis was circumscribed by Sufi theories of the time, most specifically the tradition of Ibn 'Arabī and his commentators, whose writings they saw as canonical. I will also discuss the Yazıcıoğlus' purported apocalypticism at length, concluding that Aḥmed Bīcān believed in an ahistorical, traditional apocalypse even as he ascribed an eschatological role to Sultan Meḥmed II and the Ottoman Conquest of Constantinople.

Chapter 5 attempts to understand the Yazıcıoğlu family's preoccupation with natural philosophy. This has proven more difficult than expected, as Aḥmed Bīcān does not seem to have been interested in systematising or harmonising a few apparently contradictory systems of knowledge about the natural world. However, as in other cases, he was truly concerned with personal piety as an ordering principle in a disordered world. Man as microcosm, then, is the organiser of the natural cosmos.

On behalf of the reader, I must express my frustration about finding real knowledge about the mentalities of this study's subjects and their social world quite elusive. My attempt at an intellectual biography of the Yazıcıoğlus has shown me the limitations that a historian faces when studying individuals who are reticent about their lives, living in a historical moment when documentary evidence is scarce. In a parable about the journeys of Alexander the Great across the Encircling Ocean, Aḥmed Bīcān warned the reader of these limitations. Having learned of the existence of a country on the sea's far side, Alexander struggled for years to decipher the language of one of its inhabitants. Eventually he came to understand the speech of this person from the far lands: 'There are many of the Exalted God's creatures whom you do not know of and who do not know of you [. . .] It is necessary to know one's own incapacity [. . .] and to see or hear about the wonders of the world'. Let this study then affirm this limitation as it also invokes curiosity and wonder in the reader.

Notes

1. Aḥmed Bīcān, *Kitābü'l-Müntehā*, Süleymaniye Kütüphanesi, Kılıç Ali Paşa 630, fol. 113a. This address alludes to Qur'an 89:27-30, 'Oh, soul at peace! Return unto thy Lord, content in His good pleasure! Enter among my servants! Enter my garden!'
2. 'Akbarian' has entered Western scholarship as a term denoting the tradition of Ibn 'Arabī, who was labelled *al-shaykh al-akbar* (the greatest *shaykh*) by his followers across subsequent generations.
3. Latifi, *Tezkiretü'ş-Şu'arâ ve Tabsıratü'n-Nuzamâ: İnceleme, Metin*, ed Rıdvan Canım (Ankara: Atatürk Kültür Merkezi Başkanlığı, 2000).
4. İlker Evrim Binbaş, *Intellectual Networks in Timurid Iran: Sharaf Al-Dīn 'Alī Yazdī and the Islamicate Republic of Letters* (New York: Cambridge University Press, 2016).

5. See İhsan Fazlıoğlu, 'İlk Dönem Osmanlı İlim ve Kültür Hayatında İhvânu's-Safâ ve Abdurrahmân Bistâmî', *Divan* 1, no. 2 (1996), pp. 229–40.
6. Biancamaria Amoretti, 'Religion in the Timurid and Safavid Periods', in *Cambridge History of Iran*, vol. 6 (Cambridge: Cambridge University Press, 1986), pp. 610–55. This inspired article describes the flowering of religious thought in greater Iran during the fifteenth century and thereafter.
7. The essential problems of fifteenth-century political theology are briefly laid out in John E. Woods, *The Aqquyunlu: Clan, Confederation, Empire* (Salt Lake City: University of Utah Press, 1999), pp. 3–10.
8. Hüseyin Yılmaz, *Caliphate Redefined: The Mystical Turn in Ottoman Political Thought* (Princeton: Princeton University Press, 2019).
9. Âmil Çelebioğlu (ed.), *Muhammediye* (İstanbul: Millî Eğitim Bakanlığı, 1996).
10. Aḥmed Bīcān, *Envārü'l-'Āşıqīn*, Üsküdar Hacı Selim Ağa 467.
11. Abdullah Uğur, *Yazıcıoğlu Aḥmed Bīcān and his Envārü'l-'Aşıḳīn* (Cambridge: Department of Near Eastern Languages and Civilizations, Harvard University, 2019).
12. Ahmet Bican, *El-Müntehâ: Fusûsu'l-Hikem Üzerine bir Çalışma*, ed. Ayşe Beyazit (İstanbul: İnsan Yayınları, 2011).
13. Siyabend Ebem, 'Ahmed Bîcân'a Atfedilen Bir Eser: Rûhü'l-Ervâh', *Türk Dünyası İncelemeleri Dergisi / Journal of Turkish World Studies* 14, no. 1 (2014), pp. 49–74.
14. Fatma Kutlar, 'Ahmed-i Bican'ın Manzum Cevahir-Name'si', *İnsan Bilimleri Araştırmaları* 7 (2002), pp. 59–68.
15. Carlos Grenier, 'Reassessing the Authorship of the *Dürr-i Meknun*', *Archivum Ottomanicum* 35 (2018), pp. 193–212.
16. '*Dürr-i Meknūn turkī mushtamil 'alā thamāniyat 'ashar bāban fī ba'ḍi khawāṣṣ al-mawālīd wa basā'iṭ wa 'ajā'ibihā li-Aḥmad ibn al-Kātib al-shahīr bi-Bījān*'. Kātib Çelebi, *Kitāb Kashf al-Ẓunūn 'an Asāmī al-Kutub wa al-Funūn* (İstanbul: Maṭba'at al-'Ālem, 1892), p. 488.
17. *Envārü'l-'Āşıqīn*, Süleymaniye Kütüphanesi, Pertev Paşa 229-M, fol. 3a.
18. For example, Aḥmed's signed writings nearly all include a *sebeb-i te'lif*, or 'reason for composition', which includes fixed phraseology such as 'Know that the compiler and translator of this great book and noble address is Yazıcıoğlu Aḥmed Bīcān [. . .] Praise God that this work was finished in Gelibolu . . .' and 'This poor one brought together in this very book all of the sacred *ḥadīth* and holy words and whatever kinds of divine addresses are in the Torah and Psalms and Gospels and Qur'an, as well as whatever similar Lordly words may be in the texts of the Prophets', alongside praise of Ḥācı Bayram as 'Pole of the World' (*quṭb-i 'ālem*). None of these are present in the *Dürr-i Meknūn.*
19. Stéphane Yerasimos, *La fondation de Constantinople et de Sainte-Sophie dans les traditions turques: Légendes d'Empire* (Istanbul; Paris: Institut français d'études anatoliennes; Librairie d'Amérique et d'Orient J. Maisonneuve, 1990).

20. The text mentions the death of Abdurrahman Bistami (d. 1456), and the language of the text appears to be consistent with the Turkish of the mid-fifteenth century. The author is most likely a contemporary of Aḥmed Bīcān. See Grenier, 'Reassessing the Authorship of the *Dürr-i Meknun*', pp. 210–12.
21. Yerasimos, *La fondation de Constantinople et de Sainte-Sophie dans les traditions turques*.
22. Ahmed Bican, *Dürr-i Meknun: Kritische Edition mit Kommentar*, ed. Laban Kaptein (Asch: Selbstverl. Laban Kaptein, 2007); Laban Kaptein, *Apocalypse and the Antichrist Dajjal in Islam: Ahmed Bijan's Eschatology Revisted* (Asch: privately published, 2011).
23. Kaya Şahin, 'Constantinople and the End Time: The Ottoman Conquest as a Portent of the Last Hour', *Journal of Early Modern History* 14, no. 4 (2010), pp. 317–54.
24. Quoted in Laban Kaptein, *Apocalypse and Antichrist Dajjal in Islam*, p. 4.
25. Elias John Wilkinson Gibb, *A History of Ottoman Poetry* (London: Luzac, 1900), vol. 1, p. 404.
26. Ibid. p. 405.
27. Edith Ambros, 'Yazidji-Oghlu', and V. L. Ménage, 'Bīdjān', *Encyclopedia of Islam, Second Edition*.
28. Evliya Çelebi, *Evliya Çelebi Seyahatnâmesi*, ed. Orhan Şaik Gökyay et al. (İstanbul: Yapı Kredi Yayınları, 1996).
29. Âmil Çelebioglu and Kemal Eraslan, 'Yazıcı-oğlu', *İslam Ansiklopedisi*.
30. Çelebioğlu, *Muhammediye*.
31. Âmil Çelebioğlu, 'Yazıcı Salih ve Şemsiyye'si', *Atatürk Üniversitesi İslami İlimler Fakültesi Dergisi* 1 (1976), pp. 171–218.
32. Kutlar, 'Ahmed-i Bican'ın Manzum Cevahir-Name'si'.
33. Ahmet Bican, *El-Müntehâ*, ed. Ayşe Beyazit.
34. Yerasimos, *La fondation de Constantinople et de Sainte-Sophie dans les traditions turques*.
35. Ahmed Bican, *Dürr-i Meknūn*, ed. Laban Kaptein.
36. Kaptein, *Apocalypse and Antichrist Dajjal in Islam*.
37. Ibid. p. 53
38. Ibid. p. 56.
39. Tobias Heinzelmann, *Populäre religiöse Literatur und Buchkultur im Osmanischen Reich: Eine Studie zur Nutzung der Werke der Brüder Yazıcıoğlı* (Würzburg: Ergon-Verlag, 2015).
40. Abdullah Uğur, *Yazıcıoğlu Aḥmed Bīcān and his Envārü'l-'Aşıḳīn* (Cambridge: Department of Near Eastern Languages and Civilizations, Harvard University, 2019).
41. Shahzad Bashir, *Messianic Hopes and Mystical Visions: The Nūrbakhshīya between Medieval and Modern Islam* (Columbia: University of South Carolina Press, 2003).
42. Shahzad Bashir, *Fazlallah Astarabadi and the Hurufis* (Oxford: Oneworld, 2005).

43. Fatih Usluer, *Hurufilik: İlk Elden Kaynaklarla Doğuşundan İtibaren* (Topkapı, İstanbul: Kabalcı Yayınevi, 2009).
44. Orkhan Mir-Kasimov, *Words of Power: Ḥurūfī Teachings between Shi'ism and Sufism in Medieval Islam: The Original Doctrine of Faḍl Allāh Astarābādī* (London: I. B. Tauris, in association with the Institute of Ismaili Studies, 2015).
45. Matthew S. Melvin-Koushki, 'The Quest for a Universal Science: The Occult Philosophy of Sa'in Al-dīn Turka Isfahani (1369–1432) and Intellectual Millenarianism in Early Timurid Iran' (unpublished doctoral dissertation, Yale University, 2012).
46. Binbaş, *Intellectual Networks in Timurid Iran*.
47. Christopher Markiewicz, *The Crisis of Kingship in Late Medieval Islam: Persian Emigres and the Making of Ottoman Sovereignty* (Cambridge: Cambridge University Press, 2019).
48. Yılmaz, *Caliphate Redefined*.
49. Mehmet Fuat Köprülü, *Early Mystics in Turkish Literature*, ed. and trans. Gary Leiser and Robert Dankoff (London; New York: Routledge, 2006).
50. Abdülbâki Gölpinarli, *Melâmîlik ve Melâmîler* (İstanbul: Devlet Matbaası, 1931).
51. Irène Mélikoff, *Hadji Bektach: Un mythe et ses avatars: Genèse et évolution du Soufisme populaire en Turquie* (Leiden: Brill, 1998).
52. Ahmet T. Karamustafa, *God's Unruly Friends: Dervish Groups in the Islamic Later Middle Period, 1200–1550* (Salt Lake City: University of Utah Press, 1994).
53. Ahmet Yaşar Ocak, *Zındıklar ve Mülhidler Yahut Dairenin Dışına Çıkanlar: 15.-17. Yüzyillar* (İstanbul: Türkiye Ekonomik ve Toplumsal Tarih Vakfı, 1999).
54. Dina Le Gall, *A Culture of Sufism: Naqshbandīs in the Ottoman World, 1450–1700* (Albany: State University of New York Press, 2005).
55. Hasan Karataş, 'The City as a Historical Actor: The Urbanization and Ottomanization of the Halvetiye Sufi Order by the City of Amasya in the Fifteenth and Sixteenth Centuries' (unpublished doctoral dissertation, University of California, Berkeley, 2011). John Curry, *The Transformation of Muslim Mystical Thought in the Ottoman Empire: The Rise of the Halveti Order, 1350–1750* (Edinburgh: Edinburgh University Press, 2010).
56. Zeynep Oktay Uslu, 'The Şathiyye of Yunus Emre and Kaygusuz Abdal: The Creation of a Vernacular Islamic Tradition in Turkish', *Turcica* 50 (2019), pp. 9–46.
57. Richard Repp, *The Müfti of Istanbul: A Study in the Development of the Ottoman Learned Hierarchy* (London: Published by Ithaca Press for the Board of the Faculty of Oriental Studies, Oxford University, 1986).
58. İsmail Hakkı Uzunçarşılı, *Osmanlı Devletinin İlmiye Teskilâti* (Ankara: Türk Tarih Kurumu Basımevi, 1965).

59. Abdurrahman Atçıl, *Scholars and Sultans in the Early Modern Ottoman Empire* (Cambridge: Cambridge University Press, 2018).
60. Derin Terzioğlu, 'Where *'İlmihal* Meets Catechism: Islamic Manuals of Religious Instruction in the Ottoman Empire in the Age of Confessionalization', *Past & Present* 220, no. 1 (2013), pp. 79–114.
61. Tijana Krstić, *Contested Conversions to Islam: Narratives of Religious Change in the Early Modern Ottoman Empire* (Palo Alto: Stanford University Press, 2011).
62. Sara Nur Yıldız, 'From Cairo to Ayasuluk: Haci Paşa and the Transmission of Islamic Learning to Western Anatolia in the Late Fourteenth Century', *Journal of Islamic Studies* 25, no. 3 (2014), pp. 263–97; Sara Nur Yıldız, 'A Hanafi Law Manual in the Vernacular: Devletoğlu Yūsuf Balıḳesrī's Turkish Verse Adaptation of the Hidāya-Wiqāya Textual Tradition for the Ottoman Sultan Murad II (824/1424)', *Bulletin of the School of Oriental and African Studies* 80, no. 2 (2017), pp. 283–304.
63. A. C. S. Peacock, Bruno de Nicola and Sara Nur Yıldız (eds), *Islam and Christianity in Mediaeval Anatolia* (Farnham: Ashgate, 2015); A. C. S. Peacock and Sara Nur Yıldız (eds), *Literature and Intellectual Life in 14th-15th Century Anatolia* (Würzburg: Ergon Verlag, 2016).
64. Gülru Necipoğlu, Cemal Kafadar and Cornell H. Fleischer, *Treasures of Knowledge: An Inventory of the Ottoman Palace Library (1502/3–1503/4)* (Leiden; Boston: Brill, 2019).
65. A. C. S. Peacock, *Islam, Literature and Society in Mongol Anatolia* (Cambridge: Cambridge University Press, 2019).
66. Ibid. pp. 199–217.
67. Ibid. pp. 147–87.

Chapter 1

The Scribe and his Sons

'Praise God that Yazıcıoğlu Aḥmed Bīcān, white of beard and dark of face, completed this book in Gelibolu in the month of Muḥarram in the year 870 [1465]', wrote the author at the close of his final major work, the second *Müntehā*. If the elderly Aḥmed Bīcān had chosen to recall the trajectory of his own life at that moment, it would have appeared quite stable, even static. Aḥmed seems not to have left Gelibolu during his later years, not even to visit the new capital of Istanbul; looking further back, before his brother Meḥmed's death after 1451, the two may have spent some years in Edirne and Ankara, but as soon as they could, they returned to the provincial frontier town where they had spent their youth. In social standing, these scholars and Sufis occupied a position not so different from that of their own father Ṣāliḥ, since 1388 a scribe in the employ of various borderland *ġāzīs*. For eighty years, the Yazıcıoğlu brothers and their father Ṣāliḥ lived their lives as scholars often do – as observers, not actors in the flow of history. Perhaps it is for this reason that after their deaths their readers immediately transfigured them into hagiographical myth: their lives became remarkable after their deaths, through their writings, rather than through their inspired but somewhat uneventful journeys on earth.

While the Yazıcıoğlus themselves seemed to have stood still, the world in which they lived was changing around them. In a sense, the family's stability was only an apparent one, as it relied on the forceful dynamics of political, social and cultural change that altogether allowed their lives to proceed so quietly. Seen from a global perspective, much of the Islamic world experienced the effects of the rise and dissolution of the Timurid empire, which in itself can be thought of as an experiment bringing to a close the protracted post-Mongol political crisis. From a material viewpoint, the Ottomans, alongside the rest of western Eurasia, were also acquiring the technical and economic capacity to create and sustain what historians now call an 'early modern empire'. On a more local level, the Ottoman principality, once Tīmūr's vassal most distant from his empire's heartland of southern Central Asia, began to adopt its own unique political and cultural ideals and practices. These processes were felt in Gelibolu, the 'key to Rum', as much as anywhere else. Ṣāliḥ, moving to Gelibolu not long after it was reconquered from Christian powers in the late fourteenth century, saw first-hand the development of the Ottoman rule over the Balkans, its near-disintegration during the Timurid and Civil War years, and finally its reconstitution as a regular Ottoman *sancaq*. Ṣāliḥ's sons Aḥmed and Meḥmed lived through the reigns of Murad II and Meḥmed II and the Conquest of Constantinople, and they participated in the transformation of the Ottoman state into an empire. They could stay put in Gelibolu only because in this city and region were felt all the energies of this new sociopolitical formation. Thus, much like the content and shape of their intellectual endeavours, the contours of their lives were products of both local and global factors.

In order to understand the Yazıcıoğlus' role in Ottoman and Islamic history, one must first understand how they interacted with their transforming setting. In other words, we must rely on their biographies to throw into relief the details of their environment. Unfortunately, the Yazıcıoğlus are difficult subjects, for several distinct reasons. One prominent obstacle limiting many historians of the early Ottoman Empire is the general scarcity of the period's documentary and archival legacy. The many documentary types on which historians of the sixteenth century and later can rely – such as *tapu taḥrīr* registers, imperial *mühimme*s and *qāḍī* court records, to mention but a few – are for the first half of the fifteenth century incomplete at best, or had not yet become common Ottoman practice and are thus completely absent at worst. Important genres of literary writing typically mined by historians are also rare or missing: No contemporaneous biographical dictionaries and few historical works guide the modern scholar reconstructing the social networks or political history of the second century of the Ottoman principality. It is for this reason that the fourteenth and the first half of the fifteenth centuries are often labelled the 'dark ages' of Ottoman historiography, as scholars must traverse a terrain with little to light their way. Over the course of this passage, historians in search of reliable sources around which to hinge their narratives are forced to do a particularly dangerous sort of reconstruction, inferring earlier situations on the basis of the state of affairs in later decades, a process that calls for more speculation and unsupported inferences than many historians would find acceptable. Nevertheless, this is a method followed in this study, and for this reason its conclusions must be classified as tentative.

There exists a second, equally serious difficulty in reconstructing the Yazıcıoğlus' social relations. This is the authors' very conventional reluctance to provide comments on their own lives and circumstances. This is not in any way particular to the Yazıcıoğlus, who did not display this tendency to an unusual degree – one may recall that the biographical data of litterateurs no less successful than Niẓāmī or Firdawsī are known mainly through elliptical self-references, dedications and chronograms. This convention, inseparably connected to the notion of scholarly modesty,[1] is breached only in exceptional cases. Unless writers harboured a specific autobiographical impulse, which the Yazıcıoğlus certainly did not, they tended to efface their own life story, except when revealed by dedicatory passages, panegyrics or other details alluding to social surroundings.

Given these significant constraints, it is challenging for the contemporary scholar to assemble a satisfying biographical narrative of the Yazıcıoğlu family. Avoiding first-person narration, the Yazıcıoğlus only occasionally offered comments on their own life history or subjectivity, and thus the historian searches in vain for enough internal detail to give their biographies texture. In fact, there is only one way to reconstruct their history: by learning more about the people with whom they interacted, especially their patrons and employers. Over the course of their lives they encountered individuals who taught, employed, or befriended them, and they left records of these interactions in their writings. By stringing together these brief mentions of their employers and friends, the silhouette of a life may emerge. A biography thus reconstructed is not quite as thin as one may fear. While it may lack the documentary richness and the sense of personal drama that self-narrative can provide, a prosopographical biography is quite informative for another dimension important to historians. It preserves vital data on the authors' social relations. With every mention of an employer or teacher, the Yazıcıoğlus exposed one building block of a much larger hierarchy or network.

Of these networks, three are distinct. The first is the hierarchy of Ottoman command, with the sultan and sultanic pretenders from Murād Ḫüdāvendigār to Fātiḥ Meḥmed at its pinnacle, then moving down through the ranks of *emirs* and *beg*s to local commanders and notables. Over the course of the lives of Yazıcı Ṣāliḥ and his sons, it was the men inhabiting the middle and lower rungs of this hierarchy who directly sustained their material existence, employing them in various capacities connected to their scholarly and spiritual attainments. The second is the network of religious scholars, or *'ulemā*, of the Ottoman lands. The academic institutions of the Ottoman capitals of Edirne and Bursa linked this network to the momentum of the political centre – yet, these institutions were still quite fluid during the Yazıcıoğlus' time, only gradually acquiring a hierarchical character. The third hierarchy, which may overlap with the second, consists of the community of Sufi teachers and students. As a collection of loose groupings of mystical guides and adepts stretching across the Islamic world, the nature of these secretive communities is particularly hard to characterise, even though the interpersonal bonds they created were often extremely strong and enduring. The Yazıcıoğlus, then, were positioned at various nodes in these three evolving networks – military and political leaders, scholars and Sufis. As the following biographical sketch gains its outlines, the differences of these three networks and the character of the relationships that sustained them will become apparent.

The limited sources on the Yazıcıoğlus' lives mean that this study will rely on an analysis of the same restricted set of clues that previous scholars of the Yazıcıoğlus have also utilised. As such, this study is destined to partially recapitulate the findings of the pioneering Âmil Çelebioğlu, who also attempted to reconstruct a biography of Meḥmed Yazıcıoğlu, by using a prosopographical method in the introduction to his 1996 critical edition of the *Muḥammediyye*.[2] To the late Çelebioğlu belongs the credit to be the first to model the trajectory of the Yazıcıoğlus' lives; hence, the following will inevitably retrace his work. Therefore, this chapter cannot claim originality, and it is my hope that it does justice to Çelebioğlu's earlier work. Still, important additions to Çelebioğlu's reconstruction can now be made, and this also makes it possible to dispute several of his conclusions.

Themes

The various stages of the two-generation trajectory of Ṣāliḥ and his sons reveal different aspects of the Ottoman frontier. With respect to the hierarchy of the Ottoman state, Ṣāliḥ, Meḥmed and Aḥmed served multiple generations of Thracian frontier lords; they did not enjoy any direct connection to the Ottoman sultan or his court. Between the 1380s and 1456, the three men worked for or were otherwise paid by four different political-military notables who lived in the region of Malkara and Thrace – Qaṣṣāboğlu ʿAlī, İskender b. Ḥācı Paşa, Qaṣṣāboğlu Maḥmud and Aḥmed-i Ḫāṣṣ. In serving them, the Yazıcıoğlus represented a second, sub-courtly tier of provincial litterateurs bound to local leadership. Only briefly in Meḥmed's *Muḥammediyye* and more extensively in Aḥmed's *Müntehā* of 1465 did the Yazıcıoğlus write words in praise of the Ottoman sultans. The brothers thus gave testimony to the decentralisation of literary patronage during that period.

Yet, in terms of their intellectual community the Yazıcıoğlus enjoyed a position of greater centrality. In the 1410s or 1420s, Meḥmed Yazıcıoğlu appears to have been educated at least in part by one member of a group of international scholars who convened in the Ottoman capital of Edirne and were associated with the prestigious schools of Ḥanafī scholarship of Timurid Iran and Central Asia. In this way, the *'ulemā* of the capital connected the brothers to the scholarly currents of the central Islamic lands. Just as importantly, both Meḥmed and Aḥmed were disciples of Ḥācı Bayram Velī of Ankara, the focus of an Anatolian Sufi community that would grow into the geographically widespread Bayramī and Melāmī *ṭarīqas*. This community included individuals such as the poet Şeyḫī, as well as the Sufi tutor of Sultan Meḥmed II and 'patron saint' of the conquest of Constantinople, Aqşemse'd-dīn. The brothers Aḥmed and Meḥmed reserved their most fervent statements of identification for this community of Ḥācı Bayram Velī, whose spiritual guidance seems to have structured their adult lives. Through these two sets of affiliations, the Yazıcıoğlus were able to participate in the prestigious centre of Anatolian and Rumelian intellectual life, despite their peripheral political and material position. And, in the story of their lives, one also perceives echoes of changes in the way in which the Muslims in the borderlands of Gelibolu lived: the containment of *ġāzī* lords such as Ṣaruca Beg and their replacement by Ottoman viziers like Qaṣṣāboğlu Maḥmūd or regular officers like Aḥmed-i Ḫāṣṣ; the appearance of mainstream Ḥanafī scholarly networks with an international scope; and the branching out of Anatolian Sufi communities such as the Bayramīyye into Thrace and the rest of Rumelia.

Yazıcı Ṣāliḥ and the Ġāzīs *of Rumelia*

The story of the Yazıcıoğlus begins with Ṣāliḥ, father of Meḥmed and Aḥmed. Just as with so many early Ottomans, we know Ṣāliḥ only through the traces left in his writings: who his works reveal him to be, rather than by testimonies in the works themselves. Ṣāliḥ was the author of the *Şemsiyye*, a Turkish-language verse almanac of astrological and divinatory lore, dedicated in 1423 to one İskender b. Ḥācı Paşa, a Gelibolu notable. What we can say most certainly about this author is that he was a Muslim and a speaker of Anatolian Turkish and that he had received an eclectic education. This latter point is made clear by the unusual choice of topic and source material for his work, which required the mastery of a unique body of knowledge: the omen science of *malḥama*, drawn mostly from Abu Ḥubaysh al-Tiflisī's *Uṣūl al-Malāḥim*, written in Persian.[3] There also exists definitive evidence for a second basic element of his identity – that is, his native Muslim, as opposed to convert, origins. Ṣāliḥ's son Meḥmed once mentioned his father as 'Ṣāliḥ ibn Süleymān', thus explicating the Muslim name of his own grandfather.[4] Ṣāliḥ's choice of subject-matter dictated the frequent use of words of Greek origin for months, numbers, planets, ancient sages and technical terminology. Ṣāliḥ read all of these Greek names through their renditions in Arabic and Persian.[5] It is clear, then, that Yazıcı Ṣāliḥ did not directly avail himself of Greek sources while writing his *Şemsiyye*, but making use of a profusion of Arabic sources and deftly deploying Qur'anic terminology and references. Hence, Ṣāliḥ educated, to some extent, in Arabic and Persian. E. J. W. Gibb's picturesque characterisation of Ṣāliḥ as 'a quiet student' is pure speculation, but it is consistent with the evidence.[6]

Ṣāliḥ's geographic origins are much harder to determine. However, persistent traditions link Ṣāliḥ to Ankara. The famed scholar-bureaucrat Gelibolulu Muṣṭafā 'Ālī, in his *Künhü'l-Aḫbār* dating to the close of the sixteenth century, stated that 'it is probable that his birthplace was Ankara or one of the towns of the province of Rum'.[7] 'Ālī's own origins in Gelibolu give this statement some added credibility. However, the textual foundation of this assertion, if there is one, is not presently available. Another, more compelling indication of an Ankara origin is the fact that Ṣāliḥ's two sons were disciples of Ḥācı Bayram Velī; the *shaykh* spent nearly his entire life in Ankara, where he had built and lived in a still-extant *tekke* in the city's centre. As I will subsequently argue, Aḥmed and Meḥmed's relationship to Ḥācı Bayram Velī was so substantive that it suggests the brothers' physical residence in Ankara for a period of time prior to Ḥācı Bayram's death in 1429. The commonly-cited account given in Ṣarı 'Abdullāh's seventeenth-century *S̱emerātü'l-Fuād*, which claims that Ḥācı Bayram instructed the Yazıcıoğlu brothers over the course of a few days as he passed through Gelibolu *en route* to Edirne for an audience with Sultan Murād II, does not seem to account for the depth of attachment that the brothers developped toward the master Sufi.[8] Did Yazıcı Ṣāliḥ know of Ḥācı Bayram Velī and introduce his sons to him? Did the brothers have other business in Ankara, perhaps related to their father's family, and encounter the Sufi there incidentally? All of these possibilities remain viable.

Two more connections to Ankara may be suggested. Ṣāliḥ dedicated his work to one İskender b. Ḥācı Paşa b. Nāṣiru'd-dīn b. Ḫüsrev Şāh, a wealthy notable of Gelibolu, active around the turn of the fifteenth century The twentieth-century historian İsmail Hakkı Uzunçarşılı, in a brief discussion of the Yazıcıoğlu family in his *Osmanlı Tarihi*,[9] has asserted that İskender and his forefathers were members of the Devletḫan family, one of the most powerful aristocratic families of Ankara and known as temporary beneficiaries of Tīmūr's defeat of the Ottoman army in 1402. Unfortunately, Uzunçarşılı did not cite his evidence for this claim, nor can this author find any trace of the origin of this assertion. Finally, the great seventeenth-century Ottoman traveller and memoirist Evliyā Çelebi, without providing any further details, asserted that Ṣāliḥ's tomb is in Ankara.[10]

Ġāzīs of Rumelia: Qaṣṣāboğlu 'Ali and İskender b. Ḥāci Paşa, ~ 1388–1423

The 'quiet student' appears to the historian's gaze only through the *Şemsiyye*, his sole surviving written work. A manuscript at Leiden University seems to provide a clear date for its own completion – 14 Jumādā al-Awwal 826 AH (24 April 1423 CE) – with these chronogrammatic lines: 'The day was Saturday, when I finished this book [. . .] This worthy book was written / on the fourteenth of Jumādā-i Awwal [. . .] To all who ask of its date, give / *mesned baḥr 'aṭā ṣāḥib 'eyyār*'. The *abjad* sum of this chronogram totals 826, providing what appears to be a secure fixed point on which to pin the rest of Ṣāliḥ's biography. However, this runs counter the conclusions of Âmil Çelebioğlu and Atila Batur, who have dated the work to 811/1408–9 on the basis of a line found elsewhere in the work – the only date present in the more widely-used Pertevniyal 766 manuscript.[11] But upon examining the context in which this date is provided, it becomes clear that it simply serves as an example for the specific hemerological prognosticatory technique.[12] The 826/1423 date also makes more sense for historical reasons. Elsewhere in the *Şemsiyye*, Ṣāliḥ discussed his thirty-six years of service to his master Qaṣṣāboğlu 'Alī Beg. If one counts backwards from 1408–9, then he would have begun serving Qaṣṣāboğlu in 1372 or 1373 at the latest – when Gelibolu was out of Ottoman hands, under the rule of Amadeo of Savoy and the Byzantines. However, if the date 826 AH is taken as vantage point, then his service could have begun as late as 789–90/1387–88, a decade after Gelibolu was retaken. This later date now appears far more likely. Ṣāliḥ, then, arrived in Gelibolu within a decade of the end of its ten-year occupation by Amadeo and the Byzantines, was thus part of the first generation of Turkish and Muslim settlers to reoccupy the city and then spent thirty-six years serving Qaṣṣāboğlu 'Alī in Rumelia. Ṣāliḥ described his life as a scribe for Qaṣṣāboğlu with the following lines:

I shall tell news of the [my state]
Listen with love, O master of art.
This Qaṣṣāboğlu ʿAlī Beg, immaculate in faith,
pure of heart, liberal in trust,
disposed towards perfect generosity and intellect,
a person of companionship, who listens and speaks,
God's elect, a leader of men,
his heart is full of light, jewel of the begs –
[. . .].
Though I was neither a *beg* myself, nor clearly a slave
I was accepted in whatever I would say or do.
For thirty-six years he never left me.
Not for one day did he intentionally hurt my heart.
Nor was I lacking in my service.
I served him day and night.
Happy or grim, however time passed,
Together we turned sadness into joy.[13]

This passage gives us a window into the nature of Ṣāliḥ's service to Qaṣṣāboğlu ʿAlī. It tells us, for example, that Ṣāliḥ was no aristocrat ('I was neither a *beg* myself . . .'), nor was he, as already suspected, of the non-Muslim origin required to be 'clearly a slave'. Rather, he joined Qaṣṣāboğlu ʿAlī's service as a scribal employee – a *kātib* or *yazıcı*, the profession that gave him and his sons the names by which they came to be known. Ṣāliḥ would have been charged with drafting correspondence from Qaṣṣāboğlu ʿAlī to other *beg*s and also performing administrative book-keeping of all kinds. One may attain some idea of a *yazıcı*'s tasks from the unrelated historian Yazıcıoğlu ʿAlī, who had acquired his identical name by performing the same service only slightly later, for Sultan Murād II. In his *Tevārīḫ-i Āl-i Selcūq* he glorified the 'swift-handed scribes [*yazıcılar*] and accountants who can take the measure of the sea in its greatness and in their smallness discern a miniscule speck or atom of dust or grain of barley'.[14] ʿAlī then listed a scribe's duties: 'An accountant, to be skilled in his art / must be capable of arithmetic and numeric shorthand [*sıyāqāt*]', and with this skill, . . .

Account for the requirements of the troops
and record it in a book for the king.
Let not a farm plot or arable field
be excluded, for certain,
but written in some register.
The scribe is needed for his writing.
Every year soldiers come forth
to each have their own *tīmār* granted.

The administrators' intellect sees
what the income of each one is.

Although this author described duties, such as the granting of *tīmār*s, that were pertained to the Ottoman central administration under Murād II, with a few adjustments 'Alī's verses may very well describe a career like Ṣāliḥ's. In performing these administrative duties, Ṣāliḥ joined the ranks of the 'scholar-bureaucrats' who provided an important service to the Turkic *amīr*s of the late medieval and early modern periods.

Turning once again to Ṣāliḥ's verses on his service to Qaṣṣāboğlu, one is struck by the subjective sense that they transcend the customary expressions of praise for a patron and indicate a strong personal friendship between the two men. It is likely, too, that Qaṣṣāboğlu 'Alī employed Ṣāliḥ for another, second purpose – the education of his own son Qaṣṣāboğlu Maḥmūd, later the patron and friend of Yazıcıoğlu Meḥmed. In any case, the thirty-six years of service sufficed to establish a multi-generational bond between Ṣāliḥ 'the scribe' and the Qaṣṣāboğlu family, which would later be renewed.

Qaṣṣāboğlu 'Alī, Ṣaruca Beg and the Civil War

Qaṣṣāboğlu 'Alī is invisible in the chronicles. However, he was clearly an important man. We know this on the basis of a piece of information that unlocks the Thracian context of Qaṣṣāboğlu 'Alī's and Ṣāliḥ's lives, an entry in a *taḥrīr* register from the region of Gelibolu and Malkara in 1519/925.[15] Describing the Thracian village Qırıq-'Alī whose income was entrusted to the *vaqf* of an *'imāret* in the Yedikule neighbourhood of Istanbul, this entry mentions that the village income was at one time at the disposal of Qaṣṣāboğlu Meḥmed, who later sold it. The entry goes on to make clear that this Meḥmed was the son of both Qaṣṣāboğlu 'Alī and a woman named Cevher Ḫatun, daughter of Ṣaruca Beg, a military-political leader of the first rank.

Ṣaruca (d. 1454) was one of the foremost *ġāzī* lords of Murād I and Bāyezīd II's reign. He conquered the Thracian town of Çirmen (modern Ormenio) from the Serbs and, holding the title of *ṣancaqbegi*, ruled its hinterland as a personal fief; in 1386 he brought soldiers from Çirmen to fight for Murād in Karaman, and in 1388 he led infantry in a battle at the Danube. In the first Battle of Kosovo of 1389, he commanded the Aydınlı and Ṣaruḫanlu soldiers on Murād I's behalf. At Ankara in 1402, he led the Ottoman army's wing comprised of Rumelian soldiers.[16] Moreover, Ṣaruca is perhaps most famous as an early commander of the Ottoman navy, one of the first figures to hold the title of *qapudān-i deryā*.[17] In 790/1390, he took charge of several captured Byzantine vessels and set up Gelibolu as the base of the first Ottoman fleet. To do so required a restructuring of the town's urban plan: The city's outer walls were torn down, and its citadel was enhanced with two towers protecting the harbour. Before he died around 818/1415, he built a *ḥammām*, a *kervānseray* and other buildings in Gelibolu, similar buildings in Hasköy, as well as two mosques, one in Çirmen and another in Yeni Zagra.[18]During the reigns of Murād I and Bāyezīd II, Ṣaruca Beg was one of the most powerful men in Rumelia, particularly identified with the city of Gelibolu and the Thracian hinterland.

If Ṣaruca gave his daughter Cevher Ḫatun in marriage to Qaṣṣāboğlu ʻAlī, as the *taḥrīr* says, then one can infer that ʻAlī had reached a high position among his fellow frontier lords. This detail also reveals where Qaṣṣāboğlu ʻAlī and his employee Ṣāliḥ were living in the period after 1388. To be precise, they were attached to the enterprise of Ṣaruca Beg in Thrace, a venture comprised of the twin activities of inland conquest, centred on frontier regions such as Çirmen, and maritime-naval development, focused on Gelibolu. One can imagine Qaṣṣāboğlu ʻAlī accompanying Ṣaruca Beg during the latter's activities: from the frontier regions of Kavala, Serez, İşkeçe, Dimetoka and Çirmen in western Thrace, through Ipsala, Keşan and Malkara, where the Via Egnatia passed, to the port of Gelibolu with its new fleet, whence one could cross to Lapseki and pass over land to the capital of Bursa. As a member of Ṣaruca's coalition, Qaṣṣāboğlu ʻAlī would have provided troops for his father-in-law and campaigned alongside him. Did he also bring along with him his scribe, Ṣāliḥ, much like Lala Muṣṭafā Paşa who two centuries later brought along another resident of Gelibolu, the scribe Muṣṭafā ʻĀlī?

Ṣaruca's power on the Rumelian frontier may have been self-sufficient, but this does not mean that the Ottoman sultan was absent from the picture. For much of the period in question, Murād I and Bāyezīd I were based in Edirne, not far from Ṣaruca's strongholds in Gelibolu and Çirmen. Indeed, the sultan often passed through Gelibolu and Malkara with his army. Murād I passed through Gelibolu and Malkara multiple times, the last time in 1389, the year of his death, when Neşri recorded that 'it so happened that at that time it was quite cold and a contrary wind blew; the emperor stayed a few days, and then left the ships in the hands of the lord of Gelibolu, Yence Beg [. . . Prince] Bāyezīd also came, crossed at Gelibolu, and joined up with the Emperor'.[19] Ṣaruca, too, seems to have been a loyal soldier for the Ottoman house: No trace of conflict appears in the sources, and he was entrusted with important duties on behalf of the sultan in Kosovo, Ankara and several other battles.

Matters of loyalty to the state became more complex after 1402. The party of Ṣaruca Beg, which included Qaṣṣāboğlu ʿAlī and his entourage, occupied a definite place within the factions of the Ottoman Civil War that followed the disastrous Battle of Ankara in 1402. When Tīmūr captured Yıldırım Bāyezīd there and set the sultan's sons fighting among each other, the Rumelian provinces fell under the domain of Bāyezīd's oldest living son, Süleymān, under the terms of a *yārlıġ* vassalage granted by Tīmūr. Emir Süleymān continued to control most of the Ottoman Balkans for eight years, and Ṣaruca Beg served him, as did most other Rumelian *begs*. The chronicler Konstantin the Philosopher wrote that in 1410 Ṣaruca Beg was serving as Süleymān's governor in Yambol in what is now south-central Bulgaria, when he was defeated at the hands of Süleymān's younger brother Mūsā, captured and carried to Edirne.[20] There, his presence as a hostage seems to have opened up the gates of that city. Ṣaruca was killed when Mūsā took Gelibolu.[21] Without the help of his general, Süleymān was sure to fall to Mūsā. Mūsā held Rumelia until his brother Meḥmed was ultimately able to defeat him and reunite the Ottoman realm within its pre-1402 borders. Ṣaruca, Qaṣṣāboğlu and the scribe Ṣāliḥ were thus part of a losing faction in the war.

Some time during the period of service to Qaṣṣāboğlu ʿAlī, Ṣāliḥ's older son Meḥmed was born. Three much later sources mentioning Meḥmed's birthplace may preserve the precise location of Ṣāliḥ's residence in Thrace. Writing in the early eighteenth century, Ismāʿīl Ḥaqqı Bursevī asserted that Meḥmed 'was not born of his mother in Gelibolu, but rather was raised in a village called Kadıköyü attached to the town of Malkara'. A page inserted at the beginning of some nineteenth-century printed editions of the *Muḥammediyye* repeats this information, stating: 'The one known as Yazıcıoğlu Meḥmed Efendi [. . .] was born in a village called Kadıköyü attached to a town called Malkara in Rumelia and settled later in Gelibolu . . .'[22] Finally, Bursalı Meḥmed Tahir in '*Osmanlı Mü'ellifleri* repeated this a third time: 'Though his birthplace is Kadıköyü in the district of Malkara, it is accepted that his place of residence was Gelibolu'. The fact that the latter two statements were probably based on Bursevī's original assertion does not necessarily discredit the historicity of that claim; Bursevī was a famous member of the Bayramīyye Sufi *ṭarīqa* that upheld the Yazıcıoğlus' legacy and may have had access to evidence we no longer possess. If we trust Bursevī, then it is possible that Ṣāliḥ and his wife, beginning sometime in the 1380s, lived in the still-extant village of Kadıköyü a short distance from Malkara and that he served Qaṣṣāboğlu ʿAlī from there.[23] The village of Kadıköyü ('the judge's village'), a mere twenty-five kilometres from Malkara and sixty from Gelibolu, is a unique one in the political geography of southern Thrace. This village served as the *tīmār* of the *qāḍı* (judge) of Gelibolu – that is, the income of the village was managed by the *qāḍı*, who would partially use it for the upkeep of his own household and deliver a certain quantity as tax. The *taḥrīr* register of the environs of Gelibolu from 879/1475 also mentions that in Kadıköyü there was a *zāviye*, already well in ruins, bearing the name of *Qāḍı Ṣalāḥu'd-dīn*.[24] We are now left with a suggestive question: Was Yazıcı Ṣāliḥ serving – at Qaṣṣāboğlu 'Alī's request – as judge of the Gelibolu region?

As for the identity of Ṣāliḥ's wife, the mother of Meḥmed and Aḥmed, there is only a single apocryphal clue, this time from an oral source recorded by Âmil Çelebioğlu: She was a woman from Müctebe, another village in the area.[25] The inability of this study to speak about the mother and wife of its subjects is a lamentable gap.

İskender ibn Ḥāci Paşa

Whether in battle – for instance, in the 813/1410 battle at Yambol that led to Ṣaruca Beg's final demise, or in Emīr Süleymān's campaigns for Bursa and Ankara, or during the course of his generals' feuds with Mūsā in Rumelia – or from natural causes, Qassaboğlu 'Alī passed away during the Civil War years. After thirty-six years and well into his middle age, Ṣāliḥ had to seek new employment as a scribe. His personal philosophy, developped over long years of scribal service, gave him a roadmap with which to navigate this challenging transition: 'Great is war and altercation in the land of Rum, but through knowledge, one has a path to all things'. Nevertheless, the search for a new employer and protector seems to have been difficult. Ṣāliḥ wrote:

> Since my separation from him, I have felt no joy.
> Always occupied, I found no repose.
> I tried to make my heart understand and be happy,
> and to be freed from sadness, and at ease.
> Eventually I came to know my intellect again.
> I told my heart to come back to life.
> I said to it, what can we do?
> What is the remedy, where should we go?[26]

Ṣāliḥ's expression of grief reflects the limited market for scribes writing in Turkish. Ṣāliḥ framed these 'lost years' as a dialogue between his despairing heart and the methodical optimism of his intellect. The intellect reassures his heart, reasoning that God will eventually provide him with a new patron: 'For God's decree is destiny's path. / Why sigh with pain at whatever it holds?' Eventually, Ṣāliḥ roused himself and began the difficult search for a new patron: 'I inquired extensively and searched. I swallowed my fears and encouraged myself. I thought, "I wonder what I'm doing"'. 'I don't know where I'm going!' Ṣāliḥ said, describing the confusion of his journey at the edge of destitution and in the midst of war. Ṣāliḥ's account of this search is worth quoting in full:

The intellect joined with the heart and left,
    And went searching for a while in the world,
Among city-dwelling *qāḍı*s and *ḫoca*s and *sipāhī*s,
    Seeing all of them, both strangers and locals.
Ketḫüdā, notable ['*ayān*], *beg*, king [*şāh*] and *vezīr*,
    The head of the merchant guild, the worker, the scribe [*debīr*]
[I] saw some *ṣubaşı*s,
    and asked how they could favour me.
I travelled the world from end to end,
    [Until] a dear one bestowed a privilege . . .[27]

Here Ṣāliḥ gives us a view of the classes of elite Ottomans society which could employ a scribe. This world was an urban world, where local intellectuals and religious scholars ('city-dwelling *qāḍı*s and *ḫoca*s') occupied high positions in cities and where urban tax-paying classes (merchants, workers, administrative scribes) also held some measure of independent wealth and power. Although the political structure attached to the Ottoman state was represented by the '*ketḫüdā*, notable, *beg*, king [*şāh*] and *vezīr*', the manner in which each of these titles are listed, mixed with each other and with the lower classes, somehow suggests a decentralisation of power, as if each social class operated with some degree of independence. This political world appears as a sequence of notables, each with enough wealth and power to employ a scribe, but also without a visible hierarchy or myth of state.

In the end, Ṣaliḥ finally found a new patron and protector in the person of one İskender b. Hācı Paşa. This individual is not a complete cipher, although his family is more obscure than the Qaṣṣāboğlus. We know, first of all, İskender's parentage:

He bears the name of Sikender, and his name is well-known.
    His company is desirable; he is perfect, kinglike.
His father is Ḥācı Paşa, pole of the age,
    The son of Naṣru'd-dīn, without doubt.
Ḫoca Naṣr was a moon in the world,
    and his father was Ḫüsrev Şāh.[28]

Modern historians have speculated on İskender's identity in two ways. To some early readers of the *Şemsiyye*, the name Ḥācı Paşa suggested Ḥācı Paşa of Germiyan (d. 1424), a contemporary who studied in Mamluk Egypt with Ottoman luminaries such as Molla Fenarī, Şeyḫ Bedre'd-dīn and the poet Aḥmedī, before returning to the Aegean cities of Ayasuluk and Birgi where he wrote works of medicine on behalf of the Aydınoğlu lord 'Īsā Beg and later for Murād II.[29] While this fascinating individual is consistent with Ṣāliḥ's biography in terms of chronology, prosopography and even intellectual interests, Ḥācı Paşa's autograph manuscript of his *Kitābu's-sa'ada wa'l-iqbāl* lists his own name as 'Ḥācı Paşa b. Ḫoca 'Alī b. Murād b. Ḫoca 'Alī b. Hüsāme'd-dīn el-Qunawī'.[30] Since one cannot presume that either Ḥācı Paşa of Germiyan wrote his father's name incorrectly, or that Ṣāliḥ was mistaken as to the lineage of his own employer, these cannot be the same Ḥācı Paşa.

İsmail Hakkı Uzunçarşılı advanced another possibility. Ṣāliḥ's praise of İskender in the form of the reference 'and his forefathers [*ebā-'an-cedd*] were viziers' recalls another Ḥācı Paşa: an Ottoman vizier who held his post in 1348–49 under the reign of Sultan Orḫan.[31] Unfortunately, this vizier is not listed in the historical calendars or anywhere else, and Danışmend has reminded us that 'his real name is not even clear'. Uzunçarşılı went one step further, using unknown sources to identify Ḥācı Paşa with the Devletḫan family of Ankara. Based on Uzunçarşılı's assertion of an origin in Ankara, others have inferred that the vizier Ḥācı Paşa was from an '*aḫi*' background, or that he was a scholar.[32] Yet, without the information to which Uzunçarşılı was privy, we can go no further in pursuing this avenue of inquiry.

The real answer to the question of İskender's identity is written in stone in Gelibolu itself. In the Hamzaköyü neighbourhood of the city, there stands an elegant marble prayer platform (*namāzgāh*) overlooking the Dardanelles, close to the cave where, according to later narrations, Meḥmed Yazıcıoğlu composed the *Muḥammediyye*. Described by the architectural historian Ekrem Hakkı Ayverdi as 'the finest of the country's extant *namāzgāhs*',[33] this platform was built in 1407 in a distinctive Persianate style in order to serve the needs of *'azeb* infantry soldiers passing through Gelibolu *en route* to campaigns in Rumelia and Anatolia. In fair weather, it provided a site where they could congregate and pray as they began or ended their march or embarked on or disembarked from their ships. Thus, it is a perfect architectural comment on the ethos of the maritime *ġazā* that shaped Gelibolu's character. Most importantly, an Arabic inscription on the left *minbar* reads: 'This built structure [*al-'imārat al-ma'mūra*], a *qibla* for the *'azabs*, was completed by İskandar ibn al-Ḥājj Bāshā'. This is clearly Ṣāliḥ's patron. His identity is now less mysterious.

İskender, builder of the *namāzgāh*, must have been a military man. Another inscription in the *namāzgāh* invokes 'God, opener of doors / O You of secret graces – protect us from what we fear!', calling up a familiar description of Gelibolu as the 'door' of Rumelia and Anatolia that would be repeated by Meḥmed II's construction of the immense fortress of Kilidü'l-baḥr ('the sea's key') at the tip of the peninsula of the Dardanelles. Ṣāliḥ's own verses corroborate this image of a patron of soldiers: 'He grants the partaking of food and drink / His gifts perfect, his words without error / Inwardly and outwardly a commander of his intellect, love and enthusiasms / And, as head of the [skillful ones], a fine commander'.[34] This is the extent of our knowledge on İskender b. Ḥācı Paşa. It is for him that Ṣāliḥ wrote his astrological poem *Şemsiyye*.

We know no more of Ṣāliḥ after his composition of the *Şemsiyye*. About Ṣāliḥ's final years and death there exist no clues, except for Evliyā Çelebī's passing reference to Ṣāliḥ's tomb in Ankara.[35] If Evliyā's assertion is true, then perhaps Ṣāliḥ retired to his city of origin.

Meḥmed and Aḥmed, Sons of the Scribe

The tradition, reaching us through Ismā'īl Ḥaqqı Bursevī, that Meḥmed Yazıcıoğlu was born in Kadıköyü south of Malkara is particularly plausible in light of the fact that it was during this period that Ṣāliḥ worked for a Thracian *ġāzī* under Ṣaruca Beg, who was often based in Malkara. But this hypothesis cannot take us far in establishing a chronology of the early life of Meḥmed Yazıcıoğlu and his younger brother Aḥmed. Just as the *Şemsiyye* offers the only tool for studying the life of Ṣāliḥ, for Meḥmed's life we must rely on the *Muḥammediyye*, which mentions a handful of acquaintances in the opening and closing sections of the work and is thus the primary means for piecing together the brothers' lives. Moreover, both Aḥmed and Meḥmed also discussed literary works written by living individuals and thereby showed themselves as participants in contemporaneous intellectual networks. In the absence of external narratives on their lives, these references comprise the raw material for the prosopographical chronology that follows.

Connected Families

Meḥmed wrote in the *Muhammediyye* that it was for the sake of Maḥmūd Paşa ibn Qaṣṣāb that 'in Gelibolu [he] made [his] home'. We can definitively link the context of Meḥmed's and Aḥmed's early life to Qaṣṣāboğlu Maḥmūd, the son of 'Alī, the long-time employer of their father. Maḥmūd, as we will see, grew up to become an important historical personage in his own right, a vizier to Murād II, discussed in chronicles and documentary records. By the time of his death, which occurred before 1456, he was the owner of many properties around Gelibolu and earned many thousand *aqçe* a year. But before 1423, when Meḥmed and Aḥmed were children, adolescents and young men, Maḥmūd and his own brother Qaṣṣāboğlu Meḥmed, of similar age, still lived in their father's household. It is likely that, while they all were together in Qaṣṣāboğlu 'Alī's home before 1409, Ṣāliḥ served as tutor for all of them, instructing Maḥmūd and Qassaboglu Meḥmed alongside his own two sons. Âmil Çelebioğlu has convincingly suggested that Meḥmed Yazıcıoğlu and Qaṣṣāboğlu Maḥmūd were childhood friends. By 1449, when Meḥmed wrote the *Muḥammediyye* and indicated his financial dependence on Maḥmūd, the bond between the two men had endured at least forty years, even longer than the bond that had united their fathers.

Dervīş Bāyezīd

In adolescence or later, Meḥmed must have left the household of his father and the Qaṣṣāboğlus and struck out on his own. The next individual mentioned by Meḥmed Yazıcıoğlu is someone named Dervīş Bāyezīd, described with the following ambiguous lines:

> To the tomb of the trustworthy one, the *shaykh* Dervīş Bāyezīd
> Comes ever-increasing exaltation.
> How in his time he made the earth smile,
> When Dervīş Bāyezīd was entrusted with it!
> Because of him Gelibolu became Bisṭām,
> And Bisṭām again found its Shaykh Bāyezīd.[36]

Meḥmed here played on the name and reputation of the ninth-century figure Bāyazīd of Bisṭām as an exemplar of Sufi wisdom. In fact, in these lines Dervīş Bāyezīd of Gelibolu is so over-shadowed by the time-worn image of Bāyazīd Bisṭāmī, the Sufi of myth, that one may be forgiven for assuming that the former does not exist at all – were it not for the fact that Dervīş Bāyezīd of Gelibolu is attested in multiple biographical and documentary sources as a prominent resident of the town during the late fourteenth and early fifteenth centuries. Dervīş Bāyezīd is mentioned in Taşköprüzāde's and Mecdī's biographical dictionaries, the latter asserting that 'this able, wise person was appointed as teacher to prince Sultan

Meḥmed Han, son of the Ottoman Sultan Bāyezīd'.[37] The 870/1475 *taḥrīr* register from Gelibolu adds corroborating evidence: Accordingly, a Dervīş Bāyezīd founded a Sufi lodge in a village near Gelibolu named Seydī Kavaği, and the funding for this *zāviye* came from three *kervānsarāys*, two *ḥammāms*, a pasture with fifteen cows, one farm, one salt mine and several other properties in the vicinity of Gelibolu and nearby Bolayır. By 1475, so the *taḥrīr* adds, many of these properties had been sold or had fallen into ruin, and the *taḥrīr* register of 1519 mentions neither the *zāviye* nor its properties.[38] All of this implies that the foundation of the *zāviye* took place in the 1390s and that its founder could have been acquainted with prince Meḥmed Çelebi before his father's capture in 1402; thus, he could have instructed Meḥmed Yazıcıoğlu during his youth.[39] Did the well-connected Dervīş Bāyezīd, a tutor to the sultan, introduce Meḥmed and his brother to the concepts of Sufi doctrine and practice in the closing years of the fourteenth century?

Zayn al-'Arab

The historicity of the next name mentioned by Meḥmed in the *Muḥammediyye* is more problematic:

> My teacher was Zeyn-i 'Arab
> Who was cultured both inside and out.
> He directed my ambitions,
> Until I reached Ḥaydar-i Khvāfī.
> [. . .]
> Intercede, O beloved of God, lord,
> and give them unto the highest heaven.[40]

Çelebioğlu, Yerasimos and all other scholars of Meḥmed Yazıcıoğlu have taken this name to refer to 'Alī b. 'Abdullāh Zayn al-'Arab al-Nakhchivānī al-Miṣrī, a fourteenth-century scholar of *ḥadīth* famous for his commentaries on the *Maṣābīḥ al-Sunna* by the medieval traditionist al-Baghawī. In support of this identification, Çelebioğlu has also cited an architectural historian who situated the tomb of this Zayn in Gelibolu proper.[41] This building seems to be no longer extant. Yet, this identification poses significant chronological and contextual problems. Firstly, Kātib Çelebi and the rest of the Arabic and Ottoman bio-bibliographical tradition insisted that Zayn's major works were written around 750/1350, more than half a century before the years in question. Secondly, it is believed that he built his career in Mamluk Egypt, not in Rum, as his work is dedicated to the Mamluk Sultan Badr al-dīn Ḥasan. Beyond this purported tomb, which is now unrecoverable without the aid of archaeology, there is nothing whatsoever to indicate his residence in Gelibolu, or even in Rum or Rumelia. Thus, it is hard to imagine a time when the famous Zayn could have physically instructed Meḥmed. The so-called Tomb of Zayn may have been retrospectively attributed to him after the rise to fame of the *Muḥammediyye* and the names within it.

It then becomes difficult to know what exactly Meḥmed meant when he brought up the name of Zayn al-ʿArab. It will subsequently be argued that Meḥmed read, studied and extensively used Zayn's commentary on the *Maṣābīḥ al-Sunna* in his own *Maghārib al-Zamān* and *Muḥammediyye*. Citing Zayn as his 'first teacher' is then an acknowledgment of his own intellectual debt to Zayn's work, although not, it seems, an indication that Zayn personally was his tutor.

THE SCHOLARS OF EDIRNE

In the above verses Meḥmed asserted that his period of academic study, which began with the works of Zayn and the *Maṣābīḥ* tradition, ended with his 'last teacher', Ḥaydar-i Khvāfī. This figure marks an important endpoint to this stage of Meḥmed's life and, as we will discover, integrated him fully into the world of the internationally-minded intelligentsia of Rum. At first glance the identity of Ḥaydar-i Khvāfī appears ambiguous. No Ottoman biographical source refers to a scholar of this name, and he is also absent from the *taḥrīr* and *vaqfiyye* registers that help us populate so much else in the Yazıcıoğlu family's biography. Thankfully, Ismāʿīl Haqqı Bursevī, as he also attempted to discover the identity of this Ḥaydar in the early eighteenth century, concluded with a clue that may lead us to his identity: 'What is intended by this [name]', Bursevī said, 'is Ḥaydar Haravī, who was one of the students of Saʿd al-dīn Taftazānī and gave the *fetvā* for the killing of Şeyḫ Bedre'd-dīn the Executed'.[42]

This assertion is particularly interesting. This Ḥaydar Haravī, properly known as Burhān al-dīn Ḥaydar b. Muḥammad al-Harawī al-Khvāfī (d. 1427), is described by Mecdī as . . .

> a student of Saʿd al-dīn Taftazānī. He was learned and virtuous and wise and scrupulous and excelled among the ranks of high virtue. I saw his annotations of the *Sharḥ Kashshāf* of his teacher Molla al-ʿAllāma Saʿd al-dīn Taftazānī [. . .] And he has a commentary on the *Īḍāḥ al-Maʿānā*, and I heard that he has a commentary of the *Farā'id al-Sirajiyya* . . .

Mecdī added that 'he drafted annotations to Saʿd al-dīn's *Kashshāf* commentary and composed replies to Sayyid Sharīf [Jurjānī]'s criticisms';

furthermore, he extended his entry to claim that 'it is recorded that this virtuous one studied with Mevlānā Muḥammad Kāfiyajī and Mevlānā Ḫüsrev'.[43] Kātib Çelebi also recorded Ḥaydar's commentaries on the *Sharḥ Kashshāf*, the *Īḍāḥ*, the *Farā'id al-Sirajiyya*, as well as al-Ījī's *al-Mawāqif*.[44] Each of these works of Ḥaydar survive to the present and were reproduced many times.

According to the biographical dictionary tradition, Burhān al-dīn Ḥaydar Haravī was a Khurasani intellectual with roots in Khvāf near Nishapur, or in Herat. In the last quarter of the fourteenth century he moved to Tīmūr's Samarqand for schooling, where he became part of the circle of Ḥanafī scholars that orbited around the rivals Sa'd al-dīn Taftazānī and Sayyid Sharīf Jurjānī. From the perspective of subsequent Ḥanafī jurisprudence, this cadre constituted the absolute apotheosis of their own Ḥanafī scholarly tradition and models for generations of Ḥanafī legists in the Ottoman Empire, as in Central Asia and India. Many of their works, such as Jurjānī's dictionary (*Ta'rīfāt*) and Taftazānī's *Sharḥ Kashshāf* and *Sharḥ Talkhīs*, functioned as mandatory components of Ḥanafī *medrese* curricula across the *dār al-islām* of the early modern period.[45] This enduring legacy is partly owed to the tendency of many of Taftazānī's and Jurjānī's students to migrate out of Khurasan and Transoxiana and, thanks to the pedigree of the schools of Timurid Samarqand, quickly climb to the top of local scholarly hierarchies and establish lasting institutions in their new regions. In the Ottoman realm under Çelebi Meḥmed and Murād II, these Timurid scholars forged close connections with native Rumi *'ulemā* such as Meḥmed Şāh Fenarī; from this union, what was to become the Ottoman scholarly establishment emerged.[46]

Burhān al-dīn Ḥaydar Haravī was part of this process. After studying with Taftazānī and the Māturīdī-aligned scholars of Samarqand, he travelled to Rum, where he taught Molla Ḫüsrev and possibly Meḥmed Yazıcıoğlu and others. His fellow migrants included Fakhr al-dīn 'Ajamī, one of the earliest Ottoman *şeyḫü'l-islām*s and a student of Jurjānī; Sayyid 'Alī 'Ajamī, also a student of Jurjānī; and Molla Ṭūsī, a later *şeyḫü'l-islām*.[47] Edirne was their base where, for instance, Fakhr al-dīn was appointed to preach at the Dārü'l-ḥadīs Mosque Complex built by Murād II and where, in 1444, he decreed the execution by fire of a Ḥurūfi missionary.[48] Edirne, too, was the place where Haravī must have been residing when he was called to issue a *fetvā* for the execution of Şeyḫ Bedre'd-dīn Simavī in 1420.

Returning to the life of Meḥmed Yazıcıoğlu, we may conclude that he travelled from the Gelibolu-Malkara region to Edirne between approximately 1410 and 1425 in order to further his studies in the religious sciences, and that he found instruction with the Khurasani teacher Ḥaydar Haravī who had arrived from the Timurid east. This instruction most likely was conducted entirely in Arabic and focused on the works of Ḥanafī jurisprudence that Haravī had learned from Taftazānī, specifically the *Kashshāf* of al-Zamakhsharī and its various commentaries. The ample discussion of these works in the Yazıcıoğlus' own writings, including those of Taftazānī himself, whose lifetime may even have overlapped with Meḥmed's, as well as those of Jurjānī who died somewhat earlier, comprises further evidence of the scholarly connection between the senior Khurasani *'ālim* and the provincial student from the Rumelian frontier.

We see, then, that Meḥmed Yazıcıoğlu was in contact with the core of Ottoman orthodox scholarship. Within one degree of separation from Haravī and two from Meḥmed were the following intellectuals: the Fenarī family, the founding family of the Ottoman *'ulamā* system; Musannifek, a Khurasani scholar of approximately the same age as Meḥmed Yazıcıoğlu, who served as instructor to Sultan Meḥmed; the *muftī*s Fakhr al-dīn 'Ajamī and Molla Ṭūsī; the Rumi student Molla Ḫüsrev who would become a prominent scholar in Meḥmed II's reign; Muṣliḥu'd-dīn Hocazāde Rūmī, a famous scholar of natural philosophy famed in both Transoxiana and Rum for his expertise in logic, astronomy and mathematics; and Molla Gürani, who originated from the Kurdish region, studied in Cairo and then came to found a *medrese* in newly-conquered Istanbul.[49] All of these scholars spent considerable time in Edirne when Ḥaydar Haravī was there and when Meḥmed Yazıcıoğlu may have been his student.

The Bedre'd-dīn Question

The most controversial event in the biographical profile of Burhāne'd-dīn Ḥaydar Haravī consists of his role in the execution of the Ottoman religious intellectual and political rebel Şeyḫ Bedre'd-dīn Simavī at Serez in 1420. Our sources on this famous event – the culmination of several years of political insurrection on the part of Bedre'd-dīn, former *qāḍi-'asker* and famous international scholar of Rumelian origin – attribute the execution to a *fetvā* issued by Ḥaydar Haravī upon the request of Sultan Meḥmed and his powerful vizier Bāyezīd Paşa of Amasya.[50]

The unanimity of these sources may tempt the scholar to posit some stark ideological contrast between Şeyḫ Bedre'd-dīn and his followers, on one hand, and Haravī and his Timurid Ḥanafī peers, on the other hand. This is indeed the thrust of some secondary scholarship, which attributes the execution to a fundamental incompatibility between Bedre'd-dīn's insurrectionary 'heterodoxy' and collaborationist orthodoxy.[51] However, it is worth pausing to remember a series of facts: Bedre'd-dīn had studied in Cairo with Sayyid Sharīf Jurjānī ; in Cairo he knew 'Abdurraḥmān Bisṭāmī, the famed occultist of the reign of Murād II; he was also closely acquainted with the Fenarī family there and in Rum; he taught theology in Edirne along with several Timurid immigrants, including, perhaps, Haravī himself; he participated in the Ottoman Balkan regimes of Süleymān Çelebi and then Mūsā Çelebi, as had done Ṣaruca Beg and his entourage which included Yazıcı Ṣāliḥ and the Qaṣṣāboğlus; and sources record a certain amount of dismay among the *'ulema* at the news of his death.[52] In short, Şeyḫ Bedre'd-dīn's life story and education parallel and at several points intersect with those of Ḥaydar Haravī, the man who killed him, as well as with the lives of the Yazıcıoğlus; all of these men shared a related social and intellectual context. Therefore, it is difficult to divide this context into factions or camps, each with distinct ideologies and political agendas that may somehow be read from the opposition between Çelebi Meḥmed and Şeyḫ Bedre'd-dīn. Haravī's role in the events of 1420 tells us little of the political-intellectual alignment of the Yazıcıoğlus. This is indeed part of the message of Ahmet Yaşar Ocak's comments on Bedre'd-dīn, who argues for the conflict's fundamentally economic basis.[53]

While no study on the Yazıcıoğlu family mentions Bedre'd-dīn by name, the Bayramī-Melāmī Sufi community that counts the Yazıcıoğlus as founding members over the centuries has tended to express a skeptical attitude toward the *shaykh*. 'Azīz Meḥmed Ḫüdāyī, founder of the Celvetī off-shoot of the Bayramīyye, said that Bedre'd-dīn's famous *Vāridāt* 'damaged the faith of believers and contradicted the doctrine of the community of Sunnis'. The *Muḥammediyye* commentator İsmā'īl Ḥaqqı Bursevī, coming from the same Celvetī off-shoot of the Bayramīs, wrote more ambiguously, both condemning and praising Bedre'd-dīn.[54]

In conclusion, Meḥmed Yazıcıoğlu likely studied with scholars who lived at the centre of early Ottoman intellectual life, as its learned hierarchies emerged. His own works, as will subsequently be discussed, carry the mark of the intellectual style of the Ḥanafī Timurid thinkers who occupied the pinnacle of the educational hierarchy of Edirne during the late 1410s and 1420s. But, it must be noted, Meḥmed did not strictly imitate them: He would later characterise people like Haravī as 'interpreters, legists and theologians' and juxtapose their views against the views of the Sufis who would occupy the next phase of his life. There is some truth to Bursalı Meḥmed Tahir's insight that 'while [Meḥmed], in order to bring his education to completion, benefitted from well-known individuals such as Ḥaydar Khvāfī and Zayn al-'Arab [. . .] he took his essential spiritual nourishment from Ḥācı Bayram Velī'.[55]

Anatolian Sufism: Ḥācı Bayram Velī

Before 1429, Meḥmed Yazıcıoğlu came face to face with Ḥācı Bayram Velī of Ankara, who would profoundly change his life and leave an indelible stamp on his own biography and that of his brother. The Yazıcıoğlus implied that this meeting offered each of them the profoundest illumination. Meḥmed said that he considered him 'the sultan of *shaykhs* and the seal of the *shaykhs* – the moon Ḥācı Bayram, pole of the world, the *shaykh* of the world, its king Ḥācı Bayram'. Aḥmed introduced him as 'sultan of the *shaykhs*, threshold of thresholds, pole of the truth-seekers, the most perfect of the proximate ones, guide to the people, Ḥācı Bayram'. It seems impossible to overstate the centrality of this Sufi *shaykh* to the lives of both Yazıcıcoğlu brothers. To set the brothers' first meeting with their teacher in the context it deserves, one must first locate Ḥācı Bayram's life within late-fourteenth- and early-fifteenth-century Anatolia.

Ḥācı Bayram Velī of Ankara was the most renowned mystical figure of Anatolia during his lifetime. Around such a figure biographical information tends to proliferate and grow unreliable, as later writers levy the saint's prestige in the service of contemporary concerns. Accordingly, many of his putative associations, such as the story of his friendship with the poet Eşrefoğlu Rumi of İznik, seem to be based only on much later sources of dubious reliability.[56] Yet, all these hagiographical sources preserve a core story.[57] According to common narrative elements shared by several sources, Ḥācı Bayram was born around 1350 in the town of Ṣolfaṣl (*Dhū al-faḍl*) near Ankara. His Sufi teacher was Ḥamīdu'd-dīn Aksarayī, a student of Khvāje 'Alī Ardabīlī, grandson of Ṣafī al-dīn Ardabīlī, the founder of the Ṣafavī Sufi order that would become so important to global history over the following centuries. Of south-central Anatolian origin, Ḥamīdu'd-dīn studied in Ardabil in Azerbaijan, then ruled by Tīmūr, in a pattern also shared by the founders of the Ḫalvetī order. The *Mir'ātü'l-'ışq* refers to Ḥamīdu'd-dīn's migration from Ardabil with the phrase 'in the time of Khvāje 'Alī Ardabīlī, *the secret of love*', revealed by the Prophet first to 'Alī, 'flew [from Iran] to Rum' in his person.[58] Ḥamīdu'd-dīn is said to have gone to Bursa and there to have given a sermon at the opening ceremony of Bursa's Ulu Cami in 1399, on the seven ways of understanding the *Ṣūrat al-Fātiḥa*, which impressed Molla Fenarī.[59] In that city he became known as Ṣomuncu Baba, the 'Loaf-making father', for the bakery he operated there. Leaving Bursa for reasons attributed to Tīmūr's invasion – or more likely, considering the direction of travel, because of possible competition with the Naqshbandī-aligned Sufi leader of the city, Emir Sulṭān Buḫārī – Ṣomuncu Baba spent time in a certain village in the

Çukurova region of southern Anatolia near Sis and Adana, called Nebī Sūfī, where Ḥācı Bayram met him around 1402, addressing him as 'my sultan'.

Ḥācı Bayram himself had spent the previous years as a teacher in the Melike Ḫatun Medrese in Ankara; the *Semerāt* asserts that he then rose to serve as *qapucubaşı*, a high courtly rank, for Sultan Bāyezīd I – but this assertion is not upheld by any other evidence. Similarly dubious is the claim, advanced by both Michel Balivet and Fuat Bayramoğlu, that the elderly Muslim *müderris* who encountered the Byzantine emperor Manuel II Palaiologos in Ankara in 1391 and is immortalised in his record of their lengthy mutual debate, the *Dialogues with a Persian*, was Ḥācı Bayram himself.[60] Both scholars accepted Manuel's claim that his Turkish interlocutor was 'the most famous scholar of the land' and 'acquainted with the sultan' and concluded from this that he could be none other than the famous saint before his Sufi initiation. However, Palaiologos' *müderris* mentioned having recently arrived from Babylon – in Manuel's archaicising idiom, this could mean Baghdad, Tabriz, or Cairo – and that he was already an old man. In 1391, Ḥācı Bayram was neither old, nor had he come from abroad.

After Ṣomuncu Baba gave Ḥācı Bayram the red *tāc* of his own parent order, the Ṣafaviyya, they travelled together to Syria and the Hijaz, performing the Hajj jointly, before Ṣomuncu Baba sent Ḥācı Bayram to Ankara to continue his mission. According to the *Mir'ātü'l-'ışq*, Bayram asked Ḥamīdu'd-dīn: 'But how shall I earn my keep there? I know no arts. What should I do?' Ḥamīdu'd-dīn told him to raise crops, particularly legumes.[61] By the time Ṣomuncu Baba died around 1412 in Aksaray, Ḥācı Bayram's community had grown to a significant size and had sponsored the construction of a major mosque-*zāviye* complex for his followers in Ankara. This mosque-*zāviye*, which still stands today, shares its site with the remains of the Roman Temple of Augustus, constructed in 25 BC to celebrate the emperor's conquest of Galatia; throughout the pre-Christian Roman period, the temple had served as focus of the imperial cult. Ḥācı Bayram Velī's own foundation, by contrast, seems to have evoked the *aḫī* history of Ankara, alongside the resistance to the imperial cult of Murād II.[62] According to the *Semerāt*, Ḥācı Bayram had even spent a period in spiritual retreat alongside Şeyḫ Bedre'd-dīn Simavī. Having grown alarmed at the growing following of a Sufi in an independent city outside his central lands, Murād summoned him to Edirne in 825/1422 by sending, according to this text, a *subaşı* to retrieve him. In the *Semerāt*'s telling, by the time they had crossed into Rumeli, the *subaşi* had become Ḥācı Bayram's disciple, and when they reached Edirne, the sultan, seeing the *shaykh*'s forthrightness, apologised for troubling him and requested that he give a sermon at the Eski Cami. He also exempted the Bayramiyye from taxes.

The *Semerāt* states that it was during this journey that Ḥācı Bayram passed through Gelibolu and made the acquaintance of Meḥmed and Aḥmed Yazıcıoğlu. There is some plausibility to this legend – the date of 825/1422 seems appropriate; Gelibolu was a likely transit point; and Meḥmed was probably in Gelibolu at that time. However, a look at the Yazıcıoğlus' own writings makes this seem less likely. In the final edition of his *Müntehā*, written in 870/1465, Aḥmed Bīcān used a phrase that makes such a brief meeting seem highly implausible: '[My brother Meḥmed] held the secrets of Şeyḫ Ḥācı Bayram. And this wretched one would often say to their presences [*ben meskīn her dem anlarıñ ḥażretlerine eydürdüm ki*] that the world has no permanence, and destiny has no fixity . . .'[63] Although there is considerable grammatical ambiguity here, this sentence seems to imply two things: first, that there was a moment when Aḥmed, Meḥmed and Ḥācı Bayram were all three together and, secondly, that these moments occurred more than once. Meḥmed used a similar wording in the *Maghārib al-Zamān*. The depth of Sufi attachment signals that the education of the brothers under the famous saint of Ankara was serious and sustained and more than the work of few days or weeks in Gelibolu.[64]

The most likely conclusion is that the brothers studied with Ḥācı Bayram in Ankara. We already know other threads linking the Yazıcıoğlu family to that city – namely, the possible connection of Ṣāliḥ's second patron İskender b. Ḥācı Pasa to the Devletḫan family of Ankara, as well as Muṣṭafā 'Ālī's assertion that Meḥmed was born there; to this we can add Evliyā's reference to Ṣāliḥ's tomb. Although it has been established that Ṣāliḥ was in Thrace as early as 790/1388, an Ankara family origin remains possible. If this is the case, an attractive hypothesis posits that Meḥmed and Aḥmed maintained some family links to that city and returned there in the late 1410s or early 1420s, becoming involved in Ḥācı Bayram's thriving community. Nowhere else could the brothers have lived as students and disciples of Ḥācı Bayram in a sustained way.

The Meaning of Ṭarīqa

What did this connection, which they held so dear, signify in the brothers' daily life? From Central Asia to Rumelia, the fifteenth century was for Sufi groups a time of growth and social significance. The institutionalisation of Sufi commitment can be seen clearly in the *Ṭarīqatnāme* of Eşrefoğlu Rūmī of İznik, a contemporary of the Yazıcıoğlus who wrote a well-known *dīvān* and several widely-read Sufi works. He was probably not a Bayramī Sufi; although later stories insist that he married Ḥācı Bayram Velī's daughter, his works do not mention such an event and instead show a deep connection to the distinct tradition of the Qādiriyya. In any case, his *Ṭarīqatnāme* expresses the bond of the *ṭarīqa* in words that may implicitly underlie the relationship between Meḥmed and Aḥmed Yazıcıoğlu and their common master:

> The great *shaykh*s, those guides who are said to 'have command' (*ulū'l-amr*), are deputies in the Prophet's place [. . .] And those who 'have the power' after the Prophet are those who are the finest among the people and are perfect in knowledge in [either] the exoteric and esoteric. Being thus, those who exoterically 'have command' are the *beg*s, while in truth those who 'have command' are the guides [*mürşidler*]. So, it being so, it is incumbent upon the believers not to rebel against their *beg*s, and to follow their guides, for the Messenger declared, *he who has no guidance has no religion*, that is to say, that person who has no guide has no religion.[65]

Here Eşrefoğlu ventured into Qur'anic exegesis in order to theorise the idea of Sufi guidance, in a manner more explicit than is to be found anywhere in the Yazıcıoğlus' works. He stated that a Sufi *shaykh*, as the primary inheritor of the Prophet's powers, was not simply a source of instruction and knowledge, but a leader to whom loyalty was due as if by the law of a temporal lord. Like a head of state, the fifteenth-century *mürşid* regulated the activity of a group of hierarchically-organised subordinates, directing their individual actions towards the interests of the community. To disobey, it is implied, is to betray one's faith. The Yazıcıoğlu brothers accordingly treated their *shaykh* as their ultimate leader. Nowhere in their works is any other leader accorded such a role, not even a sultan.

Early Bayramī texts such as Aqşemse'd-dīn's *al-Risālat al-nūriyya* and later ones like 'Abdurraḥmān el-'Askerī's *Mir'ātü'l-'ışq* give us the roster of those who participated in this Bayramī community in Ankara in the 1420s.[66] The innermost core of disciples was made up of those who remained in the Ankara region for most of their lives, even after the death of their master. Aqşemse'd-dīn, as is well-known, was closely associated with Sultan Meḥmed II and joined him during the Conquest of Constantinople in 1453; after returning to Göynük outside Ankara, he composed numerous important works of Sufi theory, which will be discussed below for their comparative value. Dede 'Ömer Sikkīnī broke off from Aqşemse'd-dīn's faction to lead the Melāmiyye order, which came to be a perennial fount of religious dissent in subsequent Ottoman centuries.

Not so far afield was another famous Bayramī, the poet Şeyḫī of Kütahya, the most important Turkish poet of the middle of the fifteenth century. According to the *Menāqıb* of Aqşemse'd-dīn, Şeyḫī, once a physician, was guided to the poetic arts and even given his pen-name by Ḥācı Bayram himself. Aqşemse'd-dīn purportedly claimed that in his own spiritual journeys to heaven he saw that even the angels loved to recite Şeyḫī's Turkish verses. Furthermore, in Bursa, two disciples named Aqbıyıq and Ḥıżr Dede practised Sufism; Aqbıyıq would accompany Sultan Murād II in the 1444 Battle of Varna and, around 1465, establish a *tekke* in the Istanbul neighbourhood of Cankurtaran below the Hagia Sophia. In Bolu, a certain Ṣālaḥu'd-dīn (occasionally confused with Yazıcı Ṣāliḥ) taught students; so did Molla Zeyrek, a notable scholar favoured by Sultan Meḥmed II, who studied and collaborated with many of the *'ulemā* already mentioned and therefore, like the Yazıcıoğlus and perhaps Bedre'd-dīn, himself constituted a point of intersection between the academic scholars of the capitals and the currents of Anatolian Sufism. Fātiḥ Meḥmed allowed Zeyrek to transform Constantinople's Church of Christ Pantocrator into his own *medrese*. Finally, the notable Ḥurūfī poet Seyyid Nesīmī, whose quatrains are arguably some of the finest specimens of both Ḥurūfī expression and early-fifteenth-century popular Turkish poetry, is alleged in more than one source to have studied with Ḥācı Bayram.

Considering this geographic distribution, one should note that it is north-central and northwestern Anatolia that served as home for the first generation of Bayramī disciples, with the Yazıcıoğlus of Gelibolu constituting a kind of Rumelian outpost. Other major Sufi communities occupied different geographies. Rum proper –that is, the region centred on Amasya, Sivas and Tokat – was the cradle of the Ḫalvetī order that would thrive there during the 1460s; like the Bayramīyye, the Ḫalvetiyye was also a sister order of the Ṣafaviyya, with a *silsila* extending to the *shaykh*s of Ardabīl.[67] Non-Ottoman Karaman, with its capital at Konya and reaching the port-city of Antalya and the inland centres of Kayseri and Aksaray, produced Ṣomuncu Baba, as well as later individuals belonging to the Zeyniyye order; it also was the region of birth of the Bektaşiyye. Finally, there are the 'Ottoman' cities of Bursa and Edirne, centres without an ancient Sufi tradition. In some sense, the *ṭarīqa* dynamics of the early fifteenth century was one of contest between regional Sufi groups over the allegiances of these new capitals.

This bond of *ṭarīqa* did not only imply a geographically localised political community, but also a literary and intellectual one. Once again, a comparison with the words of Eşrefoğlu Rumi helps illustrate the Sufis' context. As a Qādirī Sufi and clearly not a Bayramī despite later attributions, Eşrefoğlu discussed his own intellectual influences in the *Ṭarīqatnāme* and his *Müzekki'n-nufūs*, which lists the canon of the Qādiriyya order founded by ʻAbd al-Qādir Gīlanī in the twelfth century.[68] By contrast, one observes that the Yazıcıoğlu brothers listed individuals such as ʻAṭṭār, Ibn ʻArabī, al-Qunawī and Jandī as their Sufi ancestors – a list exactly adhered to by Aqşemse'd-dīn in the chronologically earliest Bayramī text, *al-Risālat al-Nūriyya*; they also added a number of famous names (the Turkish poet ʻĀşıq Paşa, the Persian poet ʻIrāqī, Jalalu'd-din Rumi, Shihābu'd-dīn Suhrawardī and several others) not found in Eşrefoğlu's Qādirī list.[69] Although it is certain that, sociologically speaking, the Bayramīs and Qādirīs and other orders shared a common environment, they seem to have preserved private 'reading lists' for their initiates. This is to say nothing of the canon of those orders that were more ideologically distinct, such as the Bektaşiyye.

The Ottoman Administrators

Ḥācı Bayram died in 1429, and it is impossible to know what the two brothers did next. Because all of their works written from 1448 onwards claim to have been composed in the city of Gelibolu, perhaps they moved there within a few years of the passing of their *shaykh* and lived as teachers of religious sciences and mysticism. It was during this period that Meḥmed Yazıcıoğlu may have married and fathered a child, as an amusing story in Muṣṭafā ʻĀlī's *Künhü'l-aḫbār*, cited by Çelebioğlu, relates:

> It is recounted that the *shaykh* [Meḥmed] was famous for his poverty. One hungry day when he and his young children's rations were scarce, his wife went to the bath with the little children. And she put a bit of broth into a pot [to boil] and indicated, 'watch it, so when I come back I can put in a bit of rice' [. . .] . After some time, a beggar came by, saying 'Anything for God?' and looked straight at the pot through the saint's doorway. Although the pot was reserved for his offspring and children, the kitchen of the *shaykh*'s trust in God was full of all kinds of bounties. Because of this he was not happy to see the beggar leave unsatisfied and took the pot by its handle and gave it to him, without remarking how his children would fare that night. He viewed the kind consideration of a beggar as a good thing in every respect. But when his wife came back from the bath she inquired about the pot. The saint told her point by point about the coming of the beggar and that he had given him the pot. But this woman, lacking in intellect, showed her total vexation, saying: 'But this is unfair – now what will the little children eat tonight?'[70]

Advising patience, Meḥmed later opened his front door to see that an envoy from the sultan, passing through Gelibolu on campaign, had given him a basket full of all kinds of 'delicious and sweet foods', thus illustrating the wisdom of the Qur'anic dictum: 'Whoso bringeth a good deed will receive tenfold the like thereof'.[71] Admittedly, this only weak evidence that Meḥmed had children and the text of the *Muḥammediyye* are equivocal on this point. In this connection it is worth remarking that Evliyā Çelebi claimed that he met a descendant of Meḥmed in Yenice-i Vardar in southern Macedonia.[72] Çelebioğlu also noted the testimony by the sixteenth-century poet 'Āşıq Çelebi, that one Qara Memi Celebi, a scholar from Gelibolu, claimed to be Meḥmed's relative.[73] Furthermore, Bursalı Mehmet Tahir remarked that the seventeenth-century poet and Mevlevi *shaykh* Ġavs̱ī Aḥmed Dede was of the Yazıcıoğlus' family.[74] Presently, in both Gelibolu and Bursa exist families who claim the Yazıcıoğlus as ancestors and preserve cognate surnames.[75]

The brothers' residence in the city during the later 1440s and the 1450s was sustained by the goodwill of two prominent Gelibolu political figures. We have already met one of them: Qaṣṣāboğlu Maḥmūd Paşa, son of Qaṣṣāboğlu 'Alī. By 1449, when Meḥmed mentioned him, Maḥmūd Paşa (d. ~860/1456) had become a major figure at the court of Murād II in Edirne and Bursa. He is remembered in chronicles for having personally delivered a letter from the assembled *begs*, requesting that Murād II return from retirement in 1444, as the Byzantine emperor threatened to release the captive Ottoman prince Orḫan to contest the throne against the young Meḥmed II. He is portrayed here as a loyal vizier possessing the full trust of Murād II and his son Meḥmed, as well as of the *begs* of Rumelia.[76]

It is no surprise that a man of such prominence was a great builder of public monuments in Malkara, the hometown of his family. Documentation of one of his constructions survives in a *vaqfiyye* from 860/1456, which approximates the year of his death. It describes Maḥmūd's building of a *zāviye* and lists several properties whose incomes were set aside for its upkeep: a *ḥammām*, a *kervānsarāy*, a few shops and a small orchard. This *zāviye*'s expenditures included the daily wages of an imam, a *müez̲z̲in* and a cook, as well as the purchase of a considerable amount of foodstuffs.[77] Furthermore, two villages presumably named after their founders – Qāsim-veled-Ṣōfū and Qaraca Beg – along with part of the village of Qırıq-'Alī, already mentioned as being in the hands of his brother Meḥmed, contributed to the trust of this *zāviye*. Considering the uncertain differentiation between *zāviye* and mosque in this period and especially in Rumelia, this *zāviye* mentioned in the *vaqfiyye* is probably the same as the mosque recorded in the *taḥrīr* of 1475 as 'the mosque of Maḥmūd Beg son of Qaṣṣāb' in Malkara, which also mentions a salaried 'imam and *müderris*', as well as a *müez̲z̲in*.[78]

Maḥmūd, the man who may have been a childhood friend of the Yazıcıoğlu brothers, was funding public buildings in the Malkara-Gelibolu region, while he simultaneously functioned as vizier for Sultan Murād II. Meḥmed Yazıcıoğlu makes explicit that he moved to Gelibolu for his sake:

He was a vizier, a light of munificence.
His name was Maḥmūd Paşa ibn Qaṣṣāb.
For the sake of his love I settled.
Gelibolu I made my home.[79]

It is likely that Meḥmed Yazıcıoğlu returned to Gelibolu to renew the long-term connection between the Qaṣṣāboğlu family and his own. The *Muḥammediyye* describes it only in the vaguest of terms. It is possible that Maḥmūd employed Meḥmed as a scribe, repeating the arrangement between their fathers. It is equally possible that Maḥmūd allotted Meḥmed or his brother a stipend attached to one of Maḥmūd's foundations, such as the *zāviye* described above. It is even possible that this connection amounted to nothing more than an informal renewal of friendship. But friendship with such a powerful man as Maḥmūd was certainly remunerative in some way.

The next figure mentioned in the *Muḥammediyye* is more obscure. Aḥmed-i Ḫāṣṣ is discussed in the following five couplets, asking for God's blessings on his behalf:

Especially [bless] Subaşı Aḥmed-i Ḫāṣṣ.
Everyone's king, leader Aḥmed-i Ḫāṣṣ
When the Opener created the land of Rum,
he made Gelibolu into its key.
He put this key in his [*i. e.*, Aḥmed's] hand,
His hands reached from the earth to the sky.
In this way he is the dearest of the world,
the sultan of all the *ġāzīs*.
So distinguish him among your friends,
may he be an intimate in your presence.[80]

These couplets establish Aḥmed-i Ḫāṣṣ as the *subaşı* of Gelibolu, the commander of its garrison. In emphasising the imagery of *ġazā* and evoking the continued importance of Gelibolu as 'the key' of Rum, Meḥmed showed himself to be attached to a later generation of *ġāzī*s. Whereas Ṣaruca Beg and those of his generation had experienced the conquest of Thrace from the Byzantines, the following generation of Aḥmed-i Ḫāṣṣ grew up in a more thoroughly Ottoman environment.

Aḥmed-i Ḫāṣṣ leaves a documentary trail similar to that of Maḥmūd, and he seems to have owned even more property. The 1475 *taḥrīr* mentions a *zāviye*-mosque bearing his name in Gelibolu, with an income of 18,000 *akçe*,[81] while his own *vaqfiyye* document, also from 860/1456 (which must post-date the year of his death), states that 'the deceased Ḫāṣṣ Aḥmed Beg built a *zāviye* in Gelibolu proper and to it are attached two apartments and a mosque, and besides this he built another mosque', before listing the many properties that supplied these with income.[82] These included half of the Topçu (cannoneer's) *ḥammām* in a neighbourhood where soldiers were quartered (*'azebler maḥallesinde*), several shops (including three grape-sellers and four perfumers), a few storage rooms, a *kervānserāy* 'near the docks' and many agricultural plots of various kinds scattered throughout the region. His two mosques employed two imams and two muezzins, while his *zāviye* employed a cook, a keeper of the pantry, a baker and a few other staffers. This *vaqfiyye* confirms a total income of 18,800 *akçe*, a considerable sum.

Another, later *vaqfiyye* mentions that Sultan Murād II bestowed on Aḥmed-i Ḫāṣṣ a large farm called Tekfurpınarı as a gift of private property (*hibbe ve temlīk*) in the year 855/1451–52. We also learn here that his own son was named Muṣṭafā Çelebi, that his second mosque was in the neighbourhood of Çuqurbostan and that the Topçu *ḥammām*'s income was split between Aḥmed-i Ḫāṣṣ's *vaqf* and that of the contemporary 'Terzi' Ṣaruca Pasa – a Gelibolu political figure and naval captain of the mid-fifteenth century not to be confused with the *ġāzī* Ṣaruca Beg. It is quite obvious that Aḥmed-i Ḫāṣṣ was a powerful *subaşi*, and – to judge by the location and name of his *ḥammām*, as well as his association with Terzi Ṣaruca Paşa – he considered himself a patron of the soldiers and sailors of Gelibolu. His wealth seems to have far outstripped that of Qaṣṣāboğlu Maḥmūd, at least in documents related to Malkara-Gelibolu.[83]

As commander of the Ottoman garrison of Gelibolu, Aḥmed-i Ḫāṣṣ was a representative of the Ottoman state around the time of the Conquest of Constantinople, a position that earned him wealth and power. He performed some important service for the Yazıcıoğlu brothers, resulting in Meḥmed's effusive praise in the *Muḥammediyye*. But just as in so many other cases, we cannot say what this service was – employment, material gifts, protection and advocacy, or even spiritual discipleship are possible.

Writing and Seclusion

It was only three years before Meḥmed Yazıcıoğlu's death in 1451 that he completed his earliest written work, the *Maghārib al-Zamān*, from which both the *Muḥammediyye* and his brother's *Envārü'l-'Āşıqīn* are derived. Regarding these remarkably prolific years, when his fame was greatest and his legacy cemented, oral legends and later accounts describe a period of seclusion., Travelling in Gelibolu in 1658–59, Evliyā Çelebi stated that 'Meḥmed Efendi entered a cave in a rock at the seaside and fasted there. There he composed the *Muḥammediyye*', adding that 'it was this cave in a single rock at the sea's edge where Meḥmed Efendī fasted and composed the book *Muḥammediyye*. Still the noses of those who enter this cave smell his verdant herbal musk and amber. It is a place for the soul's comfort'. Ismā'īl Ḥaqqı Bursevī added more detail: 'His will chose seclusion and isolation, since those who find unity's secret find it by first cutting away multiplicity [. . .] For this reason the author of the *Muḥammediyye* dismissed himself from the people and performed pieties and [*çīleler*] in his own cell in Gelibolu at the seaside, and in this state of isolation composed the *Muḥammediyye* . . .'[84] A modern oral tradition that now enjoys the support of the Gelibolu Municipality identifies this *çīleḫāne* with a two-by-two-meter hand-dug cave located at the base of a cliff within view of the Dardanelles and the Gelibolu *namāzgāh* built by İskender b. Ḥācı Paşa. Both the *çīleḫāne* and the *namāzgāh* are prominent tourist attractions in Gelibolu today.

Before Meḥmed died, he set up a *tekke* of his own. The 1519 *taḥrīr* of Gelibolu discusses a *tekke* of 'Muḥyīu'd-dīn Yazıcıoğlu', clearly an error for Meḥmed, with four warehouses and two stores attached to its *vaqf*. Interestingly, one of these warehouses was said to be 'close to the *ḥammām* of Aḥmed Beg-i Ḫāṣṣ'.[85] Evliyā Çelebi claimed that 'the Yazıcızāde *tekke* was a great hearth and its dervishes of the Bayramī path were numerous'[86], clearly implying that the rites of the Bayramī Sufi *tariqa* were carried on there. Ṭaşköprüzāde wrote that Meḥmed 'built a mosque. And they call this place the place of Ḫıżr and İlyās, and the following Turkish excerpt was composed in this regard: "This is the place of Ḫıżr and İlyās / He prayed and they give their greetings / Yazıcızāde saw them here / and this is why he made this exalted place"'. This legend is consistent with remarks by Muṣṭafā 'Alī that claim that, 'while he composed [the *Muḥammediyye*], he was visited by, and in some way consulted with, Ḫıżr himself'. According to the oral sources of Celebioğlu, between 1940 and 1945 this building, the 'place of Ḫıżr and İlyās' and an early Bayramī centre, was sold by the Municipality of Gelibolu for 250 lira and destroyed by its new owner.

Whether in seclusion in his cell or present in his *tekke*, Meḥmed Yazıcıoğlu composed, in sequence, three major works. Each was prompted by a specific stimulus: The *Maghārib* came about in a conversation with his brother and friends; the *Muḥammediyye* was encouraged by not just one, but three dreams of the Prophet; and the *Sharḥ Fuṣūṣ al-Ḥikam* was written after the Prophet appeared in another dream and promised to teach him the contents of Mu'ayyad Jandī's *Sharḥ Fuṣūṣ*.

Aḥmed's Later Years

Meḥmed passed away in 'the same year as the death of Sultan Murād II', in 1451. A tomb in Gelibolu purports to hold his remains, and as early as during the time of Ṭaşköprüzāde this tomb was a site of pilgrimage ('The people regard his noble tomb as a site of prayerful visitation [*mezār-ı icābet-i ed'iyye*]'). With Meḥmed's passing, his brother Aḥmed Bīcān emerged from his elder brother's shadow, writing works of his own. These works give scant information on his life and activities before his death shortly after 1466. Aḥmed listed no names of associates, as his brother had done in the *Muḥammediyye* or his father in the *Şemsiyye*. His datable statements refer only to major political events – the Crusade of Varna, the second battle of Kosovo, the reigns of Murad II and Meḥmed II, and the latter's Conquest of Constantinople and other areas – rather than to any local occurrences. Any biography of Aḥmed Bīcān between 1451 and 1466, then, is strongly conjectural.

Yet, even as Aḥmed Bīcān himself gives us scarce new data to work with, he was also more forthcoming with personal comments on his life and times. For example, Aḥmed said that around 1449 he 'sat with his brother' and conversed with him about their respective literary legacies. Later, as he discussed Sultan Meḥmed II and his conquests of Constantinople, Bosnia, Albania and the Aegean, he claimed that 'in history none will match these achievements'.[87] For now, these two general statements should suffice to characterise Aḥmed *vis-à-vis* Meḥmed. Aḥmed Bīcān, perhaps more so than his brother, lived a life centred on the practice of Sufism. He expanded his brother's major Sufi work, the *Sharḥ Fuṣūṣ*, into the *Müntehā*, twice over, once in 1453 and then again in 1465. He composed his own original *Rūḥu'l-Ervāḥ*, a short distillation of anthropocentric aspects of Sufi theory. His exaltation of poverty and condemnation of worldly vanity is a constant feature. The pervasive Sufi ideology in the works written after his brother's death makes it likely that he continued living or working in the *tekke* founded by his brother in Gelibolu, or in the cave-cell nearby.

A second special trait of Aḥmed Bīcān is his new proximity to the Ottoman state. While it is true that Meḥmed included some lines of praise for Sultan Murād II in his *Muḥammediyye*, Aḥmed Bīcān, in his 1465 edition of the *Müntehā*, was effusive in his gratitude to Meḥmed II, 'Sultan of the World and King of Kings', in pages not devoid of apocalyptic expectation. Moreover, it is possible that Aḥmed visited Istanbul at least once after its conquest, as in the 1465 *Müntehā* he stated that 'many fine mosques and *'imāret*s [were built] within it, which nothing in the

Arab lands and in Persia resembles'. Indeed, Fātiḥ Meḥmed's conquests, 'especially of Istanbul, which, with force and sword, he took from the unbelievers',[88] seem to have deeply affected Aḥmed Bīcān, perhaps marking an inflection point of his intellectual arc towards more original speculations. After 1453 Aḥmed retreated from the themes of prophetic stories and religious instructional material which his brother had favoured and moved towards the natural philosophy of the 1466 *Būstānu'l-Ḥaqā'iq* and *Cevhāhīrnāme*, as well as the theoretical Sufism of the 1453 *Müntehā*, the undated *Rūḥu'l-Ervāḥ* and the 1465 *Müntehā*.

After the 1465 *Müntehā*, Aḥmed completed his last known work, the *Būstānu'l-Ḥaqā'iq*, an adaptation of his father's *Şemsiyye*, in 1466. We cannot say what in Aḥmed's life occupied the moments between these works' composition. We only know that sometime after the completion of the *Būstānu'l-Ḥaqā'iq*, over a century after the birth of his father, a *ġāzī*'s scribe, Aḥmed Bīcān, a dervish writer, passed away in what was now not a frontier, but the *sancaq* capital of Gelibolu. His tomb still stands there.[89]

Summary

Although certainly falling short of a complete prosopography, this list tells a clear tale. Yazıcı Ṣāliḥ entered the service of a *ġāzī beg* at Malkara, a *beg* who was the client of one of the most powerful of all fourteenth-century Thracian frontier lords, Ṣaruca Beg. When this personal arrangement with Qaṣṣāboğlu 'Alī came to an end upon the latter's death, Ṣāliḥ drifted into the employ of İskender Paşa, another Gelibolu *beg* of similar, though less prominent profile. Meanwhile, his sons grew up around the *ġāzī* household of the Qaṣṣāboğlus and associated with local Sufi notables such as Dervīş Bāyezīd, before travelling to Edirne for their introduction into another social sphere, that of scholars. There, Meḥmed, through his teacher Ḥaydar Haravī, came into contact with the circle of Ḥanafī scholars that included many migrants from Timurid Iran and Central Asia, as well as men of Rumī origin. In Ankara, both brothers were inducted into the central body of Anatolian Sufism, the circle of Ḥācı Bayram. Returning to Gelibolu some years after 1429, they renewed their relationship with the Qaṣṣāboğlu family, specifically with 'Alī's son Maḥmūd, by then a vizier to Murād II. There, too, the wealthy Ottoman officer Aḥmed-i Ḫāṣṣ played a role in their lives. After Meḥmed's passing in 1451, and after the death of Aḥmed-i Ḫāṣṣ and Maḥmūd around 1456, Aḥmed Bīcān continued to live near his brother's *tekke* and *çileḫāne* and occupied himself with writing and mystical endeavours of an increasingly independent nature for at least the following ten years.

PROBLEMS

Several unsolved issues problematise this chronology and require explicit comment:

1. 'Abdurrahmān Bisṭāmī and the neo-Ikhwān al-Ṣafā

It is alleged, based on a section in the *Dürr-i Meknūn* that discusses the works of 'Abdurrahmān Bisṭāmī and acknowledges his recent death,[90] that Aḥmed Bīcān and Bisṭāmī were acquaintances or friends. However, as I have argued elsewhere, the *Dürr-i Meknūn* is probably not a work by Aḥmed Bīcān. Still, it is indeed possible to construct a chain of acquaintances by which Aḥmed (or rather his brother) could have known Bisṭāmī – through Ḥaydar Haravī, who taught alongside several of Bisṭāmī's known acquaintances, notably Meḥmed Şāh Fenarī and Molla Güranī or, equally likely, through Ḥācı Bayram Velī and one of his disciples such as Molla Zeyrek. Yet, this likelihood is balanced, and perhaps even outweighed, by Bisṭāmī's own writings, namely the contents of the *Kitāb Durrat Tāj al-Rasā'il wa Ghurrat Minhaj al-Waṣā'il*, a record of people he met on his travels across Rumelia, Anatolia, Syria and Egypt in the years from 1402 to 1442. This book has served İhsan Fazlıoğlu[91] and İlker Evrim Binbaş[92] as a template for reconstructing the hypothetical fifteenth-century intellectual network of the 'Ikhwān al-Ṣafā' – named after the medieval Basran intellectual circle – which centred on Bisṭāmī and Ḥusayn Akhlāṭī in Cairo. Yet, of the over forty individuals whom Bisṭāmī mentions as having shared words and ideas with him over these forty years – individuals whose homelands ranged from the Balkan frontier over Aleppo to Cairo – not one is known to be a first-order acquaintance of any member of the Yazıcıoğlu family.[93] Although the Yazıcıoğlus may have known Bisṭāmī, they were neither prominent nor interesting enough for Bisṭāmī to have discussed them. Therefore, to posit a direct connection of the Yazıcıoğlus to the international Ikhwān al-Ṣafā network is not yet tenable – provided that, as my own work argues, the *Dürr-i Meknūn* was not written by Aḥmed Bīcān.[94]

2. Meḥmed's Travels Outside of Rum

Certain nineteenth-century printed editions of the *Muḥammediyye* include a biographical notice that states: 'In pursuit of knowledge and art he went to the kingdoms of Iran and Transoxiana and for the acquisition of wisdom and the comprehension of truths he travelled throughout the world [*geşt ü güzār*] and shared food and conversation with the *shaykh*s of the era such as [Zaynu'd-dīn] Khvāfī and Zaynu'l-'Arab and found what he sought'.[95] Evliyā Çelebi also asserted that Meḥmed travelled to Bukhara and Balkh.[96] The provenance of this claim is unclear, but it may perhaps derive from the *Muḥammediyye*'s statement that 'whatever wonders there are in the world / I looked for them in the Arab and Persian lands and in Rum'.[97] Since this statement could easily be taken to mean that Meḥmed scanned a broad literature in various languages and since in the Ottoman lands a Sufi's travels to Iran, Khurasan and Central Asia had already become a well-worn trope, the claim that Meḥmed travelled outside of Rum cannot be readily accepted.

3. Aḥmed's Hajj

The final pages of Aḥmed's 1453 *Müntehā*, in the 1003/1594–95 manuscript, considered the most complete by Ayşe Beyazit, present the following narrative:

> The reason for writing this book is this: One day I was coming from the Ka'ba and on the road I dreamed that I saw the Prophet. He said to me, 'struggle so that knowledge and wisdom and love may come from you'. On account of these blessed words I assembled this book over three years. And in the year 857 [1453] when Sultan Meḥmed b. Murād Ḫān [. . .] conquered Istanbul, I completed this book on the twentieth day of Jumādā al-Ūlā.[98]

This seems to say with very little ambiguity that Aḥmed Bīcān performed the Hajj to Mecca in the year 854 AH (1450 or 1451 CE), three years before the completion of the 1453 *Müntehā*. Yet, this claim is not easy to accept. The 1465 *Müntehā*, present in a manuscript that appears to be written much earlier than the 1453 *Müntehā*'s copy from 1594–95, omits any mention of the pilgrimage in its closing paragraphs which are otherwise closely analogous. Moreover, Aḥmed dated the completion of two of his major works, the *'Acā'ibü'l-Maḫlūqāt* and the *Envārü'l-'Āsıqīn*, to 1451; this is when he would have been on the Hajj and not working on them. It is hard to reconcile these two facts with the 1453 *Müntehā*'s claim of a pilgrimage.

This story should be read alongside another one at the beginning of his brother Meḥmed's earlier Arabic *Sharḥ Fuṣūṣ al-Ḥikam*, the work on which Aḥmed's *Müntehā* is based. Here Meḥmed said:

> I saw the Prophet in all his good tidings in the year 853 [1449–50]. He was sitting, and in his hand was a book. He raised his head and looked at me and said to me, 'I shall teach you'. Then I found my heart illuminated with his light. He said to me, 'My heart is "the bezels" [*al-fuṣūṣ*]', and these are elevated signs for the hearts of the righteous and trials for the hearts of the treacherous.[99]

The Prophet handed Meḥmed the book, which was the *Sharḥ Fuṣūṣ* of Mu'ayyad al-dīn Jandī, an early commentary on Ibn 'Arabī's *Fuṣūṣ al-Ḥikam*. The *Muḥammediyye*, written slightly earlier, discusses three similar dreams.

This raises the likelihood that Aḥmed – or later copyists – produced a formulaic vision of the Prophet's appearance to the younger brother, in imitation of the vision of the elder's, so that the former's commentary on the *Fuṣūṣ* may match the latter's. This does not settle the issue of the Hajj, but it increases the likelihood that the story is a later fabrication.

Conclusion

We have seen how an Anatolian scribe, entering the service of a second-tier Thracian *ġāzī* around 1388, was the first of a family of scholars who would continue to work for Thracian notables until we lose sight of them after 1466. To return to the ideas laid out at the beginning of this chapter, the continuity displayed across nearly a century belies the changing nature of their world, and this change is manifested in the three hierarchies in which the Yazıcıoğlus were embedded.

For their livelihoods, the Yazıcıoğlus depended on military and vezieral notables connected to the Ottoman state enterprise. This prosopographical investigation reveals that this group was not homogenous and, in fact, transformed radically. From the late fourteenth century until the death of Ṣāliḥ, the family was attached to an early generation of Thracian *ġāzī begs*, represented by Qaṣṣāboğlu 'Alī, by his superior Ṣaruca Beg who conquered part of western Thrace and, later, by İskender b. Ḥācı Paşa who built a *namāzgāh* for soldiers. All three of these men were connected to Gelibolu and Malkara in the years before the reign of Murād II; they sided with Emir Süleymān in the Ottoman Civil War and were oriented towards the frontier. It is not strictly correct to classify these men as 'Ottomans'; rather, they participated in frontier life in an apparently autonomous way. Later on, however, the brothers Meḥmed and Aḥmed worked in the service of a generation of Gelibolu notables represented by Aḥmed-i Ḫāṣṣ and Qaṣṣāboğlu Maḥmūd. These two men were wealthy and powerful in Gelibolu during the reigns of Murad II and Meḥmed II; unlike the earlier *ġāzīs*, they were directly appointed by the Ottoman state: Maḥmūd was a prominent vizier for Murād II and Aḥmed a *subaşı* of Gelibolu. After their deaths around 1456, we know nothing of Aḥmed's associations.

The second major hierarchy is that of the Ottoman scholarly elite. We have less evidence of the diversity of this group. Apart from the local teachers emerging from a Sufi milieu – of whom we only know

Dervīş Bāyezīd by name – the developping class of Ottoman scholars in Edirne educated the Yazıcıoğlus. Ḥaydar Haravī, the primary figure in Meḥmed's education and himself a migrant from Transoxiana, connected the Yazıcıoğlus to the international Timurid intellectuals of Edirne and Bursa during the reign of Murād II. This cadre of primarily Ḥanafī scholars helped structure the early Ottoman scholastic hierarchy.

The third network in which the Yazıcıoğlu family was embedded is that of the Anatolian Sufi community of Ḥācı Bayram Velī of Ankara. Claiming spiritual heritage in the early Ṣafavī *ṭarīqa* of Ardabil, the Bayramī community united many Turcophone scholars and writers of north-central and northwest Anatolia; we must consider these individuals to be the Yazıcıoğlus' closest peers throughout the 1420s.

The sequential association of Ṣāliḥ, Meḥmed and Aḥmed with local *ġāzīs*, international intellectuals, Anatolian Sufis and Ottoman officials teaches us that the three lived at arm's length from the Ottoman sultan and the centre he represented. Instead, the Yazıcıoğlus enjoyed the favour of four separate lords located at a political distance from Edirne, Bursa and Istanbul – yet, this distance decreased over time. This pattern of patronage from Qaṣṣāboğlu 'Alī to Aḥmed-i Ḫāṣṣ was consistent and multigenerational. The Yazıcıoğlus' local roots were deep and stable. And, despite their location at a distance from the political and economic centre, the Yazıcıoğlus came into contact with two of the most vital groupings of scholars and writers of the broader region – the elite jurisprudents of Edirne and the Bayramīyye of Ankara. That the Yazıcıoğlu brothers, provincial men, came be involved with both and felt free to move from the Gelibolu region to Edirne, Ankara and back to Gelibolu, without special pedigree or official dispensation, suggests a degree of personal independence. It also shows us that the circles in which they moved were not mutually exclusive, attesting to a kind of social fluidity. Finally, these biographies show the participation of strictly local actors – individuals such as Dervīş Bāyezīd or the frontier lords – as well as individuals from as far away as Samarqand. The scope of the Yazıcıoğlus' lives, here as in other aspects, interweaves the provincial and the cosmopolitan. Of all these groups, the brothers expressed their sincerest loyalties to Ḥācı Bayram and his Sufi community. As the following chapters will show, the worldview of the Yazıcıoğlus is best understood in terms of the way in which they were able to channel the rest of their activities into a Sufi framework.

Notes

1. Self-effacement in writing is typical of both Sufis and scholars, and one common way of displaying this is the customary omission of the first-person pronoun in favour of terms such as *faqīr* or *maskīn* ('poor' or 'wretched').
2. Çelebioğlu, *Muhammediye I*, pp. 1–42. Çelebioğlu gathered a substantial array of sources on the Yazıcıoğlus, but, out of caution, refrained from collating them into a proper biographical narrative. This chapter is, in large part, an attempt to harmonise Çelebioğlu's findings with what was transpiring around the Yazicioglus' lives, while adding several new pieces of documentary evidence.
3. *Malhama* will be discussed further in Chapter 5.
4. Çelebioğlu, 'Yazıcı Salih ve Şemsiyye'si', p. 174.
5. For instance, he uses the word 'Filūris' where a Greek might use something closer to 'Febrouarios'; *Şemsiyye*, Süleymaniye Kütüphanesi, Pertevniyal 766 (henceforth *Ş*), fol. 44a.
6. Gibb, *A History of Ottoman Poetry*, p. 389.
7. Muṣṭafā bin Aḥmed 'Âlî, *Künhü'l-Aḫbār* (Istanbul: Darü't-Tıba'ati'l-āmire, 1277), vol. 5, p. 237.
8. See Sarı 'Abdullāh Efendi, *S̱emeratü'l-fuād fi'l-mebde ve'l-me'ād* (Istanbul: Matba'a-i Amire, 1288 [1871–82]), pp. 233–38. The *S̱emerat*, a Sufi history of the Ḫalvetī order, states that 'since [Meḥmed] was confused by some things and disturbed by the contamination of wine, he continually caroused and drank. Ḥācı Bayram Velī recognized his gifts, and when he saw him, turned this clouded droplet into a precious jewel, inviting him into his noble presence [. . .] and banished the love of all that was *other than God* from his heart, and his heart and soul grew intoxicated and bewildered by the wine of divine love [. . .] Yazıcızāde Efendi was released from the dark dungeon of [carnal] nature into the open space of the light of belief, and was counted among the saved ones'. This tale follows a redemptive template that is extremely common in Sufi biographies and does not need to be given special credence.
9. İsmail Hakkı Uzunçarşılı, *Osmanlı Tarihi* (Ankara: Türk Tarih Kurumu, 1947), p. 282.
10. Evliya Çelebi, *Evliya Çelebi Seyahatnâmesi*, p. 161.
11. *Ş*, fol. 121b.
12. In this particular passage, the number 811 was used to demonstrate a technique by which the year is to be divided by eight, with the remainder (in this case, three) used to refer to a prognosticatory table labelled by letters. This kind of hemerological technique was common in both the West and the Islamic world, inherited from a shared Hellenistic science. The study of this kind of Islamic magic is to an extent still framed by Toufic Fahd, *La divination arabe: Études religieuses, sociologiques et folkloriques sur le milieu natif de l'Islam* (Paris: Sindbad, 1987), pp. 483–88.

13. *Ş*, fols 9a–9b.
14. Yazıcızâde Ali, *Tevârîh-i Âl-i Selçuk*, ed. Abdullah Bakır (İstanbul: Çamlica, 2009), pp. 386–89.
15. '*Vaqf-i Muṣṭafā Paşa İstanbulda Yediqule cānıbında vāqi' olan 'imāretine ṣarf olunur. Qariye-yi Qırıq-'Alī tābi'-i Ebrī mezkūr qariye aṣlda Qassāboğullarından Meḥmed vālidesi Ṣaruca Beg qızı Cevher Ḫatunuñ mülki olub Qassāboğlu 'Ali Begüñ mezkūr Meḥmed Begden Muṣṭafā Paşa bey'-i şer'iyye ala-ṣatun alub vaqf etmişdir*'. Başbakanlık Osmanlı Arşivi, Tapu Tahrir Defterleri 75, p. 279, quoted in M. Tayyib Gökbilgin, *XV.-XVI. Asırlarda Edirne ve Paşa Livâsı: Vakıflar, Mülkler, Mukataalar* (İstanbul: Üçler Basımevi, 1952), p. 443.
16. See İdris Bostan, 'Saruca Paşa', *İslam Ansiklopedisi*, for a reconstruction of this figure's life.
17. This and the following assertions were developped by İsmail Hami Danışmend, in *Osmanlı Devlet Erkânı: Sadr-ı-a'zamlar (Vezir-i-a'zamlar), Şeyh-ül-islâmlar, Kapdan-ı-deryalar, Bas-defterdarlar, Reîs-ül-küttablar* (İstanbul: Türkiye Yayınevi, 1971), p. 172, as well as İsmail Hakkı Uzunçarşılı, *Osmanlı Devletinin Merkez ve Bahriye Teşkilâtı* (Ankara: Türk Tarih Kurumu Basımevi, 1948).
18. His *ḥammām* in Gelibolu stands as one of the city's most notable early Ottoman monuments.
19. Neşri, *Kitâb-ı Cihan-nümâ*, ed. Faik Reşit Unat and Mehmet Altay Köymen (Ankara: Türk Tarih Kurumu Basımevi, 1995), p. 239. Yence Beg must have been the administrator of the city prior to Ṣaruca's arrival in 1390.
20. Dimitris J. Kastritsis, *The Sons of Bāyezīd: Empire Building and Representation in the Ottoman Civil War of 1402–1413* (Leiden; Boston: Brill, 2007), p. 143. This monograph is the most detailed reconstruction of this tumultuous Civil War period.
21. Ṣaruca was buried in Gelibolu where his monumental tomb still stands.
22. Mehmed Yazıcıoglu, *Muhammediyye* (İstanbul: Matba'a-i Osmaniyye, 1300/1882–83), p. 1.
23. Muṣṭafā 'Ālī of Gelibolu advanced a different thesis. He stated that Yazıcıoğlu Meḥmed 'was born in Ankara and settled in Gelibolu and passed away after composing the *Muḥammediyye*'.
24. 'Tapu Tahrir Defteri T. T. 0012', Başbakanlık Arşivi, T. T. 0012, p. 195.
25. Çelebioğlu, *Muhammediye I*, p. 16.
26. *Ş*, fols 9b–11a.
27. *Ş*, fol. 10b.
28. Ibid.
29. For a recent study on this figure, which shows his connections to wider Islamic scholarly networks, see Yıldız, 'From Cairo to Ayasuluk'.
30. Cemil Akpınar, 'Hacı Paşa', *İslam Ansiklopedisi.*
31. Danışmend, *Osmanlı Devlet Erkânı*, p. 8
32. Aydın Taneri, *Osmanlı İmparatorluğu'nun Kuruluş Döneminde Vezir-i*

a'zamlık, 1299–1453 (Ankara: Ankara Üniversitesi Dil ve Tarih-Coğrafya Fakültesi, 1974); İsmail Hakkı Uzunçarşılı, *Osmanlı Tarihi 1* (Ankara: Türk Tarih Kurumu Basımevi, 1947).

33. Ekrem Hakkı Ayverdi, *Osmanlı Mi'mârîsinde Çelebi ve II. Sultan Murād Devri, 806–855 (1403–1451): II* (İstanbul: Baha Matbaası, 1972).
34. *Ş*, fol. 10a.
35. Evliya Çelebi, *Evliya Çelebi Seyahatnâmesi*, vol. 2, p. 228.
36. Çelebioğlu, *Muhammediye II*, p. 603.
37. Mehmed Mecdi Edirneli, *Hadaik üs-Şakaik* (Istanbul: Dar üt-tibaat ül-amire, [n. d.]), p. 85. For another, modernised text, see Mehmed Mecdi Efendi, *Ḥadā'iq al-Shaqā'iq*, ed. Abdülkadir Özcan (İstanbul: Çağrı Yayınları, 1989).
38. 'Tapu Tahrir Defteri T. T. 0012', pp. 197–98.
39. Çelebioğlu insisted that this Dervīş Bāyezīd of Gelibolu is the same as Dervīş Bāyezīd, author of a work entitled *Sırr-ı Cānān*, which survives in the Millet Library in Istanbul (Çelebioğlu, *Muhammediyye I*, p. 36.). This long *mesnevi* of Sufi aphorisms and prophetic narratives does appear at first sight to participate in the same Sufi milieu as the Yazıcıoğlus themselves. However, Celebioğlu's conclusion is rendered incorrect by the final pages of *Sırr-ı Cānān*, which repeatedly make mention of Sultan Selim's confrontation with the Mamluk sultan (referred to as 'the Circassian'), while using verses that function as chronograms for 922 AH (1516–17 CE), the year of the Ottoman conquest of Egypt and Syria ('Sırr-ı Canan', Millet Kütüphanesi, Manzum 937.3, fol. 227). This definitively establishes the *Sirr-i Cānān* as a work written a century after the time of Dervīş Bāyezīd of Gelibolu.
40. Çelebioğlu, *Muhammediye II*, p. 603.
41. Çelebioğlu cites Serap Özler, *Gelibolu'daki Türk Mimari Eserleri* (unpublished doctoral thesis, İstanbul Üniversitesi, 1967). This book could not be consulted for this study.
42. '*Bundan murād Ḥaydar Hereviden ihtirāẕdır ki ol Sa'de'd-dīn Taftazānī şāgirdlerindendir ve Şeyḫ Bedre'd-dīn el-maṣlūbuñ qatlına fetvā vermişdir*'. İsmail Hakkı Bursevi, *Şerh ul-Muhammediye el-Müsemma bi-Ferah ür-Ruh*, Süleymaniye Kütüphanesi, Hacı Mahmud Efendi 2241, fol. 239.
43. Meḥmed Mecdi Edirneli, *Hadaik üş-Şakaik*, p. 83.
44. Kātib Çelebi, *Kitāb Kashf al-Ẓunūn*, p. 408.
45. Shahab Ahmad and Nenad Filipovic, 'The Sultan's Syllabus: A Curriculum for the Ottoman Imperial Medreses Prescribed in a Fermān of Qānūnī I Süleymān, Dated 973 (1565)', *Studia Islamica*, no. 98/99 (2004), pp. 183–218.
46. This trajectory is outlined in Atçıl, *Scholars and Sultans in the Early Modern Ottoman Empire*.
47. See Repp, *The Müfti of Istanbul*, for more on the development of this institution.
48. The 1444 execution of a Hurūfī missionary who had been preaching to

the young Mehmed II has been described by both Ottoman historians and Venetians; for more than sixty years, this event has attracted scholarly attention. See Franz Babinger, 'Von Amurath zu Amurath', *Oriens* 3, no. 2, (1950), pp. 229–65. Recently, the Hurūfī messianic sect has been the subject of two sophisticated monographs: Usluer, *Hurufilik*, and Mir-Kasimov, *Words of Power*.

49. The cohort of Jurjānī's and Taftazānī's migrant students in the Ottoman lands deserves a comprehensive study. These scholars have been studied in individual monographs, dissertations and encyclopedia entries, without having been treated as a unit. An exemplary study that deals with this community as part of the longer-term formation of the Ottoman *'ulemā* is Atçıl, *Scholars and Sultans in the Early Modern Ottoman Empire*. A holistic perspective on this migration in the broader context of Islamic civilisation is found in Giv Nassiri, 'Turco-Persian Civilization and the Role of Scholars' Travel and Migration in Its Elaboration and Continuity' (unpublished doctoral dissertation, University of California, Berkeley, 2002).
50. For a historical overview of Bedre'd-dīn and the movement associated with him, see Michel Balivet, *Islam mystique et révolution armée dans les Balkans ottomans: Vie du cheikh Bedreddin, le 'Hallâj des Turcs', 1358/59–1416* (Istanbul: Editions Isis, 1995), p. 88–89. Taşköprüzade wrote that Bedre'd-din was executed at the command of 'Molla Haydar, a scholar recently arrived from Iran'.
51. Ibid. p. 88. According to Balivet, the chronicler İdrīs Bidlisī claimed that the *'ulemā* accused him of violating the law, of heresy (*zindīq*) and atheism.
52. Ibid. p. 89.
53. Ocak, *Zındıklar ve Mülhidler*, pp. 159–232.
54. Bursevī reported that his own *shaykh* said that Bedre'd-dīn's *Vāridāt* 'is worthless and in it are many faults'. In his own writings he declared: 'And in his book, the Varidat, there are some faults which are not justified by his incomplete conscience and knowledge . . .' See Kameliya Atanasova, 'The Sufi as the Axis of the World: Representations of Religious Authority in the Works of Ismail Hakki Bursevi (1653–1725)' (unpublished doctoral dissertation, University of Pennsylvania, 2016), p. 83, as well as Nuran Döner, 'İsmail Hakkı Bursevi'nin Kitab-i Kebir'i ve Bursevi'de Varidat Kültürü', *Tasavvuf: İlmî ve Akademik Araştırma Dergisi* 6 (2005), p. 328.
55. Mehmet Tahir Bursalı, *Osmanlı Müellifleri*, ed. A. Fikri Yavuz and İsmail Özen (İstanbul: Meral Yayınları, 1972), p. 222. Mehmet Tahir Bursalı also claimed that Mehmed had been sent by Sultan Murad I as ambassador to Egypt to announce the Ottoman conquest of Konya. This claim is not corroborated anywhere else and implausible for chronological reasons.
56. Nihat Azamat, 'Ḥācı Bayram-i Velī', *İslam Ansiklopedisi*.
57. The most comprehensive biography of the *shaykh* is still Fuat Bayramoğlu, *Hacı Bayram-ı Veli: Yaşamı, Soyu, Vakfı* (Ankara: Türk Tarih Kurumu Basımevi, 1983).

58. İsmail E. Erünsal (ed.), *XV-XVI. Asir Bayrâmi-Melâmiligi'nin kaynaklarindan Abdurrahman Elaskeri'nin Mir'âtü'l-ışk'ı* (Ankara: Türk Tarih Kurumu Basımevi, 2003), p. 200.
59. Haşim Şahin, 'Somuncu Baba', *İslam Ansiklopedisi*.
60. The origins of this claim are in Bayramoğlu, *Hacı Bayram Veli*. The dialogues themselves have been published in Erich Trapp, *Manuel II. Palaiologos: Dialoge mit einem 'Perser'* (Wien: Österreichische Akademie der Wissenschaften, Kommission für Byzantinistik, Institut für Byzantinistik der Universität Wien; in Kommission bei H. Böhlau's Nachf., Graz, 1966).
61. See Erünsal, *XV-XVI. Asir Bayrâmi-Melâmiliği'nin kaynaklarindan Abdurrahman Elaskeri'nin Mir'âtü'l-ışk'ı*, p. 203.
62. Scholars of the twentieth century have ventured to describe Ankara in the fourteenth century as a 'republic' governed by the *aḫīs*, the Anatolian adaptation of the *futuwwa* tradesmen's brotherhoods widespread in the late medieval Islamic world. For a thorough discussion of the *aḫī* phenomenon and its relationship to the state and to Sufism, see Peacock, *Islam, Literature and Society in Mongol Anatolia*, pp. 118–44. Important prior studies inlcude G. G. Arnakis, 'Futuwwa Traditions in the Ottoman Empire: Akhis, Bektashi Dervishes, and Craftsmen', *Journal of Near Eastern Studies* 12, no. 4 (1953), pp. 232–47, and Franz Taeschner, 'Beiträge zur Geschichte der Achis in Anatolien', *Islamica* 4, no. 1 (1929); Claude Cahen, 'Sur les traces des premiers akhis', in *60 Yıldönümü Münasebetiyle Fuad Köprülü Armağanı* (Istanbul: [n. p.], 1953); and Deodaat Anne Breebart, 'The Development and Structure of the Turkish Futuwa Guilds' (unpublished doctoral dissertation, Princeton University, 1961).
63. *KM870A*, fol. 3a.
64. E. J. W. Gibb comes to the same conclusion in his *History of Ottoman Poetry*, p. 391.
65. Eşrefoğlu Rumi, *Tarikatname*, Süleymaniye Kütüphanesi, Hacı Mahmud Efendi 4667, fols 1b–2b. This text has also been published; see Eşrefoğlu Rumi, *Tarikatname*, ed. Esra Keskinkılıç (Istanbul: Gelenek, 2002).
66. See A. İhsan Yurd, *Fatih Sultan Mehmed Hanın Hocası, Şeyh Akşemseddin: Hayatı ve Eserleri* (Istanbul: Yurd, 1972); Erünsal, *XV-XVI. Asır Bayrâmi-Melâmiliği'nin kaynaklarından Abdurrahman Elaskeri'nin Mir'âtü'l-ısk'ı*.
67. For an overview of the Halvetiyye, see Curry, *The Transformation of Muslim Mystical Thought in the Ottoman Empire*.
68. Eşrefoğlu Rumi, *Tarikatname*. For information on the Qādirī canon, see Thierry Zarcone, *The Qâdiriyya Order* (İstanbul: Simurg, 2000).
69. See the translation of the *Risālatu'n-Nūriyya* in Yurd, *Fatih Sultan Mehmed Hanın Hocası, Şeyh Akşemseddin*.
70. 'Âlî, *Künhü'l-Aḫbār*, vol. 5, p. 236
71. Qur'an 6:160.
72. Evliya Çelebi, *Evliya Çelebi Seyahatnâmesi*.

73. Çelebioğlu, *Muhammediye I*, pp. 24–25
74. Bursalı, *Osmanlı Müellifleri*, p. 101.
75. Private correspondence.
76. Colin Imber, *The Crusade of Varna, 1443–45* (Aldershot; Burlington: Ashgate, 2006).
77. Gökbilgin, *XV.-XVI. Asırlarda Edirne ve Paşa Livâsı*, pp. 292–93.
78. It is tempting to infer that the 'Mevlānā Aḥmed' listed as this '*imām* and *müderris*' of Qassāboğlu Maḥmūd's mosque in the 879/1475 *taḥrīr* is Aḥmed Bīcān himself. This conclusion cannot be correct, however, because for this to be the case Aḥmed must have been extremely old – far over seventy – and because he also stated as recently as 1465 that his place of residence was Gelibolu, not Malkara where this mosque is located.
79. Çelebioğlu, *Muhammediye II*, pp. 596–97.
80. Ibid. p. 602.
81. 'Defter-i esāmī-i sancaḳ-i Gelibolu (Awā'il Shawwāl 879/February 1475)', Atatürk Kitaplığı, Cevdet Collection no. 79.
82. Gökbilgin, *XV.-XVI. Asırlarda Edirne ve Paşa Livâsı*, p. 231.
83. Çelebioğlu has noted a story describing the first encounter between Aḥmed-i Ḫāṣṣ in the *Mecmu'a* of Gebrekzade Hafiz Hasan. The sources of this story are unknown. Çelebioğlu, *Muhammediye I*, p. 35.
84. This narrative has been repeated by nineteenth- and twentieth-century commentators. Aḥmed Rif'at's *Luğat-i Tarihiyye ve Coğrafiyye* repeats this story: 'Yazıcıoğlu, a great *shaykh* of the Bayramīyye and author of the famous *Muḥammediyye*, passed away in the year 855 (1451). In a stone cave he had hollowed out himself by the seaside in Gelibolu, he secluded himself in a corner and was peerless in worship. Instead of a house, he built a *medrese* in the city centre. And there was also a place of worship dug by his brother in the same area'. Ahmet Rifat, *Luğat-i tarihiyye ve coğrafiyye* (Istanbul: Mahmut Bey Matbaası, 1881).
85. İbrahim Sezgin, 'Gelibolu Kazasının Sosyal ve Ekonomik Tarihi' (unpublished doctoral dissertation, Marmara Üniversitesi, 1998).
86. Evliya Çelebi, *Evliya Çelebi Seyahatnâmesi*, vol. 5, p. 163–66.
87. *KM870A*, fols 2b–3a.
88. *KM870A*, fols 2a–4b.
89. See Çelebioğlu, *Muhammediye I*, pp. 40–42, for information on the later fate of the tombs associated with Meḥmed and Aḥmed.
90. Şahin, 'Constantinople and the End Time'.
91. See İhsan Fazlıoğlu, 'İlk Dönem Osmanlı Ilim ve Kültür Hayatında İhvânu's-Safâ ve Abdurrahmân Bistâmî', pp. 229–40. Fazlıoğlu's work, along with the articles by Fleischer, Melvin-Koushki and Gardiner, has opened up the study of this intellectual vanguard. See Noah Gardiner, 'The Occultist Encyclopedism of ᶜAbd al-Rahman al-Bistami', *Mamluk Studies Review* 20 (2017), pp. 3–38.
92. Binbaş, *Intellectual Networks in Timurid Iran*, is a landmark monograph that

details the context, interconnections and philosophies of the members of this far-flung 'republic of letters'.

93. Abdurrahman Bistami, 'Dürret Tacü'l-Resail', Süleymaniye Kütüphanesi, Nuruosmaniye 4905.
94. Grenier, 'Reassessing the Authorship of the *Dürr-i Meknun*'.
95. See, for instance, the lithographed *Kitab-i Muhammediyye* (İstanbul: Bosnavî Hacı Muharrem Efendi'nin Taş Destgâhı, 1280 [1863]), fol. 1a.
96. Evliya Çelebi, *Evliya Çelebi Seyahatnâmesi*, vol. 5, p. 163.
97. Çelebioğlu, *Muhammediye II*, p. 597.
98. *KM857*, fol. 116b.
99. *ShF*, fol. 1b.

Chapter 2

The Textual Genealogies of Ottoman Popular Islam

To an Ottoman of the seventeenth and eighteenth centuries, there was, after the Qur'an itself, arguably no book as holy as Meḥmed Yazıcıoğlu's 1449 devotional poem, the *Muḥammediyye*. Evliyā Çelebi (d. 1682) tells of the *Muḥammediyye*-reciters (*Muḥammediyye-ḫvān*) who sung the poem to audiences throughout Anatolia and Rumelia. The work's autograph – kept where it was written, in Gelibolu – was considered a relic worthy of pilgrimage. Meḥmed Yazıcıoğlu's younger brother Aḥmed Bīcān, too, gained a saintly reputation, since his *Envārü'l-'Āşıqīn*, a Turkish prose rendition of the same basic text, was almost equally potent in the popular imagination. It was read and memorised, according to Evliyā, in primary schools across Anatolia.[1] In the seventeenth century it was studied by Muslims in Hungary;[2] by the twentieth century, it was read as far away as in Kazan and Kashgar.[3] Both brothers, disciples of Ḥācı Bayram Velī in Ankara and formally educated in Edirne during the reign of Murād II (r. 1421–44, 1446–51), transcended their provincial upbringing by producing what would become a kind of international codification of populist Ottoman Sunnism.

Seemingly inseparable from these books' holiness was the notion that they emerged *ex nihilo* from a process of saintly inspiration and divine guidance. According to Evliyā Çelebi, the younger Aḥmed Bīcān used only three mythical and occult tomes to compose his work: '['Abdu'r-raḥmān Bisṭāmī's] *Kitāb-i Cifr-i Camī'* and the wisdom of 'Ali and the *jafr* of Muḥyīu'd-dīn [ibn] al-'Arabī's *Fuṣūṣ* and from them signs and secrets were revealed as the book *Envārü'l-'Āşıqīn . . .*' The early commentator İsmā'īl Ḥaqqı Bursevī, for his part, said that Meḥmed 'dismissed himself from the people and performed self-discipline in his own cell in Gelibolu at the seaside, and in this state of isolation composed the *Muḥammediyye . . .*'[4] These statements grow out of a collective memory that is symptomatic of public remembrance within Ottoman pious history – its protagonists are sacralised into archetypal figures and their views fossilised into a timeless and universal wisdom. In fact, the reality of the Yazıcıoğlus' intellectual heritage is much less dramatic.[5] The Yazıcıoğlus used a conventional library of chiefly Arabic and Ḥanafī sources that reflected their own upbringing as fifteenth-century intellectuals of Gelibolu and, by extension, described the intellectual horizons of the first generations of Ottoman scholars writing in Turkish.

Here I aim to analyse the textual origins and intellectual pre-history of these texts that came to epitomise Ottoman popular piety. An account of the sources of the Yazıcıoğlus' texts allows one to understand what was read and valued in Gelibolu during the 1440s and to contribute some detail to our knowledge of the fifteenth-century scholarly culture in which the brothers lived – what, at this crucial period of Ottoman history, did a provincial scholar's repertoire encompass? Moreover, because of the works' intense popularity, this account will also inform us about the constituent components of the populist Sunnism that is so visible in the history of the Ottoman centuries from Qāḍīzāde to Nursī. Ottoman historians have yet to perform a serious analysis of the material from which fifteenth-century piety – the immediate ancestor of the Sunnī consensus of the age of Kānūnī Süleymān and Ebū's-Su'ūd – was fashioned. Notwithstanding several excellent recent studies on the social and legal articulation of Ottoman Sunnism in subsequent periods,[6] its basic textual provenance, especially as it relates to piety on the vernacular register, remains largely unexplored. There are obvious reasons for this neglect. During the fifteenth century, the Ottoman frontier polity, and especially a provincial town like Gelibolu, was still somewhat marginal in the academic landscape of the Sunnī religious sciences centred in Timurid lands and in Mamluk Egypt and Syria. Apart from the linguistic isolation of Anatolian Turkish pious writing, its relative marginality often discourages Arabists and general Islamicists. Conversely, the necessity of imagining early Turkish vernacular writing as, among other things, the adaptation of an Arabic corpus has deterred specialised Ottomanists. As a result, we know something of *'ulemā* hierarchies and of the patterns of proliferation of Sufi *ṭarīqa*s,[7] and we have a (very) general image of fifteenth-century political and mystical philosophy, but we possess limited information on what ordinary Ottoman Muslims in newly conquered lands read and believed.

Fortunately, the three (essentially athological) texts under consideration here – Meḥmed's Arabic *Maghārib al-Zamān* (1448), Aḥmed's Turkish prose translation of this work, the *Envārü'l-'Āşıqīn* (~1449–51) and Meḥmed's Turkish verse rendition of the above, the *Muḥammediyye*

(1449) – permit this kind of analysis. The former two texts function as compilations of various kinds of lore, presenting listed *ḥadīth*, prophet stories and some argumentative passages lifted, with little modification, from their original souces. These sources are cited by one of several means. First, specific texts are cited using a simple bibliographical formula.[8] For prophetic traditions, a very short *isnād* is employed.[9] Another feature simplifying this analysis is the close textual relationship between *Maghārib*, *Envār* and *Muḥammediyye*, which are so interconnected that even their authors think of the three texts as a single corpus of translations, abridgments and versifications of each other. We are fortunate to have access to a passage in Aḥmed's *Envār* where he candidly describes how he and his brother worked together to write their masterpieces:

> [My brother Meḥmed said] 'O Aḥmed Bīcān, obeying your suggestion, I collected all of the world's laws and truths in one place. You should come, too, and translate this book, which is the *Maghārib al-Zamān*, into the Turkish language, so that the people of our land may thus gain wisdom and make use of the light of knowledge'. I, this wretched one [Aḥmed], in compliance with his blessed words, completed this book called the *Envārü'l-'Āşıqīn* in Gelibolu, finest of towns, abode of *jihad*. Now both my *Envārü'l-'Āşıqīn* and my brother's book of verse, called the *Muḥammediyye*, emanate from the *Maghārib*. That book is in verse, and this book is in prose, and thus they were written in two ways – one was versified so that it may be sweet, and the other was written in prose so that it may be easily understood. And both styles are fine and respected by the righteous. It is as if the Encircling Ocean boiled up and overflowed on both sides and made visible whatever kinds of pearls there may be. If you seek the 'hidden pearl' [*dürr-i meknūn*], study the *Envārü'l-'Āşıqīn*, and if, unhappy, you seek further satisfaction [*ecr-i ġayr-ı memnūn isterseñ*], study the *Muḥammediyye*. Praise God that we have compiled these two books, for we have suffered many frustrations on this path so that the people may say, 'Have mercy upon the Yazıcıoğlus!'[10]

There is no reason to doubt this story, for the three works truly do parallel each other in terms of their sources, structure and message. Aḥmed in this way makes it clear that with substantively identical but formally varied content these three works targeted three different audiences: those who preferred to read in Arabic, in the case of the *Maghārib*; those who sought the pleasure of a 'sweet' Turkish poetic expression, in the case of the *Muḥammediyye*; and those Turkish-speakers who, in the *Envār*, would find a clear prose rendition of religious sciences that could be 'understood'.

The three books are difficult to classify in generic terms; hence, it is easier to say what they are *not* than to describe what they are. On the basis of the connections between the Yazıcıoğlus' writings and the earlier

Muqaddime of Quṭbu'd-dīn İzniqī, to be discussed below, they possess a certain relationship and shared Ghazālian heritage with the *'aqā'id* catechistic literature and its Anatolian manifestation, the so-called *'ilm-i ḥāl* texts, but they are not *'ilm-i ḥāl*s. The books are also not strictly about the history of the Muslim community, nor solely about the end of time, nor exclusively concerned with heaven or the cosmos. They are neither collections of *ḥadīth*, nor of folk or Sufi argumentation. What can be said is that all three are texts of catechistics and dogmatics, written in terms suitable for a general – though not utterly basic – understanding of the beliefs and practices necessary for the salvation of an ordinary Muslim.

The *Maghārib* and *Envār* are divided into five major sections. The first and shortest deals with the creation of the world, systematically describing the traditional cosmology of God's Throne and Footstool and the Pen and Tablet, which lie above the levels of Heaven, Hell and the celestial spheres; this is followed by a briefly-sketched geography of the earth. The second and longest section is a chronological account of twenty-six prophets, ranging from Adam to Muḥammad and including ambiguous figures such as Dhū al-Qarnayn and Luqmān. This section culminates in lengthy heroic biographies of Muḥammad and his righteous successors. (In the *Muḥammediyye*, this section is the work's focus and eclipses some of what follows.) The third section discusses angels. The fourth section, by far the most complex, unites a kind of primer or manual for pious Muslims, outlining the requirements of prayer, fasting, charity and so on, before ending with an elaborate and detailed narrative on the Day of Judgment. The final section is a geography of heaven that discusses its various gardens, terraces, trees, rivers, fine foods and beautiful beings. Thus, in a rough sense, this structure constitutes a chronology from the creation to the end of time. It also has a protagonist: the righteous person who, created by God in his image, is represented by the sequence of prophets, obeys the Law they receive and enjoys the benefits of heaven for eternity. The works create, from a patchwork of source material, a clear cosmic narrative containing an assigned role for the believer within it.

As this variegated structure indicates, the *Envār*, *Maghārib* and *Muḥammediyye* are highly synthetic and the two prose works especially appear as lively compilations rather than original argumentation. As such, they easily lend themselves to the kind of basic source criticism I will perform. The compiled source materials can be grouped into several primary categories. Some sources serve as narrative patterns – the templates from which the *Maghārib* and *Envār* derived the structure and content of their narrative sections. Another cluster of source-texts can be considered their reference materials: the *ḥadīth* collections and Qur'an commentaries that the authors used to give these narratives additional meaning and to provide the narrative with moral lessons – sources that were used time and time again. We can presume that they sat by the Yazıcıoğlu brothers' side as they composed their works, and that their pages were heavily marked and dog-eared. Indeed, most of the *Maghārib* and *Envār* are comprised of strung-together narrations from these sources. Thirdly, a small but important set of texts of philosophical and mystical argumentation that systematically present original discussions of certain topics were utilised, such as al-Ghazālī's *Ihyā 'Ulūm al-Dīn*. Finally, the Yazıcıoğlus employed many other miscellaneous texts, ranging from legal theory (*fiqh*) and legal rulings (*fetāvā*) to manuals of preaching (*va'ẓ*). These texts may not have been always present at the time of composition but furnished important quotations and passages.

With their sources so easily discernible, it becomes impossible to agree with the testimonies of Evliyā and Bursevī, because the Yazıcıoğlu brothers' writings draw almost exclusively from a moderately sized and hyper-canonical set of Arabic *tafsīr*, *ḥadīth* and *fiqh* writing, a library that in an uncomplicated way reflected the brothers' own education, as they had received it from the *'ulemā* of Edirne and the urban Sufi community of Ḥācı Bayram Velī of Ankara. The horizons of these provincial intellectuals extended to the jurisprudential and exegetical works of a certain Ḥanafī canon, and not far beyond. Although one has a right to be skeptical of Meḥmed's claim that he 'studied 3,999 books',[11] the Yazıcıoğlus wrote while using the library of competent, if unexceptional *ḥadīth* and Qur'ān scholars, which I will now outline.[12]

Narrative Sources

QIṢAṢ AL-ANBIYĀ

One article of belief they intended to communicate was faith, in sequential prophetic dispensations culminating in the moment of Muḥammad's revelation. To convey this prophetic history, the Yazıcıoğlus created an abridgment and translation of the well-known cycle of *qiṣaṣ al-anbiyā*, stories of the prophets. The *qiṣaṣ* stories draw from the body of Islamicised Biblical apocrypha and legend that was retrospectively classified as *isrā'īliyyāt*, or 'Israelite lore'. The path by which this lore entered Islamic *ḥadīth* tends to pass through two figures: Ka'b al-Aḥbār and Wahb ibn Munabbih, the former a learned Jewish convert from Yemen and the latter a Persian from Yemen familiar with Judaic lore.[13] Because of these alleged origins in the words of two early converts who had been educated in Jewish learned environments, *isrā'īliyyāt* had long been viewed suspiciously by some *ḥadīth*-oriented Muslims.[14]

The Yazıcıoğlus had no qualms about using *qiṣaṣ* that proceed from the *isrā'īliyyāt* narrations of Ka'b al-Aḥbār and Wahb ibn Munabbih. This offers one clue that the brothers made use of populist compilations of prophet stories, rather than draw from, for example, Ibn Kathīr's very orthodox version of the prophet stories, *al-Bidāya wa al-Nihāya*, which studiously avoids all dubious *isrā'īliyyāt* narrations. To determine which of the popular *qiṣaṣ* compilations was the one used by the Yazıcıoğlus requires an examination of a particular story. In the Yazıcıoğlus' account, the story of Ṣāliḥ, a Qur'anic prophet that is not shared by Judaic or Christian tradition, rests on the authority of Ka'b al-Aḥbār. He recounted that the people of Thamūd asked Ṣāliḥ to produce, out of a certain stone, 'a she-camel [. . .] whose body is of gold and feet of silver and head of emerald and eyes of ruby and tail of coral and a hump that is a dome of pearl, and all adorned with square rubies of various kinds. If you bring a camel of this description out of this stone, we will believe you'. Perplexed, Ṣāliḥ was relieved when Gabriel came and informed him that God had already placed such a camel inside that particular stone forty years earlier, on the day of Ṣāliḥ's birth. Ṣāliḥ then prayed and, as 'the day of Bayram began', the stone moved and a majestic she-camel emerged, made from precious stone 'seven hundred cubits from nose to tail, and five hundred between its hooves'. Before the wonder-struck populace the camel loudly testified: 'There is no god but God, and Ṣāliḥ is his messenger!' The people of Thamūd then came to faith, but soon thereafter they turned away from it and killed the camel. Ṣāliḥ cursed them and called for their punishment in hellfire: 'The first day your faces will turn yellow, and on the second they will turn red, and on the third day they will turn black . . .' God called for Gabriel to destroy them, saying: 'Raise up the fires of hell and scatter them upon it'. Gabriel destroyed Thamūd 'with his shouts', and Ṣāliḥ, having lost his tribe but retained his faith, retired to Mecca where he died.

When one compares this account to a medieval *qiṣaṣ* collection in wide circulation across the Islamic world in the fifteenth century, the *Arā'is al-Majālis fī Qiṣaṣ al-Anbiyā* by Abū Isḥāq Aḥmad al-Tha'labī (d. 427/1036), one encounters enormous differences.[15] Al-Tha'labī mentions dozens of proper names for various members of the tribes of Thamūd, none of which appear in the Yazıcıoğlus' account. A few pages, rather than a few sentences, are dedicated to a description of the torments that God then inflicts on the tribe. There are also many details found in Yazıcıoğlu but absent from al-Tha'labī. Most strikingly, the image of the giant bejewelled camel that confronts the reader so forcefully in the

Yazıcıoğlus' version is absent from al-Tha'labī. Nor does Ṣāliḥ's curse appear anywhere in the *Arā'is*.

A side-by-side comparison shows that, of the many *qiṣaṣ* produced from *isra'iliyyāt* materials between the eighth and fourteenth centuries, the particular compilation that the Yazıcıoğlus chose was an especially populist and vivid *qiṣaṣu'l-anbiyā* by one Muḥammad ibn 'Abdullāh al-Kisā'ī, composed shortly before 1200.[16] One can clearly observe al-Kisā'ī's relationship with the Yazıcıoğlus' stories at a fine-grained textual level. For example, while Aḥmed Bīcān wrote that 'the tribe of Thamūd inhabited the land, to the extent that they became ten tribes. And each tribe was 70,000 people', al-Kisā'ī wrote that 'Thamud inhabited a land. They were a nation of ten tribes, each of which was composed of ten thousand men, under each of whom were ten thousand others'.[17] Except for the discrepancy in the size of the ten tribes, the passages are identical. Al-Kisā'ī's camel is likewise marvellous: 'In her eyes were rays of light, on her were reins of pearl; from her hump to the tip of her tail was seven hundred cubits'.[18] Yet, the Yazıcıoğlus' version is heavily abridged. The brothers leave out many of the original's details, those that were perhaps superfluous to the story, while preserving the original's colourful passages, such as Ṣāliḥ's prediction that the faces of Thamūd's tribesmen 'turned red; and the morning after their faces were black as coal'. Along with many other passages, the Yazıcıoğlu's close dependence on al-Kisā'ī's work is clear.[19] This conclusion, however, does not completely solve the issue of provenance, because al-Kisā'ī's *qiṣaṣ* in itself is a highly variable text. The variability of the *qiṣaṣ* alongside the anonymity of the mysterious al-Kisā'ī has led some modern scholars to believe that, rather than being the work of a single man, it 'reflects Arabic folk literature in the twelfth and thirteenth centuries'.[20] Changes such as Meḥmed Yazıcıoğlu's reduction of the population of the tribe of Thamūd from al-Kisā'ī's ten tribes of 10,000 to ten tribes of 70,000 is certainly the kind of distortion that may occur across chains of oral transmission.

Sīra Sources

The *qiṣaṣ al-anbiyā* sequence of the *Envār* and *Maghārib* ends with the ascent of Jesus to heaven. After some brief comments on the esoteric significance of each prophet's mission, which are indebted to Ibn 'Arabī's in *Fuṣūṣ al-Ḥikam* (a foretaste of both Meḥmed and Aḥmed's commentaries on that work), the Yazıcıoğlus turned to the life of the Prophet Muḥammad and the story of the first Muslims. This section differs from the previous by its habit of not citing any sources at all. Instead, they pull the narrative away from an academic style, recasting it as a heroic epic. Far from being a new invention, this is inherited from the well-known genre of *sīrat al-nābīy*, the biography of the Prophet and His Companions. This genre grows out of the early *maghāzī* ('battles') texts on the campaigns of Muḥammad and his successors. Once refashioned into biography and supplemented with stories from contemporaries and even the Qur'an, the *maghāzī* became *sīra*, the life of Muḥammad, whose classic expression was the *Sīrat al-Nābīy* by Ibn Isḥāq, preserved for posterity in the version of Ibn Hishām (d. 833). From the *sīra* of Ibn Isḥāq/Ibn Hishām, a diverse array of derivative texts grew, ranging from commentaries on the *sīra* to tracts on the 'signs of prophethood' (*dalā'il al-nubūwwa*) – that is, prophetic miracles.[21] Turkish adaptations of the life of Muḥammad had already been produced by the Yazıcıoğlus' time. The *Mevlīd* of Süleymān Çelebi, written in 1409, is perhaps the most familiar *sīra* narrative in Turkish vernacular, but there exists an earlier example.[22] The first known Turkish biography of Muḥammad was produced by Mustafa Ḍarīr, a writer from Erzurum who wrote in Turkish while in the employ of the Mamluk Sultan Barqūq in Cairo. Ḍarīr's *Sīretü'n-nebīy*, written around 1388, contributed part of the text of the *Mevlīd*.[23] When the Yazıcıoğlus used *sīra* elements, they drew from a genre that was flourishing in Turkish.

In any case, it is a very mixed assortment of *sīra*-type stories that enlivens the Yazıcıoğlus' version. The *Envār/Maghārib* and the *Muḥammediyye* do not enter the conventional *sīra* narrative from the beginning. Rather, they skip the first part of Ibn Hishām's story, which describes the history of Mecca and the Quraysh, as well as the discussion of Muḥammad's early life. We learn nothing of Muḥammad's birth as the *sīra* describes it, nor of his childhood and his wet-nurse Amina, nor of his marriage to Khadīja. In place of the mass of details narrated and carefully sourced by Ibn Hishām, the Yazıcıoğlus transmit tales of a more scattered provenance. The following passage will suffice to indicate both the general flavour of this section and reveal some of its antecedents:

> When God's beloved [*ḥabībi'llāh*] came into the world, the people of the seven levels of heaven all came to see him [. . .] That day the domes of a thousand churches fell to the ground, and the arch of King Khusraw [*Kisrā padişāh ṭāqı*] cracked and was destroyed and Lake Sāwa dried up and the flames of the fire-worshipping Magi were extinguished. [Muḥammad] cast no shadow, because from his head to his feet he was light – certainly light casts no shadow. Above his head was the fragment of a cloud. Wherever he walked, it would go with him. Just as he could see what was before his eyes, in the same manner he could see what was behind him. At the same time, he could see the east and the west. And just as his ears can hear while awake, his ears could hear while he was

> asleep. And the miracle of his nose was as follows: When Gabriel would come to give him [divine] inspiration, he could perceive a scent from heaven. His teeth shone light that illuminated paths at night. If one were to lose something, it could be found with this light. On his back was the mark of prophethood, the size of a dove's egg. When he sweats, his sweat has the odor of rosewater and musk [. . .] One day the moon descended from the sky and rocked his cradle.[24]

These details each have different origins. The story of the itinerant cloud comes directly from Ibn Hishām's *sīra* where it is attributed to the monk Bahīra.[25] The egg-sized mark of prophethood appears in the *Ṣaḥīḥ Muslim* and other *ḥadīth* collections,[26] as does the prophet's ability to see what is behind him. Narrations on the pleasant smell of the prophet's sweat appear in the *Ṣaḥīḥ Bukhārī.*[27] The light from Muḥammad's teeth is described in al-Tirmidhī's *Shamā'il,* as well as in the *dalā'il al-nubūwwa* genre. Without a doubt, each of these reached the Yazıcıoğlus through intermediary texts, some of which will be discussed below. The essential *sīra* story is thus both condensed and embellished.

Ḥadīth *and* Tafsīr *Sources*

After this Turkish redaction of al-Kisā'ī's *qiṣaṣ* and the synthesis of the life of Muḥammad that followed, the Yazıcıoğlus turned away from narrative. Upon the conclusion of the Prophet's mission and the deaths of the first generation of Companions, the Yazıcıoğlus abandonned narrative story-telling and devoted the second half of the *Maghārib* and *Envār* to a series of loosely-linked conversations on angels, salvation, orthodox praxis, Resurrection, the rewards of heaven and torments of hell. The structure of all these discussions is largely the same: They are constructed from brief *ḥadīth* narrations and short pieces of Qur'anic exegesis, each connected by a loose logical link to the ostensible subject-matter of the chapter. Yet, it is in these more disorganised sections that the authors incorporated the most particular and personal mix of source-texts, using writings that most characteristically conform to local scholarly fashions. Here I highlight the most important of the Yazıcıoğlus' *ḥadīth* and *tafsīr* sources, those that must have accompanied the scholars throughout the writing process.

AL-BAGHAWĪ'S *ḤADĪTH* AND *TAFSĪR*

Of these, the most frequently referenced source in the *Maghārib* and *Envār* is one described as *'tefsīr-i Baġevī'*, which can only be the *tafsīr* and *Maṣābīḥ al-Sunna* by the traditionist Abū Muḥammad al-Baghawī

(d. 1117 or 1122), a Shāfiʿī of Marv. Specifically, citations of al-Baghawī most likely refer to one of the commentaries and extensions of al-Baghawī's work, which were much more widely read than was the work itself. We have already encountered, in the previous chapter, the author of one such text: Zayn al-ʿArab al-Nakhchivānī al-Miṣri (fl. 1360), the name mentioned in the *Muḥammediyye* as 'my teacher' of 'inner and outer knowledge'.[28] Zayn apparently influenced Meḥmed through his own well-read *Maṣābīḥ* commentary, his *Sharḥ Maṣābīḥ al-Sunna*, a sizeable volume of which many copies still survive; Kātib Çelebi wrote that this extant *Sharḥ* is only one of three written by Zayn, each for a different audience. Zayn's *Sharḥ Maṣābīḥ al-Sunna* was widely read until at least 1565, when it appeared in a *medrese* syllabus endorsed by Sultan Süleymān.[29] For the Yazıcıoğlus, the body of al-Baghawī's corpus, read through Zayn's commentary, functioned as a basic framework for exegesis and *ḥadīth* interpretation.

Zayn's *Sharḥ Maṣābīḥ* was only one of a long tradition of works based on al-Baghawī's *Maṣābīḥ*. Walī al-Dīn Muḥammad al-Tabrīzī's *Mishkāt al-Maṣābīḥ*, written contemporaneously with Zayn's work, was a widely-copied *ḥadīth* commentary. A specific and common feature of works such as the *Mishkāt* and the *Sharḥ Maṣābīḥ* coming from the al-Baghawī tradition is that they each seem to have been written for lay use, synthesising a kind of simplified consensus from the mass of *ḥadīth* sciences.[30] The *Maṣābīḥ* and its commentaries omit long *isnāds* for the traditions they transmit and, in the service of readability, only discuss a subset of them that is deemed *ṣaḥīḥ* (sound) or *ḥasan* (good). It seems, then, that one of Meḥmed Yazıcıoğlu's own introductions to religious sciences was provided by Zayn's commentary on the *Maṣābīḥ*, a comprehensive but nevertheless simplified and readable summary of uncontroversial *ḥadīth* narrations.

AL-ṢAMARQANDĪ'S *TAFSĪR*

Another common *tafsīr* quoted in the *Maghārib* and *Envār* consists of the *tafsīr* of the Ḥanafī scholar Abū-Layth al-Ṣamarqandī (d. 373/983 or 393/1002–3). It, too, enjoyed a long commentary tradition, although it is less clear in this case as to which particular commentary the Yazıcıoğlus were using, citing him only with the phrase 'it is transmitted by Abū-Layth'. Yet, there were many possible options. Not far from the time and place of the Yazıcıoğlus' writing, the famous Damascene historian Shihāb al-Dīn ibn ʿArabshāh (791–854/1392–1450) translated al-Ṣamarqandī's *tafsīr* into Turkish at the request of Sultan Meḥmed I in Edirne and produced a Turkish commentary on it; upon the sultan's death in 1420, he returned to Syria and then Egypt, where he served the Mamluks and finished his major history.[31] Ibn 'Arabshāh's edition was not the only Turkish translation of al-Ṣamarqandī circulating in Ottoman lands at the time of the Yazıcıoğlus' writing. One Mūsā İzniqī (d. 838/1438), a Sufi who, like Yazıcı Ṣāliḥ and his sons, worked for various Rumelian and Anatolian *begs* during the reigns of Çelebi Meḥmed and Murad II completed a Turkish translation of al-Ṣamarqandī's *tafsīr* as well.[32] This work is often confused with another Turkish *tafsīr* of al-Ṣamarqandī, that of Aḥmed-i Dā'ī, a famous poet of a similar social profile, who died in Bursa in the 1420s.[33] Aḥmed-i Dā'ī's record of service was complex, having been employed to write in many different genres by the *begs* of Germiyan, by Emir Süleymān, by his victorious brother Çelebi Meḥmed, by the grand vizier Ḫalīl Paşa and, finally, by Murād II. However, his Turkish translation of the *tafsīr*, written for the Ottoman warlord Umur b. Demirtaş, was translated from a Persian edition rather than from the Arabic original. What the above makes clear is that the early and mid-fifteenth-century Ottoman lands, the time when the Yazıcıoğlus were writing, witnessed a golden age when it came to the production of commentaries and translations of the *tafsīr* of al-Ṣamarqandī.[34]

AL-ZAMAKHSHARĪ'S *KASHSHĀF*

A *tafsīr* only slightly less prominent in the *Envār* and *Maghārib* is the famous *al-Kashshāf* of the Ḥanafī scholar Abū al-Qāsim Maḥmūd al-Zamakhsharī (d. 1144). The strikingly successful *Kashshāf* reigned as a pre-eminent Qur'anic exegesis for centuries, despite its slightly controversial reputation. It was believed by scholars such as Ibn Ḥajar al-'Asqalānī and Abū al-Fidā that 'Mu'tazilite doctrine appears clearly within it', with regard to polarising issues such as the createdness of the Qur'an.[35] However, as Andrew Lane has persuasively argued, it is unclear how the *Kashshāf* acquired its Mu'tazilī reputation, as this is not supported by the text itself. Rather, al-Zamakhsharī's *Kashshāf* constitutes a 'traditional' *tafsīr* with limited theological argumentation, largely composed of philologically-oriented exegetical passages supplemented by an eclectic set of *ḥadīth*. Compared to other *tafsīrs*, it is rather short, condensed into two volumes in order to serve *medrese* instruction.

It is not difficult to guess how the Yazıcıoğlu brothers accessed the *Kashshāf* of al-Zamakhsharī, as a local tradition of Anatolian commentaries emerged in the wake of *Anwār al-Tanzīl*, Qadi al-Bayḍāwī's (d. 685/1286) popularising (and Shāfi'ī) abridgment of *al-Kashshāf*.[36] Specifically, in the fourteenth century a gloss on *al-Kashshāf* was written by Cemālu'd-dīn Muḥammed al-Aqsarayī (d. 791/1388–89), a native of the *beglik* of Karaman centred in Konya.[37] Aqsarayī gained wide-spread fame in his lifetime, even travelling to Cairo and befriending Sayyid Sharīf Jurjānī, a meeting that presaged the enduring connection between the Khurasani and Ottoman schools. His legacy was long-lasting: The most famous of his own students was Molla Şemsü'd-dīn Fenarī, the man described as the founder of the Ottoman *'ulemā* and probably an acquaintance of the brothers, while his own great-grandson Çelebi Ḫalīfe was to found the Cemālī branch of the Ḫalvetī Sufi order, one of the region's most vital brotherhoods.

Scholarship on *al-Kashshāf* reached the Yazıcıoğlus in another way as well: straight from Iran and Transoxiana. Sayyid Sharīf Jurjānī (d. 816/1413) of Samarqand himself produced a commentary, which did not prove to be as popular as the *Kashshāf* commentary written by Jurjānī's rival in Tīmūr's court, the renowned Sa'd al-Dīn Taftazānī; the latter's *Ḥāshiya al-Kashshāf* was perhaps the most widely copied of all *Kashshāf* commentaries within the Ottoman realms, and the one most often cited by the Yazıcıoğlu brothers. These works of scholarship were brought to Anatolia by the migrant students of Taftazānī and Jurjānī in the early and mid-fifteenth century; under the leadership of Aqsarayī's student Molla Fenarī, these emigrés comprised the faculty of the first elite Ottoman *medreses* of Bursa and Edirne. For the purposes of this study, it is most significant that one of these migrant students of Taftazānī was Ḥaydar Haravī, whom the previous chapter suggests to have taught Meḥmed Yazıcıoğlu in Edirne; he himself authored a commentary on Taftazānī's *Ḥāshiya*. Fenarī, too, produced his own *Ta'līq 'alā Awā'il al-Kashshāf*, as did Musannifek, the Persian scholar favoured by Meḥmed II, who served as teacher and jurisconsult in Istanbul. Molla Ḫüsrev, an important Ottoman *qaḍī-'asker*, *müderris* and *şeyḫü'l-islām* during the same period wrote a commentary on al-Bayḍāwī's commentary on *al-Kashshāf*. It is through the Yazıcıoğlus' own extensive use of al-Zamakhsharī, as well as their citation of Taftazānī's *Ḥāshiya*, that we are able to see most clearly their involvement in the international intellectual network spear-headed by the Ḥanafī scholars of Timurid Khurasan.[38] All three of these *tafsīr*s indicate the Yazıcıoğlu brothers' genuine – if unadventurous – contemporaneity, their conformity with the trends of their time and place.[39]

AL-RĀZĪ'S *TAFSĪR AL-KABĪR*

Although not as frequently cited as the above three, the *Mafātīḥ al-Ghayb* of the twelfth-century Shāfi'ī scholar Fakhr al-Dīn Rāzī constituted an important source for the Yazıcıoğlu brothers. The *Mafātīḥ*, known to the Yazıcıoğlus by its common name of *al-Tafsīr al-Kabīr*, is a massive work of Ash'arī exegesis with a strong influence in many realms, from *kalam* disputation to the theology of Ibn Sīnā. As al-Rāzī's Shāfi'ī affiliation may lead one to expect, he was less popular than the Ḥanafīs in Anatolia and Rumelia, yet was never anathametised. In fact, the above-mentioned Cemālu'd-dīn Muḥammed al-Aqsarayī claimed personal ancestry from al-Rāzī. The Yazıcıoğlus used the *Mafātīḥ* primarily as a reference for clarifying terminology.

Al-Saghānī's *Mashāriq al-Anwār*

The Yazıcıoğlus said that 'God created the earth and mountains on Sunday, the trees on Monday, the skies on Tuesday, the Light on Wednesday, animals on Thursday, and Adam at mid-afternoon on Friday', citing *al-Mashāriq al-Anwār* by Raḍīy al-Dīn Ḥasan al-Saghānī (d. 1252) as the basis for this claim. Al-Saghānī, in his lifetime primarily a scholar of Arabic linguistics, is famous for being one of the first major authors of a *ḥadīth* work from the Indian subcontinent.[40] The *Mashāriq* was noted for its attempted synthesis of al-Bukhārī's and Muslim's two *ṣaḥīḥ ḥadīth* collections and immediately became copied far beyond India. In patterns of textual transmission, it seems to move alongside al-Baghawī's *Maṣābīḥ*: In the late sixteenth century, the Ottoman scholar Bergamalı İbrāhīm used the *Maṣābīḥ al-Sunna* as the basis of his super-commentary on another *Mashāriq* commentary.[41]

This source would not be considered a noteworthy one worth, were it not for the fact that Kātib Çelebi wrote that Meḥmed's *Maghārib* is 'based on the *Mashāriq* of Saghānī'. This claim merits criticism, however, since the *aḥādīth* of al-Saghānī's text, as befits the work of a lexicographer, are listed simply according to the word with which they begin; thus, its organisational scheme cannot be compared to Aḥmed or Meḥmed Yazıcıoğlu's.[42] This does not mean that the Yazıcıoğlus made no use of the work, however. In fact, considering al-Saghānī's practice of conveniently organising the major *aḥādīth* of al-Bukhārī and Muslim in two slim and handy volumes, *al-Mashāriq* is a good candidate for an intermediate text between the Yazıcıoğlus and these two basic collections. Many of the brothers' unattributed narratives that are found in Bukhārī and Muslim – including parts of the description of the Prophet mentioned above – may have proceeded from al-Saghānī's *al-Mashāriq*.

LEGAL TEXTS

Certain short but important passages in the Yazıcıoğlus' works are indebted to readings of legal argumentation (*fiqh*) and templates for legal opinions (*fetāvā*). Their interest is in three specific works: the *Fatāwā* of Fakhru'd-in Hasan Qādīkhān (d. 1196), *al-Fatāwā al-Ẓāhiriyya* of Muḥammad al-Ḥanafī al-Bukhārī and a work entitled the *Jawāhir al-Fiqh*, probably the book by that name by Niẓām al-Dīn al-Marghinānī.[43] Of the three, Qādīkhān's is the best-known and would endure as a legal source-text into the later Ottoman period. As volumes of Ḥanafī legal scholarship, these works probably reached the Yazıcıoğlus circulating alongside the likewise Ḥanafī al-Zamakhsharī and al-Ṣamarqandī. These citations are concentrated in the fourth chapter on the Day of Resurrection, which comprises highly abbreviated *fetvā* rulings on the subject of who counts as a believer or unbeliever, taking forms such as 'He who scorns the Qur'an, who belittles it and who places his feet above the Scripture is an unbeliever', or 'He who knows the direction of the *qibla* but turns to pray in another direction is an unbeliever', or 'He who says that a mosque is the same as a wine-house and that to disbelieve is the same as to believe is an unbeliever'. In their source texts, these actions and their accompanying 'profane words' (*alfāẓ al-kufr*) are taken to indicate a lapse into unbelief. Chapter 3 will return to the relevance of these abbreviated *fetāvā* to the broader question of confession-building and deal with them at length.

Miscellaneous Sources

Many other sources remain unidentified or were used for only one or two direct quotations. Although the influence of al-Ghazālī runs deep, his name is only mentioned a handful of times. The same can also be said of the writings of Ibn al-ʿArabī and Naṣīr al-Dīn Ṭūsī. (However, in the case of Ibn al-ʿArabī, this silence may be explained by the fact that the Yazıcıoğlus reserved separate works, most importantly Aḥmed's *Kitābü'l-Müntehā*, for the interpretation of that mystic's thought.) The *Envār* and *Maghārib* are at many points intruded by aphoristic digressions with a popular flavour. Pious exhortations, often numbered or classified as 'sacred words' (*qudsī kelīmeler*), exalt the virtues of poverty and self-negation and call for a constant attention to God's strict demands. As no names of other works or writers accompany them, it is next to impossible to ascertain the sources of all these anecdotes. One presumes that some of them were part of the body of orally transmitted knowledge taught by Ḥācı Bayram Velī or other Sufi figures in the Yazıcıoğlus' environment. Others may be original paraphrases of Qur'anic text or *ḥadīth* narrations.

The Yazıcıoğlus were also familiar with a select few sources of a more argumentative and belles-lettristic nature. The *Mahabbatnāme* of Abū Hāmid al-Ghazālī, a section of his famous *Iḥyā 'Ulūm al-dīn* (possibly read in Persian, to judge by the use of the above Persian title), furnished an important quotation near the beginning of the *Envārü'l-'Āşıqīn* on the necessity of Sufi love.[44] Excerpts from the *Iḥyā* appear several times more, in an often technical role: Ghazālī's arguments, for instance, are quoted in regard to the issue of the immortality of the body after death and prior to Resurrection. He appears again to claim that patience is a primary virtue, because 'to patiently endure suffering is a particularity of man'.[45]

Most of the above sources never fell out of favour with Ottoman religious writers of later centuries. However, not all the Yazıcıoğlus' sources would remain part of the Ottoman Sunnī canon. Perhaps the most interesting of the minor sources is a quite obscure one: a mysterious preachers' manual called *Zahrat al-Riyāḍ*, repeatedly cited by Meḥmed and Aḥmed throughout the *Maghārib*, *Envārü'l-'Āşıqīn* and both versions of the *Müntehā*. The author of this long and heterogeneous Arabic text refers to himself as 'Sulaymān ibn Dawūd al-Saqsīnī', or sometimes 'al-Sūwarī'. These two *nisba*s appear in Maḥmūd al-Kashgharī's *Dīwān lughāt al-Turk*: Saqsīn is a city near Bulghar and Suwūr the tribe that inhabits it as one of the components of the Bulghar confederacy. Based on this, Zeki Velidi Togan has concluded that Sulaymān ibn Dawūd was from Saqsīn and wrote for the Muslims of the steppes.[46] Saqsīnī's text itself is a fascinating manual on the art of preaching; it compiles various stories on diverse subjects ('Fish' or 'Stones') that can be used at the pulpit.[47] Kātib Çelebi, writing in the seventeenth century, compared the *Zahrat al-Riyāḍ* to the famous Ḥusayn Vā'iẓ Kāshifī's *Majālis-i Va'ẓ*, adding that, unlike Kāshifī's work, the book was 'famous, but not valuable'. This comparison does seem to be a valid one, as Kāshifī's much later work shares the same explicit aims and organisational logic. But perhaps the most interesting feature of the *Zahrat al-Riyāḍ* is that it is strongly influenced by Shī'ism. From the *Zahrat al-Riyāḍ*, the Yazıcıoğlus chose the following excerpt:

> And it is transmitted in *Zahrat al-Riyāḍ* that Ja'far-i Ṣādiq said that, when Adam was living with Eve in heaven, God spoke to Gabriel and said: 'Take Adam's hand and circumambulate heaven'. So Gabriel and Adam together circumambulated heaven until they came to a fine palace. One brick was gold, and one brick was silver, and its balconies were green emerald. There was a throne in that palace of ruby. Above that throne was a dome of light, and in the midst of that dome there was a fine figure [*ṣūret*], and there was a crown of light

on its head, and two earrings in its ear, made of pearl, and around its waist a belt of light. Adam saw it and was amazed and forgot Eve's beauty. And Adam said, 'O Lord, what kind of figure is this figure?' God said, 'It is the figure of Fāṭima, and on her head is the Crown of Muḥammad Muṣṭafā, and around her waist [the belt is] is 'Alī, and the two earrings are Ḥasan and Ḥusayn'.

And Adam saw that there were five doors in this dome, made of light, and [on each] a word was written. On the first door, 'I am the Praised, and this is Muḥammad (*anā al-Maḥmūd, wa hādhā Muḥammad*)'. On the second door, 'I am the Exalted, and this is 'Ali (*anā al-'Alīy, wa hādhā 'Alī*)'. On the third door, 'I am the Creator, and this is Fāṭima the Brilliant (*anā al-Fātir, wa hādhihi Fāṭimat al-Zahrā*)'. On the fourth door, 'I am the Benefactor, and this is Ḥasan (*anā al-Muhsin, wa hādhā Ḥasan*)'. On the fifth door, 'And of me is the Excellent One – this is Ḥusayn (*wa minnī al-Aḥsan, wa hādhā Ḥusayn*)'. Gabriel said, 'O Adam, preserve these names. One day you will need them'. When Adam went down to earth, he cried for three hundred years. A voice came that said, 'O Adam, look at the Protected House'. Adam looked at it and saw that those noble names were written there. Adam bowed and said, 'O Praised One, I am a trustee for the sake of Muḥammad, may he accept my repentance'. God said, 'O Adam, if all of your descendants repent, I will forgive you out of respect for these names'.[48]

Although this is not indicated in the Yazıcıoğlus' text, the *Zahrat al-Riyāḍ* claims that this story comes from 'one of the sayings of Ja'far-i Ṣādiq', the sixth Shī'ī *imām*. Indeed, this narration is found in several Shī'ī compilations of the sayings of the *imāms*.[49] This story uses his authority to make the strikingly Shī'ī claims that Fāṭima was in Heaven prior to the Fall of Man, and that her existence and that of her husband and sons, 'Alī and Ḥasan or Ḥusayn (incarnated as jewellery), take priority, both temporal and moral, over the rest of creation.

Another Shī'ī-tinged quotation comes from the Twelver scholar Naṣīr al-Dīn Ṭūsī, who claimed: 'On the day of judgment, four people will be first before the throne and four people last before the Throne. Of the first-comers, one is Noah, one is Abraham, one is Moses, and one is Jesus. Of the last-comers, one is Muḥammad Muṣṭafā, one is 'Alī, one is Ḥasan, and one is Ḥusayn'. The issue of Shī'ism in the Yazıcıoğlus' works will be explored in a subsequent chapter.

Notes on Compositional Method

With our image of the brothers' sources and library beginning to take shape, a few comments on the process of its composition are in order. A particular chapter of the *Envārü'l-'Āşıqīn*, one that is representative of the brothers' style, may serve as an example of how they used their library. This third chapter, somewhat misleadingly entitled 'On the Words with which God Inspired the Angels', is composed of discrete transmissions of *ḥadīth* testimonies and *tafsīr* interpretations of Qur'anic verses, usually beginning with the phrases 'it is transmitted' or 'it is said', all of which have something to do with angels.[50] Over twenty-two pages, the number of separate transmissions totals approximately ninety. Of these ninety narrations, forty-four are fully unattributed, while thirty-five are attributed to first-order *ḥadīth* transmitters of the generation of the *saḥāba*, most commonly Ibn 'Abbās, followed closely by Abū Ḥurayra, with 'Alī, 'Āisha, 'Abdullāh b. 'Umar, Ka'b al-Aḥbār and others some distance behind. Because these do not indicate the source from which the narrations were taken, they can be considered unattributed as well. Nine narrations are assigned attributions from the by now familiar names of al-Baghawī, al-Rāzī, al-Ghazālī, al-Saqsīnī and al-Saghānī; several unattributed passages are also likely taken from al-Ṣamarqandī.

This chapter on angels opens with an overview of the four archangels Michael, Gabriel, Isrāfīl and 'Azrā'īl; they are each described with short narrations. As this theme broadens, we realise that the theme of angels is only the loosest of organising principles and often serves to introduce other subjects. For instance, Yazıcıoğlu cites a *ḥadīth* describing an enormous angel whom God places under his celestial throne and who has 70,000 wings on each side; he then cites another *ḥadīth* describing 70,000 angels that sit in front of His throne and eternally recite the *Ṣūrat al-Fātiḥa*, adding that Muslims who recite it will also be forgiven in Afterlife. Then Aḥmed Bīcān mentions a third *ḥadīth*, describing a column of ruby that bisects the cosmos and supports the Throne, which trembles each time the *shahāda* is recited; the column, personified, refuses to be still unless God forgives those who affirm God's unity, so God forgives them and calls upon the angels to bear witness. There is, then, a kind of thematic continuity of these three *ḥadīth*, which move smoothly from the Throne to the *Fātiḥa* to forgiveness, each with a reference to the angels that are ostensibly the chapter's subjects. By stringing together ordered narrations around a thematic centre – in this case, angels – they are able to circle all of the subjects they wish to include and guide the reader on a kind of pious tour up and down the space between the lowly human soul and God's immediate presence.

This tour ends, appropriately, with the image of 'Azrā'īl, the Angel of Death. 'Azrā'īl allows the Yazıcıoğlus to ruminate on death and the afterlife, engaging matters such as the resurrection of the body in the End Times, the permanence of both higher spirit and carnal soul, and so on. An emotional sermon, taken from al-Saqsīnī, describes how God transforms angels into the image of a dying traveller's estranged family in order to comfort the traveller on his deathbed. The final line offers an elegant conclusion:

> And it is transmitted that God created an angel. It circumnavigates the Throne. Since the moment the universe was created it has been saying *lā ilāha*. When at last he says *illā Allāh*, the Resurrection Day will arrive. Thus, it is that the beginning and end of the world's duration is contained in the single breath of an angel.[51]

The Yazıcıoğlus' compositional method should by now have become visible. First, they established a theme and purpose, which in this case consists of an overview of pious topics, with the idea of the angel as its unifying centre. Each source-text is then approached and scanned for relevant *aḥadīth* and other discussions, and each is copied down separately. In this particular case, Meḥmed searched for all discussions of angels. (The *tafsīr*s of al-Baghawī and al-Ṣamarqandī are organised in such a way as to make this search easy, whereas the structure of al-Saqsīnī and al-Saghānī must have made this considerably more difficult.) With these *aḥādīth* and arguments in hand, Meḥmed's task was to string them together meaningfully, and he did so in the way we can see above.

Patterns

This completes an overview of the sources at the Yazıcıoğlus' disposal as they wrote the *Maghārib al-Zamān*, *Envārü'l-'Āşıqīn* and *Muḥammediyye*. What patterns can be discerned? All of the works in the apparent bibliography of the Yazıcıoğlus were written in Arabic, with the possible exception of al-Ghazālī's *Iḥyā*, which may have been read in Persian translation, parts of the *sīra* narrative and uncited Sufi sources. The most obvious feature of this Arabic library is that the majority of the brothers' sources were written in Khurasan and Central Asia between the eleventh and thirteenth centuries The earliest were from Marv, others from the area of Tus and Nishapur, and a large contingent from Samarqand. The rest of the Islamic world is very sparsely represented. Only Ṭūsī and Ghazālī had careers in western Iran or Iraq; only al-Saghānī was from India, and only Zayn al-'Arab died in Egypt, wherever he was from. Amazingly, Ibn al-'Arabī appears to be the only named source with a career in Syria. Molla Fenarī's *Miṣbāḥ al-Uns* alone represents Anatolian Arabic writing. In other words, the bulk of their library derives from the period and place of the institutional development of Ḥanafī scholarship under the auspices of the Seljuq and

Khwarazmian states. It follows that the *madhhab* orientations of most of these texts are also Ḥanafī.

Yet, even this minority of the Yazıcıoğlus' major sources that come from other regions seem to exist on the margins of this main Khurasani cluster. Al-Saghānī's *Mashāriq* is a Ḥanafī work that compiles the *aḥādīth* of the Bukhārī and Muslim, both from Khurasan, while the author himself, although Punjabi, was educated in Transoxiana. Zayn al-'Arab, perhaps an Egyptian (or, alternately, from Nakhchivan), was a commentator on the text of the Khurasani al-Baghawī. Even Naṣīr al-Dīn Ṭūsī, although he worked elsewhere, had origins in Khurasan. The only true exceptions to this geographic rule are Muḥyī al-Dīn ibn al-'Arabī, an Anadalusian, the contemporary Molla Fenarī of Bursa and the mysterious al-Saqsīnī of the Bulghar steppes. The majority of the books which the Yazıcıoğlus were able to study and which they then valued highly enough to use as sources for their major works as they composed them in Gelibolu came from the lands between central Iran and the Syr Darya.

This overall homogeneity rests on two historical events: The first is the legacy of the importation of Seljuq Ḥanafism into Anatolia, which came along with Islam itself in the eleventh and twelfth centuries. Unlike the Bukharan scholar Maḥmūd al-Faryābī studied by Shahab Ahmed, whose bibliography consists of books entirely from his own region, the Yazıcıoğlus did not write from a local tradition of religious scholarship rooted in their homeland of Thrace and western Anatolia.[52] They could benefit from no pre-existing regional *ḥadīth* and *tafsīr* literature, but rather were among the first generation of western Anatolian and Balkan Muslims to create this literature themselves. There was no option but to look to Khurasan, the region that is the source of Anatolian Islam. As Anatolia was Islamised and governed by elites who followed the Seljuq armies from cities such as Nishapur and Bukhara, the region inherited these scholarly preferences. In this regard, it is useful to address the question of *madhhab*. From its earliest expansion into Iran, the Seljuq state had adopted and attempted to promulgate the Ḥanafī school of law and tried to suppress the Shāfi'ī in the lands under its control. Ḥanafism thus came to dominate the Seljuk schools set up in Konya, Sivas, Kayseri and other Anatolian cities, and its scholars preserved a durable intellectual partnership between the heartland of Ḥanafism, Khurasan and Mawara'n-nahr, and Rum, a region that under the early Seljuqs had once been its political extension.

A second, more immediate cause of this Khurasani Ḥanafī tendency was the transmission of scholars and texts from Timurid Iran and Transoxania in the decades during which the Yazıcıoğlus lived; as the pages of Taşköprüzāde's *al-Shaqā'iq al-Nu'māniyya* make clear, these revitalised the Ḥanafism of Anatolia when they migrated into the centres of Edirne and Bursa.[53] 'Classical' Ḥanafī writers like al-Ṣamarqandī and al-Zamakhsharī were often studied by means of a later set of 'post-classical' Ḥanafī scholars, namely the Timurid 'school of Samarqand' of the late fourteenth century, led by Jurjānī and Taftazānī. This international Timurid connection, a kind of second wave of Ḥanafī scholarship to sweep over Rum, is in this instance embodied in the person of Ḥaydar Haravī Khvāfī. Thus it is no surprise that six of the nine Khurasani sources of the Yazıcıoğlus were of the Ḥanafī *madhhab*, and the only sources dedicated to the highly *madhhab*-specific field of legal reasoning were Ḥanafī ones of Khurasani or Transoxanian provenance – Qāḍīkhān, Marghīnānī and the legist Bukhārī.[54] It is thus unsurprising that the Yazıcıoğlus' bibliography bears similarities with the curricula current in Khurasan during the reign of Shāhrukh (1409–47), as reconstructed by Maria Eva Subtelny and Anas Khalidov on the basis of *ijāza* documents.[55]

The relative lack of texts connected to Egypt and Syria requires some explanation, although none can be confidently offered here. The scholars of these two Shāfi'ī regions simply may not have been carried along with the 'Ḥanafī migrations' and had not reached currency in western Anatolia and Rumelia at this time. More remarkable is the fact that the brothers appear *not* to have been a party to the known intellectual transmission between the Mamluk lands and Anatolia and Rumelia from the fourteenth through mid-fifteenth centuries. The Yazıcıoğlus' careers do not have much in common with, for example, the earlier career of Ḥācı Paşa, who travelled from the Aydınid lands of western Anatolia to Cairo and returned to Ayaṣoluk, with the authority to write Shāfi'ī theological commentaries on al-Bayḍāwī and al-Rāzī.[56]

Another figure who typifies this commerce is Shaykh Ḥusayn Akhlāṭī of Cairo, about whom little information is known, but who remarkably figures in the biographies of two individuals within the broader orbit of the Yazıcıoğlus, 'Abduraḥmān Bisṭāmī and Bedre'd-dīn Simavī. The scholar Kāfiyajī, who was born in Anatolia but lived and died in Cairo, is another visible representative of this pattern. However, this pattern of scholarly exchange may have taken shape socially, as it is not visibly represented in the texts read by the Yazıcıoğlus. All of this should serve as a powerful reminder that Anatolia – and now Rumelia – even in the fifteenth century was a kind of outpost of Khurasani academic culture, as it had been since the Seljuq conquests.

A further feature of this library is that, from among the vast Khurasani Ḥanafī inheritance, the brothers used only the most basic and agreed-upon works (except in the case of al-Saqsīnī's Shī'ī-tinged preachers' manual), almost never straying outside the bounds of *shar'ī*-minded Sunnism. In other words, their library was an extremely conventional one, even by the standards of the time. In this regard, it is interesting how similar the brothers' library was to the official *medrese* curriculum of Sultan Süleymān's schools, codified a century after the Yazıcıoğlus' lifetimes, in 1565. This list, discussed by Shahab Ahmed and Nenad Filipovic, enumerates a long sequence of textbooks that largely overlap with the Yazıcıoğlus' reading materials: al-Zamakhsharī is paramount, and al-Baghawī, Zayn al-'Arab and Taftazānī are also to be found on the sultan's list.[57] But the Yazıcıoğlus' list is both smaller and more narrowly canonical, omitting, for example, the many super-commentaries on the *Kashshāf* and al-Bayḍāwī that dominate the royal curriculum.

An even greater degree of overlap can be seen when the Yazıcıoğlus' library is compared with Khayr al-din al-'Atūfī's inventory of the palace library of Sultan Bāyezīd II in 1502/3–4/5. Mohsen Goudarzi has noted the prominence of al-Zamakhsharī's *Kashshāf*, al-Bayḍāwī's *Anwār al-Tanzīl* and Fakhr al-Dīn al-Rāzī's *Mafātīḥ al-Ghayb* among the sultan's holdings, as well as Taftazānī's and Jurjānī's glosses on al-Zamakhsharī;[58] these are among the most important *tafsīr*s for the Yazıcıoğlus as well. The same can be said of *ḥadīth* collections. As Recep Gürkan Göktaş has shown, the *Masābīḥ al-Sunna* of al-Baghawī and al-Saghānī's *Mashāriq al-Anwār* are present in more than three copies in the sultanic archives.[59] As for the texts of other categories, Bāyezīd kept copies of al-Marghinānī's *al-Hidāya*,[60] several works by al-Ghazali[61] and the key writings of the mystics of the Ibn 'Arabī tradition cherished by the Yazıcıoğlus.[62] In short, the canon that the Yazıcıoğlus inherited was carried into the sixteenth century largely intact. Nearly every work they read and used continued to be important a century hence.

Keeping these features in mind, we can conceive of the Yazıcıoğlus' intellectual heritage as both a part of the regional inheritance of Khurasani Ḥanafism, as renewed by the influx of Timurid scholars, and a forerunner of the Ottoman standard *medrese* culture, as it was to crystallise in the following century. But we do not see what Evliyā Çelebi and Ismā'īl Ḥaqqı Bursevī suggested when they reminisced about these two saints of Gelibolu: two hermit-dervishes crafting masterpieces using only their inspired imagination. I instead offer the vaguely counter-intuitive proposal that some of the most celebrated mystics in Turkish history and the authors of some of popular Ottoman Islam's most vital dogmatic texts assembled their works from utterly conventional material. Their writings, in this sense, serve as a more or less perfectly reflective mirror of a provincial, *shar'ī*-minded scholar's intellectual world. And this world was exactly what one would expect it to be.

The brothers' uniform 'orthodoxy' may call on us to make an important historiographical revision, by re-assessing what has now become almost conventional wisdom in the study of fifteenth-century global Islamic intellectual history: that this period was an era of rampant doctrinal experimentation empowered by the introduction of Sufi, Shī'ī and philosophical ideas into new contexts. While such a trend was certainly displayed in the writings of elite international intellectuals such as 'Abduraḥmān Bisṭāmī of Bursa, Sharaf al-dīn 'Alī Yazdī of Herat and Sa'īn al-dīn Turka of Isfahan,[63] this experimentation is not in evidence in the works of the humble brothers of Gelibolu, preachers and Sufi guides to a crowd of sailors and recruits. In transmitting the heritage of Islamic scholarship to this frontier congregation, they drew from the acceptable core of that heritage, not from its margins. The inclusion of al-Saqsīnī's text about Fāṭima and her family is perhaps the only reminder that the Yazıcıoğlus wrote during a period of looser doctrinal policing than what was to emerge in the sixteenth century.

If the brothers did not innovate or notably re-synthesise, it remains to be asked why their works remained so enduringly popular in the sixteenth century and thereafter.[64] As a preliminary and personal answer, I suggest that these works wildly succeeded because they happened to reinforce the sensibilities of those later centuries, while bearing the valuable pedigree of the heroic age of the early Rumelian frontier. In their straightforward popular Sunnism derived from strictly canonical sources, the Yazıcıoğlu brothers are in this sense the fifteenth-century Ottoman exemplars of the famous aphorism of Jules Michelet: 'Each epoch dreams the one to follow'.

Notes

1. Evliya Çelebi, *Evliya Çelebi Seyahatnâmesi*, vol. 2, p. 225.
2. Gábor Ágoston, ''Muslim Cultural Enclaves in Hungary under Ottoman Rule',' *Acta Orientalia Academiae Scientiarum Hungaricae* 45, no. 2/3 (1991), pp. 203–4.
3. There also exist manuscript copies from Kashgar translated into Eastern Turkic, such as 'Muhammediye', Lund University Library, Box 3, Jarring Collection 55; the Kazan edition, still available in Central Asian and Russian libraries, has been published as *Anwar al-Ashiqin* (Kazan: [n. p.], 1898).
4. Yazıcıoğlu Mehmet, *Muhammediye*, pp. 77, 64–101.
5. In this regard not all Ottoman commentators followed Evliyā and Bursevī.

As Heinzelmann has noted, Taşköprüzade asserted that Meḥmed Yazıcıoğlu wrote from reliable sources. See Heinzelmann, *Populäre religiöse Literatur und Buchkultur im Osmanischen Reich*, for the most comprehensive study of the later uses and readership of the Yazıcıoğlus' writings.

6. See, for instance, Derin Terzioğlu, 'How to Conceptualize Ottoman Sunnitization'. *Turcica* 44, (2012/13): 301–38, and Guy Burak, *The Second Formation of Islamic Law: The Hanafi School in the Early Modern Ottoman Empire* (New York: Cambridge University Press, 2015).
7. Two English-language monographs on the Naqshbandiyya and Halvetiyye are Le Gall, *A Culture of Sufism*; Curry, *The Transformation of Muslim Mystical Thought in the Ottoman Empire*. See also Nathalie Clayer, *Mystiques, état et société: Les Halvetis dans l'aire balkanique de la fin du XVe siècle à nos jours* (Leiden: Brill, 1994).
8. Typically this follows the form of '*S̱el'ebī* Tefsīr*inde eyitdi, Peyġāmber 'aleyhi's-selām eyitdi*' ('Tha'labī in his *Tafsīr* said that the Prophet [upon him be peace] said . . .'). Aḥmed Bīcān, 'Envarü'l-Aşıkin', Süleymaniye Kütüphanesi, Pertev Paşa 229-M (henceforth *EA*), fol. 275a.
9. These *isnād*s usually extend only one or two nodes from the Prophet. '*İbn-i 'Abbās eyitdi Peyghāmber buyurur ki* . . .' ('Ibn 'Abbās said that the Prophet said . . .'), *EA*, fol. 17b.
10. *EA*, fols 2b–3a.
11. Meḥmed Yazıcıoğlu, *Meğarıbü'z-zaman*, Süleymaniye Kütüphanesi, Nuruosmaniye 2596, fol. 4.
12. This study complements another attempted reconstruction of a Yazıcıoğlu library: Kaptein, *Apocalypse and the Antichrist Dajjal in Islam*, esp. pp. 191–204. While my focus is on the *Envārü'l-'Āşıqīn*, Kaptein centres his study on another work traditionally attributed to Aḥmed, the *Dürr-i Meknūn*.
13. A recent synthesis of generations of scholarship on Wahb is found in Michael Pregill, 'Israiliyyat, Myth and Pseudepigraphy: Wahb b. Munabbih and the Early Islamic Versions of the Fall of Adam and Eve', *Jerusalem Studies in Arabic and Islam* 34 (2008), pp. 215–84.
14. Aḥmad ibn Hanbal condemned their use by implying that they have no *aṣl*, or revealed basis; Ibn Ṭaymiyya, centuries thereafter, levied a similar charge. In response to these objections, a *ḥadīth* was often cited which claimed that the Prophet said: 'Narrate [traditions] concerning the Children of Israel and there is nothing objectionable [in that]'. M. J. Kister, '*Haddithu 'an Bani Isra'ila wa-la Haraja*: A Study of an Early Tradition', *Israel Oriental Studies* 2 (1972), pp. 215–39.
15. William M. Brinner, *'Arā'is al-majālis fī qiṣaṣ al-anbiyā' or 'Lives of the Prophets'* (Leiden: Brill, 2002).
16. Muḥammad ibn 'Abd Allāh al-Kisā'ī, *The Tales of the Prophets of Al-Kisā'ī*, trans. Wheeler M. Thackston (Boston: Twayne Publishers, 1978).
17. al-Kisā'ī, *The Tales of the Prophets of Al-Kisā'ī*, p. 118.
18. Ibid. p. 123.

19. The nature of the dependence on al-Kisā'ī is proven not only by the sequence of prophet stories, but also in both works' introductory sections on the scope of creation. Compare, for instance, al-Kisā'ī's description of the seven parallel planets that God created besides our own, with the one written by Aḥmed Yazıcıoğlu; see the Appendix. These passages are almost identical.
20. Brinner, *'Arā'is al-majālis fī qiṣaṣ al-anbiyā' or 'Lives of the Prophets'*, p. xxi.
21. Particularly famous compilations include the *Maghazi* of al-Zajjāj (d. 923), the *Ṣifat al-Nabīy* of Muḥammad al-Bustī (d. 965), the *Sīra* of Ibn Ḥazm (d. 1064) and the *al-Durar fī ikhtisari al-maghāzī wa al-siyar* of Ibn 'Abd al-Barr (d.1071). See M. J. Kister, 'The Sīrah Literature', in *Arabic Literature to the End of the Umayyad Period*, ed. A. F. L. Beeston, T. M. Johnstone, R. B. Serjeant and G. R. Smith (Cambridge: Cambridge University Press, 1983), pp. 352–67.
22. Süleyman Çelebi, *Mevlid*, ed. Neclâ Pekolcay (Ankara: Türkiye Diyanet Vakfı, 1993); Süleyman Çelebi and Ahmed Ateş, *Mevlid: Vesîletü'n-necât* (Ankara: Türk Tarih Kurumu Basımevi, 1954).
23. Mustafa Erkan, 'Mustafa Darir', *İslam Ansiklopedisi*; Yorgo Dedes, 'Süleymān Çelebi's Mevlid: Text, Performance, and Muslim-Christian Dialogue', in *Şinasi Tekin'in Anısına: Uygurlardan Osmanlıya* (İstanbul: Simurg, 2005), pp. 305–49.
24. *EA*, fols 166b–167a.
25. 'Abd al-Malik Ibn Hishām, *The Life of Muhammad*, trans. A. Guillaume (London: Oxford University Press, 1955), p. 80.
26. Muslim Ibn al-Ḥaǧǧāǧ al-Qušayrī, *Ṣaḥīḥ Muslim* (Liechtenstein: Thesaurus Islamicus Foundation, 2000), vol. IV, p. 856.
27. Muḥammad ibn Ismā'īl, *Sahih al-Bukhārī* (Liechtenstein: Thesaurus Islamicus Foundation, 2000), vol. IV, p. 6.
28. Yazıcıoğlu, *Muhammediye*, p. 603
29. Ahmed and Filipovic, 'The Sultan's Syllabus'.
30. See Muḥammad ibn 'Abd Allāh Khaṭīb al-Tibrīzī, *Mishkāt al-Maṣābīḥ*, ed. Muḥammad Mahdī Sharīf (Beirut: Dar al-Kutub, 2012), for a recent edition of this work.
31. Robert McChesney, 'A Note on the Life and Works of Ibn 'Arabshah,' in *History and Historiography of Post-Mongol Central Asia and the Middle East: Studies in Honor of John E. Woods*, ed. Judith Pfeiffer, Sholeh Quinn and Ernest Tucker (Wiesbaden: Harrassowitz, 2006), p. 226.
32. M. Kamil Yaşaroğlu, 'Mûsâ İznikî', *İslam Ansiklopedisi.*
33. For details on Dā'ī, see İsmail Hikmet Ertaylan, *Aḥmed-i Dâ'î: Hayatı ve Eserleri* (İstanbul: Üçler Basımevi, 1952).
34. Yet, while the patronage of al-Ṣamarqandī translations came to a halt, the work's relevance never ceased: The sixteenth-century Ottoman reformist scholar Meḥmed Birgivī not only relied heavily on al-Ṣamarqandī's *tafsīr* for the composition of his *al-Tariqa al-Muhammediyya*, but also on other works

by Abū-Layth, especially the paraenetic *Bustan al-'arifin* and the *Tanbih al-ghafilin*, which were so valued by Birgivī that they may be considered Birgivī's 'source of inspiration and model'. See Katharina Anna Ivanyi, 'Virtue, Piety, and the Law: A Study of Birgivi Meḥmed Efendi's *Al-Tariqa Al-Muḥammadiyya*' (unpublished doctoral dissertation, Princeton University, 2012).

35. For an excellent overview of al-Zamakhsharī and his thought, see Andrew J. Lane, *A Traditional Mu'tazilite Qur'an Commentary: The Kashshāf of Jār Allāh Al-Zamakhsharī (d. 538/1144)* (Boston; Leiden: Brill, 2006). Lane disputes the author's Mu'tazilism as alleged by medieval scholars such as Abū'l-Fidā (p. xxi).
36. Al-Bayḍāwī's major theological work, *Ṭawāli' al-Anwār min Maṭāli' al-Anẓār*, was the subject of a commentary by the Anatolian scholar Ḥācı Paşa, written in Ayas̱oluk in the later fifteenth century. See Yıldız, 'From Cairo to Ayasuluk'. Although there is no direct evidence that the Yazıcıoğlus accessed this commentary, it provides clear evidence of the transmission of Shāfi'ī theology from Mamluk lands to the Anatolian marchlands in the generations prior to the period under consideration here.
37. Mustafa Öz, 'Cemaleddin Aksarayi', *İslam Ansiklopedisi*. Irène Mélikoff, 'D̲jamāl al-Dīn Aḳsarayī', *Encyclopaedia of Islam, Second Edition*.
38. The outline and history of the early Ottoman intellectual hierarchy is discussed in Atçıl, *Scholars and Sultans in the Early Modern Ottoman Empire*, as well as in the classic works by Uzunçarşılı, *Osmanlı Devletinin İlmiye Teskilâti*, and Repp, *The Müfti of Istanbul*. All of these heavily rely on the Ottoman biographical dictionary tradition epitomised by Taşköprüzāde's *al-Shaqā'iqu'n-nu'māniyya*.
39. For comments on the continuing relevance of *al-Kashhaf* and of *tafsīr* writing in the Ottoman system, see Susan Gunasti, 'Political Patronage and the Writing of Qur'ān Commentaries among the Ottoman Turks', *Journal of Islamic Studies* 24, no. 3 (2013), pp. 335–57.
40. Ramzi Baalbaki, 'al-Ṣag̲h̲ānī', *Encyclopaedia of Islam, Second Edition*.
41. Metin Yurdagür, 'Bergamalı İbrahim', *İslam Ansiklopedisi*.
42. See al-Ḥasan ibn Muḥammad Ṣaghānī, *Mashāriq al-anwār* (Dersaadet [Istanbul]: Matbaa-yı Reşadiye, 1911).
43. The more famous Burhān al-dīn al-Marghīnānī was the author of the well-known *Hidāya*, an important eleventh-century manual of Ḥanafī *fiqh*. The Yazıcıoğlus were familiar with the *Hidāya* and cited it occasionally. As Yıldız has discussed, the *Hidāya* was even translated into versified Anatolian Turkish by one Devletoğlu Yūsuf Balıkesrī during the reign of Murad II, slightly ante-dating the Yazıcıoğlus' careers. The vernacularising aims of its translator resonate strongly with the Yazıcıoğlus' project. As Yıldız writes, 'His translation thus involves not only linguistic movement from Arabic to Turkish, but also the localization of his narrative in his own time and place. This strategy not only made Hanafi *fiqh* principles more concrete, but also, in

essence, indigenized classical Hanafi practice'. For more on this fascinating text, see Yıldız, 'A Hanafi Law Manual in the Vernacular'.

44. *EA*, fol. 7b.
45. For a summary of the Ottoman reception of al-Ghazali in later centuries, see M. Sait Özervarlı, 'Ottoman Perceptions of Al-Ghazālī's Works and Discussions on His Historical Role in Its Late Period', in *Islam and Rationality: The Impact of al-Ghazālī. Papers Collected on His 900th Anniversary*, ed. Frank Griffel (Leiden: Brill, 2016), vol. 2, pp. 253–82.
46. See V. F. Büchner and P. B. Golden, 'Saḳsīn', *Encyclopaedia of Islam, Second Edition.*
47. Süleyman b. Davud es-Suvari, 'Zehretü'r-Riyad', Süleymaniye Kütüphanesi, Aya Sofya 4329.
48. *EA*, fols 35a–36a. An identical passage, in Arabic, is found in 'Zehretü'r-Riyad', Süleymaniye Kütüphanesi, Aya Sofya 4329, fol. 123a.
49. See Mohammad Ali Amir-Moezzi, *The Divine Guide to Early Shiism: The Sources of Esotericism in Islam* (Albany: State University of New York Press, 1994), p. 30. Amir-Moezzi finds this story attributed to the sixth imam, according to the Shi'i scholars Ibn Bābūya, Ibn al-Bitrīq and al-Hurr al-'Āmilī.
50. *EA*, fols 230a–252b.
51. *EA*, fol. 252b.
52. Shahab Ahmed, 'Mapping the World of a Scholar in Sixth/Twelfth Century Bukhāra: Regional Tradition in Medieval Islamic Scholarship as Reflected in a Bibliography', *Journal of the American Oriental Society* 120, no. 1 (2000), pp. 24–43.
53. Pertinent comments on mobility as made visible in Taşköprüzade are found in Ertuğrul Ökten, 'Scholars and Mobility: A Preliminary Assessment from the Perspective of *al-Shaqāyiq al-Nu'māniyya*', *Journal of Ottoman Studies* 41 (2013), pp. 55–70.
54. Yet their *madhhab*-consciousness was not of an exclusive sort. Some of the most important of the Yazıcıoğlus' sources – al-Baghawī's *Maṣābīḥ*, Fakhr al-Dīn Rāzī's *tafsīr* and al-Ghazālī's *Ihyā*, for example – are explicitly Shāfi'ī in *madhhab* orientation. So is the *tafsīr* of Qadi Bayḍāwī, admittedly a somewhat less often used source.
55. Subtelny has noted that a core part of the Timurid curriculum consisted of al-Zamakhsharī's *al-Kashshāf*, al-Baghawī's *Maṣābīh al-Sunna*, al-Saghānī's *Mashāriq al-Anwār* and al-Marghīnānī's *al-Hidāya*, all of which the Yazıcıoğlus also use. Maria Eva Subtelny and Anas B. Khalidov, 'The Curriculum of Islamic Higher Learning in Timurid Iran in the Light of the Sunni Revival under Shāh-Rukh', *Journal of the American Oriental Society* 115, no. 2 (1995), p. 223.
56. See Yıldız, 'From Cairo to Ayasuluk'.
57. Ahmed and Filipovic, 'The Sultan's Syllabus'.
58. Mohsen Goudarzi, 'Books on Exegesis (*tafsīr*) and Qur'anic Readings

(*qirā'āt*): Inspiration, Intellect, and the Interpretation of Scripture in Post-Classical Islam', in *Treasures of Knowledge: An Inventory of the Ottoman Palace Library (1502/3–1503/4)*, ed. Gülru Necipoğlu, Cemal Kafadar and Cornell H. Fleischer (Leiden; Boston: Brill, 2019), pp. 267–308.

59. Recep Gürkan Göktaş, 'On the Hadith Collection of Bayezid II's Library', in *Treasures of Knowledge: An Inventory of the Ottoman Palace Library (1502/3–1503/4)*, ed. Gülru Necipoğlu, Cemal Kafadar and Cornell H. Fleischer (Leiden; Boston: Brill, 2019), pp. 309–40.
60. Himmet Taşkömür, 'Books on Islamic Jurisprudence, Schools of Law, and Biographies of Imams from the Hanafi School', in *Treasures of Knowledge: An Inventory of the Ottoman Palace Library (1502/3–1503/4)*, ed. Gülru Necipoğlu, Cemal Kafadar and Cornell H. Fleischer (Leiden; Boston: Brill, 2019), pp. 389–422.
61. Abdurrahman Atçıl, 'The Kalam (Rational Theology) Section in the Palace Library Inventory', in *Treasures of Knowledge: An Inventory of the Ottoman Palace Library (1502/3–1503/4)*, ed. Gülru Necipoğlu, Cemal Kafadar and Cornell H. Fleischer (Leiden; Boston: Brill, 2019), pp. 309–88.
62. Cemal Kafadar and Ahmet Karamustafa, 'Books on Sufism, Lives of Saints, Ethics, and Sermons', in *Treasures of Knowledge: An Inventory of the Ottoman Palace Library (1502/3–1503/4)*, ed. Gülru Necipoğlu, Cemal Kafadar and Cornell H. Fleischer (Leiden; Boston: Brill, 2019), pp. 439–507.
63. For studies of these figures and their contexts, refer to Melvin-Koushki, 'The Quest for a Universal Science', alongside Binbaş, *Intellectual Networks in Timurid Iran*, and articles by İhsan Fazlıoğlu and Cornell Fleischer.
64. Without being primarily concerned with this question, Heinzelmann, in his *Populäre religiöse Literatur und Buchkultur im Osmanischen Reich*, deals with the readership and uses of the Yazıcıoğlus' works. In Turkey, the Yazıcıoğlu manuscript tradition is the subject of excellent ongoing work by Abdullah Uğur of Marmara University, to whom I am deeply grateful.

Chapter 3

Religion on the Frontier

Let us return to the *çīleḫāne* where Meḥmed Yazıcıoğlu, in popular legend as in Evliyā Çelebi's *Seyāḥatnāme*, composed the *Maghārib* and the *Muḥammediyye* between 1444 and his death in 1451.[1] Through a small window carved into its inner room, Meḥmed could see the Dardanelles plied by Ottoman warships and Italian traders, and across the straits Asia and Lapseki whose fortress, first raised by Murād I in 1376, he saw destroyed by Murād II on the eve of a battle with Venice's fleet. Above and behind him loomed Gelibolu's own castle with its garrison recently held by the pretender Muṣṭafā's Byzantine allies, where now men like Meḥmed's patron Qassāboğlu Maḥmūd Paşa gathered and set out for the now-distant Balkan frontiers. To the west, near the harbour, spread out the large neighbourhood of Greek oarsmen, workmen and sailors recorded in the 879/1475 *taḥrīr*.[2] To the east, a few hundred yards from Meḥmed's cave and atop another cliff facing the straits, was an open-air mosque, a marble prayer platform commissioned by İskender, the man with whom his father had spent his final years in scribal service; it had been built for soldiers and seamen, so that they could pray as they marched from the garrison to their ships, to war in Anatolia and Rumelia.[3] Along the ridge that led into the new Muslim quarter of town behind these cliffs were the tombs of several warriors: Bayraqlı Baba (d. 1410), who according to legend swallowed Sultan Orḫan's banner to prevent its desecration; Emīr 'Alī Baba (d. 1356), the captain who ferried the daughter of John VI Kantakouzenos from Constantinople so she could become Orḫan's wife; and the admirals Terzi Ṣaruca Paşa and Sinān Paşa. Meḥmed Yazıcıoğlu's own *tekke* and, later, his own tomb and that of his brother was to be built among them. This heroic landscape, today extended by the peninsula's monuments to 1915, was taking shape as Meḥmed and Aḥmed worked in their cave to write the works that gave them enduring fame.

Historiographically speaking, the writing of Sunnī catechistics and dogmatics within this geography defined by a history of holy war situates the Yazıcıoğlu brothers and their works at the intersection of two debates in the study of the first Ottoman centuries. From the perspective of the '*ġāzī* thesis' debate, which has preoccupied Ottoman scholars since Paul Wittek's *Rise of the Ottoman Empire* in 1939, we are made to wonder how the Yazıcıoğlu brothers participated in and affected the political and ideological dynamics of frontier warfare, and how this was reflected in their works. From the perspective of the debate on the consolidation of an Ottoman Sunnī Islam – a process often called 'confessionalisation', borrowed from the terminology of Reformation historiography[4] – we are prompted to assess how the brothers and their writings comprised a stage in the growth of this religious consensus; a consensus born, in part, from this unique frontier environment.

In the context of both the '*ġāzī* thesis' debate and the confessionalisation debate, we see the Yazıcıoğlu brothers working in the same direction, in a single process. They participated in the 'centripetal' impulse of early Ottoman ideology, aiming to resolve the ambiguities of borderland life by drawing out the matrix of a popular piety that could be nourished in the hearts of ordinary Muslims, in order to sweep away the confusion of earlier conceptions of religious difference and of *ġazā*, and to replace it with a clear proscriptive understanding of the Muslim-Christian confessional border. The Yazıcıoğlus wrote a '*ġāzī* theology' that could render this ceaseless warfare in pursuit of the straits' control and the resulting fallen soldiers and martyrs sensible.

Scholarly debate on Ottoman origins has been re-animated by the 1996 publication of Cemal Kafadar's *Between Two Worlds.*[5] Kafadar has argued that the very concept of *ġazā*, often translated as 'holy war',[6] in fact masks several historically distinct ideologies across the course of the fourteenth and fifteenth centuries, even as it remained a defining term of the Ottoman political culture throughout the whole period. Not all *ġazā* was for Islam, while not all Muslims believed in the same kind of *ġazā*. Furthermore, he has argued that the evolution of the moving concept behind the term *ġazā* followed the dynamics of Ottoman political practice, transforming across the period from the reigns of Bāyezīd I to Meḥmed II, from a discourse serving the *ġāzī beg*s of the frontier, to a discourse responding to the centralising demands of the sultan in Istanbul. This broadest possible definition of *ġazā* – that it was not just fighting for Islam against the Christians, and not just the 'feigned cooperation' called *müdārā*, but a general and mutable style of borderland coexistence – is the definition that will be used here.

In lieu of reviewing the theories of Ottoman origins[7] with which Kafadar's thesis stands in dialogue – theories presented in studies such as Rudi Lindner's anthropologically informed revision of the organisation of Osman's tribe,[8] the works of Heath Lowry,[9] the influential tribal theory of Fuad Köprülü[10] and the original *ġāzī* thesis of Wittek – I will merely state that a point of departure of what follows is Kafadar's important insistence that '[a]n ideological commitment to *gaza* was in all likelihood common to [1300 or 1330 or 1360 or 1410], but its character and intensity kept changing, just as inclusivism was never fully abandoned by the Ottomans but was constantly redefined'.[11] To paraphrase, different phases of early Ottoman history called for different conceptions of what defined the frontier and theories of religious difference.

By the 1440s and early 1450s, when the Yazıcıoğlus were writing, the borderlands had already undergone important transformations. These include the victory in the Ottoman Civil War of the most Anatolian and least Balkan of Bāyezīd's sons and the marginalisation of the early state's Balkan elites; the defeat, soon thereafter, of Şeyḫ Bedre'd-dīn's ecumenical Sufi movement; and Murād II's defeat of the Hungarian expedition of Varna, which was commemorated in the *Ġazavātnāme* as a victory of *ġazā* over crusade.[12] One factor affecting the development of *ġāzī* ideology is comparatively understated: This is the entry of the Ottoman Empire, for the first time, into the mainstream of Islamic intellectual life. The vehicle of this integration has already been described in Chapter 2: the group of scholars mostly from the Timurid centres of Iran and Central Asia, who found careers in the schools of Murād II's Edirne and Bursa. They brought to the Ottoman frontier a worldview legalist in character, which had long ago been worked out in *fiqh* and other religious sciences.

The Yazıcıoğlus themselves were of the first generation of Ottoman intellectuals who could participate in this wave of Timurid and Mamluk scholarship, and accordingly they propagated an orthodox, traditionally Islamic ideology of confessional identity that they had received from their teachers. Nevertheless, they were not simply repeating Ḥanafī consensus indiscriminately. Rather, they were also participating in another, more local discourse that transpired at the same time – an inter-confessional one, actualised in the innumerable conversations that Christians had with Muslims and *vice versa* about what their respective faiths meant. While the brothers were informed by a strictly Islamic set of texts, the questions that they answered were, I will argue, local to the frontier and to Gelibolu, and particular to their time. Out of this discourse the Yazıcıoğlus created an ideology of confessional difference. The creation of this ideology from Muslim-Christian frontier dialogue will be the focus of this chapter.[13]

In order to demonstrate this emergence, I will first dwell on the nature of the Gelibolu frontier and the Marmara region in the fourteenth and early fifteenth centuries, initially focusing on its role as a centre of the military frontier. A consequence of this strategic importance was the transformation of the city and region into ones that had a dual character, deeply conscious of the politico-religious division that bisected them, but also profoundly heterogeneous in an ethno-religious sense. This, in turn, stimulated a pattern of dialogue between Muslims and Christians, a dialogue that was structured by a discrete set of questions on the distinction between the two faiths. The reader will have to indulge this excursus into fourteenth- and fifteenth-century political and intellectual history, which may seem to have little bearing on the lives of the Yazıcıoğlus. Yet, if, as this study has consistently maintained, the Yazıcıoğlus' works are best conceived as a dialogue between the local and the cosmopolitan, then the cultural setting that produced them in Gelibolu deserves a detailed exposition as part of the history of the Yazıcıoğlus' writings.

The second part of this chapter will focus on the ideology of the Yazıcıoğlus themselves, seen as a response to this environment. Immersed in these frontier conversations even as they received orthodox Islamic educations, the brothers displayed a preoccupation with countering the dogmatic fixed points of Christianity and tried to rectify ambiguities between Islam and Christian beliefs. A major feature of this apologia is a defense of the superiority of Muḥammad over Jesus, which directs the flow of much of the texts' narrative. Following this, I will delineate the brothers' attempt to counter this ambiguity: the foundations of a kind of lay Muslim catechism. The mechanisms by which this basic 'textbook Islam' gained traction with ordinary believers include the acquisition of *s̱evāb*, or divine favour, to the status of arch-metaphor and foregrounding the imagery of death, as well as the rewards and punishments in the Hereafter. Finally, I will bring this discussion back to the tangible life of Gelibolu, a city that was then sustained by the industry of naval *ġazā* for the Ottoman enterprise.

The Nature of the Borderland

> Gallipoli, the Muslim throat that gulps down every Christian nation, that chokes and destroys the Christians . . .
>
> Düzme Muṣṭafā, according to Doukas.[14]

Since the publication of Frederick Jackson Turner's *The Frontier in American History* in 1893, historians have seen value in treating the borderland as a geography greatly distinct from the heartlands on either side. It has become commonplace, for example, to oppose the frontier Turkoman polities of medieval Anatolia, such as the Danışmend state, to the Seljuq kingdom in Konya: While the latter, recognizing a common sedentary and bureaucratic culture, usually made common cause with the Byzantines, the former pursued its own aims and raided large parts of the peninsula with a motley convert army, providing an outlet for the marginalised elements of the interior.[15] Frontiers were also porous, encouraging certain kinds of intellectual commerce. As Linda Darling has argued, the Ottoman marches of the early modern Mediterranean may be reinterpreted as inclusive borderlands rather than fortified frontiers.[16] It is clear that the city of Gelibolu shared the characteristics of both a separating frontier and a uniting borderland. The sites of contact and exchange were also the sites of religio-political polarisation, and the repelling and attracting impulses of the interlocutors on both sides of the Byzantine-Ottoman frontier gave it its character. What follows explores the nature of the Gelibolu frontier until the time of the Yazıcıoğlu brothers, as they wrote in the middle decades of the fifteenth century, on the eve of the Conquest of Constantinople. Gelibolu, it can be said without exaggeration, was the city that embodied these frontier characteristics most typically.

The meaning of the name of the Byzantine city of Kallipolis, 'the fine town', was apparently preserved as one of the Arabic epithets that the Yazıcıoğlus used for their city: *aḥsanu'l-bilād*, 'finest of towns'. By the medieval period, the fortress, situated on a natural harbour at one of the Dardanelles' narrowest points, had outgrown the older stronghold of nearby Abydos, where in the fifth century BCE Xerxes had built his bridge of boats in order to attack the Greek states. In the twelfth century, the Spanish Jewish traveller Benjamin of Tudela claimed that Kallipolis was large enough to have a resident community of 'two hundred Jews'.[17] Yet, despite its prosperity, for centuries its political fortunes were subsidiary to those of Constantinople, its mother city, and fell under its jurisdiction or that of inland Adrianople.

At the beginning of the fourteenth century, the city would come to earn another of the Yazıcıoğlus' favorite epithets: *dārü'l-cihād*, 'abode of holy war'. In 1305 the Catalan Grand Company of mercenaries entered Byzantine service and occupied Kallipolis, bringing with it Turkish mercenary allies from across the straits, the so-called *tourkopoloi.*[18] Instead of serving Emperor Andronikos II, the Catalans and Turks held fast to the city and used it as a base to plunder Thrace and march west to Thessaloniki, pillaging on the way. With the Turcopole presence, Gallipoli and the straits, instead of separating the Byzantines from the contested terrain of Anatolia, became a gateway that opened it up to Anatolia's nomadic populations, as a prelude to the ultimate Ottoman invasion of inland Thrace. The *Crónica* of Ramón Muntaner, a Valencian soldier who took part in this campaign and served as the town's garrison commander, stated that the city was the key to the mainland territories: 'Gallipoli is the maritime capital of Macedonia, just as Barcelona is the maritime capital of Catalonia and Lérida of the hinterland'.[19] During his seven-year adventure, when Gallipoli was the administrative centre of 'the Host of Franks who are ruling the Kingdom of Macedonia', the city was the site of incessant intrigues among Aragonese nobles, exiled Constantinopolitans and mercenary Turks. The 'Turks and Turcopoles' in particular got along well with the Catalans, 'and they never called me anything else than *ata*, which in Turkish means father'.[20] In 1312, more *tourkopouloi*, led by one Ḫalīl Paşa whose name suggests that he may have remained Muslim, occupied the peninsula and were only ousted when Emperor Michael IX summoned a Serbian army.

While the Ottoman *beglik* was still confined to Bithynia, another regional power showed an interest in Kallipolis and its peninsula: the Aydınoğulları of the region of Ephesus and Ayas̱oluk (Theologos), whose naval exploits under their leader Umūr Beg were commemorated in the fifteenth-century epic *Düstūrnāme* by Enverī. In 1332, Umūr's father Meḥmed Beg raided Kallipolis and confronted the Thracian governor Andronikos Asen in what Enverī, using a terminology of religious warfare that anachronistically reflects his own fifteenth-century moment, described as a great battle. At the point of defeat, Aydın's general dismounted from his horse in the thick of the battle and prayed: 'O Creator, pity us / we are hopeless and lost and afflicted. If you don't help us at this moment / we will not repel these many unbelievers'. But God heeded his call: 'The wind blew dust upon the unbelievers / earth struck and filled their eyes / The unbelievers were defeated in disarray / and the *tekfūr*[21] Asen was shamed / The plain was filled with the bodies of unbelievers / in one *dönüm* there were five thousand dead . . .'[22]

Although the *Düstūrnāme* makes it clear that the forces of Aydın won the day in 1332, they were unable to control the fortress itself and soon crossed back to Anatolia. By 1352, Kallipolis and its peninsula were in the hands of the embattled Emperor John VI Kantakouzenos. In a consequential sequence of events whose precise chronology remains in dispute, Kantakouzenos invited Ottoman forces to Thrace in order to help him in his struggle against John V Palaiologos. After occupying Tzympe (Çinbe) Castle on the peninsula, the Ottoman troops refused to return to Anatolia once Kantakouzenos had consolidated control; in 1354, a fortuitous earthquake toppled the walls of Kallipolis' fortress and allowed Sultan Orḫan's son Süleymān Paşa to occupy and convert it into an Ottoman base for Rumelian conquests. The historian George Arnakis, citing a Bulgarian chronicle from 1561, proposed that this was a gradual process in the course of which Turkish soldiers and colonists over time overwhelmed the Greek population and garrison.[23] Regardless of the nature of this hand-over, Gelibolu immediately acquired central importance to the Ottoman state. The new *sancaq* was named *Paşa sancağı* in testimony to the lasting memory of Süleymān Paşa, whose own residence was at nearby Bolayır.

When Süleymān Paşa predeceased his father in 1357, Gelibolu became a residence for the future Sultan Murād I. During the decade between the first Ottoman conquest of Gelibolu in 1354 under Süleymān Paşa and its fall to Amadeo VI of Savoy in 1366, the city was one of the pre-eminent Ottoman strongholds in Rumelia – only Dimetoka (Didymoteichon), conquered in 1361, and the future capital of Edirne (Adrianople), conquered in 1362, surpassed it as population centres of the early Ottoman realms in Europe. It is doubtful, however, that most of these Turkish settlers were 'Ottoman' in a meaningful sense. The Turks of the former *beglik* of Karesi, which bordered the Ottoman heartland to the west and populated the Asian side of the Dardanelles until the Ottomans took it in 1345–46, were the best-positioned to colonise Gelibolu and its peninsula once Süleymān Paşa opened it up to settlement.[24] The populace of the old *beglik* of Saruḫan, further south, may have taken part as well: The 879/1475 *taḥrīr* records a neighbourhood of '*Saruḫanlu*' residents in nearby Malkara.[25] The Ottoman chronicler 'Aşıqpaşazade mentions 'families of recruits' ('*azeb evleri*, often read as '*arab evleri*) sent from Anatolia to repopulate Rumelia, which were likely from these same western *begliks*, rather than from the heartland of the Os̱mānoğulları in inland Bithynia.[26]

This era ended abruptly in 1366, with Amadeo's arrival at the head of a minor crusade against both Murād I and Tsar Ivan Alexander of Bulgaria. Taking the city back from the Ottomans in a battle that goes unremarked in the Ottoman chronicles, Amadeo returned Gelibolu to Emperor John V Palaiologos, who ruled the city in relative tranquility for a decade. This conquest effectively cut off the Ottoman frontier domains in Rumelia from the Anatolian heartland, setting the former upon a separate trajectory for some time and causing a decade-long break in the continuity of the city's and the region's Muslim rulership. The young *beglik* was now effectively two and thus less capable of concerted expansion. This situation stimulated the Byzantine intellectual Demetrius Kydones to compose *De Non Redenda Gallipoli* in Latin for a Western audience; in it, he urged all Christian powers to ensure that Gelibolu never be returned to the Turks on account of its immense strategic value for the whole of Christendom:

'We have long considered Gallipoli the most precious of our possessions and the most able to be of assistance in the war against the barbarians'.[27] Until the Conquest of Constantinople, similar expressions concerning the precarious dependence of Ottoman expansion on the control over the Dardanelles and its fortress were to become refrains on both sides of the political border.

In 1376 Andronikos IV, revolting against his father John V, handed the city and fortress of Gelibolu over to Sultan Murād. With this second reconquest, logistical coordination across the straits could resume and, along with it, the process of cultural Islamisation and political Ottomanisation of the city and its Thracian hinterland.[28] Certain figures appeared on the scene in Gelibolu during this time. One was Ṣaruca Paşa; attached to his household was Qassāboğlu 'Ali, the patron of Yazıcı Ṣāliḫ. This moment of Turco-Muslim stability was also the period during which Yazıcı Ṣāliḫ moved to Thrace. While most of the first generation of Thracian settlers were from the western *begliks*, Ṣāliḫ, who may have been from Ankara, is perhaps a token of a newer wave of settlers from central Anatolia who came at this point in time.[29] Gelibolu had become an Ottoman town and its region an Ottoman province, and Yazıcı Ṣāliḫ, father of Aḥmed and Meḥmed, was among its settlers.

It was at this time that the city's centrality to the wars of Ottoman expansion on both land and sea seems to have given rise to a certain polarising atmosphere, illustrated in contemporaneous European travel accounts. Johannes Schiltberger, a Bavarian soldier in Hungarian service taken captive after King Sigismund's defeat at Nicopolis in 1396, described how he, along with other captives (including Duke Phillip of Burgundy), was confined for two months in the tower of Gelibolu's citadel. Testifying to the adversarial outlook of many in this military city, Schiltberger said that, when King Sigismund's ship passed through the straits, '[the Turks] took us out of the tower and led us to the sea, and one after the other they abused the king and mocked him, and called to him to come out of the boat and deliver his people; and this they did to make fun of him . . .'[30] A sectarian consciousness, political in its origins and expression, and sustained by a military presence, is evident here.

This tense atmosphere persisted throughout the period following the Battle of Ankara and the Ottoman Civil War. In 1402, the Castilian diplomat Ruy Gonzáles de Clavijo was sent from Madrid to Samarqand to serve as ambassador to Tīmūr; his account gives us a glimpse of Gelibolu immediately following Bāyezīd's defeat, with a focus on the city's military and logistical capabilities:

> Here the Turks have all of their fleet of galleys and other ships where also they have made a great arsenal [. . .] the castle of Gallipoli is very strongly garrisoned with many troops and a large guard [. . .] It was through [taking Gallipoli] that the Turks conquered all the Greek lands that they had won: and should they ever come to lose Gallipoli, they would indeed lose all the lands they have conquered in Greece. Since they have come to possess this port, where they station their fleet of galleys and other ships, this for them is the passage across from the Turkish homelands both for their troops, and for supplies; and this fortress of Gallipoli is the base by which the Turks oppress the empire of the Greeks.[31]

One wonders whether Clavijo, in expressing the city's strategic value to the Ottoman enterprise, may have become aware of Kydones' earlier statements, which after all had been written in Latin.[32] Indeed, during and after the Ottoman succession war, the city was the target of Byzantine and Venetian raids in 1410 and 1416 – well within the lifetime of the Yazıcıoğlu brothers.

Although the facts of these battles and the testimonies of Kydones, Schiltberger and Clavijo play up the rigidity of the politico-religious border, it is clear from other sources that the population of the region itself was characterised by mixture. Illustrating both dimensions is the account given by the Greek historian Doukas of the cooperation between Düzme Muṣṭafā, the pretender to the throne of Murād II, and the Byzantine Emperor Manuel II Palaiologos along with Cüneyd, ruler of Aydın. Doukas described how in 1420 Muṣṭafā, Cüneyd and the emperor's general Demetrios Leontarios fought side-by-side to conquer Gelibolu from Murād's troops. After battling Sultan Murad II's troops to a stalemate, Muṣṭafā and Demetrios addressed the gathered population of the city, who then surrendered to 'the force of heavily armed Romans and Turks' and acclaimed Muṣṭafā as ruler. However, several months later, when Muṣṭafā agreed to hand the city over to the Byzantine Emperor Manuel II Palaiologos, the town's Muslims were dismayed: 'The Turkish populace was thrown into a state of confusion and turmoil at the unwanted and unexpected Roman takeover'.[33] Using words that precisely echo the earlier remarks of Kydones and Clavijo, Muṣṭafā then argued: 'As for surrendering this city, that is, Gallipoli, the Muslim throat that gulps down every Christian nation, that chokes and destroys the Christians, never could such an absurdity enter my mind!' He claimed that he could not in good conscience '[deliver] the pious into the hands of the impious, by making a free people slaves, and by putting the nation which is consecrated to God into the hands of the infidels who do not know the One God of heaven and earth'.[34] Nevertheless, the operational alliance between Manuel Palaiologos and these two Muslim lords persisted until it was defeated near Gelibolu by Murād II, who had allied himself with the Genoese and other Italians. This history is meaningful. We see that the life of the city permitted cooperation between 'Romans and Turks' within certain parameters before it transformed into a discourse of opposition. This paradoxical combination reflects the essential character of the Gelibolu frontier.

The *taḥrīr* registers provide more concrete evidence of the heterogeneity of Gelibolu's population. The earliest of them, from 879/1475, notes many groups of Greeks organised into legally-overseen workers' associations attached to the Ottoman navy in the city, including rowers and arbalesters. Greeks seem almost as common in this *taḥrīr* as Muslims or Turks; when names such as 'Yorgi son of Yanis', or 'Teodoris son of Kosta' appear as leaders of naval workmens' regiments, one can be certain that Gelibolu's navy and the rest of its military was an integrated force. A 'mosque of the church' appears here as well, indicating architectural re-use.[35] A later *taḥrīr*, from 925/1519, separates Greek neighbourhoods into those pertaining to individual churches, such as St. Nicholas, St. Demetrios and many others, which certainly had existed before Ottoman occupation.[36]

The famed Italian humanist Cyriaco of Ancona disembarked in Gelibolu on 29 January 1444 during his long investigation of the remains of classical antiquity. Reminding us that the city was a mercantile as well as military centre, he met two Genoese and one Anconan trader who 'happened to be doing business with the barbarian settlers [that is, the Turks]'. His attention was then drawn by the re-use of a piece of inscribed ancient marble within an Ottoman mosque. 'I found this inscription on a marble altar of the barbarian superstition, that you might see a sample of the venerable antiquities of this ancient town', he stated, before quoting the ancient Greek text of this inscription in honour of a long-gone Roman administrator.[37] It is a pleasing historical coincidence that Cyriaco and the Yazıcıoğlu brothers – one the prototype of the Italian humanist, and the others of Ottoman populist litterateurs – walked the same streets for a time that winter.

This combination of political polarisation invoked by incessant warfare, along with cultural mixture and transit, gave rise to a characteristic phenomenon of frontier zones: dialogue, requiring both a strong sense of difference and an intimacy of contact. While countless conversations on the differences between Islam and Christianity certainly occurred across individual fourteenth-century encounters – in the conversations, for example, between Ramón Muntaner's Catalans and their Turkish comrades-in-arms, or between Christian and Muslim members of 'Os̠mān's and Orḫan's forces – perhaps the first with a clear written testimony is that of Gregory Palamas, archbishop of Salonica and one of the foremost intellectuals of the Orthodox Church.[38] In 1354, Palamas, while travelling between Constantinople and Salonica, was captured aboard his ship outside of Gelibolu. His Ottoman captors held him in Gelibolu (which had recently 'come under the yoke of the Achaemenidae') for a few days and then allowed him to preach in a church across the straits in Lapseki, before leading him across Ottoman Bithynia into Bursa. There, and later in Orḫan's camp further inland and in İznik (Nicaea), Palamas was made to engage in a dialogue on religious fundamentals with a set of learned Muslim interlocutors.

These dialogues present a concise summary of the forms of Islamo-Christian disputation typical of the region, a list that encompasses a few points of dispute between the religions. The scholars first asked Palamas: 'How do you call Christ a God since he was born a man?' Secondly, the Muslims were dismayed that Palamas refused to acknowledge the prophethood of Muḥammad while they themselves acknowledged that of Jesus. As a veteran *ġāzī* inquired, 'We believe in your prophet, why do don't you believe in ours?' Finally, Palamas' Ottoman interlocutors accused Christians of engaging in idolatry, in violation not only of Qur'anic injunctions against the worship of images, but of the Second Commandment, which the Muslims were able to recite. Both Palamas and 'a Turk' then brought the conversation to a close by voicing hope for a reconciliation between the faiths, stating 'there will come a time when we will agree with each other'.

These points, as well as the conciliatory sentiment that closes the dialogue, embedded in a broadly common rational theology and framework of Abrahamic prophetology, would recur over the coming century. In 1391 the Byzantine Emperor Manuel II Palaiologos, in his role as Ottoman vassal, was transported to Ankara to assist in Sultan Bāyezīd's fight against the ruler of Sivas. According to his own *Dialogues*, it was there that he spoke at great length with a 'learned Persian' *müderris* on the incompatibilities as well as sympathies between his faith and the Islam of his interlocutor, recording these dialogues in the form of an account that is by now well-known in the history of Muslim-Christian polemics.[39] Over the course of several days and nights, the two peaceably discussed 'the Muslim conception of Paradise, the nature of plants, animals and human beings, Muhammad and his doctrines, the prophets and Moses, the Holy Spirit, the substance of faith, considerations of the Holy Trinity or polytheism by the Muslims'.[40] The arguments of both Manuel and the 'Persian' encompass typical issues of Christian-Muslim polemic: They asked each other, for instance, about the sequence of revealed law – how is your Law better than the detested Law of the Jews? How can the doctrine of the Trinity be reconciled with monotheism? Here, too, in the friendly tone of the debate and in the shared emphasis on a unitary divinity amid consecutive prophetic cycles, there can be felt a sincere desire for the possibility of reconciliation – or, more deeply, a merging – between the two faiths. The Yazıcıoğlus' contemporary Gemistos Plethon manipulated these same ideas when he felt obliged to integrate his idiosyncratic Hellenic system (in which Zeus and Zoroaster both played roles) with the historical sequence of Abrahamic revelation. Such were the contours of regional religious experimentation.[41]

In fact, this prospect of a common faith emerging from the areas of overlap between Islam and Christianity – a kind of revived philosophical Abrahamism growing from a mixed community of native Christians, Anatolian migrants and converts – arises as a separate and powerful theme across multiple contexts in the first decades of the fifteenth century, when the Yazıcıoğlu brothers were growing up. Sharing a broad structure, linguistic register and pattern of subsequent popularity with Meḥmed Yazıcıoğlu's *Muḥammediyye* is the *Mevlid* of Süleymān Çelebi, an account of the Prophet's life written in 1409.[42] Recently, Yorgos Dedes has drawn attention to an entry in the sixteenth-century biographical dictionary of Laṭīfī concerning the composition of this text. According to Laṭīfī, in Bursa's Ulu Cami, the largest mosque of what was then the Ottomans' most important city, a preacher claimed that, as a prophet, Muḥammad was not superior to Jesus. An Arab in the congregation challenged this preacher, arguing that, if this were the case, how could the Qur'anic line 'And those Messengers, some We have preferred above others'[43] be understood? The people of the Ottoman capital, however, sided with the preacher, while the Arab went back to Syria to get a ruling supporting his argument, returning with an order for the preacher's death. But the Bursans still upheld the arguments of their preacher claiming that Jesus was equal to Muḥammad, until the Arab uttered the threatening prediction that, if the preacher did not retract his views, the land of Rum would be overrun by infidels.

Laṭīfī wrote that Süleymān Çelebi, who witnessed these events, composed these Turkish lines of his *Mevlid* in response to the dangerously Christian sympathies of Bursa's congregation:

> And Jesus did not die but rose to heaven
> That was so that he be of this community [that is, Islam].
>
> [. . .]

They pleaded with God
That they might be of Muḥammad's community
For they have messengers too.
But Aḥmed [that is, Muḥammad] is most perfect and superior,
for he is the most deserving of superiority.
Only a simpleton [*ahmaq*] does not know that.[44]

Thus, it seems that even in Bursa, the oldest and most significant Ottoman city, Muslims were curious about the relative rankings of Jesus and Muḥammad and unwilling to demarcate anathematising lines between the two confessional communities. Also worth noting is the fact that this narrative was attached to an entry dealing with the composition of Süleymān Çelebi's *Mevlid.* Just as was the case with the Yazıcıoğlus, an atmosphere of confessional fluidity prompted the production of popular Turkish vernacular writing, as a way to dispel the misconceptions of a naive population.[45]

From another witness we hear of a similar conversation among Muslims. In 1455, a Serbian soldier named Konstantin Mihailović was captured by Ottoman forces and then joined them. In his memoirs he tells how a preacher in a mosque rejected the claim that Christ had been crucified, saying: 'You must not believe that. Jesus was of such holiness that nobody could really touch him'. He was raised to Heaven and, on Judgment Day, will look with dismay at both Christians and Jews, saying to the former 'You called me God' and to the latter 'You wanted to torture and crucify me'. In another instance, Mihailović witnessed a gathering of what he called 'monks' under the leadership of a *shaykh* in the presence of the vizier Maḥmūd Paşa. They argued over whether Jesus was just a prophet or 'an archprophet alongside God the Creator' and whether some good Christians have 'faith but no religion' and thus may still be registered alongside Muslims on Judgment Day. Mihailović said that this argument got so heated that 'having raised a cry one against another, they began to throw books at one another. Indeed I thought they would give each other blows to the head with those books'.[46] It is significant that it was Maḥmūd Paşa who convened this gathering – a vizier of Greek and Slavic aristocratic origin who certainly held in his heart his own questions as to the connections between his adopted faith and the faith of his childhood.

Perhaps the most complete dialogue of this type comes from Maḥmūd Paşa's own cousin, the philosopher George Amiroutzes of Trebizond (1400–70). A contemporary of the Yazıcıoğlu brothers, Amiroutzes, an attendee of the Council of Florence and holder of high office in Comnenian Trebizond, began a second career after his hometown's 1461 conquest, as companion and advisor to the sultan.[47] Most relevant to this discussion is the fact that the sultan and Ottomanophile philosopher[48] engaged in theological debate during the 1460s, a conversation preserved only in Latin as *De fide uel Philosophus*. Generally, this record had not been regarded as authentic until the recent work of Óscar de la Cruz Palma, who has used newly found manuscript evidence to argue for its authenticity.[49]

The subject-matter of this dialogue is familiar. Sultan Meḥmed takes on the role of a rationalist interlocutor opposed to the notion of miraculous and arbitrary divine intervention in the world; he advocated reasoning about God from rational principles alone while denying miraculous divine intervention. He expressed this in the following passage:

> If your ideas [. . .] are proven not from principles customarily known, but from your own suppositions, how will we know those which are true and those which are invented? Even the pagans, just as the Jews, Christians, *and Arabs*, can specifically prove the items of faith of their religion by using things they suppose [to be true].[50]

Here, with remarkable commitment to rational method, the sultan explicitly placed the Islamic revelation alongside those of the Christians and Jews, thereby implying a certain interchangeability between all religions that believe in a God that can be deduced through reason. After defending revealed knowledge, Amiroutzes tried to defuse this tension by returning to a principle upon which he suspected both would agree. 'Doubtless, sultan', the philosopher said, 'we consider Man to be the noblest of all creations produced by God that can be perceived by the senses. And on behalf of Man all other things have also been created . . .' The sultan replied, 'I easily affirm that it is so. On this matter we believe the same thing'.

The common ground, then, was substantial. The sultan and the philosopher shared a debating mode as they jointly acknowledged a tension between prophecy and rational theology – and, unlike the figures discussed thus far, they also affirmed an anthropocentrism. In contemporary Sufism, one finds echoes of this anthropocentrism in the principle of *al-insān al-kāmil*, 'the Perfect Man', developped from the works of the Andalusian Sufi Ibn 'Arabī and his immediate successors; it posits that Adam and his descendants microcosmically embody universal creation and constitute the polar focus of divine self-consciousness. Marshall Hodgson suggested that the anthropocentrism of the Ibn 'Arabī school, nearly ubiquitous among Sufis of the period, stimulated experimentation in the arena of religious and political thought generally during the fourteenth and fifteenth centuries, rendering permissible expressions of universalism in novel ways.[51]

Through anthropocentrism appears another well-known opening towards an Islamo-Christian fusion. This is the revolutionary ecumenical Sufi movement led by the Ottoman scholar and Sufi Şeyḫ Bedre'd-dīn in 1416. Bedre'd-dīn's movement has proven difficult to characterise with any scholarly rigor. Ahmet Yaşar Ocak, who reserved a chapter for Bedre'd-dīn in his important work on Ottoman heretical movements, has remarked that characterising the nature of his rebellion 'still presents an unsolved historical problem' on account of the extreme ideological variety in evidence in the *shaykh*'s own texts, in those of his followers and in contemporaneous historical accounts.[52] While Bedre'd-dīn's own surviving writings leave the movement's ideological basis somewhat obscure, the actions of his disciples, according to the writings of Doukas and those of the *shaykh*'s grandson Ḥāfiz Ḫalīl, hint that its appeal rested on the proposal of a shared monistic basis of a common piety, a universalism that existed side-by-side, if not in tension with a legalistic piety.[53] Thus, the rebellion that Bedre'd-dīn led against the rule of Meḥmed I seems to constitute an actual fusion of the *shaykh*'s own academic Sufism with the pieties of the first-generation Muslims and native Christians of Thrace and the Aegean littoral. Within the flexibility afforded by Bedre'd-dīn's Sufi framework, the frontier's ecumenical feeling found yet another expression.[54]

Thus, we can see that in a general sense Gelibolu and its Marmara and Aegean hinterlands constituted a central and contentious node on the political frontier, in which curious parties on both sides conversed in an atmosphere of heightened sectarian consciousness. According to multiple extant accounts, these conversations took the form of disputation about the rudiments of faith, in a manner that shared common outlines. And several times within the Ottoman domains, the outcome of these dialogues revealed a degree of ambiguity regarding basic religious tenets. By the time the Yazıcıoğlus were able to intervene in this conversation, debate had not yet died down.

'To Know the Bond of Islam': From Sacred Knowledge to Communal Identity

> Turn this into Turkish so that the people of our land may see the benefit of wisdom and of the lights of knowledge . . .[55]

The response of the Yazıcıoğlu brothers to the confessional ambiguity of their place and time was one of reaction. Where Palamas, the Bursan preacher, Maḥmūd Paşa's entourage, Meḥmed II and Bedre'd-dīn saw the potential of reconciliation, agreement and even a union of faiths, the

Yazıcıoğlus, like the Arab in the Ulu Cami, were alarmed and feared that their own religion would disappear into incoherence, and together with it all that gave their community identity and meaning. All of the frontier's conversations and potential for syncretism were dangers that could 'send astray' (*azıtmaq*) wayfarers currently on the 'straight path' (*ṣırāṭ-ı mustaqīm*). For this specific reason they wrote directly to the population of the frontier and gave them the narrative tools to reaffirm the distinctness of Islam.

In the introduction to his *Envārü'l-'Āşıqīn*, Aḥmed Bīcān wrote that his brother told him to 'Turn this into Turkish so that the people of our land may see the benefit of wisdom and of the lights of knowledge . . .'[56] It is of crucial importance that Aḥmed Bīcān used the phrase 'our people of this land' *(bizüm ilüñ qavmı)*. For a pre-modern and especially an Islamic author, to target an explicitly local population suggests that the author discerned a particular local problem, specifically that the religious needs of Gelibolu and its frontier hinterland were not being met. That their community, 'our people of this land', was not well-defined and, in fact, permeable to what was around it seems to underlie Aḥmed's wording. Thus, 'our people of this land' were both audience and object of the *Envār* and the *Muḥammediyye*.

Their strong sense of the disintegrating boundaries of the Turkish Muslim community of the border region can be seen in the third 'reason for composition' (*sebeb-i te'līf*) of the *Envārü'l-'Āşıqīn*. Aḥmed wrote:

> A group of God's people said to me that in these times there are many who advance ignorance and imitation. Some of them are occupied by whims, while I am law-abiding [. . .] Some abandon the arguments of Law and Truth and do not discern faith and *madhhab*, and say '*all people know their drinking-place* [mashrabahum]'.[57] But [in doing so] they lead both themselves and the people astray [*azıtdılar*] from God's path, and with vain imaginings debar themselves from truths. Thus it is necessary that a book be written and that in it the ways of the prophets [*aḥvāl-i enbiyā*] and the rulings of law [*aḥkām-i şer'*] be exoterically explained, and these truths and mandates esoterically affirmed . . .[58]

He then transitioned to a passage from Abū Ḥāmid al-Ghazālī's *Iḥyā 'Ulūm al-Dīn* ('Revival of the Religious Sciences'), a twelfth-century classic of Islamic religious thought that is partially rendered here in Turkish.[59]

Upon initial reading, it seems that the target of this address is the familiar figure of the hypocritical scholar and that the Yazıcıoğlu brothers, along with other Ottomans on the same frontier, participated in a kind of *ġāzī* anti-clericalism.[60] However, this identification cannot be sustained if we remember that Meḥmed Yazıcıoğlu himself was a student of Ḥaydar Haravī, a scholar trained in Timurid Samarqand by leading figures of Ḥanafī jurisprudence.[61] It does not seem that the Yazıcıoğlus held an attitude of skepticism towards the religious elite. Upon closer inspection it seems that the brothers were instead addressing another group with the phrases 'those who advance ignorance and imitation' and those who 'abandon the arguments of Law and Truth and do not discern faith and *madhhab*'. When the Yazıcıoğlus charged that the 'hypocrites' employed the Qur'anic phrase 'All people know their drinking-place', which ostensibly describes the way in which the twelve tribes of Israel drank from Moses' spring, to allude to the validity of all styles of worship and behaviour (*mashrab*), they seem to indicate that their greatest worry was irreligiosity and an antinomian, universalising piety. Alongside 17:84, 'each works according to his manner', the phrase could be used to defend a pluralistic approach to religious practice.

Here Aḥmed Bīcān appears to be targeting individuals and groups with a local, even syncretistic understanding of Islam, like those Ottoman scholars whom Mihailović saw in the presence of Maḥmūd Paşa, who argued that Jesus was superior to Muḥammad, or the masses of Bursa who did not object when similar comments were made during Friday sermons. Just as Süleymān Çelebi was moved by the incident in Bursa to draft verses arguing Muḥammad's superiority over the other prophets, the Yazıcıoğlus must have been prompted by the conversations of the frontier to clarify the Islam of Gelibolu and to turn the beliefs of its people into doctrines and practices that were in line with the Ḥanafī Sunnism they had learned. Recalling the points of objection enunciated by Muslims over and over again during frontier debates, it becomes possible to read much of the Yazıcıoğlus' *Envārü'l-'Āşıqīn* and *Muḥammediyye* as a set of apologetics intended to counter these points of Christian dogma and deepen the convictions of wavering or new Muslims. As Aḥmed said, he wished for the people of his land to 'hold law and truth in their hearts and their convictions and *know the bond of Islam*'.

It would be easy to mistake the brothers' writings for simple instruction manuals on the daily duties of a pious Muslim. This kind of text had, in fact, already existed under the genre label '*ilm-i ḥāl*, the name given to a family of writings concerned with basic doctrinal elaboration and guidelines for ritual practice. This Turkish genre in fourteenth- and early-fifteenth-century Anatolia grew out of the older *aqā'id* tradition and proliferated across the early Ottoman centuries, as Derin Terzioğlu has discussed at length.[62] Terzioğlu has shown how the genre began to expand rapidly in the fifteenth century, when it acquired its generic identity. Around 1403, Qutbu'd-dīn İzniqī, the author of one of the earliest such texts in Turkish, the *Muqaddime*, described his own *'ilm-i ḥāl* as 'an introduction to the knowledge of obligatory duties in Turkish [. . .] that is read by the novice and to the boys and girls who are about to reach maturity, until they retain the commands of law . . .'[63] İzniqī's *'ilm-i ḥāl* is concerned, above all, with these obligatory duties and their technically proper performance – the motions of prayer, the timing of fasting, the rules of pilgrimage and the like. The fifteenth century saw a flourishing of similar works, each with generic variations. *Ṭarīq-i Edeb* ('The Path of Propriety'), a fifteenth-century text by one 'Alāe'd-dīn el-Amasī, is apparently a kind of primer of basic religious knowledge for parents to teach to their children. Furthermore, it seems to be aimed at new Muslims, or those who only have a very vague understanding of legalistic faith, as it contains advice mostly irrelevant to any other audience. 'Three things are necessary in order for the male child about to be born to become a monotheist believer [that is, a Muslim]', 'Alae'd-dīn wrote. 'One is that he be given a name from one of the Most Beautiful Names [of God]. The second is that he be circumcised. The third is that he be sent to school to study knowledge'.[64]

In contrast, the Yazıcıoğlu brothers aimed at an audience of slightly higher educational attainment than İzniqī and el-Amasī, although perhaps one with equally shallow roots in normative Islam. The brothers aimed to communicate doctrinal elements that extended beyond praxis, turning the merely practising Muslims who had read texts such as İzniqī's and el-Amasī's, who knew how to pray and act like Muslims, into Muslims who also understood the sequence of prophets and believed in the revelation of the Qur'an, in the Day of Resurrection and other basic tenets. As Aḥmed stated, 'in this book I have scattered and strung all the pearls of Revealed Law [*teşrī'*]'. The Yazıcıoğlu brothers consciously wrote the *Envār* and *Muḥammediyye* in order to expand the practical proscriptions of the *'ilm-i ḥāl* into lessons on dogma and the meaning that lies behind ritual. This is demonstrated by an interesting transformation in the parallel passages at the beginning of İzniqī's 1403 *Muqaddime* and Aḥmed Bīcān's *Envār*. In this passage, which is also derived from the introduction to Abū Ḥāmid al-Ghazālī's *Iḥyā 'Ulūm al-Dīn*, İzniqī wrote: 'Know that there are differences of opinion regarding obligatory duties [*farż-i 'ayn*]. The theologians say that knowledge of obligatory duties is known by the signs of God's unity and attributes. The jurists say that it is obtained by knowing the science of law, that is, the things God obligates and what is forbidden and permissible . . .'[65] Aḥmed Bīcān repeated this paragraph almost identically, but replaced the term 'obligatory duties' with a much more interiorising term: 'the basis of knowledge' (*aṣl-ı 'ilm*).[66] And while

İzniqī continued quoting from al-Ghazālī as he elaborated on the differences between esoteric and exoteric and between belief and praxis, the Yazıcıoğlus departed from al-Ghazālī and entered a discussion of creation and the nature of God's unity. By advancing the *'ilm-i ḥāl*'s concern with duties to a more intellectual intent to regularise religious knowledge, the Yazıcıoğlus hoped that their readers would 'hold truth in their hearts and convictions'.

How, then, did the Yazıcıoğlu brothers describe what it means to be Muslim? They did so by writing a 'salvation history', to use a term favoured by John Wansbrough. In his studies of the *sīra* (prophetic biography) of Ibn Isḥāq in the ninth-century recension of Ibn Hishām, Wansbrough has emphasised how the story of the Prophet provides the faithful with a dynamic set of stories to which they can connect and then animate the 'grid of the Qur'an'.[67] This historicising narrative complementing the scripture portrays salvation as the outcome of a historical process, so that Muslims could identify themselves, politically and personally, as members of the *umma* of the time. The Yazıcıoğlus, as editors and commentators of the very same *sīra*, shared some of these traditional preoccupations while adapting them to the circumstances of the fifteenth-century environment. They extended the scope of salvation history from the *sīra* through the popular medieval compilations of prophet stories known as the *qiṣaṣ al-anbiyā*, in particular the popularising and colourful edition attributed to the anthologist al-Kisā'ī;[68] each prophet story, including that of Muḥammad, shares a common template that establishes the stages of prophetic time. This extended salvation history allows the brothers to address in more detail, for example, the divine intention behind the prophethood of Jesus and to expound on the status of Muḥammad according to the understandings that had emerged during the course of Islamic theological debate since its first centuries. All of these are supplemented by elements taken from several branches of Islamic literature, which bring sophistication and topicality to this salvation history.

The question of Muḥammad's primacy over Jesus is addressed at the very beginning of the *Maghārib*, *Envār* and *Muḥammediyye*. In fact, one of the most important themes of all three works is that the person of Muḥammad is more worthy of respect than all other created things. (Yorgos Dedes, writing about similar qualities in Süleymān Çelebi's *Mevlid*, has wondered whether such a preoccupation with Muḥammad 'may be related to the contacts between Muslims and Christians . . .')[69] The brothers opened each of their three works with a grand cosmology of heavenly objects that emphasises how the prophethood of Muḥammad is in fact the purpose of the entire remaining creation. 'The Pen which writes the world's destiny first wrote first upon God's throne, "There is no God but God and Muḥammad is His messenger"'. Universes of angels were created, 'who do not know who Adam or Iblis are', but continually recite Muḥammad's name.[70] The brothers recited the *ḥadīth* story of a 'white handful' of luminous earth brought by Gabriel for God to mould into the body of Muhammd before even creating Adam – a story that figures in the earliest *mawlid* texts on Muḥammad's birth.[71] Adam even said to God: 'Lord, do not withhold from me the love of Muḥammad, for which you have created all of Creation [. . .] O Lord, I saw Muḥammad's name written at the foot of the Throne and at the base of the Tablet, and from this I knew that there is none more beloved than him'. And it was Muḥammad who, at the time of Adam's fall, interceded on his behalf to give him a place on earth rather than in hell. The figure who distinguishes Islam from Christianity becomes the centre of creation. The Yazıcıoğlus, by highlighting Muḥammad and his priority over Jesus, emphasised this distinction.

History thus starts and ends with Muḥammad, and what structures the sacred history in between the Fall from Paradise and Resurrection Day are the stories of each of the righteous prophets who parallel the outlines of his own prophetic mission. In each story, a sinful or idolatrous population first rejects the newly-sent prophet in favour of a corrupted law, or worse, a false god. Ultimately, however, this community either perishes or accepts the new dispensation. The stories of Noah and Moses enact this drama on a grand scale, but it can be seen in simple outline in the stories of the 'minor prophets'. The story of Hūd, prophet of the tribe of 'Ād, is perhaps the starkest: Hūd preached that 'beside God there is no god', but the tribe of 'Ād refused and, thus, God vanquished them with 'a barren wind' (*rīḥ-i 'aqīm*).[72] All of these stories share a strong structural congruence with the story of Muḥammad's life – first rejected at Mecca, then victorious – in a manner that is certainly intentional. And while the prophethoods of Abraham, Moses and Solomon follow more elaborate plot lines, their essential pattern is similar: Each prophetic dispensation enacts the dramas of Mecca and Medina and foretells it.

Jesus, in this story cycle, is a forerunner to Muḥammad. After Jesus proved his authenticity to the skeptics by bestowing life to a clay bird or bat, God reminded him that he was not His own most beloved, and that this honour belonged to 'the heart of my messenger Muḥammad'. Jesus then advised his apostles to instruct the people to await the coming of the final Prophet foretold by his own Gospel, saying that 'Muḥammad's community will come. They will be wise, just, and God-fearing people'.[73] It is noteworthy that these details are *not* found in al-Kisā'ī's *Qiṣaṣ*, the Yazıcıoğlus' source for this section: They are the Yazıcıoğlus' own addition. Inserting this material that is extraneous to the brothers' chief textual source highlights their underlying preoccupation with countering Christian points of belief. In this context, also, Meḥmed Yazıcıoğlu's *Muḥammediyye*, by focusing primarily on the Prophet's miraculous biography, may have intended – like Süleymān Çelebi's *Mevlid* – to aggrandise the Prophet and to argue against the lingering devotion to Jesus among the new converts to Islam. For a fifteenth-century reader, this and countless other moments would suffice to drive home the point that apparently confused the congregants in Bursa, or the book-throwing dervishes that Mihailović saw, and to affirm the distinct character of what the brothers consistently called 'the community of Muḥammad' (*ümmet-i Muḥammed*).

Just as they exalt Muḥammad, these prophet narratives also replay the experience of the convert – a significant part of the Yazıcıoğlus' audience – and thereby heighten the power of the reader's own conversion. This conceptual linkage is perhaps clearest in the tale of Shu'ayb, another of the so-called 'Arab prophets' not present in the Biblical tradition. Shu'ayb is given the burden of prophethood to the idol-worshipping tribe of Madyan. Shu'ayb, a Madyanite himself, preached to the chiefs of the tribe, whose names – Abjad, Ḥavvāz, Huttī, Kalamān and Qarīshat – are formed from the letters of a magical alphabet. They refused to believe his call and persisted in the worship of idols; thus, God sent Gabriel to suggest that he 'depart from among them, and consider [God's] wrath against them'.[74] God cast a shadow over the tribe, then a hot wind; finally, a cloud rained fire down on them. Shu'ayb saw what happened to his former clan and thanked God, 'crying for three hundred years', that he had been spared because he had left his tribe for the righteous faith. This story theatrically enacts the heroic self-narrative of converts to Islam on the Ottoman frontier, converts whose convictions compelled them to leave the people of their birth. Righteousness, in the story of Shu'ayb and others, is pared down to a matter of changing identity and initiating social separation.

Most of these discussions about the distinguishing features of being Muslim were not new to the era, but, like the Yazıcıoğlus' own sources, were rooted in long-established Muslim responses to Christian doctrines. A lengthy portion of the *Envārü'l-'Āşıqīn*, for example, discusses Jesus' ascent to heaven in the manner established in the Islamic tradition. Interestingly, Aḥmed Yazıcıoğlu used this occasion to present a very anachronistic typology of Christian sects – drawn, through his source-texts, from the religious landscape of ninth- through twelfth-century Syria and Iraq. This typology, which does not distinguish Catholic from Orthodox, also became a way for him to address the doctrine of the Trinity. Nestorians, so he stated, believed that Jesus is God's son; Jacobites believed that Jesus is God himself, while the Melkites (Chalcedonians) believed that God is the third of three, as Jesus and Mary are the other two. One does wonder how, despite his easy access to Chalcedonian Christians in Gelibolu who could have corrected him, he did not remove Mary from this trinity. In any case, all three Christologies are refuted in a time-honoured way, by referring to the Qur'an's *Ṣūrat al-Mā'ida*, which unequivocally states that 'there are unbelievers who say "God is the third of three"', and *Ṣūrat Maryam*, which says, 'it is not for God to take a son unto Him'. With these and similar arguments, the brothers provided their readers with a scripturally-established refutation of both the doctrine of the Trinity and the Virgin Birth.

Subtle warnings of the perils of accommodating Christian devotional practice appear in the story of Solomon. Solomon first took the daughter of 'the lord of the land of Saydon in Europe [*Firengistān*]' as a wife, and this European princess crafted an idol (*ṣūret* or *resm*) in the shape of her own father, which she would worship in secret. Solomon discovered this, broke the idol, banished her and fled to the desert for forty days to mourn.[75] As Stéphane Yerasimos has argued in reference to the contemporaneous *Dürr-i Meknūn*, which contains a similar story, this idol-worshipping European princess was a topical addition to the story of Solomon.[76] Some of its details are not found in the Yazıcıoğlus' source for the rest of this section, al-Kisā'ī's *qiṣaṣ*, and for this reason should be considered a special comment on divisive contemporary issues such as the veneration of images in churches or the taking of unconverted Christian wives.[77] Again, the *qiṣaṣ* is crafted into an apologia.

The notion that the Yazıcıoğlus' presentation of the *sīra* and *qiṣaṣ* constituted a specific response to their confessional environment requires some additional justification, since an emphasis on the sacrality of Muḥammad vis-à-vis other prophets was not a new feature of Sufi and devotional writing. On the contrary, such a template had been a feature of devotional narratives throughout the central Islamic lands for centuries. Naturally, in these environments the drawing of inter-confessional boundaries was not a vital concern. How then can the Yazıcıoğlus' identical narratives be read as literature of the frontier and as a product of its local setting? To address this question one can first turn to the brothers' own statements about the intentions of their works and what we know about their audience. The Yazıcıoğlus did not present themselves as innovators with respect to either generic form or content. They described themselves as only 'gathering' (*cem' eylemek*)[78] or 'arranging' (*düzmek*) pre-existent materials. Rather, their importance lay in their presentation of material that this local audience could 'utilise'. That is, they emphasised that their works were aimed directly at the faith of 'the people of our land' and not at a broader audience. As such, their renditions of the *qiṣaṣ* and *sīra* cannot be separated from the way in which their readership of converts and unlettered Muslims would interpret these very standard stories. These texts were shaped by their sense of how their readers would connect the stories of the prophets and of Muḥammad to their own lives. Any analysis of the Yazıcıoğlus' writings should proceed in this direction – from the needs of its readership to the content of its formulaic narratives. Such an approach shows how the Yazıcıoğlus' prophetic histories, although fundamentally derivative and formulaic, retain contemporaneity.

Even though their works might echo older Sufi literature, they also contained new elements that more explicitly addressed local concerns. One of the most remarkably topical passages in the combined writings of the Yazıcıoğlu brothers also comes from the *Envārü'l-'Āşıqīn*, in one of the work's later sections ostensibly concerned with the trials of Judgment Day. Here Aḥmed was interested not only in addressing inter-confessional ambiguities, but also in countering the notion that ambiguity should even exist within the faith of the righteous. Simply entertaining a confusion as to the nature of Islam, he seemed to argue, was a departure from Sacred Law. The author compiled a list of abbreviated *fetvās*, or legal opinions, using several classical Ḥanafī *fetvā* compilations, including the *Fatāwā* of Qāḍīkhān and the *Jawāhir al-Fiqh* of al-Marghīnānī.[79] The *fetvās* chosen out of the many contained in these volumes appear to have been selected to address ambiguities in basic confessional allegiance. Several of them essentially answer the question of how to determine if the questioner is a Muslim or non-Muslim, the clearest of which boldly declares: 'If a person says, "I don't know if I am a Muslim or an unbeliever", then they are an unbeliever'. Some address the position of other faiths, as in the *fetvā* declaring 'If a person says, "the religions of the Jews and Christians are the truth", then he is an unbeliever'. Some abridged *fetvās* refer to the nature of faith itself: 'If a person says that he is both Muslim and an unbeliever at once, then he is an unbeliever'. Another, alluding to Christian practice, asserts: 'If a person knows the prayer direction but worships in another, then he is an unbeliever'. An amusing *fetvā* seems to refer to the presence of people who openly mock the seriousness of the faith: 'If a person, while drinking alcohol, climbs to a high place and makes as if to preach [. . .] and laughs, whoever hears him and laughs too are all unbelievers'. One last *fetvā* hints that existential doubts may have run even deeper than the matter of confusion between the faiths: 'If someone says, "Now is the era of unbelief: faith has been taken away", then they are unbelievers'. All of these *fetāvā* recall the words that Aḥmed used in the *Envār's* introduction: 'Some abandon the arguments of Law and Truth and do not discern faith and proscriptive dogmatics, and say "All people know their drinking-place"'.[80] By rejecting the confusions of the frontier, turning their back on points of harmony between Islam and Christianity, and directly countering many of these points in the form of a targeted prophetic history, the brothers participated in a traditionalist reaction, purveying the concept of a unitary, homogeneous faith.

A Simple Islam

We have discussed one role of the brothers' writings in their frontier context, theorising how their inter-confessional boundary-drawing was stimulated by the encounter with Christian interlocutors. Behind these clear boundaries discussed above, they drafted a vision of what being a Muslim entailed and expressed this content in a simplified manner. The prophet stories, pared down to their identity-affirming cores, paved the way for a dogmatic discussion of the beliefs required for salvation. Importantly, the *Maghārib*, *Envār* and *Muḥammediyye*, as they sought to reassure the faithful of their attachment to the 'bond of Islam', emphasise the *ease*, rather than difficulty, of the 'straight path'. This, too, may betray the implicit presence of Christian dogmatic disputation in the Yazıcıoğlus' milieu: By making Islam also about salvation, predicated on a set of beliefs and practices valid without church or clergy, the Yazıcıoğlus advertised the simplicity of Islam to the converts and reassured the common readers that they were, in fact, good Muslims. Salvation, for Aḥmed and Meḥmed, was in fact quite easy; as this amusing narration shows, a simple *shahāda* often was enough:

> The Prophet said that when one says *lā ilāha illā'l-llāh, Muḥammadun rasūlu'l-llāh*, a white bird comes out of this person's mouth, with two wings of pearl and ruby. That bird goes to heaven. It buzzes like a bee. [The angels] tell the bird, 'be quiet', and the bird says, 'I will not, until the person who said *lā ilāha illā'l-llāh, Muḥammadun rasūlu'l-llāh* is saved'. God says, 'I have saved this person'. Then God gives this bird seventy tongues with which to ask the servant's forgiveness until Resurrection Day. And on Resurrection Day [the bird] takes this servant's hand and guides him to heaven.[81]

Yet, despite God's liberal attitude towards his believers, the brothers found it necessary to advance a straightforward understanding of the essentials of Islamic dogma, with the stipulation that these requirements be followed conscientiously. This mandate appears in many formulations throughout the works, most definitively enunciated by the structure of the chapter ostensibly on Resurrection Day. Here the brothers number Friday prayer, praying in mosques, *zekāt* (almsgiving), Ramadan and supererogatory fasting, Hajj (pilgrimage), *jihād* (armed or spiritual exertion) and *ẕikr* (verbal remembrance) as requisite duties, in addition to the *shahāda*. It is unsurprising that to the traditional Five Pillars the Sufi *ẕikr* is added, having become an indispensable component of even the most this-worldly forms of piety – Aḥmed Bīcān dwelled on *ẕikr* at length in the first sections of the *Envār*, claiming that '*ẕikr* is the greatest form of worship' and that the greatest of *ẕikr* formulae is the one sanctioned by Fakhr al-Dīn Rāzī in his *Tafsīr*: *lā hūwa illā hūwa*, 'there is no He but He'. Each of these recommendations are expressed in compilations of *ḥadīth* narrations and are said to be rewarded with various numbers of *s̱evāb*, or units of divine compensation.

In fact, *s̱evāb* and the straightforward way in which a believer can acquire it by means of satisfying ritual obligations seem to have been a consistent principle of the Yazıcıoğlus' catechistic impetus. Providing a simplified, quantitative metric for proper behaviour, *s̱evāb* turns religion into a proscriptive habit and restructures it as a matter of obeying any set of the many directives arrayed across hundreds of *ḥadīth* narrations. With enough *s̱evāb* accumulated, even the most half-hearted of believers could gain an assured place among the saved elect and bypass the rigors of ascetic renunciation as well as the externalising legalism of the traditionally orthodox. Even the act of reading the *Envār* apparently gave *s̱evāb*: 'God gives ten *s̱evāb* for every letter of those who learn and read, and every day [of learning] gives the *s̱evāb* of one thousand circumambulations of the Ka'ba'.[82] Religion was to be felt as a matter of private ritual and prayer, the more frequent the better. Salvation was within everyone's reach.

To be sure, their insistence that Islam is simple and their stark positioning of belief against unbelief was not necessarily unique to the Ottoman frontier, but common to the multi-confessional environment of Rum and Rumelia across the previous century of its Islamisation. To illustrate this, Tijana Krstić has drawn attention to the parable of Munkar and Nakīr, the two angels who interrogate the dead about their faith, seeing the contents of this dialogue as a kind of metric of the changing demands of Islamisation. The *Risāletü'l-İslām* from the mid-fourteenth century had these angels refrain from quizzing the dead about doctrine, asking only for faith in God, while in the fifteenth-century *Muqaddime* by İzniqī, the two angels were more demanding, asking the deceased to pronounce the six articles of faith.[83] Looking at an earlier period, A. C. S. Peacock has found the same story in two fourteenth-century Anatolian recensions of the catechistic text *Siraj al-Qulūb*, in both Persian and Turkish. In these, the angels simply ask for the deceased to name his or her god, religion and prophet.[84] In Aḥmed's *Envārü'l-'Aşıqīn*, this is precisely what the angels also ask,[85] contrasting with the more stringent angels of İzniqī, but not with those of the earlier *Risāletü'l-İslām*. Here Aḥmed followed precedents that grew from the specific demands of Anatolian Islamisation in other eras and locales. A concern with unbelief, and Christianity in particular, was also present in earlier Anatolian vernacular texts. Peacock has observed how the poet Gülşehrī's *Manṭıqu't-Ṭayr* reworks 'Aṭṭār's poem by introducing themes of conversion from Christianity to Islam. Various *Cenknāme*s on the exploits of 'Alī ibn Abu Ṭālib frame 'Alī's enemies as in league with the Byzantines.[86] Along these dimensions, the Yazıcıoğlus, addressing belief and *kufr* by tacitly emphasising the contrast between Islam and Christianity, seem to have inherited a typical Anatolian pattern. Yet, even as they drew on precedents and analogues in the literature of pre-Ottoman Anatolia, the importance of the Yazıcıoğlus' works lies not in its innovation, but in its timeliness. Directing older language and tropes towards their specific audience, the Yazıcıoğlus gave voice to a developing Ottoman frontier Islam.

Dealing with Death

The above discussion has run the risk of trivialising the Yazıcıoğlus and their pious impulse into a shallow 'national' ideology performing the basic function of justifying a new communal identity. But this was far from the case. The brothers, with genuine poetic sensitivity, addressed the problems of living in a time of turmoil. To take one illustrative example, a primary theme of the three writings under discussion here is the inevitability of death and the nature of Afterlife. There may be a reason for this. Uli Schamiloglu has proposed that the fourteenth-century global bubonic plague pandemic, as it spread across Eurasia, had profound cultural and political effects on the Turkic world, stimulating the creation of a vernacular pious literature in particular. 'As in Europe, there is evidence of an increase in religiosity as seen from a vernacular literary work entitled *Nehcü'l-Ferādis* (whose Turkic subtitle *Uştmaxlarnıñ açuq yolu* may be translated as 'The Clear Path to Heaven'), a work produced during a plague year in the Golden Horde (1358)', so he has argued.[87] In a fascinating manner, Schamiloglu has drawn an analogy from 'The Clear Path to Heaven', not only with Boccaccio for whom the plague famously provided a setting for his vernacular masterpiece, but also with Süleymān

Çelebi's similarly-named *Veṣīletü'n-necāt* ('The Path of Safety') from early-fifteenth-century Bursa, which we have encountered under the more common title *Mevlid* as a counterpart of the Yazıcıoğlus' *Envār*, *Maghārib* and *Muḥammediyye*.

It is perhaps possible to extend Schamiloglu's insights. We know, first of all, that the bubonic plague struck Gelibolu intensely around the time of the Yazıcıoğlu brothers' birth, when Clavijo wrote that in 1402 a merchant ship avoided the city because 'the plague was raging in Gallipoli, and with very great mortality'.[88] The plague that struck Bursa in 1429 and 1430 most likely reached Gelibolu as well. Oruç wrote of a plague that caused 'terrible deaths' in Rumelia in 1435.[89] A major epidemic struck the entire region in 1466, devastating Istanbul before passing to Gelibolu and across the Dardanelles into Anatolia: Kritovoulos wrote that in Istanbul the dead were so numerous that sometimes coffins would have to hold two.[90] Plague was not the only bringer of death. We have already seen that war never left Gelibolu for long between the Catalan invasion and the reign of Meḥmed II. Enverī's *Düstūrname* and Doukas' history both refer to the depopulation that occurred with each conquest of the city.

The Yazıcıoğlus, living at the epicentre of all this disease and violence, dwelled on the omnipresence of death and constantly strove to make it intelligible. A heavy, funereal atmosphere suffuses large parts of the texts. 'Azrā'īl, the Angel of Death, is described in vivid detail:

> 'Azrā'īl has four faces. One face is fire, and with that face he takes the souls of the unbelievers; one face is made of darkness, and with that face he takes the souls of the hypocrites; and one face is made of flesh, and with that face he takes the souls of the believers, and one face is made of light, and with that face he takes the souls of the prophets and the righteous [. . .] His voice shakes the heavens, his breath is like the fiercest of winds.[91]

The passage of a soul into death was likened to leaves falling off a tree one by one, and 'the name of every person is written on these leaves. When a person passes to eternity, one of those leaves trembles and then falls, and it falls before 'Azrā'īl. 'Azrā'īl takes it and reads it'. Because death was random, one must be mindful, the Yazıcıoğlus insisted, of the existential judgment it brings. 'The Angels said, "If the sons of Adam were to know Death, they would never eat or drink or laugh and would never occupy themselves with the world". God replied, "Endless desire makes them forget about Death"'. There is even a long technical discussion, again connected to al-Ghazāli, on the permanence of the body in the tomb – does it literally reconstitute on Resurrection Day; is it created again of new material; or does only the spirit rise? Does a soul in the tomb feel pain?

It is interesting that this precise topic was discussed by Amiroutzes and Meḥmed II, with the sultan advancing noncorporeal resurrection and the philosopher believing in the literal rising of bodies, agreeing with the Yazıcıoğlus.

The brothers' narrative of the End Times finishes with the unusual image of 'Cutting Death's Throat', this time with Death personified not as 'Azrā'īl but as an old sacrificial goat. With those deserving of heaven in heaven, and those deserving of hell in hell, God summons the angels 'to take Death and cut his throat in a place between heaven and hell'. With Death now dead, the End Times come to a close and God draws creation into eternity.

Sacralising Frontier Warfare

Aḥmed and Meḥmed Yazıcıoğlu were born into a community of Turcophone Muslim Rumelians for whom the consciousness of a global Islamic ecumene had not yet fully crystallised. In its place, they encountered a matrix of philosophical exchange between Muslims and Christians, amply testified to by Palamas, Manuel II, Mihailović and others. The Yazıcıoğlus' response was not to introduce a synthesis of these dialogues, but to step outside of them by describing a populist piety envisioned within the historical mainstream of Islamic civilisation. Why would Aḥmed and Meḥmed Yazıcıoğlu participate in such a discourse, in which each of their interventions seemed designed to strengthen confessional boundaries and heighten the distinctions between Muslim and Christian, while also reinforcing the qualities of Islam as a mass faith?

I suggest that their apologia responds to a certain mid-fifteenth-century moment on the Mediterranean frontier and within Ottoman cultural history, when the opportunistic inter-confessionalism, hinted at in certain Ottoman chronicles, was giving way to a more theoretically conceived ideology in which the notion of religious distinctiveness constituted a major pillar. That is, the expansion of the Ottoman state was on its way to being conceived as a religiously motivated process, and frontier warfare was being sacralised in a way defined and accommodated by the newly normative Ḥanafī Islam. We may follow Cemal Kafadar in naming the mid-fifteenth century and the subsequent decades the final developmental stages of the ideology of *ġazā*, as it evolved from a frontier-oriented discourse to a centralising one.[92] Along with the Yazıcıoğlus, others shared this project. We may also cite as a parallel the chronicles of Neşri or Şükrullāh, which efface the complex negotiations of early Ottoman political development and present a uniform image of the Ottomans as fighters for the expansion of Islam. In the Yazıcıoğlus' case, the matter to be revised is not the religious naiveté of the early Ottoman *beg*s, but the confessional ambiguity of the Mediterranean frontier itself. With their apologia, the Yazıcıoğlus hoped to close this frontier.

In their half-Greek hometown of Gelibolu, dependent on its fleet manned by converts and non-Muslims, the Yazıcıoğlu brothers certainly shared the state's concern with ordering identity and ideology and integrating locals into the structure of religiously-construed warfare following a single ideological model. In order to define the frontier, the *ġazā* that produced it had to be made sacred in a way that was intelligible both to the intellectual vanguard of the state – the Ḥanafī scholars patronised by the court – and the Muslim rank-and-file. We can see this in the way in which the brothers endorsed the concept of *ġazā* itself, by connecting proper religious belief and practice with the execution of frontier warfare. 'This poor one [. . .] finished [this book] in the finest of towns, the abode of *jihād*, Gelibolu', Aḥmed wrote in the final pages of the *Envārü'l-'Āşıqīn*. He went on to say:

> For in Gelibolu there are two groups of people. One of them are the *ġāzī*s, and one of them are the martyrs. And of this first group, the *ġāzī*s, there are two classes. One of them are those who conduct *ġazā* against the unbelievers, and one of them conduct *ġazā* against their own carnal souls. And of the martyrs there are two kinds. One of them are those who are martyred at the hands of the unbelievers (*kuffār*), and one of them are those who bear witness to the hand of the Forgiver (*ġaffār*). May God not hold them to account in the hereafter.

War led by the Ottoman sultans here structured the fate of Rumelian souls in life and in death. *Ġazā* seems to have fundamentally organised the brothers' sense of subjective time as well. In the *Envārü'l-'Āşıqīn*, Aḥmed connected his act of writing to Ottoman victory at Varna in 1444: 'The date [I started] this book is the time when the sultan son of sultans, Sultan Ġāzī Murād Ḫān, cut off the head of the lord of Hungary and sent it to the sultan of Egypt . . .'[93] Aside from the Conquest of Constantinople and other territories mentioned in Aḥmed's 1465 *Müntehā*, this battle is the only contemporary event mentioned in the brothers' corpus.

When we recall that the brothers lived and worked in a seaside neighbourhood and that their audience may have been comprised of sailors who prayed in the *namāzgāh* of their father's patron İskender, it comes as no surprise that they considered the truest *ġazā* to be naval war. A section of the *Maghārib* and *Envār* titled 'A chapter on *jihād*' primarily constitutes a defense of naval warfare as it was practised in Ottoman Gelibolu, delineating the sea as the greatest field of battle against the unbeliever. Aḥmed wrote, 'To conduct *ġazā* at sea is worth ten times *ġazā* on dry land'.[94] 'God's most favoured kind of war is war at sea. God grants seventy Hajj *s̱evāb*s', the brothers declared and extended this claim using dozens of similar sayings and *ḥadīth*. One *ḥadīth* even insists that one who dies at sea, unlike a soldier who dies on land, is not even judged by his beliefs and deeds, but sent directly to heaven. When Aḥmed listed different categories of martyrs – those who die of plague, those who die in fire, those who die in childbirth and so on – he remarked: 'But more so than all of these, a person who dies at sea in the territory of the unbeliever is a martyr'. The sacred enterprise of warfare on the maritime frontier is perhaps most evocatively expressed in the lines with which they closed the chapter: 'Praise God that in Gelibolu there is frequent war with the unbelievers and we perform *ġazā*. Sometimes the unbeliever comes to us, and sometimes we go to the unbeliever'.[95] The connection between boundary-drawing in the field of religious ideology and the defense and justification of maritime expansion conceived as *ġazā* is implicit here.

Conclusion

The brothers' anti-Christian polemic embedded in salvation history, their dogmatics and existential evocations of death and their defenses of naval expansion may seem like an arbitrary combination of literary ingredients. But the above has shown that this configuration was appropriate to the needs of fifteenth-century Gelibolu, as similar writings were appropriate to other settings in the multi-confessional environment of Islamising Anatolia. As such, it becomes clear that the *Maghārib*, *Envār* and *Muḥammediyye* together create a small canon of what might be termed '*ġāzī* theology'. The three works gave the new Muslim readers of the city of *jihād* just enough knowledge of their faith and of what made it distinct so as to sustain the enterprise of Ottoman expansion that was increasingly being defined in religious terms. Muslims or half-Muslims, '*ġāzī*s against the unbelievers [. . .] or against their carnal souls', could find in them their allegiance to the enterprise of the house of 'Os̱mān – and, by the end of this process, to Islam itself – clarified, deepened and defended.

The relationship between the attitudes of the Yazıcıoğlus and the early modern process of confession-building across the Mediterranean and Europe, linked to the rise of centralising states and their expanding payroll, may form an attractive subject for comparative scholarship. What is certain is that the brothers' writings, originally reactions to the political and confessional flux of the early and mid-fifteenth century, grew to become key texts of populist Ottoman Sunnism for hundreds of years to come, even after the dynamics of the frontier had changed completely. Even in the world empire of the Ottoman sultans, the *ġāzī* theology of this period, imbued at the site of its origin with the heroic mystique of pre-1453 Gelibolu, remained attractive and relevant to ordinary Muslims. In 1626, in one chapter of the long and storied afterlife of these texts, Gábor Bethlen, a Calvinist prince of Transylvania, which then was not under Ottoman rule, requested that his scribe János Házi translate into Hungarian a work that all his Muslim subjects were reading, 'in order to show the wise the light of righteousness so that they can differentiate it from the dark abyss of false teachings'.[96] This book was Aḥmed Bīcān's *Envārü'l-ᶜĀşıqīn*, and it was printed in Hungarian in Košice, in what is now Slovakia.[97] The frontier having moved this far, it is remarkable to find this text still being used for its intended purpose, two hundred years later.

Notes

1. Evliyā Çelebi, *Evliyā Çelebi Seyahatnâmesi.*
2. 'Defter-i esāmī-i Sancaḳ-ı Gelibolu (Awāʾil Shawwāl 879/February 1475)', Atatürk Kitaplığı, Cevdet Collection no. 79.
3. For information on this beautiful structure, see Ekrem Hakkı Ayverdi, *Osmanlı Mi'mârîsinde Çelebi ve II. Sultan Murad Devri.*
4. See Terzioğlu, 'Where *İlmihal* Meets Catechism', as well as Guy Burak, 'Faith, Law and Empire in the Ottoman "Age of Confessionalization" (Fifteenth–Seventeenth Centuries): The Case of "Renewal of Faith"', *Mediterranean Historical Review* 28, no. 1 (2013), pp. 1–23.
5. Cemal Kafadar, *Between Two Worlds: The Construction of the Ottoman State* (Berkeley: University of California Press, 1996).
6. Much has been made of the semantic distinction between *ġazā*, the religiously-defined fighting on the frontier, and the term *jihād*, a more general term denoting all kinds of religious warfare and struggle, including even the internally-directed struggles of the mind of the believer. This study will not linger on this difference, as the Yazıcıoğlus themselves seem to use both terms interchangeably.
7. Linda T. Darling, 'Reformulating the Gazi Narrative: When Was the Ottoman State a Gazi State?', *Turcica* 43 (2011), pp. 13–53, is a comprehensive and useful review of this debate. See also Linda T. Darling, 'The Mediterranean as a Borderland', *Review of Middle East Studies* 46, no. 1 (2012), pp. 54–63. Ottoman *ġazā* has been studied in comparison with the *ġazā* of the first Mughal emperor Babur in Ali Anooshahr, *The Ghazi Sultans and the Frontiers of Islam: A Comparative Study of the Late Medieval and Early Modern Periods* (London: Routledge, 2009).
8. See Rudi Paul Lindner, *Explorations in Ottoman Prehistory* (Ann Arbor:

University of Michigan Press, 2007); Rudi Paul Lindner, *Nomads and Ottomans in Medieval Anatolia* (Bloomington: Research Institute for Inner Asian Studies, Indiana University, Bloomington, 1983).

9. Heath W. Lowry, *The Nature of the Early Ottoman State* (Albany: State University of New York Press, 2003).
10. Mehmet Fuat Köprülü, *The Origins of the Ottoman Empire*, trans. Gary Leiser (Albany: State University of New York Press, 1992).
11. Kafadar, *Between Two Worlds*, p. 120.
12. Ottoman writers were conscious that the joint Byzantine-Catholic Crusade of Varna of 1444 entered the realm of possibility only with the ecumenical Council of Ferrara; *ġazā* was posed as its response. See the anonymous *Ġazavātnāme* translated in Imber, *The Crusade of Varna*, pp. 41–106.
13. This dynamic is not unique to this frontier. See Judith Pfeiffer, 'Confessional Ambiguity vs. Confessional Polarization: Politics and the Negotiation of Religious Boundaries in the Ilkhanate', in *Politics, Patronage, and the Transmission of Knowledge in 13th-15th Century Tabriz*, ed. Judith Pfeiffer (Leiden: Brill, 2014), pp. 129–68.
14. Doukas, *The Decline and Fall of Byzantium to the Ottoman Turks*, trans. Harry J. Magoulias (Detroit: Wayne State University Press, 1975), pp. 143–44.
15. Claude Cahen, *Pre-Ottoman Turkey: A General Survey of the Material and Spiritual Culture and History, c. 1071–1330.* (New York: Taplinger, 1968), has long provided the definitive narrative of these dynamics.
16. Darling, 'The Mediterranean as a Borderland'.
17. Benjamin of Tudela, *Itinerary*, quoted in Joshua Starr, *The Jews in the Byzantine Empire, 641–1204* (New York: B. Franklin, 1970), p. 231.
18. This venture was typical of the politics of the late thirteenth- and fourteenth-century Aegean, riven between the political aims of the Byzantines, Venice, western mercenaries and Turkish *begliks*. The most complete picture of this environment is found in the work of Elisabeth Zachariadou, esp. *Trade and Crusade: Venetian Crete and the Emirates of Menteshe and Aydin (1300–1415)* (Venice: Istituto ellenico di studi bizantini e postbizantini di Venezia per tutti i paesi del mondo, 1983); Elisabeth A. Zachariadou, *Romania and the Turks, c.1300–c.1500* (London: Variorum Reprints, 1985). For information on pre-Ottoman Byzantine-Turkish political and social contact, see also Rustam Shukurov, *The Byzantine Turks, 1204–1461* (Leiden: Brill, 2016), as well as Dimitri Korobeinikov, *Byzantium and the Turks in the Thirteenth Century* (Oxford: Oxford University Press, 2014).
19. Ramón Muntaner, *Cronica Catalana de Ramón Muntaner: Texto Original y Traducción Castellana*, trans. Antonio de Bofarull (Barcelona: Jaime Jepus, 1860), p. 402.
20. Ibid. p. 441.
21. *Tekfūr* is the term used by Muslim writers to refer to Byzantine power-holders ranging from local nobility to the emperor himself.

22. Irène Mélikoff, *Le Destan d'Umur Pacha: Düsturname-i Enveri* (Paris: Presses Universitaires de France, 1954), pp. 61–63.
23. G. G. Arnakis, 'Gregory Palamas, the Hiones, and the Fall of Gallipoli', *Byzantion* 22 (1952), p. 311.
24. For more on the early interactions between Karesi and the Ottoman *beglik*, see Elisabeth A. Zachariadou, 'The Karesi Emirate', in *The Ottoman Emirate (1300–1389): Halcyon Days in Crete 1 : A Symposium Held in Rethymnon 11–13 January 1991*, ed. Elisabeth Zachariadou (Rethymnon: Crete University Press, 1993), pp. 225–36. A slightly more recent monograph-length study of this polity is found in Zerrin Günal Öden, *Karası Beyliği* (Ankara: Türk Tarih Kurumu Basımevi, 1999).
25. 'Tapu Taḥrīr Defteri, T. T. 0012', Başbakanlık Arşivi, T. T. 0012, p. 42.
26. Aşıkpaşazade, *Tevarih-i Âl-i Osman'dan Aşıkpaşazade Tarihi*, ed. 'Ali Bey (Istanbul: Matba'a-yı Âmire, 1332 [1914]), p. 49.
27. Judith R. Ryder, *The Career and Writings of Demetrius Kydones: A Study of Fourteenth-Century Byzantine Politics, Religion and Society* (Leiden; Boston: Brill, 2010), pp. 59–60.
28. For information on early Ottoman naval leaders based in the city, see Danışmend, *Osmanlı Devlet Erkânı*, p. 172, as well as Uzunçarşılı, *Osmanlı Devletinin Merkez ve Bahriye Teşkilâtı*.
29. For a discussion of the date of Ṣāliḫ's migration, see Çelebioğlu, 'Yazıcı Ṣāliḫ ve Şemsiyye'si', as well as Çelebioğlu's remarks in his edition of Meḥmed Yazıcıoğlu's *Muhammediye* (İstanbul: Millî Eğitim Bakanlığı, 1996). My own conclusion, discussed earlier in this study, is that Ṣāliḫ moved to Rumelia in the late 1380s.
30. Johannes Schiltberger, *The Bondage and Travels of Johann Schiltberger, a Native of Bavaria, in Europe, Asia, and Africa, 1396–1427*, ed. Filip Jakob Bruun, trans. J. Buchan Telfer (London: Hakluyt Society Publications, 1879), p. 6.
31. Ruy González de Clavijo, *Embajada a Tamorlán: Estudio y edición de un manuscrito del siglo XV*, ed. Francisco López Estrada (Madrid: Consejo superior de investigaciones científicas, Instituto Nicolás Antonio, 1943), p. 53.
32. The French traveller G. de Lannoy made a nearly identical remark in 1422: 'Et qui auroit dit chastel et port les Turcs n'auroient nul sçeur passage plus de l'un àl'autre et seroit leur pays qu'ilz ont en Grèce comme perdu et defect', quoted in Halil İnalcık, 'Gelibolu', *Encyclopaedia of Islam, Second Edition*.
33. Doukas, *The Decline and Fall of Byzantium to the Ottoman Turks*, p. 143.
34. Ibid. pp. 143–44.
35. 'Defter-i esāmī-i Sancaḳ-ı Gelibolu (Awā'il Shawwāl 879/February 1475)', Atatürk Kitaplıgı, Cevdet Collection no. 79, p. 9.
36. TD Defter 725.
37. Cyriac of Ancona, *Later Travels*, trans. Edward W. Bodnar and Clive Foss (Cambridge, MA: Harvard University Press, 2003), pp. 95–97.

38. Arnakis, 'Gregory Palamas among the Turks'; Arnakis, 'Gregory Palamas, the Hiones, and the Fall of Gallipoli'.
39. Trapp, *Manuel II. Palaiologos: Dialoge mit einem 'Perser'*. For Emperor Manuel's comments on intra-Islamic affairs, see Elizabeth A. Zachariadou, 'Manuel II Palaeologos on the Strife between Bāyezīd I and Ḳāḍī Burhān Al-Dīn Aḥmad', *Bulletin of the School of Oriental and African Studies* 43, no. 3 (1980), pp. 471–81.
40. Dedes, 'Süleymān Çelebi's Mevlid', p. 334, quoting Elisabeth Zachariadou, 'Religious Dialogue between Byzantines and Turks during the Ottoman Expansion', in *Religionsgespräche im Mittelalter*, ed. Bernard Lewis and Friedrich Niewöhner (Wiesbaden: Harrasowitz, 1992), pp. 290–304.
41. Gemistos Plethon has been the subject of extensive scholarship, notably C. M. Woodhouse, *George Gemistos Plethon: The Last of the Hellenes* (Oxford: Clarendon Press, 1986), and, more recently, Niketas Siniossoglou, *Radical Platonism in Byzantium: Illumination and Utopia in Gemistos Plethon* (Cambridge; New York: Cambridge University Press, 2011). Plethon's connection to Ottoman intellectual culture has finally been explored in Maria Mavroudi, 'Plethon as a Subversive and His Reception in the Islamic World', in *Power and Subversion in Byzantium*, ed. D. Angelov and M. Saxby (Farnham: Ashgate Variorum, 2013), pp. 177–204.
42. Süleymān Çelebi, *Mevlid*; Dedes, 'Süleymān Çelebi's *Mevlid*'.
43. Qur'an 17:55.
44. This translation is based on the translation in Dedes, 'Süleymān Çelebi's *Mevlid*'.
45. This kind of incident would recur in the centuries to follow, in the form of the 'Ḥubb-Mesīḥī' movement as well as the pseudo-Christian preachers Molla Qābiż and Ḥakīm Ishāq. See Colin Imber, 'A Note on "Christian" Preachers in the Ottoman Empire', *Journal of Ottoman Studies* 10 (1990), pp. 59–67; and Ocak, *Zındıklar ve Mülhidler*, pp. 268–84.
46. Konstantin Mihailović, *Memoirs of a Janissary*, trans. Benjamin Stolz (Ann Arbor: The University of Michigan, 1975), p. 17.
47. For biographical details, see John Monfasani, *George Amiroutzes, the Philosopher and his Tractates* (Leuven; Walpole, MA: Peeters, 2011).
48. For Meḥmed he composed several panegyric poems that emphasise the continuity between the Roman tradition and the Ottoman sultanate, describing Meḥmed as emperor of the Greeks, as *autocrator* and *basileus*, and comparing him to Alexander and Hercules. One of his two Ottomanised sons took the name İskender Paşa.
49. George Amiroutzes, *El diálogo de la fé con el sultán de los turcos: Edición crítica*, ed. Óscar de la Cruz Palma (Madrid: Consejo Superior de Investigaciones Científicas, 2000).
50. Ibid. pp. 51–52. Emphasis mine.
51. This is a major contention of Marshall Hodgson in *The Venture of Islam, Volume 2: The Expansion of Islam in the Middle Periods* (Chicago: University

of Chicago Press, 1977). Indeed, the task of addressing this hypothesis has been an implied aim of many recent studies on the Islamicate late medieval and early modern period.

52. Ocak, *Zındıklar ve Mülhidler.*
53. See Balivet, *Islam mystique et révolution armée dans les Balkans ottomans*, p. 17. This point is made especially by Binbaş, *Intellectual Networks in Timurid Iran*, pp. 124–25. See also Ayhan Hıra, 'Şeyh Bedreddin'in Fıkıhçılığı' (unpublished doctoral dissertation, Marmara University, 2006).
54. For a study of Sufism along the Balkan frontiers during this period and in the following century, see Nikolay Antov, *The Ottoman 'Wild West': The Balkan Frontier in the Fifteenth and Sixteenth Centuries* (Cambridge: Cambridge University Press, 2017).
55. *EA*, fol. 3a.
56. *EA*, fol. 3a. '*Bunı Türk diline döndürgil tā kim bu bizüm ilüñ qavmı daḫı ma'ārifden ve envār-ı 'ilmden fāida görsünler*'.
57. Qur'an 2:60, 7:160.
58. *EA*, fols 3b–4a.
59. The profound influence of al-Ghazālī on Ottoman thought has yet to be fully explored. As this instance demonstrates, the Yazıcıoğlus clearly deployed his *Iḥyā 'Ulūm al-Dīn* at a close textual level. Beyond this, al-Ghazālī's comprehensive integration of popular Sufism into traditional orthodoxy appears to have provided a basic grounding for their intellectual project.
60. The suspicion that some Ottomans held for the learned *'ulema* and *ehl-i qalem* has been noted by many contemporary historians, on the basis of abundant evidence in chronicles and other historical accounts. Murat Cem Mengüç has summarised and contextualised the anti-clericalism of fifteenth-century historians from Aḥmedī to the later generation of historians that includes Neşri and Aşıqpaşazade. The classic villain in these stories is the Çandarlı family of viziers, along with the class they represented – the Persianised (if not themselves Persian) intellectuals who had maneuvred into positions of influence in the Ottoman state beginning in the late fourteenth century. Murat Cem Mengüç, 'Histories of Bayezid I, Historians of Bayezid II: Rethinking Late Fifteenth-Century Ottoman Historiography', *Bulletin of the School of Oriental and African Studies* 76, no. 3 (2013), pp. 373–89.
61. This was first suggested by Âmil Çelebioğlu in his edited *Muhammediye* (1996), on the basis of the conclusions of the text's most famous commentator, the eighteenth-century İsmā'il Haqqı Bursevī; see Chapter 1.
62. Terzioğlu, 'Where *'İlmihal* Meets Catechism'.
63. Kutbe'd-dīn İznikî, *Mukaddime*, ed. Kerime Üstünova (Bursa: T. C. Uludağ Üniversitesi, 2003), also quoted in Krstic, *Contested Conversions to Islam*, p. 25.
64. Alae'd-dīn el-Amasī, 'Tarik-i Edeb', Süleymāniye Kütüphanesi, Laleli 1876, fols 1a–4b.
65. Kutbe'd-dîn İznikî, *Mukaddime*, p. 139.

66. *EA*, fols 4a–5b.
67. This phrase, as well as the term 'salvation history' used here, were notably employed by John Wansbrough in his study of the *sīra* and Qur'an. John Wansborough, *The Sectarian Milieu* (Oxford: Oxford University Press, 1978). Wansbrough's approach to these texts has been extensively criticised by Fazlur Rahman for its implication that they are fabricated in an environment of 'intense Judaeo-Christian sectarian debate'. Fazlur Rahman, *Major Themes of the Qur'an* (Chicago: University of Chicago Press, 2009), pp. xvii-xx. Rahman has argued that the unities and symmetries of the Qur'an and the *sīra* story preclude such composite origins. My usage of Wansbrough's terminology here is not intended as a comment on this debate on the Qur'an and Islamic origins, but solely means to describe the Yazıcıoğlus' usage of the *qiṣaṣ* and *sīra* narratives.
68. For more information on al-Kisāʾī, see Wheeler Thackston's introduction to Muḥammad ibn 'Abd Allāh al-Kisāʾī, *The Tales of the Prophets*, and the discussion in this study's previous chapter.
69. Dedes, 'Süleymān Çelebi's *Mevlid*'.
70. *EA*, fols 9b–10a.
71. For information on these narrative elements in their *mawlid* contexts, see Marion Holmes Katz, *The Birth of the Prophet Muhammad: Devotional Piety in Sunni Islam* (London; New York: Routledge, 2007).
72. *EA*, fols 45b–46b.
73. *EA*, fol. 147b.
74. *EA*, fols 72a–74a.
75. *EA*, p. 121a.
76. Yerasimos, *La fondation de Constantinople et de Sainte-Sophie dans les traditions turques*. While Yerasimos, following a long-standing tradition, attributes the *Dürr-i Meknun* to Aḥmed Bīcān, this unsigned work departs from Aḥmed's style in several respects, and thus the question of this attribution needs revisiting. I have laid out the argument that Aḥmed is not the author of the *Dürr-i Meknun* in Grenier, 'Reassessing the Authorship of the *Dürr-i Meknun*'.
77. Sami Helewa has come to a similar conclusion in his interpretation of the same story, as it appears in the much earlier *qiṣaṣ* of al-Ṭabarī. For al-Ṭabarī's tenth-century readers, the story of the princess from Saydon must have evoked the concern of Muslims about 'new converts who were serving in positions close to their Muslim rulers'. Sami Helewa, *Models of Leadership in the Adab Narratives of Joseph, David and Solomon: Lament for the Sacred* (Lanham; Boulder; New York; London: Lexington, 2018), p. 155.
78. *EA*, fol. 3b.
79. *EA*, fols 266a–270a.
80. *EA*, fol. 4a.
81. *EA*, fols 242a–242b.
82. ibid.

83. Krstić, *Contested Conversions to Islam*, pp. 29–31.
84. Peacock, *Islam, Literature and Society in Mongol Anatolia*, pp. 199–200.
85. '*Man rabbuka wa mā dīnuka wa man nabiyyuka?*' *EA*, fol. 258b; '*Rabbuñ kimdür ve dīnüñ ne dīndür ve peyġāmberüñ kimdür?*' *EA*, fol. 308a.
86. Peacock, *Islam, Literature and Society in Mongol Anatolia*, pp. 204–10.
87. Uli Schamiloglu, 'The Rise of the Ottoman Empire: The Black Death in Medieval Anatolia and Its Impact on Turkish Civilization', in *Views From the Edge: Essays in Honor of Richard W. Bulliet*, ed. Neguin Yavari, Lawrence G. Potter and Jean-Marc Oppenheim (New York: Columbia University Press, 2004), pp. 255–79.
88. Clavijo, *Embajada a Tamorlán*, p. 31.
89. Nükhet Varlık, *Plague and Empire in the Early Modern Mediterranean World: The Ottoman Experience, 1347–1600* (New York: Cambridge University Press, 2015), p. 123–24. Varlık has collected evidence showing that this epidemic in the 1430s devastated the Marmara region for years. Among her sources are Oruç Beğ, *Oruç Beğ Tarihi (1288–1502)*, ed. Necdet Öztürk (İstanbul: Çamlıca, 2007), and Kritovoulos, *History of Mehmed the Conqueror*, trans. Charles T. Riggs (Princeton: Princeton University Press, 1954).
90. Ibid. p. 263.
91. *EA*, fol. 247b.
92. See the discussion in Kafadar, *Between Two Worlds*, pp. 145–46.
93. *EA*, fols 396a–396b. This sentence presents a problem. The beheading of King Vladislav occurred at Varna in 1444; yet, some manuscripts add 'at Kosovo' here, referring to the 1448 battle against János Hunyadi. The *Ḥijrī* date that Aḥmed Bīcān gives, 850, coincides with neither battle and falls almost exactly between them. In this context, the 1444 date seems the more likely one, because of the detail chosen to commemorate Varna. The English traveller Jehan de Wavrin attested that Vladislav's head was shown to the Venetian official Pietro Loredan in Gelibolu as he passed through on his way to Cairo. I consider it more likely that Aḥmed Bīcān accurately remembered the passage of the king's head through the city and that he (or a copyist) erred on the date, rather than *vice versa*. Imber, *The Crusade of Varna*, p. 133.
94. *EA*, fols 285a–285b.
95. *EA*, fol. 275b.
96. Ágoston, 'Muslim Cultural Enclaves in Hungary under Ottoman Rule', pp. 203–4.
97. János Házi, 'Machumet propheta, vallásán levő egy fő irástúdo doctornac irásából' (Cassan, 1626), Lucian Blaga Central Library, Cluj-Napoca, BMV 1795.

Chapter 4

The Yazıcıoğlus within Islam

The Yazıcıoğlu brothers relayed only a fraction of their religious ideas within the *Muḥammediyye* and *Envārü'l-'Āşıqīn*. We have seen how these Turkish catechistic masterpieces presented Islam as a surface that could be traced by a novice, just as the *sīra* and *Qiṣaṣ* once had done for earlier generations of Muslims. This was the *face* of the new religion of the Rumelian marches: respect for the Law delivered by the final prophet Muḥammad, belief in a strictly unitary God and a sense of propriety expressed by quantifiable pious actions. Beneath this surface lay the depths of their personal faith with all of its tensions and contradictions. The Yazıcıoğlu brothers were participants embedded in their own theological-dogmatic tradition, and in Edirne and Ankara they had developped sophisticated opinions about what was beyond the outer presentation of the *dīn-i muḥammedī*. Once 'submerged' within the sea of law and faith, precise guidance was still needed so that even committed, educated believers could navigate not only towards religious correctness, but towards subjective proximity to the divine. Expressed as both theology and Sufi mystical practice, the Yazıcıoğlus' Islam was situated within the discursive traditions of Islamic dogmatics.

Elaborating on and resolving dogmatic tensions constituted a motive for the composition of the family of texts that presents the brothers' most capacious and wide-ranging: the *Müntehā* works, which consist of Meḥmed's 1449 *Sharḥ Fuṣūṣu'l-Ḥikam* ('Commentary on *Fuṣūṣ al-Ḥikam*'), written in Arabic, and Aḥmed's two distinct Turkish editions with the same title, the *Kitābü'l-Müntehā* ('The Utmost') of 1453 and 1465. As the name of Meḥmed's original text suggests, the stated intent of these compositions was to serve as a commentary on the famous *Fuṣūṣ al-Ḥikam* ('The Bezels of Wisdom') of Muḥyī al-dīn ibn 'Arabī, a late medieval source-text of mystical philosophy that had already generated a specifically Anatolian (although not linguistically Turkish) commentary tradition. But if the *Müntehā* works presented commentaries, then they would be highly eccentric ones, with a circumscribed relation to the *Fuṣūṣ* itself. In fact, unlike Meḥmed's earlier *Sharḥ*, the *Fuṣūṣ* structures only a section of the *Müntehā* works, which otherwise integrate elements seen already in the *Envār* and the *Muḥammediyye,* and many other features as well. Aḥmed Bīcān's two editions of the *Müntehā* also retain the vernacularising approach of the *Envār*. Repeating a passage from his earlier work, Aḥmed wrote:

> I, the helpless Bīcān, saw that the scholars have prepared many books of exoteric and esoteric knowledge. But some of those books are in Arabic and some in the Persian language. Everyone who studies them cannot extract their fine meaning [. . .] This poor one desired to prepare a book in translation, so that the people of our land may benefit from exoteric and esoteric knowledge and become wise . . .[1]

The application of this vernacularising method to more advanced subject-matter makes the text especially rich. The *Müntehā* drifts in and out of proximity to Ibn 'Arabī's difficult text, while remaining, as always, sensitive to contemporary problems facing the Muslims, old and new, of Anatolia and Rumelia. Not for the novice and still not for the Arabic-reading specialist, the *Müntehā* texts are the Yazıcıoğlu brothers' most developped works on religious subjects.

This chapter aims to use the *Müntehā* to unravel the Yazıcıoğlus' views on four polemicised religious topics of their era: (i) the Ibn 'Arabī tradition, (ii) the lineages of Sufi communities, (iii) the question of Sunnism and Shī'ism, and (iv) apocalypticism. While the *Müntehā* touches on many themes beyond these four, these may suffice to characterise Aḥmed and Meḥmed as Muslims negotiating their worldview in the interstices between mysticism and law, Sufi communalism and universalist ethics, orthodoxy and heresy, the Ottoman present and the eschatological future.

The Meaning of the Ibn 'Arabī Tradition

In choosing Ibn 'Arabī's *Fuṣūṣu'l-Hikam* as vehicle for expressing their most sophisticated opinions, the Yazıcıoğlus participated in a textual lineage that was two hundred years old. To commentators both modern and medieval, the *Fuṣūṣ* was a work defined by its difficulty and opacity. Among the moderns, no less a scholar of Islam than A. J. Arberry said that it exemplified 'the confusion of the mental universe of Ibn 'Arabī' along with 'his heterogeneous and incoherent technical vocabulary'; Clement

Huart called it a 'disordered fantasy';[2] R. J. W. Austin, a specialist on Ibn 'Arabī and translator of the *Fuṣūṣ* into English, admitted that the *Fuṣūṣ* suffers from a 'general lack of organisation' and that the work's themes 'occur again and again from chapter to chapter in a rather haphazard way'.[3] The Yazıcıoğlus themselves acknowledged its difficulty when they stated in the *Müntehā*'s introduction: 'Although the *Fuṣūṣ* is to be highly valued by steadfast intellects, it is highly discordant to gullible hearts, according to whom some of its words contradict the Law and its ways seem not to be the ways of the Prophets'.[4]

One way in which the *Fuṣūṣ* has confused commentators and readers is through its structure, composed of chapters corresponding to the lives of twenty-seven prophets. However, with the exception of the first (Adam) and the last (Muḥammad), these prophets are not arranged according to any traditional chronology, such as that of the Yazıcıoğlus' *Envārü'l-'Āşıqīn* or the *Muḥammediyye*, nor that of their model, al-Kisā'ī's *Qiṣaṣ al-Anbiyā*. Furthermore, in most cases the connection between the lives of each prophet and the metaphysical discussion that ensues is quite obscure. In the chapter on Abraham, for example, Ibn 'Arabī used the patriarch's common epithet *al-khalīl*, 'the friend', as an occasion to elaborate on the inseparability of God and the cosmos: God permeates (*yatakhallalu*) his cosmos like colour permeates a coloured object, just as '[t]he Friend was only named "Friend" due to his permeation and encompassment of everything that the divine Essence is describable of being'.[5] The opacity of this presentation has not, however, impeded a general comprehension of the work's three central ideas, which served as starting points for later interpretations of the *Fuṣūṣ*. The first is its monism: All of creation – encompassing the physical world, the world of forms, the world of spirits and other layers of reality – is, through its existence, a manifestation of a single God, so that there is neither substance, nor form, nor action that is not some aspect of God's own Being. A reconciliation of the apparent contradictions between this absolute unity of all reality within God's self (which later commentators have customarily referred to as *waḥdat al-wujūd,* the Oneness of Being) and the visible multiplicity of the universe, as it is differentiated into attributes, substances, forms, space, time and so on, presents a concern that motivates many of Ibn 'Arabī 's arguments and those of his followers.

A second major message of the *Fuṣūṣ* is the role of mankind, more particularly, the role of the prophets and saints within this comprehensive divine reality. The *Fuṣūṣ* makes it clear that God 'manifested' humankind within Himself as a microcosm of reality as a whole; in a classic image, creation as a whole is for God/Reality a mirror disclosed by His innermost self (*ẕāt*), and mankind is the 'clearness' on that mirror that enables creation to become an image of Himself.[6] Because humankind alone, in the sum of its capabilities and limitations, participates in each of the Divine Names and attributes (unlike, for instance, the angels who through their absolute obedience only represent a set of them), Heserves as the ultimate locus of divine self-disclosure. As Ibn 'Arabī claims in the *Fuṣūṣ*' chapter on Adam, '[f]or God, [man] is as the pupil in relation to the eye through which vision occurs'.[7] As microcosmos that embodies, then perceives and, finally, interprets the whole of reality, man is entrusted with mastery over creation, acting as God's vice-regent (*khalīfa*) within the created world. Yet, while all humankind shares in this general vice-gerency, this potential can only be actualised insofar as it is focused in one specific individual at any given time, the so-called *al-insān al-kāmil*, the Perfect (or Complete) Man.

Thirdly, the means by which one comes to know these metaphysical facts and simultaneously ascend in degrees towards closeness with God and sainthood is fully supra-rational. Metaphysical knowledge, such as the one Ibn 'Arabī claimed to possess himself, is only earned experientially, through a process of 'discovery' (*kashf*) and 'verification' (*taḥqīq*) that resists rational description. As an early student of Ibn 'Arabī stated in very simple terms,

> Meanings are there
> that cannot fit into fancy –
> reason grasps nothing
> but a fable.[8]

While one can acquire a vague sense of these three cornerstones of Akbarian doctrine from an initial reading of the *Fuṣūṣ*, students have traditionally understood them through interpreters and commentators. One of the first generation of Ibn 'Arabī's students is credited with systematising the Andalusian's complex writings: an Anatolian of Persian origin, Ṣadr al-dīn al-Qūnawī, from the Seljuq metropolis of Konya. Qūnawī was the architect of a vast synthesis, essentially a companion systematisation of Ibn 'Arabī's thought, in his influential *Miftāḥ Ghayb al-Jam' wa Tafsīlihi* and other works.[9] When Qūnawī chose to comment on Ibn 'Arabī's works directly, it was the *Fuṣūṣ al-Ḥikam* to which he turned, rather than the master's more capacious *al-Futūḥāt al-Makkiyya*. When his chief student, Mu'ayyad al-dīn Jandī, built on Qūnawī's synthesis, he also chose to focus on the *Fuṣūṣ*, and this *Sharḥ Fuṣūṣ al-Ḥikam*, two generations removed from Ibn 'Arabī, became the archetype of its genre.[10]

Jandī wrote that it was during Qūnawī's instruction of the *Fuṣūṣ* that his deepest spiritual experience took place.

> At that moment [Qūnawī] exercised a mysterious influence with me, by virtue of his theurgy, such that God thereby granted me an immediate understanding of all that is contained within the entire book, simply through this elucidation of the preamble [of the *Fuṣūṣ*]. The *Shaykh* told me that he too asked his master – the author of the *Fuṣūṣ* – to expound to him its secrets, and that while he was explaining to him the preamble he exerted a wondrous influence within him, by virtue of his theurgy, such that he thereby grasped all that the book contained.[11]

Jandī here used the *Fuṣūṣ* to represent the transmission of Akbarian metaphysics in its entirety. Personal instruction of the *Fuṣūṣ*, he implied, allowed one to arrive at an inner realisation of Ibn 'Arabī's thought – furthermore, its embodiment in the *Fuṣūṣ* was what allowed this realisation to be transmitted across generations by means of an 'initiation by the book'. That is to say, the *Fuṣūṣ al-Ḥikam* was the package by which Ibn 'Arabī and Qūnawī's mysticism could be most efficiently perpetuated. This transmission was dependent on the personal tutelage of a master of the *Fuṣūṣ*; just like other forms of esoteric knowledge, the *Fuṣūṣ* could be handed down in a chain of mystical initiation.

Jandī's own *Sharḥ* and Qūnawī's reformulation proved to be the most influential carriers of Ibn 'Arabī's thought in the post-Mongol period. By the fifteenth century, it had become customary for a certain broad class of mystically-inclined intellectuals to produce a *Sharḥ Fuṣūṣ* of their own, based on Jandī's model. Jandī's student 'Abd al-Razzāq Qāshānī (d. 1329) wrote a *Sharḥ* famous for clarifying much of the terminology employed by Qūnawī and Jandī in a technical fashion. One of Qāshānī's students was another Anatolian, Dāvūd-i Qayṣerī, who met his teacher in the Iranian city of Sāva. Qayṣerī, too, was the author of a well-known *Sharh Fuṣūṣ*, one with a particular connection to Rum. In 1336, Sultan Orḫān installed Dāvūd-i Qayṣeri in a *medrese* in İznik, with a thirty-*aqçe* salary, thereby making him the first prominent commentator on Ibn 'Arabī in the western Anatolian borderlands.[12] Molla Fenarī, who later became a central figure of early Ottoman *medrese* education, composed the *Miṣbāḥ al-Uns*, a commentary on Qūnawī's *Miftāḥ al-Ghayb*, which acquired a place as 'one of the premier texts for the teaching of theoretical gnosis' in Iran during the Safavid period and afterwards.[13]

Meanwhile, at the other end of the Anatolian plateau, in Azerbaijan and its political centre Tabriz, the *Fuṣūṣ* had by the Yazıcıoğlus' lifetimes begun to signify something political and social. A sixteenth-century hagiography of Ibrāhīm-i Gülşenī (d. 1534), founder of the eponymous branch of the Khalwatiyya Sufi order in Cairo, alleged, unsurprisingly, that the saint's teacher, Dede 'Umar Rawshanī of Tabriz (d. 1487), had been a devotee of the *Fuṣūṣ* who mingled with the Aqqoyunlu lords then ruling eastern Anatolia and Iran. However, in his setting this was apparently not thought of as harmless: Scholars of the Aqqoyunlu encampment in Qarabāġ accused Rawshanī of unbelief, a charge against which he acquitted himself.[14] Later, during the 1470s, Rawshanī once again faced this charge, when his accusers condemned him with the apparently negative label of '*Fuṣūṣī*'.[15] According to the hagiographical account, in this instance his student Gülşeni stepped in to demonstrate the orthodoxy of the *Fuṣūṣ*. It seems that by this time, at least in the Aqqoyunlu lands under the influence of the reformist administrator Qāḍī 'Īsā, to be a *Fuṣūṣī* was to be a member of a faction facing opposition.[16] Yet, in the long run this opposition was ineffective: The Khalwatiyya order, to which the Yazıcıoğlus were connected from afar, maintained a strong tradition of *Fuṣūṣ* scholarship.

In Khurasan and central Iran, the *Fuṣūṣ* commentary tradition was just as strong. Shāh Ni'matullāh Valī (d. 1431), founder of one of the most widespread and enduring Sufi brotherhoods of Iran, was the author of a *Fuṣūṣ* commentary. Sa'īn al-dīn Turka, a polymath intellectual of fifteenth-century Isfahan, was immersed in the *Fuṣūṣ* tradition and wrote a commentary himself.[17] Perhaps most enduringly, the tradition of *Fuṣūṣ*-related writings persisted in the Naqshbandiyya Sufi order, whose early systematiser Muḥammad Pārsā (d. 1419) wrote yet another *Sharḥ Fuṣūṣ*.[18] As has been persuasively shown, the Naqshbandiyya, commonly perceived as ultra-orthodox, assigned an important place among its doctrines for teachings of the Ibn 'Arabī tradition prior to its reformation under the order's 'renewer' Aḥmad Sirhindī (d. 1624).[19] No less a figure than the great litterateur 'Abdu'r-raḥmān Jāmī, a devoted Naqshbandī, produced a commentary of Qūnawī's *Naqsh al-Fuṣūṣ*, titled *Naqd al-Fuṣūṣ*.[20] Like many others before him, including the Yazıcıoğlu brothers, Jāmī first encountered the original and was baffled by it, needing to turn to a commentary, in his case Qūnawī's. Having studied it for years, Jāmī found that 'there remained no ambiguous points [. . .] and some of the works that drew criticism for their apparently anti-*shar'ī* stand, shone like the sun'.[21] In Herat of the latter decades of the fifteenth century, Jāmī became a tireless defender of the doctrines of *waḥdat al-wujūd*, as did many of his fellow Naqshbandīs. Like the Khalwatiyya and the Ni'matullāhiyya, the Naqshbandiyya grew into a vital conduit for Ibn 'Arabī's and Qūnawī's ideas across the whole of their geographical scope.[22]

Needless to say, the transmission of these ideas, within and outside the structures of the *ṭuruq*, garnered strong polemical responses in each of the areas where they were popular. Tracing in the past what we have already seen regarding Dede 'Umar Rawshanī's reception among the scholars of late fifteenth-century Azerbaijan, Alexander Knysh has discussed the evolving reception of the doctrines contained in the *Fuṣūṣ* among the *'ulamā* already during Ibn 'Arabī's lifetime, distinguishing several lineages of critical response. Of these, the most central to the shape of anti-Akbari-anism (that is, criticism of Ibn 'Arabī) in the long term were the arguments articulated by the famous Ibn Ṭaymiyya of thirteenth-century Damascus.[23] However, Ibn Ṭaymiyya does not appear to have had any influence on the Anatolian and Rumelian intellectual world of the mid-fifteenth century, when the Yazıcıoğlus were writing.[24] No references to Ibn Ṭaymiyya have been discovered in the Yazıcıoğlus works, nor in those of their Anatolian and Ottoman peers. Instead, a more relevant lineage of anti-*Fuṣūṣ* writing is that from eastern Iran and Central Asia, which emerged from the critical tradition of Māturīdī *kalām* argumentation. A clear expositor of this sort of criticism was the Māturīdī intellectual Sa'd al-dīn Taftazānī, whom we already know to have exercised paramount influence in the early Ottoman intellectual zone (and the rest of the Ḥanafī world) through the wide diffusion of his students – one of which was Ḥaydar Khvāfī Haravī, most likely a teacher of Meḥmed Yazıcıoğlu.

In his *Risāla fī waḥdat al-wujūd*, Taftazānī took aim at 'Ibn Arabi and his students.[25] Interestingly, the thrust of his criticism was that they strictly based themselves on the arguments of rational theology (*kalām*) and sought to defend the *kalām* approach against the Ibn 'Arabī school, which generally rejects rational inquiry in favour of an epistemology freed from 'the shackled intellect' (*al-'aql al-muqayyad*). Strikingly, he believed that these epistemological foundations of the Unity of Being *limited* the possibilities for a human understanding of God's Law, by constraining the value of empirically-based knowledge in general. In the following sarcastic passage cited by Alexander Knysh, Taftazānī argued that, if rational inquiry could say nothing about an entirely unitary existence of which we can learn only through mystical experience, then we could discover nothing about the nature of creation, or even of man.

> Earth is identical with heaven, heaven is identical with water, water is identical with fire, fire is identical with air, air is identical with a human being, a human being is identical with a tree, a tree is identical with a donkey, a donkey is identical with man.[26]

Taftazānī took this *reductio* to be self-evidently absurd, representing a dead end to all paths for inquiry. Furthermore, he asserted that it was blasphemy against the idea that God has willed the world and its objects into discrete existence. Taftazānī insisted that, insofar as a *Fuṣūṣī* would trust the primacy of his visions that indicate a general union among all things, consubstantive with God, he would be misled into ignoring the world's multiplicity which is sustained by the particularities of God's will.

The Yazıcıoğlus among Fuṣūṣ Critics

Keeping in mind the debates that the work had by then stimulated, how did the Yazıcıoğlu brothers participate in the *Fuṣūṣ* commentary tradition? They explicitly acknowledged the controversial character of the *Fuṣūṣ* and of the lineage of commentaries to which they were adding. From the very beginning of the *Münteha* works, Aḥmed and Meḥmed positioned themselves within the almost global debate on Ibn 'Arabī's doctrines and hoped to convince readers of its validity. Aḥmed wrote:

> Although the *Fuṣūṣ* is to be highly valued by steadfast intellects (*'uqul-i rāsıḫīn*), it is highly discordant to those imitative hearts (*qulūb-i nāsıḫīn*) according to whom some of its words contradict the Law, and its ways are not the ways of the Prophets. This is why the opinions of masters of [both] reason and received tradition (*'uqūl ve nuqūl*) have abandonned it, to the extent that they claim that, if one trusts in its external aspects, one becomes an unbeliever, and if one trusts its esoteric aspects, one needs to ask forgiveness. This poor one was very puzzled (*ġāyet müteḫayyır*) by this.[27]

The two *Müntehā*s of Aḥmed Bīcān, from 1453 and 1465, resolved this puzzlement by providing a narrative. In the earlier text, Aḥmed Bīcān described the sudden arrival of a stranger from Iranian lands who 'held a book' in his hands (the resemblance of this story to Ibn 'Arabī's own description of how he received the *Fuṣūṣ* from the Prophet in a dream is probably not coincidental). This book, which is not precisely named, appears to have been a derivative of the *Sharḥ Fuṣūṣ* of Mu'ayyad al-Dīn Jandī by an otherwise obscure Jalāl al-dīn Khujandī Uzjandī. Aḥmed studied this book and found within it a passage that put his doubts on Ibn 'Arabī's orthodoxy to rest. This dialogue must be quoted here in full, because it contains the core of Aḥmed's refutation of Ibn 'Arabī's critics:

> I found in this book that Jalāl al-dīn Khujandī Uzjandī testifies that Mu'ayyad al-dīn Jandī testifies and recounts that Muḥyī al-dīn Maghribī [that is, ibn 'Arabī] said to one of his companions: 'Do you not know that I have said that some of what I have written in the *Fuṣūṣ* and other books of mine contradicts the Law?'
>
> 'I did not know', said the dervish.
>
> The *shaykh* said, 'This is because the Messenger gave me to the *umma* as both mercy and scourge (*raḥmet ü belā*), in order to test its convictions. Thus I have become the means to distinguish a heretic (*mulḥid*) from a monotheist – to

send he who is a believer to journey to God on the path of the Law, and to send the *mulḥid* astray from guidance towards the obedience of fancy'.

'O *Shaykh*, how is it permissible to guide in this way?' asked the dervish.

The *shaykh* said, 'I am appointed, and the appointee is excused. I am like those angels whom God commanded at Resurrection to say, *I am your Lord Most High*, so as to test the ideas of the wise (*efkār-i 'uqalā*). Did those angels become unbelievers? I am just like them'.

So, in finding this authentic testimony, I found success in my aim.[28]

The later text omits the story of the book but retains the rest of the conversation between Ibn 'Arabī and his disciple. The message in both cases is clear. Aḥmed believed that the *Fuṣūṣ* and Ibn 'Arabī's 'other books' deliberately skirted the edge of heresy without crossing into it; therefore, to study them would separate believer from unbeliever. As a sensitive marker for orthodoxy and heresy, those who understand the *Fuṣūṣ* while remaining properly faithful reaffirm religion deeply and securely, while those who harbour tendencies towards heresy use that same text to move even farther away from God and to fall into lawlessness. The *Fuṣūṣ*, deliberately provocative, contains temptations that can only be avoided by a proper education, given by a trustworthy guide, in the text's inner meanings.With this maneuvre, Aḥmed Bīcān thus excused the most problematic aspects of the *Fuṣūṣ* and detoured around the epistemological and metaphysical criticisms levelled by the likes of Taftazānī, while at the same time he called for education in the *Fuṣūṣ* commentary lineage. While Māturīdī critics may work from sound logic, they understand Ibn 'Arabī's corpus through the same naïve sense that a putative *Fuṣūṣī mulḥid* (heretic) would, not as a *Fuṣūṣī mū'min* (believer) should, and thus they miss the point. To defenders of the *Fuṣūṣ*, such as the Yazıcıoğlu brothers, falls the task of explaining the narrow road of true orthodoxy – of understanding the *Fuṣūṣ* within the frame of true monotheism.[29]

Hence, in describing what it is to be a *mū'min* who understands Ibn 'Arabī, they required the utter rejection of rationalist criticism like Taftazānī's, which they likened to the literalism of calling unbelievers angels whom God commanded to say 'I am the Lord Most High'. Accordingly, without engaging in any sort of pre-emptive defense, the brothers began to summarise the essence of the Unity of Existence in a series of short sections titled 'prologues' (*temhīd*), much like in Qūnawī's *Miftāḥ*. The first begins with the core claim of *waḥdat al-wujūd*: '*Existence is none other than He* [*wujūd min ḥaythu hūwa*]', who requires no preconditions; it is this absolute Reality that we call the "hidden of hiddens" and the "truths of truths"'.[30] The second *temḥīd* tells us that all sensible objects are sensible only by virtue of God's own self-knowledge, in which 'the knower and the known are one', and lays out a chain of being in which causal agency rests, at every juncture, with God as Being's sole source. The Yazıcıoğlus then proceeded to briefly mention the third major feature of the ideology of the *Fuṣūṣ*, the concept of *al-insān al-kāmil*: 'For the Muḥammedan Truth is manifest and is master of the temporal world, and manifests in human reality [*ḥaqīqat-i insāniyye*]. We call this [manifestation] "the Great Man". On account of this, mankind merits the vicegerency [*ḫilāfet*]'.[31] They opened a subsequent section with a clear statement: 'Intellect is inadequate [. . .] The external aspects [of Truth] cannot be comprehended as objects of intellect'.[32]

Within only a few pages, we have received a summary of three core elements of Ibn 'Arabī's thought, which differentiate it from Avicennan *falsafa* or Māturīdī *kalām*: a gnostic epistemology, the Unity of Existence and the anthropocentric principle of the Perfect Man. This rapid run-through of core *Fuṣūṣī* beliefs indicates for us how *little* the Yazıcıoğlus actually cared to argue directly against Taftazānī's refutations. The doctrines emerge without defense, as pure, confident declarations; the authors used for this text portions of Jandī and Qūnawī and made full use of terminology favoured by the Ibn 'Arabī textual tradition. Also drawing from Jandī, the Yazıcıoğlus then outlined another controversial doctrine, that of the 'immutable essences' (*a'yān-i s̱ābite*) which constitute a formal blueprint for the items of creation – a doctrine which critics have accused of undermining the idea of God's omnipotence.[33] Then ensues a technical discussion of the 'Five Presences', or categories of existence, that descend from the world of immutable essences and divine knowledge, through the world of 'hidden presences' and spirits, to the world of exemplary forms and dreams, then the world of visible forms, all of which are suffused with 'the hidden presence of the absolute, which is all-encompassing'. These fit closely with the Five Presences of Qūnawī.[34] Likewise, the rest of this section remains firmly within Qūnawī's and Jandī's framework.

However, we do perceive a certain defensive anxiety about *wujūdī* beliefs in the following chapter which, despite its initial appearances, amounts to a very coherent apologia for Akbarian doctrine. Organised into 'observation-places' (*mirṣad*), this second chapter at the outset diverts the reader with the highly obscure matters of the directionality of God's relationship with creation. Yet, the arc of this chapter differs from the previous in that it moves 'downward' from high theology and its abstract equations, into more familiar Yazıcıoğlu territory: testimony from various historical religious authorities and miscellaneous *aḥādīth*. Aḥmed Bīcān, in a tremendously revealing passage, stated his motivation for entering this discussion.

> O seeker of divine secrets! If you ask us, 'what is he basis of this knowledge? And why be submerged in the Unity [*tevḥīd*] of His Essence [*ẕāt*]?' These many truths have been told, but in the time of the Prophet and his Noble Companions and followers they did not speak thusly . . .
>
> The answer is this: How much have the notable scholars and the pillars of wisdom said about the Truths of Unity! Their knowledge is the most exalted knowledge and a foretaste of [divine] Glories [*eclā*]. The sign of this, first of all, is God's own Word; and after that the word of the Prophet and then the word of 'Alī and then the word of the verifiers [*muḥaqqıqlar*] whose perfections of knowledge are trusted by the scholars of the East and West . . .[35]

The sentiment that is here expressed by the questions of a hypothetical reader – that the vocabulary of Ibn 'Arabī's theology deviates from Prophetic practice – is a criticism entirely different from the objections of the Māturīdī critics. Rather, it has more in common with Ibn Ṭaymiyya's suspicion that the Sufism of the post-Mongol period constituted a rejection of the practices of the righteous early Muslims and an example of innovation without foundation in the religious sciences. Ibn Ṭaymiyya's *al-Ṣūfiyya wa al-Fuqarā*, for example, is a sustained argument that the Qur'anic terminology used by contemporary mystics – words such as *faqīr* and *walī* to describe themselves, and the concepts of intoxication and self-annihilation to describe their mystical states – was understood in the Qur'an and in the time of the Prophet in very different, less radical ways.[36] For instance, the word *walī* signified not the saints whose spiritual power, earned through knowledge and devotional exercises, brought them into proximity to God; rather, it simply meant 'the pious believers, whether called *faqīr*, Sufi, legist, scholar, merchant, soldier, artisan, *amīr*, governor, or something else'.[37] In short, Ibn Ṭaymiyya alleged that the whole Sufi, and by extension, Akbarian conceptual world was based on wishful thinking and would have been alien to the world of the Prophet and his companions. It seems that some of the Yazıcıoğlus' audience, despite the fact that they were probably unfamiliar with Ibn Ṭaymiyya, held similar views that called for the Yazıcıoğlus' response. We may venture to call this a kind of 'fundamentalist' objection to *wujūdī* teachings.

Aḥmed Bīcān and Meḥmed offered an effective response to the 'fundamentalist' objection. They stated that all respected religious masters, beginning with the Prophet himself, had, sometimes clearly and sometimes obscurely, expressed the doctrine of the Unity of Existence, and he provided quotations from these figures. According to them, the Prophet himself had said: 'In matters of knowledge there are things like a hidden body [*hey'et-i meknūn*]. None know them except the knowers of God, and they cannot be denied but by the resisting ones [*ehl-i i'tirāẓ*] who deny this'.[38] 'Alī ibn Abū Ṭālib, for his part, claimed: 'Reality [*ḥaqīqat*] is a light that shone at the dawn of pre-eternity upon the forms that had no being. All action and attributes were made manifest by means of that Reality'.[39] Ja'far al-Ṣādiq said: 'God illuminated his servants with his Word, but the people did not see it'. This argument is further developped with quotations from Bāyazid Bisṭāmī, Abū Ṭālib Makkī, Junayd Baghdādī, Abū Ḥāmid al-Ghāzalī and others, with the latest being allegedly *wujūd*ist statements by the famous Samarqand rival of Taftazānī, Sayyid Sharīf Jurjānī: 'Truly the necessary of existence is absolute existence, and by absolute existence what is meant is essence (*māhiyyet*), without any faults [. . .]. Existence lacks for nothing'.[40] Finally, they cited an exegesis by Fakhr al-dīn Rāzī in which the Qur'anic phrase 'Had there been within [the heavens and earth] gods besides God, they both would have been disordered'[41] is taken to imply that all existence must have only one divine source that is unshared and direct.

Over the course of this set of quotations, each of these great figures of the past is taken to verify a specific aspect of the Ibn 'Arabī legacy that speaks to its contemporary context. The Prophet asserts that esoteric knowledge is real and important; 'Alī implies the strong monism of Ibn 'Arabī and the priority of being over form and attribute; al-Ṣādiq predicts that not all will be able to understand it, while the latter-day scholars corroborate Akbarian metaphysics. It is interesting that all of these figures are called *muḥaqqiq*s, 'verifiers', the term used by Qūnawī and others to refer to the Ibn 'Arabī school – whether or not they predate the *shaykh*.[42] The conclusion here is that *wujūdī* mysticism is as old as Islam and that it was part of the esoteric knowledge of all generations of the righteous. A fundamentalist critique like Ibn Ṭaymiyya's is then rendered empirically untenable: the first generation of Muslims believed the same things Sufis do.

This argument also appears in the writings of the Yazıcıoğlus' closest peers within their own Sufi community, the Bayramiyye of Ankara. Particularly in Aqşemse'd-dīn's writings one can detect the same kind of concern with countering the objection that Sufi practice was a groundless innovation. Yet, his focus was quite different. Although he also used many of the Yazıcıoğlus' sources (Suhrawardī's *'Awārif al-Ma'ārif*, Fakhr al-dīn Rāzī's *Tafsīr*, al-Baghawī's *Maṣābīḥ* and others), Aqşemse'd-dīn drew from them far more practical information, dedicating more attention to the matter of what colour undergarments a Bayramī should wear or how to fold the cloth that makes up the Bayramī headgear than to the subtle polarities of God's presence throughout creation. Nevertheless, it seems that his critical interlocutors (whom he calls 'slanderers' [*maṭā'in*]) were of a familiar type, charging that there was no Prophetic precedent for mystics' beliefs and habits. In one typical example of many in his *al-Risālat al-Nūriyya*, Aqşemse'd-dīn wrote:

> A slanderer alleges, '[Sufis] hold a staff in their hands. For Sufis to carry a staff is an innovation (*bid'at*)'. [On the contrary], to carry a staff is *sunna* [. . .] as is seen in the *Büstānu'l-faqīh* [sic] of Abū Layth [al-Ṣamarqandī], which says that it is transmitted from Ibn 'Abbās that 'to carry a staff is the *sunna* of all the prophets, and is a sign to the believers'; and Ḥasan al-Baṣrī also said 'to carry a staff has six benefits . . .'[43]

Although this reference to respected early pietists may not have silenced all critics, it implies that, for practising mystics like the Yazıcıoğlus and Aqşemse'd-dīn, a turn to *ḥadīth* and the heroic characters of early Islam (such as Ibn 'Abbās and Ḥasan al-Baṣrī) was an appropriate response to those who charged that Sufi practice was a recent innovation. It is now possible to speculate on the climate of popular religious debate in the context of these two Bayramīs. For the Yazıcıoğlus' audience, much like for Aqşemse'd-dīn's, learned *kalām* argumentation in the style of Taftazānī's was less important; rather, perhaps there existed a popular sensibility in these west Anatolian and Rumelian circles that measured religious traditions against ideas about what had existed in the Prophet's time. The *Fuṣūṣ* fell within the purview of this criticism and thus required a traditionalist defense.

Having invested so much energy in defending the *wujūdī* worldview, the bulk of the Yazıcıoğlus' *Fuṣūṣ* commentary surprisingly retreats from the abstraction of the Qūnawī-Jandī tradition and returns to their most familiar source of inspiration, a very literal narrative of the sequence of prophets. This creates a dramatic contrast with both the original *Fuṣūṣ* and its other commentaries. First, each of the *Fuṣūṣ*' chapters are reordered into a chronological sequence, so that it comes to resemble the *Qiṣaṣ al-Anbiyā* structure of the *Envār* and the *Maghārib al-Zamān*. Instead of following the arbitrary order of the *Fuṣūṣ* – which, for example, places Jesus in the fifteenth chapter and Moses in the twenty-fifth – the Yazıcıoğlus' *Fuṣūṣ* commentary matches the traditional chronology, with Jesus as second-to-last.

More importantly, the metaphysical discussion occasioned by the invocation of each prophet in Ibn 'Arabī's and Jandī's texts is often shortened, summarised, or even omitted entirely in the Yazıcıoğlus' texts. In its place, the brothers revisited their *Qiṣaṣ* sources and outlined amusing or edifying anecdotes from each prophet's life. The chapter on the prophet Joseph is typical. Following Ibn 'Arabī's precedent, several pages meditate on the 'light' which is evoked by Joseph's famed physical beauty; the created cosmos is like a shadow of God's all-encompassing light for which Joseph's beauty is a symbol and which Muḥammad witnessed at the height of his *mi'rāj*. Yet, this commentary soon transforms into the familiar narrative of the life of Joseph, in which his brothers abandon him to be eaten by wolves, he makes his way to Egypt and then deals with the Pharaoh and Zulaykhā.[44] Most of this section is identical to the *qiṣaṣ* recounted in the *Maghārib al-Zamān* and the *Envārü'l-'Āşıqīn*. As such, the *Müntehā* turns long sections of the *Fuṣūṣ al-Ḥikam* into even longer sections of al-Kisā'ī's *Qiṣaṣ al-Anbiyā*.

This pattern is not uniform. The chapter on the relatively minor prophet Shu'ayb does not deal with the prophet at all, but, like the *Fuṣūṣ* and its commentaries, expounds on Ibn 'Arabī's views of man's gnostic capacity as represented by the heart, before discussing the nature of an individual's belief in God and finally dealing with God's continual renewal of creation. The Yazıcıoğlus greatly expanded on this discussion in several directions, for instance, by listing many word pairs that in their pairing represent the capacity for divine understanding – the most important of which is *'ışq* and *ma'şūq*, lover and beloved.

On the whole, however, the Yazıcıoğlus literalised the text of the *Fuṣūṣ*, using their commentary to give the reader contextual background rather than a laborious exegesis of Ibn 'Arabī's philosophical argumentation. It is risky to speculate on the motivations for turning theology into prophetic narrative. Certainly, this literalisation is not due to any lack of understanding or interest in the finer points of Ibn 'Arabī's metaphysics, which is amply demonstrated throughout the work. I may only suggest that this approach to the *Fuṣūṣ* tradition is reflective of the needs of an audience who may not be familiar with all of the extra-Qu'anic lore that is taken as common by learned readers of the *Fuṣūṣ*.

Insofar as some later Ottomans objected to Meḥmed's and Aḥmed's works, they did so because of its position on the *Fuṣūṣ* and Ibn 'Arabī. A late seventeenth-century Ottoman *fetvā* by one 'Ālim Meḥmed (Emīrzāde) recorded the following question-and-answer:

> Some scholars approve of the book *Muḥammediyye* by 'the *Muḥammediyye*'s author' Yazıcıoğlu and count it among accepted books. And some get ahold of it and do not like it [. . .] and claim on your authority that 'Ālim Meḥmed Efendi does not approve of it. If in fact the *Muḥammediyye* contains some words that contradict the Law. Please grace us with your pronouncement . . .
>
> The answer: Yazıcıoğlu, author of the *Muḥammediyye*, is of the carnal soul's *wujūdī* school. It is the school of the author of the *Fuṣūṣ*, Ibn 'Arabī. He com-

mented on the *Fuṣūṣ* and in his *Muḥammediyye* there are many forged *ḥadīth*s and falsehoods.[45]

Sufi Lineage and Community

We have seen the manner in which the Yazıcıoğlus navigated the controversial subject of Ibn 'Arabī and the *Fuṣūṣ*. This may have been at the time the most contentious, but by no means the only pietistic theme taken up by the Yazıcıoğlu brothers; the *Müntehā* is not simply a manifesto of *Fuṣūṣi* doctrine. The brothers had to navigate many other doctrinal and sociological divisions within the imagined history of mystically-inclined communities. The *Müntehā* includes several sections by which they were able to depict themselves as part of an ancient and venerable lineage of Sufi figures and institutions going back to the time of the Prophet, while also distinguishing their own identities within that continuity. A section immediately following their narrative of the prophet's life (largely identical with the one presented in the *Envārü'l-'Āşıqīn*) consists of an unattributed extract from 'Abd al-Razzāq Qāshānī's *Istilāḥāt al-Ṣūfiyya* ('Sufi Terminology'), a glossary written specifically to clarify difficult Arabic terms and concepts from the *Fuṣūṣ* and other mystical texts.[46] The Yazıcıoğlus' version is highly abridged in an idiosyncratic manner, focusing on an assortment of specifically Akbarian concepts such as *a'yān al-thābita* ('immutable essences') or *barzakh* ('isthmus' or 'interval'), but without diverging from Qāshānī's original definitions. In any case, Aḥmed Bīcān, in his 1453 edition, wrote that he provided this glossary for the following reason:

> Now, O revealers of the secrets of truth! O, he who encounters the lights of subtleties! Let it be known that for each student who studies these sagely words [. . .] and accepts these words into their hearts, there is no doubt that they will reach their goals and accomplish their aims! For there are two types of *shaykh*s. One they call the 'Easterners' [*meşārıqa*], and the other they call the 'Westerners' [*meğāribe*]. All those who are Easterners say: 'Asceticism and seclusion are necessary for all students until their souls are rescued from the world of darkness and reach the light of lights'. But the Westerners say: 'There is no doubt that asceticism and monasticism have their effects, but those who know our wisdom do not have much need for asceticism and seclusion. Asceticism, a demanding path, gives no peace to those who do not deserve it, while wisdom is the most proximate path, the path of annihilation and permanence. Sometimes immediate emanations [of wisdom] reach [a student] in a year or a month or a week and they achieve their aim. And a very talented student can do so in a day or an hour; it is even true that a perfect teacher [*şeyḫ-i*

> *kāmil*] can guide one and cause one to arrive [at proximity to God] in a single moment'. This is why I, caller to faith, Aḥmed Bīcān, have summarised these terms and brought them as an offering to the mystics ['*uṣṣāq*], so that, with God's permission, they may quickly reach [God's Presence].[47]

Aḥmed presented here a simple taxonomy of *shaykh*s, dividing them somewhat enigmatically into shakyhs of East and West. The so-called *mashāriqa* (Easterners) emphasised ascetic practice and seclusion as prerequisites for gnosis, while the *maghāriba* (Westerners) recognized wisdom itself as the only necessity. In the 'western' view, the especially talented student, under the guidance of an accomplished mystagogue, could reach gnosis in a single moment of illumination, with no need for rigorous self-denying practices. To what does this binary refer? It is reasonably clear that by 'Westerner', Aḥmed referred to Ibn 'Arabī and his disciples; the *shaykh*, coming from faraway al-Andalus, brought a discrete body of highly difficult but still practicable doctrines to his disciples in Anatolia and Syria. Along with other Andalusi mystics, Ibn 'Arabī did not create or participate in the structure of a *ṭarīqa* which could organise the practices of ascetic devotion. The 'Easterners', on the other hand, probably represented the rigorous institutional Sufism that grew out of the Khurasani Malāmatiyya of the ninth and tenth centuries – the *ṭarīqa* tradition properly understood. In the Yazıcıoğlus' day, this was best exemplified by the Ḫalvetiyye and Ṣafaviyya of Anatolia and Iran, the Mevleviyye of Anatolia, the Naqshbandiyya-Khvājagān, the Yazıcıoğlus' own Bayramiyye and various other orders, all of which were characterised by specific devotional practices such as *khalwa* (seclusion), *samā'* (musical performance and dance) and *dhikr* (recitation), respectively. There then emerges a contradiction. Aḥmed Bīcān seemed to imply that he followed the Western, and not Eastern practice, even as he claimed membership in the Bayramiyye that is explicitly linked to an 'Eastern' lineage through the Ṣafavī *shaykh*s and their forebears.

It is also difficult to contextualise this preference for the so-called 'Western' mystical tradition in light of passages elsewhere in the *Müntehā*. An illuminating chapter is entitled *Tezkiret-i Evliyā*, 'A Register of Saints', where the brothers presented a chronological list of holy personages after Muḥammad's time, which serves as a kind of internal history of the Sufi tradition of which they considered themselves a part; based on the particular individuals listed, its entries appear to have been extracted from Farīd al-dīn 'Aṭṭār's work of the same name.[48] Aḥmed Bīcān claimed that the Prophet's Companions had been written about elsewhere, so 'I myself will write about the *shaykh*s'.[49]

Following 'Aṭṭār, the first such *shaykh* is the sixth Shī'ī *imām* Ja'far al-Ṣādiq, who, as 'sultan of the nation of Muṣṭafā', is 'perfect in the knowledge of truth and wisdom, the foremost of the people of discernment and leader of the people of Love' (*zevq ehline muqaddem ve 'ışq ehline pīşvā*). We need not take this dedication as an expression of Shī'ī tendencies as they would later come to be understood: praise of Ja'far as-Ṣādiq was common in the Ottoman lands and elsewhere for centuries before and after the Yazıcıoğlus' time. Following Ja'far as-Ṣādiq, a list of well-known figures revered among *ṭarīqa* Sufism is presented: Uways al-Qaranī, Ḥasan al-Baṣrī, Mālik b. Dīnār, Muḥammad b. Wasi' (d. 751), Ḥabīb al-'Ajamī, Abu Hāzim Madanī, 'Uqbat al-Ghulām, Rābi'a al-'Adawiyya, Fuḍayl b. 'Iyāḍ, Ibrāhīm b. Adham, Bishr al-Khwāfī, Dhū al-Nūn al-Miṣrī, Bāyazīd Bisṭāmī, 'Abdullāh b. Mubārak, Ṣufyān Thawrī, Abū 'Alī Shaqīq, Jihād al-Kūfī, Imām Shāfi'ī, Aḥmad ibn Ḥanbal, Dāvūd al-Ṭā'ī, Sariy al-Saqaṭī and Junayd al-Baghdādī. To close this sequence, Aḥmed Bīcān praised his own Sufi master Ḥācı Bayram Velī, citing his *silsila* which runs from the Ṣafavī *shaykhs* through Aḥmad al-Ghāzalī, Junayd, Sariy al-Saqaṭī, Ḥabīb al-'Ajamī and Ḥasan al-Baṣrī to 'Alī and Muḥammad. 'Dervish Bīcān's *shaykh* is Ḥācı Bayram', he wrote, 'and his *shaykh*'s *shaykh*'s *silsila* and gnostic knowledge is that of Sultan Bāyazīd [Bisṭāmī], and his robe and headgear are from Junayd of Baghdad'. Manṣūr al-Ḥallāj is invoked at the close of the chapter. Each personage is described with one or two anecdotes illustrating their piety.[50]

Although the figures in this list are not obscure – indeed, almost all were universally revered in the Sunnī world as Sufis and scholars – their union here, insofar as it shortens 'Aṭṭār's more comprehensive listing, represents a particular configuration of pious memory. While Aḥmed Bīcān preserved 'Aṭṭār's broad framework of the history of sainthood – from Ḥasan al-Baṣrī and Uways to al-Ḥallāj – it is worth noting how exclusively his list harkens to the mythical genesis of Sufism in the community of *zāhids* (renunciants) of late Umayyad and 'Abbasid 'Iraq. Aḥmed Bīcān repeated only the first twenty-one figures of 'Aṭṭār's *Tazkira*, the majority of whom were Baghdadi renunciants, while omitting all of 'Aṭṭār's later pious figures with the sole exception of al-Ḥallāj. Nor are any post-Ḥallāj individuals included in this list. There is a deliberately archaic quality to his memory of his Sufi forebears.

It appears, in other words, that Aḥmed Bīcān was at pains to situate his Bayrami Sufi heritage within classical *zuhd*. His own *silsila* is presented in the same way, passing with few links from the contemporary Ṣafaviyya backwards in time to Junayd al-Baghdādī and al-Saqaṭī. Neither the Ṣafavī *shaykhs* who taught the teachers of Ḥācı Bayram, nor the revered Ibrāhīm

Zāḥid Gīlānī from whose circles the Ṣafaviyya and Ḫalvetiyye emerged, are mentioned more than in passing. An interesting consequence of this emphasis is a corresponding de-emphasis on another strand of medieval Islamic piety: the heritage of the Malāmiyya of Khurasan. Ahmet Karamustafa has characterised late medieval *ṭarīqa* Sufism partly as a merging of the ethos of early *zuhd* piety of early Baghdad Sufism with the social-mindedness of the somewhat later Khurasani tradition of the Malāmiyya, 'The Path of Blame'.[51] Malāmī ideology remained current as a strand of Persianate Sufi thought throughout the Yazıcıoğlus' time – indeed, in 1429 the name Melāmiyye was revived by Dede 'Ömer Sikkīnī (Bıçaqçı), one of the primary disciples of none other than Ḥācı Bayram Velī, as a name for one of the Bayramīs' successor communities.[52] Thus, it is striking that the Yazıcıoğlus make no mention of the original Malāmī *shaykh*s in their *Teẕkiret-i Evliyā*, but instead focus exclusively on the earlier *zāhid*s. The absence of symbolic Melāmīs such as Ḥamdūn al-Qassār and Abū Ḥafs al-Haddād, who are prominent in 'Aṭṭār's *Taẕkira*, shows a revision of the historical memory of the Malāmiyya.

Any interpretation of this *teẕkire* ventures into the realm of untestable hypothesis. By drawing a direct line from the early Sufis of Baghdad to the present-day *shaykh*s of the Bayramiyya while skipping over post-'Abbasid spiritual figures, Aḥmed Bīcān perhaps intended to ground his own Bayramī heritage in the unimpeachable prestige of the early period. The universal respect enjoyed by these politically quietist ascetics, distant from the controversies of the era of *waḥdat al-wujūd*, may have been appealing to the Yazıcıoğlu brothers, in effect placing the Bayramiyya on a stable island of sound authority in uncertain times. In another sense, this is an analogy to the traditionalist tendency to privilege the opinions and manners of the Companions or early jurists over later interpreters, especially in times of upheaval. We have seen already how 'fundamentalist' criticism of Sufi practice called for a response from the likes of the Yazıcıoğlus and Aqşemse'd-dīn (the latter made special note of his Sufi lineage extending to the unimpeachable first generations of Muslims, and even drew his own familial lineage back to Shihāb al-dīn Suhrawardī, Shaqīq al-Balkhī and ultimately Abū Bakr). It seems that the Yazıcıoğlus and their community stood at the intersection between a *ḥadīth*-centric traditionalism and the novelty of the post-Ibn 'Arabī religious sciences, always aware of an ever-present 'past-oriented' discourse on religious fundamentals in which one must either participate or against which one must defended oneself.

On the question of Sufi practice, there is no evidence that the Yazıcıoğlus advocated anything unusual. They discussed practice in a section of the *Müntehā* claiming to be an abridgement of the *Manāzil al-Sā'irīn* ('Travellers' Stopping-Places') of the eleventh-century Khurasani mystic Abū Ismā'īl 'Abdullāh al-Anṣārī al-Harawī, possibly accessed through the *Sharḥ Manāzil* of 'Abd al-Razzāq Qāshānī.[53] Aḥmed Bīcān presented this enduring spiritual guidebook as a manual for good Sufi devotional practice that presumably reflects contemporaneous Bayramī teachings. We see how Aḥmed, through the *Manāzil*, exalted such practices as ascetic penitence (*tevbe*), pious contemplation of God's unity and its verbal commemoration (*tefekkür* and *teẕekkür*), renunciation and abandonment of worldliness (*i'tiṣām* and *firār*), self-discipline (*riyāẓet*), auditory or music-related devotional routines (*sema'*), extra-sensory perception of hidden qualities (*baṣīret* and *firāset*) and fasting. 'Abdullāh al-Anṣārī also described the stages of a mystic's inner development, designated by terms such as *ğarq* (submersion) and *vecd* (ecstasy), *sekr* (intoxication) and ultimately *maḥv* (eradication) and *fenā* (annihilation), with each such term denoting a specific station (*maqām*) along a mystic's route of spiritual passage.

Since it is so universal, the *Manāzil* cannot be used to differentiate the practices of the Yazıcıoğlus and the Bayramīs with respect to other contemporary Sufi groups. At most, one can suggest affinities with other Sufis for whom the *Manāzil* was also canonical, such as the Naqshbandiyya who hold al-Anṣārī in especially high esteem. Like the Naqshbandiyya, Aḥmed Bīcān's Sufi community seems to have used the *Manāzil* as a guide to a moderately renunciant Sufism that allowed for the possibility, but not necessity, of gnosis. (However, unlike the Naqshbandiyya, the Yazıcıoğlus and the Bayramīs upheld vocal, not silent, *ẕikr*.) For further details on contemporary Bayramī practice, such as their sartorial requirements, specific prayers and guidelines on ritual purity, the more pragmatic writings of Aqşemse'd-dīn afford a better source, although they lie beyond the scope of this study.

The Shī'ī–Sunnī Question

We have been able to place the Yazıcıoğlus at a particular juncture within the controversies surrounding the *Fuṣūṣ* and among the competing lineages of fifteenth-century Sufism. What remains to be discussed is the intra-Islamic sectarian consciousness of the Yazıcıoğlu brothers. Modern scholars have characterised the fifteenth-century Persianate societies in the Timurid, post-Timurid Turkmen and Anatolian domains as being both pre- and post-sectarian, embodying a kind of Shī'ī–Sunnī inter-confessionalism that was ruptured only by Shah Ismā'īl's Safavid revolution at the century's end. Emblematic of this state of affairs are the evolution of the Kubraviyya order along doctrinal lines intermediate between the classical expressions of the two faiths, while in the long term trending towards Twelver Shīʿism,[54] and the more famous Shīʿitisation of the Ṣafavī order of Ardabil in the latter half of the century.[55] For clear examples from Timurid territories, we need look no further than Sulṭān-Ḥusayn Bayqara in Herat calling for a *khutba* in honour of the Twelve Imāms,[56] or Abū al-Qāsim Bābur's minting of coins with the names of the *imāms*; further west one encounters the ʿAlid poetry of Jihānshāh,[57] sultan of the Qaraqoyunlu domains, and any number of examples detailed in Biancamaria Amoretti's classic study on the subject.[58] In the Ottoman case, evidence of such philo-ʿAlidism is harder to come by, but the sparsity of evidence should not lead one to conclude the complete absence of these tendencies. Among the few data points that have been studied count the rapid spread of Bektaşism into western Anatolia from the thirteenth through fifteenth centuries,[59] as well as the long-term presence of social elements such as the Tekke tribe of southwestern Anatolia, who, through the Şāh-Qulu movement, would make common cause with Ismāʿīl's religiously-motivated insurrection at the beginning of the sixteenth century. These indicate that at that time strongly Shīʿī or ʿAlid-loyalist doctrines had some foothold in the Ottoman lands and bordering regions.[60] In any case, whatever experimental sectarian syntheses appeared in the continuum between an emerging modern Sunnism and Twelver Shīʿism were soon to fall victim to sixteenth-century doctrinal entrenchment on both sides of the Ottoman-Safavid frontier.

An original motivation for this investigation into the Yazıcıoğlu brothers and their pious vision was to see if it may show evidence of a 'pre-classical' Ottoman Sunnism displaying what modern eyes would see as Shīʿī characteristics. The results of this inquiry are mixed. On one hand, the Yazıcıoğlus consistently adhere to the markers of Sunnī affiliation, such as a scrupulously equivalent reverence of the four Righteous Caliphs, Abū Bakr, ʿUmar, ʿUthmān and ʿAlī. On the other hand, they appear remarkably *un*concerned with refuting Shīʿism or even identifying it as heresy, as would become standard within a half-century of their writing. And in a more subtle sense, they show evidence of having been educated in a sea of Shīʿī-influenced argumentation on the issue of religious leadership and of having absorbed such argumentation, through intermediaries, into their core beliefs. That is to say, the stamp of late medieval Shīʿism indelibly marks their works, despite their non-Shīʿī gestures.

It is easy to scan *Kitābü'l-Müntehā* and find statements that rule out doctrinaire Shīʿism. Aḥmed stated: 'The *ʿāşere-i mübeşşire* [the ten who are promised paradise] are in heaven. They are Abū Bakr, ʿUmar, ʿUthmān,

'Alī, Ṭalḥa, Zubayr, 'Abdurraḥmān [b. 'Awf], Sa'd b. Abī Waqqās, Sa'īd b. Zayd and Abū 'Ubayda b. al-Jarrāh'[61] – this list includes figures such as 'Umar and Sa'd, who are anathema to Shī'īs of any stripe. In the narrative portion, the Prophet is quoted as finding Abū Bakr and 'Umar 'the most appropriate for the imamate'. The episodes of the Sunnī origin story, such as 'Uthmān's death 'while reading the Scripture',[62] are relayed in typical ways. The four Rāshidūn are to sit, in sequence, on a throne of ruby in heaven that is 'twenty miles in length'.[63] There is no doubt that, in the broadest self-declared sense, Aḥmed Bīcān's sectarian legacy conforms to conventional Sunnism.

However, perhaps surprisingly given their consistent Sunnī signals, the Yazıcıoğlus' appear to have been completely disinterested in defining Sunnism *vis-à-vis* any other form of Islam. Not once did they refer to the term *ehl-i sünnet ve'l-cemā'at*, the conventional term for the Sunnī orthodox. Nor does *taşayyu'*, a neutral term for Shī'ism, appear in their writings. What does appear once is a derisive term for Shī'ism, *rāfiẓī* ('refusers' of the agreed-upon caliphal succession). Yet, the context in which this word appears is non-polemical, not resembling at all the anathametising stridency of later Ottoman sectarian documents, such as the *fetvā*s of Kemālpaşazāde and Ebū's-Su'ūd.[64] The term *rāfiẓi* only appears in a short excerpt of a passage copied from the heresiographical tradition exemplified by Nawbakhtī, Ibn al-Jawzī's *Talbīs Iblīs*, 'Abd al-Qāhir al-Baghdādī's *al-Farq Bayn al-Firaq* and Shahrastāni's *Kitāb al-Milal wa al-Niḥal.* It reads as follows:

> The Prophet said, 'Just as the Tribe of Israel is comprised of seventy-two groups, my community is comprised of seventy-three groups'. One of them is the *Khārijī*s, one the *Rāfiẓiyya*, one the *Qaḍariyya*, one the *Jahmiyya*, one the *Jabriyya* and one the *Murji'a*. And each of these are comprised of twelve groups, seventy-two in total.[65]

The architecture of this passage is dictated by the famous *ḥadīth* stating that Muḥammad's community will be divided into seventy-three groups, all but one of which will be misguided – a tradition that affected the totality of Islamic heresiography by forcing writers to invent spurious sects until reaching that number. What is relevant are the six classifications: All are classical heresies following the sequences of the early heresiographers,[66] and among these the *rāfiẓī* are placed without any special salience. This sect is not presented as more relevant or contemporary than, for example, the Jabriyya, whose disavowal of human moral culpability did not exert significant influence in fifteenth-century philosophy, or the universally disdained Khārijīs, remote from Anatolia and Iran. This passing reference to the *rāfıżī*s indicates that refutation of Shī'ism was not a particular concern of the Yazıcıoğlu brothers. They spent much more time describing the psychological subtleties of unbelief; rather than historical heresies, these constitute the real sources of *kufr* and, accordingly, are more carefully classified. 'One must know that there are four kinds of unbelief', Aḥmed stated, listing the *kufr* of denial, abjuration, stubbornness and hypocrisy.[67]

In place of a sustained refutation of Shī'ism, the Yazıcıoğlus displayed residues of the fifteenth-century confessionally intermediate outlook described by Amoretti. This is most visible in two passages of the *Müntehā* and the *Muḥammediyye*, of which the more notable has already been described in Chapter 2 but deserves repeating. Under the heading of their ostensibly Jandī-style commentary on the *Fuṣūṣ al-Ḥikam*'s section on the wisdom of Adam, the Yazıcıoğlus once again inserted the *qiṣaṣ* content of *Envārü'l-'Āşıqīn*, which contains an excerpt from *Zahrat al-Riyāḍ* of al-Saqsīnī describing Adam's tour around heaven – a tour whose prime attraction was the holy personage of Fāṭima and representations of her sons Ḥasan and Ḥusayn.

> And it is transmitted in *Zahrat al-Riyāḍ* that Ja'far-i Ṣādiq said that, when Adam was living with Eve in heaven, God spoke to Gabriel and said, 'Take Adam's hand and circumambulate heaven'. So Gabriel and Adam together circumambulated heaven, until they came to a fine palace. One brick was gold, and one brick was silver, and its balconies were green emerald. There was a throne in that palace of ruby. Above that throne was a dome of light, and in the midst of that dome there was a fine figure, and there was a crown of light on its head, and two earrings in its ear, made of pearl, and around its waist a belt of light. Adam saw it and was amazed and forgot Eve's beauty. And Adam said, 'O Lord, what kind of figure is this figure?' God said, 'It is the figure of Fāṭima, and on her head is the Crown of Muḥammad Muṣṭafā, and around her waist [the belt] is 'Alī, and the two earrings are Ḥasan and Ḥusayn'.

The immediate provenance of this anecdote in al-Saqsīnī's manual of sermons is, admittedly, distant from traditional sources of Imāmī lore when it was originally recorded.[68] Yet, the idea that Fāṭima, 'Alī and their sons form a tableau at the centre of heavenly geography and, in their persons, constitute a primeval promise to Adam of mankind's eternal guidance emerges from the traditions of the Imāms, the textual basis of Shī'ī piety. We can find expressions of a similar tone in both the historical narrative and the apocalyptic section of the Yazıcıoğlus' other works as well. In Meḥmed's *Muḥammediyye*, in the context of a narrative on Ḥusayn's death at Karbalā at the hands of the Umayyads, we see him defend the practice of cursing the name of the Umayyad caliph Yazīd as something appropriate for Muslims of his time:

Yazīd, in ancient times, was not cursed,
But those of us in latter days distance ourselves [from him].
For God's Messenger cursed his family,
And cursing is appropriate because they blasphemed against God.[69]

Times have changed, he claimed, and 'those of us in latter days' have seen the value of this formerly Shī'ī practice. The remainder of the passage is filled with elements proceeding from Imāmī imagination. Meḥmed Yazıcıoğlu described how Muḥammad hoisted his grandson Ḥasan onto his shoulders, granting him *isnād* (succession). The Prophet then said,

He whom I love, then, O God, love as well!
What you deduce from this is guidance [*irşād*].
He said again that Ḥusayn is from me, and I am from Ḥusayn.
He who loves him loves God, for He loves the saints [*evṭād*].[70]

In structure these verses remind the reader of the *ḥadīth* of Ghadīr Khumm, in which the Prophet is alleged to have said: 'Of whomever I had been lord [*mawlā*], then 'Alī is his lord'.

In their remembrance of Karbalā, they demonstrated not an avowed Shī'ism, but rather their emotional attachment to the figural centres of Shī'ī piety – in other words, they very typically held to the '*ahl al-bay-tism*'[71] that pervaded the Yazıcıoğlus' entire era. In this vein, alongside Meḥmed's eulogy for Karbalā, we may consider another *maqtal* produced in the generation just preceding Yazıcı Ṣāliḥ's in his probable home of north-central Anatolia: the 1361–62 *Destān-i Maqtel-i Hüseyn* by one Ṣāẕī of Kastamonu.[72] Although far less enduring than the *Muḥammediyye*, it displays the same elements. Closer to the Yazıcıoğlus' lifetime and also produced in north-central Anatolia, the early-fifteenth-century *Maqtel-i Hüseyn* by the Mevlevi poet Yūsuf-i Meddāḥ presents a loose translation of a Persian original.[73] And, at the beginning of the following century, we may liken these two to the classic *maqtal* work *Rawḍat al-Shuhadā* by the late Timurid polymath Ḥusayn Vā'iẓ Kāshifī, written in the officially Sunnī environment of Herat – or to its revered Turkish adaptation, the *Hadīqat al-Sü'edā* by Fużūlī, himself a product of the diverse sectarian environment of the early-sixteenth-century Ottoman-Safavid border country of 'Iraq.[74] Indeed, the scenes in the drama of Ḥasan and Ḥusayn, which the Yazıcıoğlus emphasise in the *Muḥammediyye*, *Envār* and *Müntehā* are the same as those of these other *maqtals*. Among them count the descent of the angel Gabriel to Muḥammad to warn him of the future deaths of Ḥasan by poison and Ḥusayn by the sword – by bestowing upon each child a yellow and red scarf, respectively. These show that the *maqtals* are the clear ancestors and descendants of the Yazıcıoğlus' Karbalā narrative; as such, their commemoration is embedded in the contemporary currents of *ahl al-bayt*ism that stand outside Sunnī–Shī'ī frameworks. Yet, as a note of caution, it is possible to read any mention of the Prophet's family too readily as related to this tendency, when in fact such statements were more general across the Islamic world. When, for instance, in the apocalyptic section of the *Müntehā* Aḥmed Bīcān claimed that 'the Mahdī will be the offspring of Fāṭima', he shared a position common in the post-Mongol Islamic world even among the most anti-Shī'ī of Sunnī commentators.[75]

At this point it is important to mention that the Yazıcıoğlus' apparently nonchalant approach to Sunnī–Shī'ī sectarianism may not be representative of or shared by all contemporaries or predecessors in Islamic Anatolia. A. C. S. Peacock has charted the complex contours of sectarian identity in Anatolia of the thirteenth and fourteenth centuries, noting that some Anatolian scholars, as well as ordinary citizens, *did* seem to worry about exactly what kind of Muslims they and those around them were. Perhaps the best example comes from the testimony of the North African traveller Ibn Baṭṭūṭa; while visiting Sinop on the Black Sea coast in 1332, locals accused him of Shī'ism because of his Mālikī custom of praying with his hands extended downwards rather than clasped, and he was only able to reassure them of his Sunnism by eating rabbit meat, which is forbidden to Shī'ī Muslims.[76] There, at least, it appears that townspeople were wary of *rāfiḍī*s. Some popular literature also seems to project a sectarian divide. Beypazarılı Ma'azoğlu Hasan's *Cenadil Qal'esi*, a fourteenth-century epic recounting the holy wars of 'Alī ibn Abū Ṭālib, explicitly identifies 'Alī and his partisans with 'the Sunnis'.[77] Ma'azoğlu's work comprises part of a larger genre of epic poems on 'Alī's exploits, called *Cenknāme*s, most of which, as Peacock has noted, seem to refrain from expressing a genuinely Shī'ī sectarian orientation despite the subject-matter. They paint 'Alī and those close to him simply as 'Muslims' or even 'Sunnī Muslims' and his opponents as unbelievers or even Christians – a rhetorical choice that may deliberately efface the potential of the story of 'Alī ibn Abū Ṭālib to advance Shī'ī ideas.[78] In contrast, poets such as Kaygusuz Abdāl (traditionally believed to have died in 1444) revered by present-day Alevīs, and the above-mentioned Şāẕī of Kastamonu expressed a traditionally Shī'ī reverence for the Twelve Imāms and encouraged the cursing of the Umayyads, respectively.[79] Thus, while the Yazıcıoğlus in the mid-fifteenth century did not appear acutely conscious of their identity as Sunnīs *vis-à-vis* Shī'īs, this generalisation cannot be extended to the Anatolian and Rumelian Muslim environment as a whole, where occasionally one's Sunnī or Shī'ī sectarian position appeared worthy of comment.

Thus it is both in keeping with and in contrast to the spirit of their time that the Yazıcıoğlus seem disinterested in differentiating the *'ehl-i sünnet'* from an unacceptable Shīʿism, or even in articulating a form of 'Sunnī 'Alīdism', although this *ahl al-bayt*ism certainly characterised their general standpoint towards the Prophet and his family and companions. This is not an incoherent position. Lamenting Karbalā and praising the *'aşeretü'l-mübeşşire* at the same time signified, as so much else does in the Yazıcıoğlus' oeuvre, a generally ecumenical and 'omnivorous' vision of Islam that incorporated ideological elements which would be considered incompatible in centuries to come and perhaps even in other contemporaneous or prior contexts. They wrote to delineate an Islam that is unitary within itself while also distinct from Christianity and other faiths. In other words, the concept of *ümmet-i Muḥammed* overshadows and dominates that of *ehl-i sünnet*.

Apocalypticism

A final subject that must be addressed with respect to the *Müntehā* is its purported apocalypticism and its contemporary – or, alternatively, ahistorical – character. This thematic current of the Yazıcıoğlus' works should be approached with great caution. As scholars have come to recognize apocalyptic thought as a connecting tissue between religious sciences and political ideology, they have also placed themselves at risk of over-historicising apocalyptic expressions that are fundamentally formulaic in nature. For this reason, one should carefully ascertain the precise characteristics of pre-modern apocalyptic pronouncements, which may mean different things in different contexts.

Apocalyptic writing must be understood within a taxonomy of apocalypses. Norman Cohn has attempted to create one in his landmark 1957 *Pursuit of the Millennium.*[80] Cohn has charted millennarian and messianic movements across the late medieval and early modern European sphere, from the Peasants' Crusade to the Anabaptists of Münster, and represented them as the violent expressions of the lower clergy's and peasantry's resentment against the High Church and nobility. For Cohn, the essence of apocalypticism was an egalitarian critique ('mystical anarchism' or 'anarcho-communism'), and its goal was the upending of a social order headed by the clerical classes. Bernard McGinn, writing twenty years later in *Visions of the End*, has disputed this thesis, arguing that the typical medieval Christian apocalypticist was, more often than not, an elite intellectual and that their apocalypticism was 'not primarily a movement from below'.[81] Rather, apocalypses were attempts by religious scholars to 'interpret the times, to support their patrons, to console their supporters

. . .'[82] According to McGinn, apocalypticism has an oblique relationship to political or social unrest: 'It is not so much crises in itself, as any form of challenge to established understanding of history, that creates the situation in which apocalyptic forms and symbols [. . .] may be evoked'. Apocalypses must then be treated as a kind of cryptic historiography, or as contemporary commentary shrouded in the language of End Times. In in a 1968 essay on the methodological challenges of approaching apocalypse, Paul J. Alexander has advocated a similar reading of apocalypses as 'chronicles written in the future tense'.[83]

There have been several attempts to apply these theoretical insights to Islamic culture. Mohammad Masad has provided an analysis of apocalyptic thought and related occult sciences among thirteenth-century *'ulemā* figures of the Mamluk lands.[84] In his *Studies in Muslim Apocalyptic*, David Cook has presented a thorough analysis of the elements of classical Islamic apocalyptic.[85] Especially useful for this investigation is Cook's classification of Islamic apocalyptic narrative elements into four types: (a) historical, (b) metahistorical, (c) messianic and (d) moral. Historical ones are those apocalyptic traditions that describe 'recognizable historical personalities, and a historical sequence of events that leaves reality at a particular point . . .'[86] In this category Cook places apocalyptic traditions on the Muslim invasions of Christian lands and Christian counter-invasions, the cycle of apocalyptic stories centring on the Syrian valleys of A'māq and on Egypt, and apocalypses dealing with the invasion of far-eastern Turks into the Arab lands. Each of these, so Cook shows (following Alexander's methodology), emerged from specific historical moments in the first few centuries of Islam and often represented adaptations of earlier Christian and Jewish apocalyptic. Some of these cycles of historical apocalyptic, especially those classified by apocalypticists under the rubric 'Signs of the Hour' (*ashrāṭ al-sā'a*), will be discussed in greater detail below, with particular reference to the Yazıcıoğlus' writings.

Metahistorical apocalypses, by contrast, are those 'unconnected with historical events [. . . and] set in the eschatological future'.[87] These metahistorical apocalypses constitute the heart of Islamic apocalyptic, including the narrative of the appearance of the false messiah Dajjāl – usually likened to the Antichrist – and the return of Jesus to combat him, the demonic child al-Ṣayyād, the emergence of the Dābbat al-Arḍ (the Beast of the Earth) and the second false messiah al-Ṣufyānī. Since each of these narratives occur largely outside of historical time, they are developped with an eye to Qur'anic justification and thus integration with the rest of the religious sciences. Although Cook has separated messianic apocalypse from this classification, it is strongly connected with metahistorical cycles as well. The appearance of the Mahdī, who will return at the end of time, is rarely separated from a similar narrative about Jesus, with whom he will join forces, or the Dajjāl, which he will help defeat. Betraying the origins of Mahdism in the ferment of proto-Shī'ism and constituting a reworking of Johannine and Jewish apocalypse, diverse and contradictory traits are ascribed to this messianic redeemer.

Finally, Cook has identified the 'moral apocalypse' as one in which the writer laments the corruption of the present day and calls for renewed piety in preparation for the coming end. This has its textual origins in the writings of the *zāhid*s. Apocalyptic writing is thus a listing of the sins of contemporaries – avarice, sexual impropriety, hypocrisy – and an invitation to the world-renouncing virtues that reject them totally. Divine retribution is an important part of these moral apocalypses. In terms of Cook's classification, the Yazıcıoğlus wrote both historical and metahistorical apocalypse with a moral component; by focusing on one and not the other, it is easy to make the brothers into very different kinds of apocalypticist. Lurking around this discussion are the problems raised by my contention, published elsewhere, that the *Dürr-i Meknūn* is not a work by either of the Yazıcıoğlu brothers.[88] How this alters prior interpretation constitutes an issue that will be discusssed below, where relevant.

Arguments for the ahistorical quality of the Yazıcıoğlus' treatment of the End Times have rested on evidence from their metahistorical apocalyptic writings. Advancing this thesis is Laban Kaptein, whose *Apocalypse and the Antichrist Dajjāl in Islam* is a focused effort to unravel the content of the apocalyptic portions of the *Dürr-i Meknūn* (which he ascribes to Aḥmed Bīcān), supplementing this analysis with Aḥmed and Meḥmed's other writings on eschatology in the *Envāru'l-'Āşıqīn*, *Muḥammediyye* and *Müntehā*.[89] Kaptein has suggested that the apocalyptic segments of Aḥmed's works (including the *Dürr-i Meknūn*) should not be taken to represent any particular 'Doomsday fever' on the part of Ottoman or Turkish society during the fifteenth century – rather, Aḥmed's eschatological images are 'taken straight from the traditional Islamic stock, with stereotypical complaints added to them and the ubiquitous longing for the good 'ole days'. Directly disputing Cornell Fleischer, who has written about apocalyptic thought as social criticism in the Ottoman fifteenth and sixteenth century,[90] Kaptein has argued that Aḥmed Bīcān's apocalypse is a standard Islamic one; among the countless others in Islamic, Christian and Jewish literature, it demonstrates that eschatology is an integral aspect of the Abrahamic historical sense of piety. Kaptein has suggested that, if such imagery generally were to to reflect a contemporary message, one would need to 'suspect apocalyptic motives [. . .] in al-Tabari, al-Mas'udi,

Muslim, and al-Yaquti'[91] and to over-politicise any pious discussion of End Times throughout Islamic literature. Kaptein is indeed correct in insisting that apocalyptic segments similar to those in the *Dürr* and *Envār* were extremely common in Islamic letters across many centuries. That is, if apocalyptic expression was so ubiquitous, then what use is it as a tool for learning about the society that produced it?

For this reading Kaptein has interpreted the *Dürr-i Meknūn*'s and the *Envār*'s apocalyptic narrative in view of classical Islamic apocalyptic literature, especially in *tafsīr* and *ḥadīth* interpretation – a reading amenable to the metahistorical apocalyptic sections that come at the end of these works. This End Times narrative, which the *Dürr* and *Envār* largely have in common, consists of a moral apocalypse: a listing of the Signs of the Hour, chapters on the coming of Jesus, the Mahdī and the Dajjāl, the emergence of the Beast of the Earth, the sun's rising in the west, the trials and tribulations of the earth and its cities, and the Resurrection and Judgment. These are, in short, the typical metahistorical apocalyptic elements identified by Cook, which are not suitable for historicised readings. Kaptein has quite adeptly situated these metahistorical narratives within the classical apocalyptic tradition and, thus, disarmed them of any contemporary apocalyptic urgency.

Conversely, to see the Yazıcıoğlus' apocalypticism as critical commentary on contemporary events requires a privileging of their historical apocalyptic writings at the expense of their metahistorical writings. An example of this is Kaya Şahin's 'Constantinople and the End Time', which discusses components of the eschatological comments of the *Dürr-i Meknūn* (and to a lesser extent the 1465 *Müntehā*'s) in view of a purported proliferation of End Times speculation and occult prognostication surrounding Meḥmed II's Conquest of Constantinople.[92] Şahin has asserted that the *Dürr-i Meknūn*, again attributed to Aḥmed, can be fruitfully interpreted as a kind of summary of different strands of the fifteenth-century Ottoman apocalyptic discourse, and above all as a topical revival of the tradition of historical apocalyptic writing on the Muslim conquest and Christian re-conquest of the Second Rome. Şahin has argued that Aḥmed in this work expressed with utmost urgency the conquest's immediate fulfillment of historical apocalyptic prophecy.

Yet, Şahin's important contribution is rendered problematic by his assumption that Aḥmed Bīcān was the author of the *Dürr-i Meknūn*. As I have shown in 'Reconsidering the Authorship of the *Dürr-i Meknūn*',[93] the remarkable 'Hidden Pearl' in its anonymity dares to be more contemporary and political than anything written by the authentic Aḥmed Bīcān or his brother. With this misattribution Şahin has connected the sustained moral and historical apocalypticism of the *Dürr* to the person of Aḥmed Bīcān of Gelibolu. For instance, Şahin has taken the section at the end of the *Dürr*, where the author says that he has taken Bisṭāmī's *jafr* and translated it into Turkish, to imply that Aḥmed Bīcān himself endorsed Bisṭāmī's numerological style of End Times prognostication – one of the latter's notable conclusions is that one 'Maḥmūd' or 'Meḥmed' will be the sultan at the time of the final tribulations. The *Dürr* author's preoccupation with astrological-calendrical cycles ending in End Times is taken to mean that Aḥmed expected the Signs of the Hour to appear shortly, at a definite time, and in a fixed relation to the cycles of the historical apocalypse. Regrettably, while these features indeed describe the apocalyptic fervour of the *Dürr*'s author, they cannot be connected specifically to Aḥmed Bīcān. Thus, the hypothesis of Şahin's article – that is, the *Dürr*'s author is commenting on the End Times – remains intact, even if it is not Aḥmed Bīcān.

In light of these two contrasting interpretive approaches, one must then inquire as to the actual nature of Meḥmed and Aḥmed Yazıcıoğlu's apocalypticism. If Kaptein is correct to deny the historical relevance of the metahistorical cycles of the Yazıcıoğlus' eschatology, and if Şahin's comments are largely misdirected at the *Dürr*, then what is left of the Yazıcıoğlus' apocalypse? The bulk of the apocalyptic writings of the Yazıcıoğlu brothers is condensed into the final chapters of the *Muḥammediyye*, *Envār* and *Müntehā*, and they each follow similar outlines. As Kaptein has correctly argued, these apocalypses are *strictly metahistorical*. They are presented as the final episode in their chronological narrative of cosmic history, the ultimate end of the story that begins with Creation. As such, they are presented as an integral part of the religious sciences, and not as a separate political statement. In the *Müntehā*'s final pages, Aḥmed described his own metahistorical apocalypse as a companion text to the apocalyptic writings of the famous Ottoman *medrese* scholar Şemsu'd-dīn Meḥmed Fenarī:

> Meḥmed Ibnu'l-Fenarī has expressed in a concisely-styled summary the Apocalypse [*qıyāmet*], from the Gathering to Hell and Heaven to the appearance of God's visage [. . .] I too have gathered into my book the events [*aḥkam*] of the Apocalypse so that its conceptualisation be simple, so that students may understand it in a simple manner [*ṭālibler āsān vechle añlayalar*].[94]

The events that precede this summary statement are part of classical religious knowledge, extending from the Signs of the Hour to the Dajjāl, Jesus and the Beast to the Gathering, culminating in the final Resurrection and humankind being transported into God's presence in Heaven or to the torments of Hell. These very same events are found in Fenarī and many of the Yazıcıoğlus' other well-known sources, including Zamakhsharī, Baghawī, Bayḍāwī and Ghazālī. Nothing about the Yazıcıoğlus' metahistorical apocalypse stands out. One must regretfully discount the relevance of the Yazıcıoğlus' metahistorical apocalypse.

Nonetheless, a historical and contemporary apocalypse emerges. Amid this lengthy metahistorical segment in the 1453 *Müntehā*, one encounters a section on the Signs of the Hour:[95]

> The *ḥadīth* scholars have said: First the Blond People [*Beniyü'l-Aṣfer*] will come from the west in alliance with the Franks and gather eighty banners with twelve thousand people under each banner. That is to say, in total, [their numbers will be] ten times one hundred thousand minus forty thousand. To make a long story short, there is a village in Syria called A'māq, and they will go as far as it. And from Medina the soldiers of Islam will arrive in three companies and fight with the unbelievers. One company will be defeated by the unbelievers, and one will break them, and it is they who will be the finest of the martyrs, and one will defeat the unbelievers. Seventy people of the Banī Isḥāq will come to Istanbul and, saying *lā ilāha illā'l-llāh wa Allāhu akbar*, destroy it from the direction of the sea; it will again be destroyed from another side by a group saying the same thing, and again destroyed from another side. Constantinople will be plundered. Satan will come and cry out, 'The Dajjāl has arrived. He has captured your sons and daughters . . .' Then they will go back to Syria and the Dajjāl will emerge, and then the signs of the Apocalypse will begin to be made clear.[96]

We see here a primary feature of Muslim historical apocalyptic appear: the cluster of stories related to the Syrian valleys of A'māq. The A'māq cycle, as Cook has described it, is 'fundamental to the study of Muslim apocalyptic, since the basic story line is repeated in most of the major traditions'.[97] The many variations of this cycle usually involve a truce between Syrian Muslims and Romans in order to battle a third party, a breaking of that truce and subsequently a major Muslim invasion of the Byzantine Empire, which ends with the Conquest of Constantinople, the ultimate symbol of Christian political power, as revenge for the Roman destruction of Jerusalem's Second Temple. (Sometimes Rome itself is then taken by a Muslim army.)

This Conquest of Constantinople is the polemical centre of this cycle, according to Cook. In some traditions, the Bosphorus parted to let the Muslims enter 'as [it was] for Banū Isrā'īl' crossing the Red Sea. The city, 'proud and tyrannical', is described in Muslim apocalyptic, in imagery perhaps derived from those describing Babylon in the Revelation of John; the extent of the justified plunder that followed the coming Muslim sack of the city is vividly depicted. As the story continues, the Romans respond with a counter-invasion through Syria, which ends with the apocalyptic confrontation at A'māq or Dābiq. Here, the A'māq cycle usually joins with the metahistorical narratives of the Dajjāl, al-Ṣufyānī, or Gog and Magog.

Aḥmed Bīcān's rendition of the A'māq cycle attributes this Roman counter-attack to the 'Blond People', or Banū al-Aṣfar. The origins of this term are intensely disputed, and even its referent appears highly variable.[98] What is certain is that the Banū al-Aṣfar appear relatively early in Arabic apocalyptic writing, along with the rest of the A'māq cycle, and tend to refer to Romans or Byzantines. Moreover, the term's mutability allowed it to denote other groups, including Christians in general, 'Frankish' Catholics, Slavs, or even Vikings. Perhaps because of this obscurity, the motif of the Banū al-Aṣfar remained relatively minor in the Islamic apocalyptic tradition, receiving little elaboration in major texts.

In the ninth century, the image of the Blond People underwent a crucial translation when, rendered as the 'fair ones' or 'blond-bearded ones', it found its way into works descending from the Syriac Christian apocalypse of one Pseudo-Methodius, which, like the Muslim apocalypses, were probably composed in northern Syria in early caliphal times.[99] The Islamic apocalypses and Pseudo-Methodius, originating at the same time and in the same areas, are thus twins; in medieval Greek and Slavonic derivatives of the latter, appearing under the title *Visions of Daniel* and attributed to the Old Testament prophet, the Blond People are described as restive allies of the messianic 'Last Roman Emperor'. The emperor 'tames' the Blond Ones, and the two cooperate to defeat the 'Ishmaelites' (that is, Muslims or Arabs). In a massive campaign, the emperor and the Blond Ones move towards Sofia and its hinterlands, and there proceed to a sortie pursuing the Ishmaelites into 'their own country', culminating in the emperor's victorious march from the west into Constantinople, 'The City of Seven Hills'.[100] There is in this text, too, a Thracian borderland.

The *Visions* and the Muslim A'māq cycle thus share a genealogical relationship and a deep compatibility. In both the *Visions of Daniel* and the Islamic A'māq cycle, a Roman or Christian army, with or without Blond People, rolls back the successful Muslim conquest of Constantinople, marches into Syria and returns to dominate the City of Seven Hills. Christians and Muslims thus shared the same historical apocalypse. This concise demonstration of the idea that Muslim and Christian apocalyptic drew from the same lore raises a further question: Why did Aḥmed Bīcān choose, from all the available options, this motif of the Banū al-Aṣfar and Constantinople, one of the most distinctive points of overlap between the

Visions and the A'māq apocalypse, as the Sign of the Hour?

The Blond People's counter-attack on Constantinople reappears in the sole indisputably historical apocalypse in the Yazıcıoğlus' oeuvre. In Aḥmed Bīcān's 1465 version of the *Müntehā*, the author inserted a passage that once again presents the drama of the Blond People and Constantinople – but he went even further by matching it with the present of the conquest and the conqueror, Sultan Meḥmed II. Aḥmed made Sultan Meḥmed into a figure destined, by virtue of his battles against the Blond People, to be a harbinger of the End Times:

> Now: This Sultan Meḥmed Khan who is presently *pādişāh* took Galata and Sinop and Samsun and Trabzon and especially Istanbul – which he took from the unbelievers with force and sword, and within which he built fine *'imāret*s and mosques the likes of which are not to be found in the lands of the Arabs or Persia [*'Acem*]. And by the lower sea [*aşağı deñizi*, – that is, the Aegean], he took Mytilene and Bosnia and the Morea and Albania with his sword. He would obtain the poll-tax [*bāc ü ḫarāc*] from the unbelievers. The *ġāzī*s would take the poll-tax. He is the king of the *ġāzī*s and the sultan of the martyrs. For the finest of the *ġāzī*s are those who would stand against the Blond People from the West and with the sword strike them and aim for Rome and Amorium [*Rūmiyye ve 'Ammūriyye*] and the Blond People. For the End Times are near [*zīrā qıyāmet yaqīn*] [. . .] Victory over the unbelievers will come from the west. The Blond People will come from the west. And behold, it is so that Sultan Meḥmed stood against the Blond People and defended against them and repelled them. Thus, the finest of the *ġāzī*s are the offspring of 'Os̱mān [*'Os̱mān oğlanları*], who face the Blond People. May God have mercy upon them and preserve their princes until Resurrection, so that in their time Law and Truth and scriptural interpretation [*te'vīl*] be strengthened.[101]

Before we turn to the heart of the matter, a new element of this narrative requires clarificiation. *'Ammūriyye*, here paired with *Rūmiyye* (Rome or Italy), is another name closely linked to the Conquest of Constantinople in the A'māq cycle literature on the Signs of the Hour. In its original usage, according to al-Idrīsī, it referred to the Anatolian city of Amorium, a major Roman town near modern Eskişehir, until at least the eleventh century. The city's starring role in the drama of the End Times is owed to its 708 conquest by the Arab general Maslama, a conquest that was considered his most notable victory *en route* to his failed siege of Constantinople in 711. Amorium entered subsequent apocalyptic literature as one of the stages of the Muslim conquests of the period of the Signs – from Amorium to Nicaea, to Constantinople and thence to Rome.[102] It is in this sense deployed as part of a fixed apocalyptic landscape, rather than a reference to the contemporary ruins of Amorium near Eskişehir.

Far more important than Amorium is the invocation of Sultan Meḥmed, for whom this passage was written primarily as praise. Aḥmed stated that Meḥmed and his victories were the sign by which he knew that 'the End Times are near'. His *ġazā* is written into the apocalypse. Yet, from the perspective of the traditional Islamic historical apocalypse Meḥmed's role is ambiguous. For in the ordinary A'māq cycle – including Aḥmed's version in the 1453 *Müntehā*, as quoted above – the Christians or Blond People appear from the West, as a force expected to *retake* Constantinople after its first conquest by the forces of Islam. The nameless leader of the Muslims who, prior to this, takes Constantinople in a re-enaction of the eighth-century sieges, later suffers the indignity of losing the city to the coalition of Christian forces in which the Blond People lead or take part. Şahin has noted that Meḥmed feared taking on the eschatological role of this doomed ruler as he deliberated his strike against the city, only to be reassured by Aqşemse'd-dīn that the Blond Peoples' reconquest would occur in the far distant future.[103]

Yet, here Aḥmed Bīcān presented Sultan Meḥmed II as an ill-destined re-enactor of Maslama's conquests; he was not the Mahdī. He 'struck' against the Blond People but required prayer to assure that he be perpetually victorious against them. It is perhaps for this reason that Aḥmed praised Sultan Meḥmed II as merely 'the finest of the *ġāzīs*', because of his fight against the Banī al-Aṣfar – and not as messiah, Mahdī or caliph. Fatiḥ Sultan Meḥmed, by conquering the city and fighting the Banī al-Aṣfar, was the harbinger of the End Times and the legitimate master of the Muslim forces that inaugurated the Final Hour – although he is not ultimately a sacred ruler of the eschatological final age. Hence, Aḥmed's final benediction – 'May God have mercy upon their princes until Resurrection . . .' – in this sense appears to voice a small amount of trepidation rather than total confidence in any Ottoman's messianic purpose.

The Blond People, by contrast, have a more definite correspondence. In Aḥmed Bīcān's telling, they strongly appear to denote the recurring coalition of European enemies that threatened the Ottoman realms throughout the reigns of Meḥmed II and his father Murād II. The Blond People who 'come from the west' and are 'in alliance with the Franks' certainly evoke the crusading coalition of the Hungarians and Venetians and other Catholics defeated at Nicopolis in 1396, at Varna in 1444 and at Kosovo in 1448, the latter two battles so strikingly evoked by Aḥmed in his *Envār*.[104]

The identification of the Blond People with a Western coalition received unexpected corroboration in the Balkan Christian discourse on the *Visions of Daniel*. Paul Alexander has cited a thirteenth-century Serbian redaction of the *Visions*, titled *Zbornik Popa Dragolia* and perhaps representative of other redactions of the *Visions* circulating in the region; these claim that the Last Roman Emperor, as he assembles his coalition with the Blond People, will march from the West through Sofia and battle the Ishmaelites at a place called Perton, identified as one of 'two hills on one side of Serdica [Sofia]'.[105] Here, the very geography of the southern Balkans, where Murād II and Meḥmed II faced Hungarian, Vlach, Serbian, Venetian and papal troops so many times, was written into the apocalypse featuring the Blond People. This identification was current enough to make it into broader Islamic historiography as well. The chronicle of the Mamluk historian al-Sakhāwī describes the events at Varna as follows: 'On Monday, 16 Shawwal 848 [27 January 1445], news came from Murād Bey son of 'Uthmān, the so-called king of Bursa and other places in Rum, that there had been a great battle between himself and a faction of the Banū Aṣfar, and that nothing like it had been seen in this age . . .'[106] The way in which Aḥmed repeatedly made use of the phrase 'from the west' may tell of the persistent geographical polarity of these military struggles, as we also see in 'Āşıqpaşazāde's telling of the accord between King Vladislav of Hungary and Emir İbrāhīm of Karaman, which preceded the Varna campaign: '"You [Vladislav] march from the west", [İbrāhīm] said, "while I march from the east"'.[107]

One final set of End Times commentary can be found in the *Tale of the Taking of Tsargrad* by one Nestor-Iskander, a Russian claiming to have been captured by Ottomans as a youth and a witness of Constantinople's final siege. At the end of his account of Meḥmed II's conquest, Nestor-Iskander invoked the 'fair ones' (*rusii rod*), a force of messianic redeemers of the city: 'For it is written: "The fair [ones] are a race who, with former creations, will vanquish all of the Ishmaelites and will inherit Seven Hills with its former laws. The fair [ones] will rise to the throne of the Seven Hills and will hold it firmly . . ."'[108] Repeating the *Visions*' and the A'māq cycle narrative in brief, Nestor-Iskander's description of these *rusii rod* entered later Russian historiography as *ruskii rod*, 'the Russian people', in this way 'giving substance to [the Muscovite] political-religious notion of Moscow as the Third Rome'.[109] In Nestor-Iskander's account as much as in Aḥmed Bīcān's, the Banū al-Aṣfar apocalypse of the Visions and the A'māq cycle was historicised in a precise manner.

Aḥmed Bīcān's historical apocalypse is thus textually distinct – it is a grandchild of the Balkan interpretations of the *Visions*, such as the *Zbornik*, and the Islamic historical apocalypse of the A'māq cycle – while also limited in scope. The Dajjāl is not imminent, nor is the Mahdī; Sultan Meḥmed and his Conquest of Constantinople are eschatologically significant but exist in undefined relation to the metahistorical schedule of

End Times. This reinforces, rather than disputes, Şahin's illustration of a cross-border sense of apocalyptic event centred on the Conquest of Constantinople and the crusading armies of the Blond People. Because Aḥmed's apocalyptic outlook is both historical and metahistorical, one cannot characterise it any more clearly than Aḥmed did himself with the simple statement: 'The End Times are near'.

Conclusion

This heterogeneous discussion has attempted to flesh out the Yazıcıoğlus' nuanced religious sensibility by means of their most ambitious text, the two editions of Aḥmed's *Müntehā*. We find in them a series of conventional elements that together paint an idiosyncratic portrait. Aḥmed Bīcān presented an Akbarian metaphysics in the style of Jandī and Qūnawī in a certain literalising manner, in response to traditionalist criticism. He asserted his membership in the Bayramī Sufi *ṭarīqa*, while also dissociating his own heritage from contemporary Sufi *ṭarīqa*s and harkening back to a timeless ascetic piety. He consistently identified himself as a Sunnī, by bringing forth old sectarian markers, while at the same time exhibiting total disinterest in refuting the tenets of pro-'Alīdisim. And his specific sense of eschatology was marked by the fixed and theoretically inevitable schedule of a distant Judgment Day, shaded by an inchoate sense that the present was hurrying towards the End, in the portentious confrontation of Sultan Meḥmed II and the Banī al-Aṣfar of Christian Europe. Aḥmed Bīcān, author of the *Müntehā* texts, was a scholar conscious of the way in which the innovations of his era called for criticism as well as defense; likewise, he was aware of the political and social undertones of modern Sufism, desiring to preserve his own mystical practice apart from these controversies. For Aḥmed Bīcān, the idea of being Muslim trumped any other sectarian division in the borderland setting. In his tumultuous times, he somehow expected the fulfillment of the End Times prophecy – without knowing exactly what was happening.

There exists in all of this, as in so much of the Yazıcıoğlus oeuvre, an interplay between universalist (or ecumenical) dogmatics in an archaicising style, on one hand, and local, frontier-oriented tendencies, on the other. In fact, these may be two sides of the same coin. While Aḥmed's universalism is explicit in his traditionalist defense of Ibn 'Arabī, his extolling of *zuhd*, and his "Alīd Sunnism', a local particularity may also be perceived in this same aspect. That is, one must entertain the hypothesis that the universalism of the Yazıcıoğlus' Sunnī dogmatics was a specific necessity for the borderland Ottoman setting, a kind of 'pan-Islamic' ideology that was at home only there, on Islam's edges. By presenting Islam, with all of its legalist and mystical approaches, as a unified totality and effacing its internal divisions, it became the creed of a new political – and more importantly, social – order on the Ottoman frontiers. From a distinct combination between innovation concerning the dogma of the central Islamic lands and reaction against the chaos of the borderlands, an Ottoman epistemology was born.

Notes

1. *KM870a*, fol. 3a.
2. Both of these characterisations are cited in Michel Chodkiewicz, 'The Diffusion of Ibn 'Arabī's Doctrine', *Journal of the Muhyiddin Ibn 'Arabi Society*, no. 9 (1991), p. 36.
3. Cited in R. W. J. Austin, *The Bezels of Wisdom* (New York: Paulist Press, 1980), p. 20. See also Caner K. Dağlı, *The Ringstones of Wisdom: Fuṣūṣ al-Ḥikam* (Chicago: Great Books of the Islamic World, distributed by Kazi Publications, 2004), for a more recent and equally scrupulous translation of the work.
4. *KM870A*, fols 1b–2a; *KM857*, fols 1b–2a.
5. Dağlı, *The Ringstones of Wisdom*, p. 59.
6. Ibid. p. 5.
7. Ibid. p. 6.
8. William C. Chittick, *Faith and Practice of Islam: Three Thirteenth Century Sufi Texts* (Albany: State University of New York Press, 1992), p. 48. Chittick's work is generally the most comprehensive English-language introduction to the thought of Ibn 'Arabī. See William C. Chittick, *The Sufi Path of Knowledge: Ibn Al-'Arabi's Metaphysics of Imagination* (Albany: State University of New York Press, 1989). Other important studies framing modern scholarship on Ibn 'Arabī are the works of Henry Corbin, especially *Alone with the Alone: Creative Imagination in the Sūfism of Ibn 'Arabī* (Princeton: Princeton University Press, 1998), as well as Toshihiko Izutsu, especially *Sufism and Taoism: A Study of Key Philosophical Concepts* (Berkeley: University of California Press, 2016). Equally vital to the field is the masterful biography by Claude Addas, *Quest for the Red Sulphur: The Life of Ibn 'Arabī* (Cambridge: Islamic Texts Society, 1993), and the remarkable work of Michel Chodkiewicz, especially *Seal of the Saints: Prophethood and Sainthood in the Doctrine of Ibn `Arabi* (Cambridge: Islamic Texts Society, 1993). All of these scholars, to one extent or another, have used Ibn 'Arabī as a vocabulary through which to navigate their own philosophical explorations; this only enhances their value.
9. Richard Todd, *The Sufi Doctrine of Man: Ṣadr Al-Dīn Al-Qūnawī's Metaphysical Anthropology* (Leiden: Brill, 2014), is a perceptive new

approach to Qūnawī, which assesses him as an independent philosopher in his own right.

10. For Chittick's work on the relationship between Qūnawī and his master, see William C. Chittick, 'Sadr Al-Din Qunawi on the Oneness of Being', *International Philosophical Quarterly* 21, no. 2 (1981), pp. 171–84; William C. Chittick, 'The Last Will and Testament of Ibn ᶜArabi's Foremost Disciple and Some Notes on Its Author', *Sophia Perennis* 4 (1978), pp. 43–58; William C. Chittick, 'Ṣadr Al-Dīn Muḥammad B. Isḥāḳ B. Muḥammad B. Yūnus Al-Ḳūnawī', *Encyclopaedia of Islam, Second Edition.*
11. Quoted in Todd, *The Sufi Doctrine of Man*, p. 25.
12. Mehmet Bayraktar, 'Dâvûd-i Kayserî', *İslam Ansiklopedisi.*
13. Seyyed Hossein Nasr, 'Theoretical Gnosis and Doctrinal Sufism and Their Significance Today', *Transcendent Philosophy* 6 (2005), p. 5.
14. Alexandra Whelan Dunietz, 'Qadi Ḥusayn Maybudi of Yazd: Representative of the Iranian Provincial Elite in the Late Fifteenth Century' (unpublished doctoral dissertation, University of Chicago, 1990), pp. 53, 136–39. This has since been published as: Alexandra Whelan Dunietz, *The Cosmic Perils of Qadi Ḥusayn Maybudi in Fifteenth-Century Iran* (Boston; Leiden: Brill, 2016).
15. Side Emre, *İbrahim-i Gülşeni (Ca 1442–1534): Itinerant Saint and Cairene Ruler* (unpublished doctoral dissertation, University of Chicago, 2009), pp. 140–43. This has since been published as: Side Emre, *Ibrahim-i Gulshani and the Khalwati-Gulshani Order: Power Brokers in Ottoman Egypt* (Leiden: Brill, 2017).
16. Woods, *The Aqquyunlu*, describes the context of the late Aqquyunlu period and its political-theological debates.
17. Melvin-Koushki, 'The Quest for a Universal Science'. See also Binbaş, *Intellectual Networks in Timurid Iran*, pp. 140–49.
18. Hamid Algar, 'Muhammad Parsa', *İslam Ansiklopedisi.*
19. Hamid Algar, 'The Naqshbandī Order: A Preliminary Survey of Its History and Significance', *Studia Islamica* 44 (1976), p. 144; Hamid Algar, 'Reflections of Ibn 'Arabi in Early Naqshbandî Tradition', *Journal of the Muhyiddin Ibn 'Arabi Society* 10 (1991), pp. 45–57.
20. Nūr-ad-Dīn 'Abd-ar-Raḥmān Ibn-Aḥmad Jāmī, *Naqd an-nuṣūṣ fī šarḥ naqš al-fuṣūṣ*, ed. William C Chittick (Tihrān: [n. p.], 1977); Jami's intellectual commitment to *waḥdat al-wujūd* has been discussed at length in Ertuğrul Ökten, 'Jami (817–898/1414–1492): His Biography and Intellectual Influence in Herat' (unpublished doctoral dissertation, University of Chicago, 2007).
21. Ökten, 'Jami (817–898/1414–1492)', p. 307.
22. Algar, 'Reflections of Ibn 'Arabi in Early Naqshbandî Tradition'.
23. Alexander D. Knysh, *Ibn Arabi in the Later Islamic Tradition: The Making of a Polemical Image in Medieval Islam* (Albany: State University of New York Press, 1999).

24. Katharina Anna Ivanyi, 'Virtue, Piety, and the Law', pp. 81–82, disputes the implied influence of Ibn Ṭaymiyya on the thought of Birgivi Meḥmed, a sixteenth-century Ottoman pietist. In doing so she finds no evidence that the former was read in the Ottoman sixteenth century or earlier.
25. The following discussion of Taftazānī's refutation of the *Fuṣūṣ* is based on Knysh, *Ibn Arabi in the Later Islamic Tradition*, pp. 143–58.
26. Ibid. p. 157.
27. *KM870A*, fols 1b–2b.
28. *KM857*, fols 2a–3b.
29. Aqşemse'd-dīn wrote to a similar effect in *al-Risālat al-Nūriyya*. Distinguishing some kinds of *wujūdī* from others, he stated that the heretical ones failed to distinguish Creation from Creator, saying that 'God is omnipresent like Nature' and that the '*mulḥid*s' among them, whom he called 'monists' (*ittiḥādīler*), pantheistically identified themselves with God. The proper *muḥaqqiq*s – whom he called the 'Sufis' – are those who asserted God's independent existence and Creation as an emanation ('shadow') of it within His domain. In other words, those who properly understand the Unity of Existence grasp how divine transcendence is preserved through emanation from an unknowable centre. Yurd, *Fatih Sultan Meḥmed Hanın Hocası, Şeyh Akşemseddin*, p. 78.
30. *KM857*, fol. 2a.
31. *KM857*, fol. 3a.
32. *KM857*, fol. 10a.
33. The critics' argument, in this instance, is that the immutable essences constrain God's creative power to those already existing essences.
34. See Todd, *The Sufi Doctrine of Man*, p. 98, for a summary of Qūnawī's theology of Presences.
35. *KM857*, fol. 8a.
36. Th. Emil Homerin, 'Ibn Taimiya's *Al-Sufiyah wa'l-Fuqara*', *Arabica* 32 (1985), pp. 219–44.
37. Ibid. p. 236.
38. This *ḥadīth* was probably learned from al-Ghazali's *Mishkāt al-Anwār*, his famous commentary on the Qur'an's 'Light Verse' (24:35), in which the author uses it to defend the value of esoteric knowledge. See Al-Ghazali, trans. David Buchman, *The Niche of Lights = Mishkat al-anwar* (Provo: Brigham Young University Press, 1998), p. 2.
39. These words attributed to 'Alī are a clear expression of the idea, dominant in Islamic philosophical piety since Avicenna, that being precedes form.
40. *KM857*, fols 8b–9a.
41. Qur'an 21:22.
42. In Aḥmed Bīcān's thought, this is a consistent distinction. For instance, he wrote in the *Envār*: 'The exotericists [*ehl-i ẓāhir*] say that for God to love one of his servants is a metaphor, an expression for God's mercy. And for a servant to love God is an expression of worship. But the verifiers [*ahl-i*

taḥqīq] say that for God to love his servant is to be close to Him, and to purify esoteric nature [*bāṭin*] instead of loving the world, and to remove the veil from the heart. For the servant to love God is to incline towards this perfection'.

43. Yurd, *Fatih Sultan Meḥmed Hanın Hocası, Şeyh Akşemseddin*, pp. 32–33.
44. *KM857*, fols 40a–42a.
45. Mehmed Emirzade, 'Majmu'a 1694–1716', Houghton Library, Harvard University, MS Arab 292. I thank Nir Shafir for bringing this manuscript to my attention and for providing access.
46. Compare *KM857*, fols 77b–79a to 'Abd al-Razzaq al-Qashani, trans. Nabil Safwat and David Pendlebury, *A Glossary of Sufi Technical Terms* (London: Octagon Press, 1984).
47. *KM857*, fols 80a–80b.
48. Farīd al-Dīn 'Aṭṭār, *Farid Ad-Din 'Attār's Memorial of God's Friends: Lives and Sayings of Sufis*, trans. and ed. Paul E. Losensky (New York: Paulist Press, 2009).
49. *KM857*, fols 96a–96b.
50. *KM857*, fols 96b–100b.
51. Ahmet Karamustafa, *Sufism: The Formative Period* (Berkeley: University of California Press, 2007). On the Malāmatiyya, see pp. 48–51. 'The encounter of Iraq Sufism with Malāmatiyya led to a merger of the two in which Sufism [. . .] emerged as the dominant party' (p. 173).
52. The latter-day Melāmī order, an outgrowth of the Bayramī community, was one of the Ottoman Empire's most successful Sufi groups. For an overview of its history, see Nathalie Clayer, Alexandre Popović and Thierry Zarcone, *Melâmis-Bayrâmis: Études sur trois mouvements mystiques musulmans* (Istanbul: Les Editions Isis, 1998). One of its key texts has been published as Erünsal, *XV-XVI. Asır Bayrâmî-Melâmîliği'nin Kaynaklarından Abdurrahman El-Askerî'nin Mir'âtü'l-ışk'ı*; an older study on the Ottoman Melāmīs is Gölpinarli, *Melâmîlik ve Melâmîler*.
53. *KM857*, fols 80b–88b.
54. Marijan Molé, 'Les Kubrawiya Entre Sunnisme et Shi'isme', *Revue Des Etudes Islamiques* 29 (1961), pp. 61–142, and 'Profession de foi de deux Kubrawis: 'Alī Hamadānī et Muhammad Nūrbakhsh', *Bulletin d'études Orientales* 17 (1962–61), pp. 133–204. For the order's later developments, see Devin DeWeese, 'The Eclipse of the Kubravīyah in Central Asia', *Iranian Studies* 21, no. 1/2 (1988), pp. 45–83.
55. Classic works on this subject are Adel Allouche, *The Origins and Development of the Ottoman-Safavid Conflict (906–962/1500–1555)* (Berlin: K. Schwarz Verlag, 1983), and Michel M. Mazzaoui, *The Origins of the Ṣafawids; Šī'ism, Ṣūfism, and the Ġulāt* (Wiesbaden: F. Steiner, 1972).
56. See, for instance, Jean Calmard, 'Les Rituels Shiite et le Pouvoir: L'imposition du Shiism Safavide, eulogies et maledictions canoniques',

in *Études Safavides*, ed. J. Calmard (Paris-Tehran: Institut Français de Recherche en Iran, 1993), p. 113.

57. V. Minorsky, 'Jihān-Shāh Qara-Qoyunlu and His Poetry (Turkmenica, 9)', *Bulletin of the School of Oriental and African Studies, University of London* 16, no. 2 (1954), pp. 271–97.
58. Amoretti, 'Religion in the Timurid and Safavid Periods'.
59. The history of the early Bektaşis has been well-studied, but still remains somewhat mysterious. See Suraiya Faroqhi, *Der Bektaschi-Orden in Anatolien: Vom späten fünfzehnten Jahrhundert bis 1826* (Vienna: Verlag des Institutes fur Orientalistik der Universitat Wien, 1981); the classic (although now somewhat dated) history is John K. Birge, *The Bektashi Order of Dervishes* (London: Luzac, 1994); see also Zeynep Yürekli, *Architecture and Hagiography in the Ottoman Empire the Politics of Bektashi Shrines in the Classical Age* (Farnham; Burlington: Ashgate, 2012), a recent monograph on Bektaşi shrines containing a useful introduction to the sect, as well as the works of Irène Beldiceanu-Steinherr. For a different perspective on the Bektaşis, particularly their material rivalry with other Sufi groups, see Judith Pfeiffer, 'Mevlevi-Bektashi Rivalries and the Islamisation of Public Space in Late Seljuq Anatolia', in *Islam and Christianity in Medieval Anatolia*, ed. A. C. S. Peacock, Bruno de Nicola and Sara Nur Yıldız (Burlington: Ashgate, 2015), pp. 309–27.
60. Overviews of these aspects of Anatolian Turkish society are given in Ocak, *Zındıklar ve Mülhidler*, and Karamustafa, *God's Unruly Friends*. For the forms of Shīʻism native to eastern and central Anatolia and north Syria, see the ongoing work of Rıza Yıldırım and Stefan Winter, especially Rıza Yıldırım, 'Turcomans Between Two Empires' (unpublished doctoral dissertation, Bilkent University, 2008).
61. *KM857*, fol. 112b.
62. *KM857*, fol. 73a.
63. *KM857*, fol. 111b.
64. For Ebū's-Suʻūd's *fetvā* condemning the doctrines of the Safavid revolutionaries, see Mehmet Ertuğrul Düzdağ, *Kanunî Devri Şeyhülislâmı Ebussuud Efendi Fetvaları* (İstanbul: Kapı Yayınları, 2012), p. 89.
65. *EA*, fol. 259a.
66. Compare with Muḥammad ibn ʻAbd al-Karīm Shahrastānī, *Muslim Sects and Divisions: The Section on Muslim Sects in Kitāb al-Milal wa'l-Niḥal*, trans. A. K. Kazi and J. G. Flynn (London: Kegan Paul International, 1984).
67. *EA*, fols 259a–259b.
68. This narration is mentioned in Mohammad Ali Amir-Moezzi, *The Divine Guide to Early Shi'ism*, p. 30, where it is sourced in Ibn Bābūya and several other Shīʻī traditionists, in each attributed to the sixth Shīʻī Imām.
69. Çelebioğlu, *Muhammediye*, p. 433.
70. Ibid. p. 434–35.
71. This term was first proposed by R. D. McChesney in *The Waqf in Central*

Asia (Princeton: Princeton University Press, 1991), p. 33, and has acquired wide currency since.
72. Şeyma Güngör, 'Maktel-i Hüseyin', *İslam Ansiklopedisi.*
73. See Kenan Özçelik, 'Yusuf-i Meddah ve *Maktel-i Hüseyn*: İnceleme-Metin-Sözlük' (unpublished MA thesis, Ankara Üniversitesi, 2008), for a transcription and critical examination of this text. A close comparison between Yūsuf's *maqtel* and the *Muḥammediyye* may yield evidence of a direct textual relationship. Yūsuf's more famous romance, *Varqa ve Gülşah*, has been explored in İsmail Hikmet Ertaylan, *Türk Edebiyatı Örnekleri: Varaka ve Gülşâh* (İstanbul: İstanbul Üniversitesi, 1945), and in Grace Martin Smith, *Varqa ve Gülşâh: A Fourteenth Century Anatolian Turkish Mesnevi (Translation, Glossary and Introduction)* (Leiden: Brill, 1976).
74. For a study of Fużūlī and his sources, see Hamide Demirel, *The Poet Fuzûli: His Works, Study of His Turkish, Persian and Arabic Divans* (Ankara: Ministry of Culture, 1991).
75. See Wilfred Madelung, 'al-Mahdī', *Encyclopaedia of Islam, Second Edition.*
76. Peacock, *Islam, Literature and Society in Mongol Anatolia*, pp. 2–3.
77. Ibid. pp. 213–15.
78. Ibid. pp. 204, 214.
79. Ibid. pp. 210–11. For more on Kaygusuz Abdal, see Uslu, 'The Şathiyye of Yunus Emre and Kaygusuz Abdal', as well as Ahmet T. Karamustafa, 'Kaygusuz Abdal: A Medieval Turkish Saint and the Formation of Vernacular Islam in Anatolia', in *Unity in Diversity: Mysticism, Messianism and the Construction of Religious Authority in Islam*, ed. Orkhan Mir-Kasimov (Leiden: Brill, 2014), pp. 329–42.
80. Norman Rufus Colin Cohn, *The Pursuit of the Millennium* (London: Secker & Warburg, 1957).
81. Bernard McGinn, *Visions of the End: Apocalyptic Traditions in the Middle Ages* (New York: Columbia University Press, 1979).
82. Ibid. p. 32.
83. Paul J. Alexander, 'Medieval Apocalypses as Historical Sources', *The American Historical Review* 73, no. 4 (1968).
84. Mohammad Ahmad Masad, 'The Medieval Islamic Apocalyptic Tradition: Divination, Prophecy and the End of Time in the 13th Century Eastern Mediterranean' (unpublished doctoral dissertation, Washington University, St. Louis, 2008).
85. David Cook, *Studies in Muslim Apocalyptic* (Princeton: Darwin Press, 2002).
86. Ibid. p. 34.
87. Ibid. p. 92.
88. Grenier, 'Reassessing the Authorship of the *Dürr-i Meknūn*'.
89. Kaptein, *Apocalypse and the Antichrist Dajjal in Islam.*
90. See especially Cornell H. Fleischer, 'The Lawgiver as Messiah: The Making of the Imperial Image in the Reign of Süleyman', in *Soliman Le*

Magnifique et Son Temps: Actes Du Colloque de Paris, Galeries Nationales Du Grand Palais, 7–10 Mars 1990, Rencontres de l'Ecole Du Louvre (Paris: Documentation française, 1992), pp. 159–77, and Cornell Fleischer, 'Seer to the Sultan', in *Cultural Horizons: A Festschrift in Honor of Talat S. Halman*, ed. Jayne L. Warner (Syracuse: Syracuse University Press; Yapı Kredi Yayınları, 2001), pp. 290–99.

91. Kaptein, *Apocalypse and the Antichrist Dajjal in Islam*, p. 53.
92. Kaya Şahin, 'Constantinople and the End Time'.
93. Grenier, 'Reassessing the Authorship of the *Dürr-i Meknun'*.
94. *KM857*, fol. 115b.
95. *KM857*, fols 102b–103a.
96. The *Muḥammediyye* versifies this. See Çelebioğlu, *Muhammediye* II, pp. 314–15:

> When the Blond People are broken in A'māq,
> The armies of Medina will rend and consume them.
> Seventy thousand of the Bani Isḥāq reach that city
> that we call Constantinople . . .
> With sword and arrow they are undefeated,
> But they are destroyed only by reciting [God's name]
> They are entirely undone.
> And in the end they recite *Allāhü ekber.*
> They will be defeated by one side from the sea
> And do the same from the other side
> And from one more side they will be defeated.
> The third time they recite God's name
> And the city is completely opened [to the armies of Muslims].
> Hear of the plunder, how it was.
> The Dajjāl's voice will be heard.
> Those who plundered will return
> And go back to the land of Syria.
> The historians have said this,
> And it is told in the prophetic histories
> That from the time when Constantinople is taken . . .
> it will be six years until the coming of the Blond People, doubtless,
> And in the seventh year will come the Dajjāl . . .

97. Cook, *Studies in Muslim Apocalyptic*, p. 49.
98. For a view of the range of interpretations of the 'Blond People', see Maribel Fierro, 'Al-Aṣfar', *Studia Islamica*, no. 77 (1993), pp. 169–81, and G. Levi Della Vida, 'The "Bronze Era" in Moslem Spain', *Journal of the American Oriental Society* 63, no. 3 (1943), pp. 183–91; see also Cook, *Studies in Muslim Apocalyptic*; Ignaz Goldziher, 'Aṣfar', *Encyclopaedia of Islam, Second Edition.*
99. See Paul Julius Alexander, *The Byzantine Apocalyptic Tradition* (Berkeley: University of California Press, 1985), for a discussion of the origins of this text, along with a translation.

100. Ibid. pp. 71–73.
101. *KM870A*, fols 2b–3a.
102. Cook, *Studies in Muslim Apocalyptic*, p. 58.
103. Şahin, 'Constantinople and the End Time', p. 326.
104. *EA*, fols 396a–396b.
105. Alexander, *The Byzantine Apocalyptic Tradition*, p. 69. The *Visions*' tale of the Last Roman Emperor who redeems the City from the Ishmaelites may also bear some relation to Sultan Meḥmed's revived claims to be the 'Caesar of Rome'.
106. Imber, *The Crusade of Varna*, p. 187.
107. Aşıkpaşazade, *Tevarih-i Âl-i Osman'dan Aşıkpaşazade Tarihi*, p. 144.
108. Nestor-Iskander, *The Tale of Constantinople: Of its Origin and Capture by the Turks in the Year 1453*, trans. Walter K. Hanak and Marios Philippides (New Rochelle: A. D. Caratzas, 1998), p. 195.
109. Ibid. pp. 19, 136–37.

Chapter 5

Wonder and Cosmos at the Edge of the World

In 1466, Aḥmed Yazıcıoğlu composed one of his last known works, the *Cevhāhīrnāme* ('Jewel-book'). It is a thirty-seven line poem on the magical properties of gemstones and metals, in its style and subject evoking an ancient discourse on talisman-making at the intersection of practical magic and natural philosophy, which since the time of al-Bīrūnī had passed in and out of textual and oral tradition for centuries.[1] It opens:

> He who dives for the pearl of meaning is wise.
> Exalted God's presence created
> for man's sake jewels of great value.
> In each one God with his power placed
> specific natures, remedies for affliction.
> This discourse from the mouth of Aḥmed Bīcān
> comes from the prophet Solomon . . .[2]

Amidst a certain atmosphere of Solomonic and Alexandrine legend, these opening lines call to mind the image of Creation as a directional act in which God imbued the matter and form of the cosmos with essences, for the humans' special use. In the subsequent lines listing jewels and their talismanic benefits, one sees a classification of the objects of the natural world along the axis between the humans and the Creator.[3]

A generation earlier, Aḥmed Bīcān's father Yazıcı Ṣāliḥ had been employed as a scribe in the same region. At that time, Gelibolu had been even more definitively located at the world's edge, and Ṣāliḥ had accompanied his warlord patrons on campaign through the forests of the southern Balkans. In his complex poem on meterological and astrological omens, titled the *Şemsiyye* ('Solar [poem]'), Ṣāliḥ described how the variety of the physical cosmos is continually dependent on the gift of divine grace: 'All of the animals, the fish in the sea, man and beasts, and the monstrous folk, all of living creatures, the birds flying in the sky, the reptiles under the earth [. . .] all of the world, the various jinn and angels and man – all these can never do without the tiniest grain of Your forgiveness'.[4] These words convey the sense that the existence, sustenance and differentiation of the physical world is a continuous divine expression. These and related questions preoccupied Ṣāliḥ and his sons for half a century, because in 1466 the now aged Aḥmed Bīcān – 'white of hair, dark of face' – put his pen to rest on the *Būstānu'l-Ḥaqāiq* ('The Garden of Realities'), a prose edition of his father's *Şemsiyye*.

These two astrological texts, the first and last works of the three scholars of Gelibolu, book-end two more natural-philosophical writings of Aḥmed Bīcān. One is the undated *Rūḥu'l-Ervāḥ* ('The Spirit of Spirits') – this compact distillation of a Sufi philosophy of man based on the Andalusian mystic philosopher Ibn 'Arabī's doctrine of *al-insān al-kāmil* ('the Perfect Man') posits that the cosmos is fundamentally ordered by man within it. The second is by far the more substantive: In 1453 Aḥmed Bīcān completed an abridged Turkish edition of the thirteenth-century Arabic cosmological masterwork by the philosopher Abū Zakariyā al-Qazwīnī, *'Ajā'ib al-Makhlūqāt wa Gharā'ib al-Mawjūdāt* ('The Wonders of Creation and the Oddities of Existing Things'), which aims to take its readers on a journey around the cosmos, from the heavenly spheres to the terrestrial climes, from the majesty of the angels to the habits of insects, each inspiring their own sort of wonder (*'ajab*). Altogether, Ṣāliḥ's *Şemsiyye*, along with his son Aḥmed's works – the *Rūḥ*, *'Acāib*, *Būstān* and *Cevhāhīrnāme* – arguably comprises the most vital body of popular natural-philosophical writings produced in Ottoman Turkish in the fifteenth century.

This raises the question as to what connects all these works – in other words, what motivated this strong cross-generational interest in the structure of nature? Could these non-elite writers at the edge of what was for them the civilised world be said to have a coherent 'philosophy of nature'? If what they wrote was science, then how did they imagine the science of the physical cosmos? There are several ways of addressing this. One is to search for their writings' common epistemological foundation, in reason or revelation, esotericism or externalist legalism, *kalām* or philosophy, Sufi vision or empirical observation. The validity of this approach rests on the presupposition that, despite the different outward concerns of their works, they are unified as a single project under a shared theory of knowledge.

A second way to connect these natural-philosophical investigations is in view of the *questions* posed by the projects themselves. One must ask what it was that Aḥmed Bīcān, the person, was trying to learn or solve when he approached the variety of the cosmos. To consider this issue is to wonder as to what extent the *'Acāib*, *Rūḥu'l-Ervāḥ* and *Būstān* betray common concerns and develop towards their own resolutions, with inquiries rather than answers representing Bīcān's own mentality. The result of this kind of investigation will not be a definitive metaphysical system, but rather a sort of existential problematic that can perhaps be historicised. In the following exploratory, tentative and incomplete search for something uniting Aḥmed Bīcān's natural philosophy, I have found that the second approach is the only possible one. Contrary to my hope, it appears difficult to admit that all the works under discussion fall within a single philosophical rubric – neither was Aḥmed Bīcān a scholar interested in building systematic consistency out of their heterogeneity.

Instead, Aḥmed Bīcān clearly demonstrates in these works a persistent concern with the position of man in the cosmos and, as a result, a profound eclecticism as to the sources of knowledge brought to bear on this problem. Through an opportunistic rather than systematic approach to his sources of knowledge, he sought to discover the human subject in a natural universe of overwhelming complexity. Like the mystical systems outlined in Chapter 4, Aḥmed Bīcān's panorama of nature, irrespective of specifics, integrates his new Muslim reader (and himself) into an ethical realm one step beyond dogma and ritual. In his three texts on nature, human moral sensibility becomes a focal point for navigating against the firmament of stars and the panorama of lands and phenomena. In the *'Acāibü'l-Maḫlūqāt*, Aḥmed Bīcān, confronted with Qazwīnī's mass of wondrous tales, reformed his encyclopedic source into a text offering lessons on ethics and pietism together with a world-tour; the *Rūḥu'l-Ervāḥ* dwells especially on the way in which human psychological features are macrocosmically projected on the universe, implying also that human moral consciousness is the orienting pole of cosmic order; the *Şemsiyye* and the *Būstān* can be seen as attempts to establish human priorities and a realm for human action against the secret of time.

Throughout all these investigations into the natural world runs like a thread an impulse to bring a humane order to his disorientation resulting from an environment of political uncertainty. In an insightful article, Gottfried Hagen has recently argued for historicising the fifteenth-century Turkish hagiographic and heroic literary tradition against its backdrop of social chaos.[5] This heroic figure, strengthened by the challenges he transcends with his exploits, becomes the hub from which the spokes of the world's moral order extends. The humanity of the saint, as well as of the pious man, unites the Muslims at the edges of the *dār al-islām* in a shared subjecthood.

The following section proposes to address the three sets of Aḥmed

Bīcān's natural-philosophical writings with these considerations in mind.

Wonder and Ethics in the 'Acāibü'l-Maḫlūqāt

In mid- or late 1453, just after the Conquest of Constantinople, Aḥmed Bīcān of Gelibolu completed a highly abridged Turkish edition of Abū Zakariyā Qazwīnī's thirteenth-century Arabic natural history *'Ajā'ib al-Makhlūqāt wa Gharā'ib al-Mawjūdāt* ('The Wonders of Creation and the Oddities of Existing Things'). Qazwīnī's work is a vivid tour of the cosmos, from the most to the least exalted of things, directed by the idea of *'ajab*, or 'wonder'. In choosing to translate the *'Ajā'ib* and abridge it (by two thirds), Aḥmed Bīcān could not have opted for a broader canvas upon which to sketch the outlines of his own approach to the variety of the natural cosmos. It is in the *'Acāib* that Aḥmed Bīcān formulated his most complete vision of the natural world and is most forthright about his own philosophical commitments. In what follows, I will try to show that Aḥmed Bīcān's *'Acāibü'l-Maḫlūqāt* departs from its thirteenth-century mode – and thereby expresses its particular local, Ottoman and frontier character – when it turns the original into a pious, Sufi and ethically-focused text.

Here one enjoys the luxury of a rich secondary literature on the *'Ajā'ib al-Makhlūqāt*, a text copied and modified from Qazwīnī's original in countless variations throughout the centuries, to the extent that it almost comprises a genre in itself. The *'Ajā'ib* has usually been understood as the most famous Islamic example of 'wonder literature' inherited from the classical *mirabilia* tradition that weaves together popular geography, folk tales, bestiaries of Plinean races and narratives from epics and romances such as the Alexander cycle. In this context, the term *'ajab* denotes these works' entertaining or unbelievable qualities, characteristics that have made some scholars label the *'Ajā'ib* 'medieval science fiction' or liken it to oral story cycles such as *Sindbad* or *One Thousand and One Nights*.[6] Recently, this has been challenged in the context of a growing scholarly interest in Arabic encyclopedism, by Elias Muhanna and others. Syrinx von Hees, who has written extensively on Qazwīnī,[7] departs from the fixation on the fantastic, unbelievable and unscientific that had adhered to the genre label of *'Ajā'ib*, arguing that scholars who have analysed the tradition from this perspective are incoherent.[8] Against earlier generations of *'Ajā'ib* scholars as well as theorists of wonder such as Tzvetan Todorov,[9] von Hees has called Qazwīnī's work – because of its systematic organisation, brevity, didacticism, accessibility and concern with scholarly justification – a 'full-fledged encyclopedia in medieval terms'.[10] Rather than a collection of wondrous, unbelievable stories, it is 'a highly scholarly text, measured according to the standards of medieval natural history'.[11] Furthermore, von Hees has asserted that, in keeping with the didactic aims of the encyclopedia genre, Qazwīnī's scientific systematicity served a program of personal edification wherein the astonishment or wonder of approaching nature through observation 'is seen as stimulating research and ultimately involving the knowledge of God'.[12] For Qazwīnī, she has argued, wonderment at nature 'embodies the beginning of the inquiring search that ultimately leads to the cognition of God [. . .] astonishment is the driving force for an alert mind and a living faith'. She has noted that al-Ghāzalī used the term in a similar sense: 'The way to the knowledge of God [. . .] is through observing his creations and contemplating the wonders of His works'.[13]

The art historian Persis Berlekamp has taken these insights into a novel direction in her recent landmark study on *'Ajā'ib* illustrated manuscripts.[14] While accepting the viability of the wonders-of-creation as a genre, she has used the visual dimension of these manuscripts to investigate the relationship of the *'Ajā'ib* to its evolving readership. Berlekamp places great importance on the fact that Qazwīnī, in Iraq, was part of a circle of scholars working in the philosophical tradition of Ibn Sīnā, specifically under the renowned scholar Athīr ad-dīn al-Abharī. An *isnād* consisting of five links from Ibn Sīnā circulated among this community, certifying the transmission of Ibn Sīnā's philosophical knowledge. Qazwīnī's *'Ajā'ib al-Makhlūqāt* must then be understood as a text grounded in Avicennan metaphysics and motivated by a desire to guide the reader in the process of learning about the world consistent with Ibn Sīnā's framework.

For Berlekamp, the key feature of Ibn Sīnā's cosmology as it relates to Qazwīnī's *'Ajā'ib* is an emanationist model of creation in which the world is instantiated and sustained as a Neoplatonic gradient from the heart of God. She has argued that this is visible first in the *'Ajā'ib*'s structure, which moves from celestial objects located nearest to God, to terrestrial ones further away, with these two categories in turn classified by their qualities. Wonder, in this Avicennan scheme, is a form of human participation in the outward radiation of God's sustaining power, a power that inspires one to investigate the causes and effects of things closer and farther from God and thus to ascertain their place within the order of created things. The wondrous things of the world make up an ordered cosmos, and the reader, by feeling wonder about them, inserts himself in a dynamic position within it.

Berlekamp's integration of Ibn Sīnā into our understanding of the

'Ajā'ib provides an excellent starting point for assessing Aḥmed Bīcān's abridged Turkish *'Acāib* of 1453. Meanwhile, it is also important to note that Aḥmed's work followed everal earlier Turkish Anatolian texts of this kind. Günay Kut has found that one 'Alī b. 'Abdu'r-raḥmān composed a text of the same title, apparently derived from the history of al-Ṭabarī and other sources. Another Turkish *'Acāib* was written by Rükne'd-dīn Aḥmed between 1413 and 1421 for Sultan Meḥmed I, also containing substantial material extraneous to Qazwīnī, especially legends about Constantinople of a more local provenance.[15] As these texts have not been studied, any statements about them remain speculative. Aḥmed's *'Acāib* from 1453 followed these as a 'free and abridged' translation of Qazwīnī and, in turn, was followed by a series of further Turkish *'Acāibs*, in a tradition that persisted until at least the eighteenth century.[16]

I suggest that Aḥmed's *'Acāib* is indeed a reflection of an Avicennan emanationist naturalism, and even more than that: His Turkish *'Acāib* is a repository of nature knowledge circulating in the early Ottoman lands, which is suffused with a pietist sensibility alien to the original. Aḥmed Bīcān transformed Qazwīnī's philosophical encyclopedia into a populist handbook on nature, imbued with local folktale material, medical knowledge and, above all, a particular Sufi ethics. It is illustrative of the place of Aḥmed's *'Acāib* in Ottoman social memory that its copies are sometimes bound together with mystical texts. In one such *mecmū'a*, earlier preserved in a Sufi *tekke* at Sütlüce in Istanbul's outskirts and dated to the early seventeenth century, the *'Acāib* is placed in the volume after a mystical text and immediately before a treatise on the numerological divinatory technique of magic squares (*vafq*).[17] This may be an indication that the compilers of this *mecmū'a* considered Aḥmed's *'Acāib* not solely a compilation of descriptive geography or cosmology, but of hidden wisdom to be read in preparation for the kinds of occult wisdom represented by the numbers in the *vafq*. More than a 'tour of the universe', the *'Acāib*'s text, according to Aḥmed's summary, became a statement of a normative orientation towards the world.

The basis of the *'Acāib*'s moral program was a cyclical process of learning informed by Sufi ideas. Aḥmed, using words that are largely Qazwīnī's, described his motivations for producing his own version of the *'Acāib*, here quoted in full:

> The reason for writing this book is that while studying created things, it occurred to my estranged [*ġarīb*] heart to compile some 'wonders of the world' ['*ālemiñ ba'żı 'acāibini*], especially those many kinds of oddities of the world [*ġarāib-i 'ālem*], from the Throne as far as the Carpet, that the worldly sages of the time of Alexander have described.

But this book [of Qazwīnī], being in the Arabic language, cannot be used by the populace of our country [*bizüm vilāyetimüz ümmīleri fāida edemezlerdi*]. With filial servitude I put this book together in one piece for my *shaykh*, the sultan of *shaykh*s, the pole of the truth-seekers, Ḥācı Bayram. I hope that the reader may not forget prayers for this poor one, God willing.

First, one must know that it does not suffice to simply observe [*naẓar*] the world with one's eyes, for animals alongside man observe with the eyes. Rather, one is to ideate based on the observation of particularities [*belki murād, maḥṣūṣāta naẓar etmekden fikr etmekdir*]. Truly, this knowledge of reality [*'ilm-i ḥaqāiq*] is the cause of both worldly pleasure and eternal enjoyment. No skills [*hünerler*] are acquired but by a person who is informed of intelligibles [*ma'qūlāt*] and by particularities [*maḥṣūṣāt*]. I composed this book when Sultan *Ġāzī* Meḥmed took Istanbul. It was the year 857.

And one must know that by 'wonder' [*'aceb*] the people of wisdom [*ehl-i ḥikmet*] mean a kind of bewilderment [*ḥayret*] in which humankind is lacking [in understanding] on account of not knowing the cause of something or not knowing the nature of the consequence of something.

Now first: Observe the size and height of this world and the heavens that turn. Observe the differences in their motions, some like a water-wheel, some like a windmill, and some like a spinning wheel. And observe how the spheres stand without supports and observe how each of them rise and set in a different place, and with varying periodicities they each travel in their appointed houses according to their position. And observe the forms of the heavens, of which some are red and some white and some silver and some gold and some ruby and some formed of pearl, and observe the path of the sun in the fourth sphere – how in one year it travels through twenty-eight constellations and returns to its place, and how the night and the day are distinguished. And observe the moon – how it acquires the light of the sun and at night is the sun's deputy, and how it becomes crescent and full, and how the moon is eclipsed and reappears and how stars fall from the sky and lightning and thunder appears and it rains fire and stones and snow. And observe the different winds and the clouds that bring water to the earth's surface and in accordance with wisdom make it rain upon the parts of the world . . .[18]

This lyrical passage, replete with Qur'anic allusions, continues in this style for several more pages, invoking plants, animals, stones and gems, serving double duty as a rapid run-through of the miracles of the cosmos and as the work's only table of contents. Several features stand out. We see, first, that Aḥmed intended to produce an *'Ajā'ib* that served the needs of a local population of Turcophone faithful (*vilāyetimüz ümmīleri*, 'our nation's common folk'). We may take *ümmī* to refer to the most unlettered of that populace – those most in need of orientation within the Islamic cosmos. He also claimed that he was inspired to fulfill the posthumous request of his late Sufi master. Thus, the text is locally situated; it is intended as a culmination of Aḥmed's mystical education and as a means to grant that education to those who lack it.

The discussion of *'ajab* that follows concatenates two much longer passages by Qazwīnī on this topic. Aḥmed states that sense perception (*naẓar*) is the beginning of the process of acquiring knowledge of truth. Our human intellect then must inquire using thought (*fikr*) into the causes and effects of these perceptions, basing this on a study of its specific particularities. Apprehension of a single true thing is the result of these two steps of observation and cognition. Sense perception is the basis for the acquisition of knowledge and the foundation of wonderment, but it is thought that transforms this material into useful understanding.

We understand more of this process as Aḥmed, closely following Qazwīnī, used a simple phrase to define wonderment: 'By *'ajab* the people of wisdom (*ehl-i ḥikmet*) denote a kind of bewilderment (*ḥayret*) in which man is lacking [in understanding] on account of not knowing the cause of something or not knowing the nature of the consequence of something'.[19] This is a customary definition of wonderment in the medieval period across both the Christian and Islamic worlds. Lorraine Daston and Katharine Park have encountered this definition of wonderment as an ignorance of cause and effect in the writings of Aquinas, Albertus Magnus, Francis Bacon and Adelard of Bath.[20] When Aḥmed Bīcān rested this definition on the authority of the people of 'wisdom' (*ḥikmet*), he most likely referred to the same classical philosophers that informed the thought of his Christian peers: Plato, who wrote that 'Wonder is the feeling of the philosopher and philosophy begins in wonder', and Aristotle, who expressed that 'For it is owing to wonder that men [. . .] began to philosophize . . .'[21]

Yet, 'wisdom' as a source of lore also possesses a secondary meaning. Ibn Sīnā often uses *ḥikma* in the sense of 'Oriental' (*ishrāqī*) philosophy which, according to some scholars, refers to an esoteric blend of his own scholastic thought with Sufism and the theosophical wisdom of diverse sources.[22] In any case, Aḥmed's own Sufi affiliation and the depth of Sufism's influence on his worldview opens the possibility for a mystical reading of the term *ḥayret* ('bewilderment') that follows. As one of Sufism's most ubiquitous concepts, *ḥayra*, in a simple sense, refers to human incapacity before divine transcendence. In a related but narrower sense, *ḥayra* is a subjective aspect of the Sufi spiritual moment of ultimate proximity to God, which the returning mystic, at a complete loss for words, can only describe as 'bewilderment'. Beyond thought and expression, the mystic in the state of *ḥayra* enacts Man's ultimate contingency in the face of overpowering divinity. The *'ajab* of marvelling at nature and the *ḥayra* of the mystics' theophanic experience are thus closely related.

In this way, the three concepts introduced by this passage – wonder, observation and cognition, phrased in a way that resonates with the language of mystical experience – delineate a kind of dialectical process for the study of nature. One feels wonderment upon observing nature; then, upon pondering the causes and effects of this wonder and discovering them, one feels a new sort of *'ajab*, which in turn produces another paired process of observation and thought. It is *'ajab* and the Sufi's bewilderment that drives this cycle forward, a mute praise of creation that compels the seeker up the steps of a ladder towards knowledge of the cosmos and of God. *'Ajab*, *naẓar* and *fikr* are the components of a method of spiritual improvement. In a classic digression on the marvel that is the beehive, Qazwīnī gives an example:

> If a person sees a beehive and has not seen one previously, he will become bewildered because he does not understand who made it. If he then learns that it is the work of a bee, he will be bewildered again by how this weak creature makes these hexagons, the likes of which a skilled engineer would be unable to make with a compass and ruler.[23]

Qazwīnī then remarked how the wax, honey and overall design of the beehive each prompt further wonderment. The more one learns, the more wonderment one feels. And it is not just beehives that are wondrous. 'Everything is like this', he added.

While the outlines of this process are explicit in Qazwīnī, the Sufi and scriptural dimension of this method comes to the forefront of Aḥmed Bīcān's *'Acāib*. This is very clear in the chapter on time and its divisions, which follows a section on the heavenly bodies and the angels. At first sticking close to Qazwīnī, Aḥmed says, 'the sages (*ḥukamā*) decree that by "time" they mean the quantity of the movements of the spheres', and these movements divide time into ages (*qurūn*), years and finer measurements.[24] Yet, while Qazwīnī, aiming for an even-handed comprehensiveness, describes not only the months of the Islamic calendar, but also the Persian and Roman months, adding for each a detail or two (usually a prophetic *ḥadīth*), in Aḥmed's text only the Islamic months are discussed in entries of a very different template. Each of Aḥmed's entries incorporate a moralising story that explains the etymology of the name of each month, usually drawn from the *isrā'īliyyāt* of the Old Testament prophets or from the mythos of pre-Islamic Arabia. The month of Sha'bān, illustrated by a few simple *aḥādīth* in Qazwīnī, has been expanded by Aḥmed Bīcān into a story on Moses, Joshua and the subsequent 'branching-out' (*tasha''ub*) of the Tribe of Israel. In the section on the month of Jumada al-Awwal, we are treated to a strange story of an ancient king named Melikşāh who, in campaign against his rival Kiyāz, set up camp in a cold and snowy mountain region. There, he and his tribe stayed the two months of Jumādā frozen in the cold (*cümūd oldu*).[25] The month of Ṣafar is so named because the pre-Islamic tribe of ‘Adnān prepared for campaign (*sefer*) during that month. Aḥmed's template then usually calls for the mention of a few edifying anniversaries from the heroic history of early Islam: ‘On the first day [of Ṣafar], the infidels took the head of Ḥusayn to Damascus'.[26] The overall effect of these changes is to remake the calendar year into a dramatic matrix of wondrous stories of prophets, kings, tyrants and saints. An ethical element is deeply embedded in the retelling of the wanderings of the Tribe of Israel and of the Prophet and his companions and family across the landscape of the months. Its language is rich in opposing pairs – infidels and believers, corrupters and holy men, tyrannical kings and pious subjects. In this calendrical text, wonder and piety are fused.

This sensibility extends across Aḥmed's work. In a superficial sense, one can see this in the ways in which the marvellous creatures of the world are described; Aḥmed deploys what may be a specific style of the fantastic distinct from Qazwīnī's, sometimes inserting scriptural imagery into the bestiary of bizarre creatures and Plinean races. The clearest example of this is a strange Mediterranean fish, one of only two wonders from his native sea that Aḥmed preserved from Qazwīnī's long list. ‘There are flying fish', he wrote. ‘Above their left ear is written *lā ilāha illā'l-llāh* [there is no god but God] and above their right ear is written *wa Muḥammad rasūlu'l-llāh* [and Muḥammad is God's Messenger]'.[27] Qazwīnī related this narrative skeptically, as the unreliable testimony of a traveller who caught a brief glimpse of the fish as it swam by to catch a sinking object. When Aḥmed piously repeats it, it becomes fact, as certain as whales and sharks. Likewise, in a passage on the *jinn*, scriptural history dominates, whereas in Qazwīnī's text *jinn* lifestyle and behaviours are the focus. In Aḥmed's version, God sent eight hundred prophets to the *jinn*, but the ungrateful creatures killed them all. Angels sent to the *jinn* were captured by them, and Satan was born from the union of a *jinn* and a captive angel. After he was returned to heaven and refused to bow before Adam, ‘God turned away from him' and cast him back down to earth, where he had five sons: ‘Some say they were born from eggs from his tail'.[28]

Wonder stories that reinforce scriptural narratives make up only part of the pious program of Aḥmed's *'Acāib*. Another strongly emphasised aspect is the practical utility of domestic animals and useful plants – wonders of the world we would not presently call wondrous. At least one third of the text is given over to these matters, some of which are not at all related to material in Qazwīnī. These entries are generally lighthearted in tone and sequenced in such a way as to mix advice of tangible utility with unusual and amusing aspects of each animal or plant. We learn, for instance, that the jackal ruins gardens and orchards, but that one who eats its meat is cured of insanity. We read that rabbit meat promotes pregnancy and that a tincture made from the tooth of a rabbit cures toothaches. The horse is the most useful of animals, and God gave Adam the horse to serve him 'so that he may reach his destinations'.[29]

Monkeys are so intelligent that an Indian king taught one of them to craft jewelry out of silver and to play chess; another monkey he taught the trade of a tailor. Aḥmed's text gives the reader the useful 'fact' that, 'if one keeps company with a monkey for ten days, melancholy departs from one's nature'.[30] Countless herbal remedies promise cures for sleeplessness and lovesickness. And, very poignantly, we learn that, of all the creatures in the wondrous cosmos, 'the camel is the strangest of all animals'.[31]

By asking us to imagine the familiar camel as the most wondrous of all creatures – by drawing attention to its strange long neck and its ability to go for ten days without water or food – Aḥmed aimed to defamiliarise the world of the reader and renew the world's *'ajab*. This key message is expanded in the form of an evocative Alexander tale, one of the few to survive from Qazwīnī's section on the 'wonders of the seas':

> King Alexander wanted to know the extent of the Encircling Ocean, so he built a ship. He sent it from the west outfitted for a two-year journey under the command of an elite captain named *Deñizoğlu* ['Son of the Sea'], crewed by seventy-two heart-entrusted men and one woman as well. That ship spent a year at sea and did not see a single thing. Then one day they saw a ship and pulled alongside it, and fought with it, but could not take it. Then they conversed with each other, and they did not know each others' language. Alexander's ship gave the other ship the woman and took from that [other] ship one man and turned back.
>
> They came before Alexander and informed him of the wonders they had seen. They offered him that person [from the other ship], and Alexander commanded that they give that person a woman. From them a boy was born, and that boy learned the language of his father and of his mother. They said to this boy, 'Ask your father, "Where do you come from? And tell of your land of lands".' The person said 'We have a king. He equipped us for a two-year [journey] and said, "Travel for one year to see if there are any other Sons of Man besides us". And when we set out, we encountered you', he said.
>
> Then they asked, 'What kind of king is your king, and what kind of kingdom is his?' The person said, 'Our king is greater than King Alexander, and his kingdom and his army are greater than Alexander's kingdom and his army. By God, what a great king he is'. Alexander said, 'I rule the whole of the East and West, there is no king greater than me'. And in the islands of the

> Encircling Ocean there is [also] a king who says he rules the whole of the East and West.
>
> *From these words it is understood that there are many of the Exalted God's creatures whom you do not know of and who do not know of you. The moral intention is that it is necessary to know one's own incapacity, to affirm God's magnificence, and to see or hear about the wonders of the world* [emphasis mine].[32]

Stranded amid countless fragmentary and formulaic notices on odd fishes and islands inhabited by headless troglodytes, this artful fable is developped from a bare Qazwīnī narrative into a cornerstone of Aḥmed's *'Acāib*. Its elegant moral conclusion, original to Aḥmed, transforms the story from one merely illustrating the immense physical size of the Encircling Ocean into a parable on the limits and potential of human knowledge. It seems to have been written with a personal attentiveness that brings into the story something of the air of the seafaring town of Gelibolu. (The Turkish name of the captain is his own addition, as is his brief evocation of the crew and the dialogue between the stranger and Alexander.) One imagines Aḥmed Bīcān reciting and embellishing the story of the strange ship to his audience of sailors and oarsmen at his seaside dervish lodge, flanked on one side by the roads to inner Rumelia and on the other by the Dardanelles and the Mediterranean crowded with enemy triremes – in the year Columbus was born.

Thus, its message is not one of epistemological caution. Rather, it conveys with directness the urgent necessity of the bewildered unknowingness of *'ajab* and *ḥayra*. The story of the most heroic of all kings – moved by the immensity of the sea to venture into it, then ingeniously transcending the obstacle of language, before finally being confronted by the reality of 'creatures whom you do not know of and who do not know of you' and, accordingly, the total revision of his image of the world – works as a profound metaphor for the process of wonderment, perception and investigation, as well as the revived, deepened mystification that is the essence of *'acab*. To 'see and hear about the wonders of the world' in order to be continually reminded of human humility in the face of God's transcendence is what drives personal and spiritual development.

The Rūḥu'l-Ervāḥ *and the Microcosm*

The outlines of another kind of philosophy of nature emerge in Aḥmed's undated work written near the end of his career, entitled *Rūḥu'l-Ervāḥ* ('The Spirit of Spirits'). This short text derives from a very large body of Sufi literature that bases its claims to truth on the visionary 'states' (*aḥvāl*) in which mystical practitioners acquire direct experiential knowledge of metaphysical truth, through their own proximity to God. In its textual heritage, it is rooted in the works of Ibn 'Arabī and later commentators of the lineage stretching from Ṣadr al-dīn Qunawī to the Anatolian proponents of his school, especially Dāvūd-i Qayseri and Şemsü'd-dīn Fenari. Familiar with these texts and a member of the living Bayramī Sufi community, Aḥmed Bīcān presented in the *Rūḥ* a Sufi philosophy of man. Its essential message is that humans, their organs and their mental faculties, as the centrepiece of the cosmos, correspond to features of other levels of creation, such as the geography of the earth, the spheres of the heavens and the events of the End Times. This anthropocentrism has explicit Akbarian foundations in the doctrine of *al-insān al-kāmil* ('the Perfect Man'), as Aḥmed wrote in a high theosophical language otherwise encountered only in portions of the *Müntehā*, his mystical magnum opus:

> One must know that God, according to his essence, desired the Comprehensive Cosmos [*kevn-i cāmi'*] that is the Perfect Man. And God manifested his mystery in the Perfect Man, for the world is like a seal and man is the image on that seal. God does not reveal Himself in His majesty [*tecellī eylemez*], but by means of the Perfect Man . . .[33]

This message is further communicated by means of a symbol: the 'Man-World' or 'World of Man' (*insān 'ālemi*). Heaven and earth and the attributes of God appear in the *insān 'ālemi* – that is, in man – as one-to-one correspondence. In a simple instance of the Man-World correspondence, Aḥmed brings forth his favourite subjects, the stories of the angels and the prophets. 'For all that exists in the Hidden World (*'ālem-i ġayb*)', Aḥmed wrote, 'there is something that resembles (*beñzer*) it in Man. For example, in the World of Man, Abraham resembles the spirit (*rūḥ*), Gabriel the intellect and Qūj the carnal soul (*nefs-i emmāre*)'. In the same way, Aḥmed claimed, 'what is meant by Jacob in the *insān 'ālemi* is the intellect, and what is meant by Joseph is the heart'.[34] It is clear that with this analogy Aḥmed Bīcān simultaneously communicated a *metaphor* of man as a hermeneutic tool to facilitate our intellectual interpretation of the cosmos as a whole and the *reality* of macrocosmic embodiment in the human being.[35]

Expanding this further, Aḥmed, in a sustained analogy, described how the physical geography of the cosmos resembled the life cycle of man:

> In one aspect the soul resembles the Throne and the heart the Footstool and the heavens between them knowledge and wisdom, and the faculties of the soul resemble the angels, and their movements resemble those of the stars, and being born from a mother resembles the stars' rising, and death resembles the

> setting of the stars, and bones resemble mountains, and limbs resemble lands, and the front [of the body] resembles the east, and the flesh resembles the earth, and hair resembles plants, and the front [of the body] resembles the east and the back the west, and the carnal soul resembles the winds, and words resemble thunder, and the smile resembles lightning, and crying resembles the rain, and wakefulness resembles life, and sleep resembles death.[36]

The angels correspond to a body part:

> In the *insān 'ālemi* [. . .] the eye is a manifestation (*mażhar*) of 'Azrā'īl, and the ear is a manifestation of Michael, and the nose is a manifestation of Azrāfīl, and the mouth is a manifestation of Gabriel. And the abilities of man are [contained] in their wings; one is the capacity for intellectual reasoning (*'aql*), and the other is the capacity for observation (*naẓar*).

The geography of Paradise, too, corresponds to aspects of the Man-World. The heavenly tree of the *sidretü'l-müntehā* is the 'holy spirit' (*rūḥu'l-quddūs*). Another monument in Paradise, the *beytü'l-ma'mūr*, is represented by the 'protected house' of the human heart, and just as the angels periodically circumambulate the *beytü'l-ma'mūr*, the heart beats with its own rhythm.[37] Each of the seven levels of Hell finds counterparts in what one would call human psychological limitations – stubbornness, disbelief and so on.

Aḥmed embarked on a unique reading of eschatological events according to their meanings in the *insān 'ālemi*. The apocalypse is internalised, here playing out as a form of spiritual psychology. One of the early stages of the apocalypse, the coming of the Blond People who inaugurate the wars of the End Times, represent 'the coming apocalypse, the triumph of the Satanic faculty (*quvvet-i şeyṭāniyye*) over spiritual power. Then the spiritual faculty (*quvvet-i rūḥāniyye*) will triumph over the satanic faculty'. Including elements of historical apocalypse from his earlier *Müntehā*, Aḥmed then added: '[In] the conquest of Istanbul one sees the faculties of belief (*īmān quvvetleri*) triumph and the greatness of Satan's cities brought down and destroyed'. The coming of the 'Smoke' among the events of the End of Days is the triumph of the 'animal darkness' (*ẓulmet-i hayvānī*) over the human soul; the arrival of the messianic Mahdī is the victory of the 'holy reason' (*'aql-i qudsī*) over it; the coming of the Antichrist Dajjal is the manifestation of the 'commanding soul' (*nefs-i emmāre*) over the 'contented soul' (*nefs-i muṭmā'inne*), which in turn prevails over it, as symbolised by the coming of Jesus who is also the 'exalted spirit' (*rūḥ-i a'lā*). The emergence of the Beast of the Earth is a manifestation of the 'self-blaming soul' (*nefs-i levvāme*). Fire raining from heaven is another appearance of the commanding soul, and the perishing of sinful humankind in this fire is, 'in the *insān 'ālemi*, an expression (*'ibāret*) of the annihilation of the souls' material embodiment in the light of Truth'. When the faces of the believers who have assembled for judgment turn white, signifying their salvation, this designates the illumination of the human heart with divine light; when the faces of the damned turn black, it is a sign (*işāret*) of 'desiring the world and being denied God's light'.[38]

Several features of these sets of correspondences stand out. The first is that the verb linking the subject of these correspondences (the natural feature, angelic being, or apocalyptic event) with the human object in the *insān 'ālemi* (the human intellect, the carnal soul, the heart, the eyes) varies substantially, implying an unclear ontological priority between the two elements. The angels' wings 'contain' human intellectual faculties; hell is a 'sign' of human obstinacy; the fires of the apocalypse are an 'expression' of annihilation of the self in God. Sometimes the two elements 'resemble' or 'are like' (*gibi*) each other; at other times they simply 'are' each other. While the confusion of predicates may imply a certain unclarity on Aḥmed Bīcān's part, more likely it is a consequence of the rigorous deployment of Ibn 'Arabī's *waḥdat al-wujūd* metaphysics. If all existing things are derived particulars of God's ultimate unity, then all subjects and objects are identical and all verbs relating them are reduced to superfluity. To emphasise a distinct form of relations between the *insān 'ālemi* and the world around it would introduce a precarious directionality to the objects subsisting within God's unity and, thereby, fracture it. The Man-World is not a lesser replica of nature – man and nature are parallel and corresponding reflections of the same divine blueprint. The image of man and the features of the cosmos ontologically coincide as the 'comprehensive creation'. [39]

A second feature can be found in how the aspects of the *insān 'ālemi* that map against nature (or the stages of apocalypse) are most often not corporeal parts of a human, but rather *psychological* components, thus implying a theory of the mind. The Islamic psychology that Aḥmed Bīcān inherited was, like many other sciences, a hybrid of traditions. The main line of this theory of mind runs from Aristotle's *De Anima* and passes through Ibn Sīnā.[40] For Ibn Sīnā, just as for Aristotle, the soul is a set of 'faculties' (*quwwāt*) of reason, observation, memory, intuition and so on. To this Ibn Sīnā added an intuitive capacity reserved for those of high development, which he called the 'holy reason' (*al-'aql al-qudsī*) emanating from the Prime Intellect or 'holy spirit' (*al-rūḥ al-qudsī*). By contrast, a different, Qur'anic model describes the individual as a hierarchy of souls, comprising the 'commanding' (*ammāra*)[41] soul that desires evil things, the 'self-blaming' (*lawwāma*)[42] soul that identifies its imperfections and the 'contented' (*mutmā'inna*)[43] soul that is at peace. A thorough exploration of this Qur'anic psychology may be found in an important manual of fifteenth-century Turkish sciences of the mind, the *Müzekkī'n-Nüfūs* ('Purifier of Souls') by the Qādirī Sufi poet Eşrefoğlu Rūmī, who may have participated in the circle of mystic practitioners around Ḥācı Bayram Velī and was a prominent figure in Aḥmed Bīcān's wider environment. The *Müzekkī'n-Nüfūs*, deeply Sufi and strictly non-philosophical in its orientation, approaches the science of the mind according to the directive of the well-known *ḥadīth* 'He who knows his soul (*nafs*) knows his Lord',[44] and it encourages a believer to examine the parts of his soul that govern his deeds.

Strikingly, Aḥmed Bīcān deployed both approaches: the philosophers' psychological vocabulary (such as 'holy spirit', 'holy intellect' and the pervasive term 'faculty') and the Qur'anic hierarchy of different types of *nafs*. We have already seen that this not very rigorous style of synthesis is typical of Aḥmed Bīcān, in this case reflecting a form of integration perhaps transmitted in Sufi circles such as the Bayramīs of Ankara. Significantly, Aqşemse'd-dīn, Aḥmed Bīcān's peer within the Bayramī order, advanced a similar blend of philosophical and Qur'anic psychology.[45] We may venture to see in this coexistence of philosophical, Qur'anic and Sufi terms a tension between an ever-shifting mapping of the microcosmic and macrocosmic levels of the mind, body and world – in this mapping, the world is a kind of fractal repeating itself at different scales from a divine template, with the densest similitude in man – and the philosophical model in which soul and cosmos alike, in ordered classes, emanate from the Prime Intellect. These provide a dual set of compatible principles for Aḥmed Bīcān's approach to a philosophy of nature: one principle is revealed in experiential mystical discovery, and the other in philosophical contemplation and observation.

Returning to Aḥmed's concern with apocalyptic imagery, one may suggest that, by making human psychology central to cosmic order, he intended to signal to his readers that the individual struggles of the soul and the triumph of its intellectual and spiritual faculties over its baser ones is a part of cosmic history. That is to say, the moral imperative of the 'purification of the soul' constitutes the very difference between the triumph of the 'satanic faculty' or the 'holy spirit' in the End Times. There is, in this sense, no more perfect instantiation of the idea of man as microcosmic embodiment than the individual's own enactment of the cosmic cycle of creation and resurrection.

Malḥama *and Esoteric Revelation*

The two texts that book-end the whole corpus, the family's first and last works – Ṣāliḥ's 1423 *Şemsiyye* and his son's 1466 *Būstānu'l-Ḥaqāiq* – are prognosticatory texts, concerned less with establishing a metaphysical relation between man, God and nature than with the proper application of a technical body of knowledge for practical aims. In terms of their textual heritage, the *Şemsiyye* and *Būstān* grew out of the *malḥama* tradition and the calendrical arts, as well as various astrological and occult writings then in fashion. The primary source was a version of the *Malḥamat Dāniyāl* ('The Omens of Daniel'), a family of divinatory writings on the portents of days and months.[46] According to its purported origin, the secrets of the *malḥama* were written on baked clay tablets by Adam in a cave in Sri Lanka (Sarāndīb) after his Fall, and the tablets were cached there. Much later, in Jerusalem, the Prophet Daniel heard of the legend of Adam's tablets and travelled to Sarāndīb to find them, copying their contents in ink on paper.[47] As Ṣāliḥ and Aḥmed's texts themselves acknowledge, the *malāḥim* do in fact derive from pre-Islamic wisdom traditions, most likely passed on through Syriac texts and Arabic and Persian translations *en route* to their encounter with the Rumelian borderlands. The scholar A. Fodor has theorised, based on weak evidence, that the origins of all *Malḥama* are to be found in the Syriac literature of early medieval northern Mesopotamia, more specifically the plateau of Tur Abidin in the hinterlands of Mardin. More verifiably, Ṣāliḥ's proximate source was Abū al-Fażl Ḥubaysh al-Tiflīsī's twelfth-century *Uṣūl al-Malāḥim* ('The Principles of Omenology'), a Persian calendar-almanac collecting the branches of this textual lineage into a single popular compendium.[48]

Ṣāliḥ spoke for *malḥama* as a whole when he said that his *Şemsiyye* aimed to predict 'feast or famine, plague or locusts / peace or war, security or uncertainty, joy or sadness / [. . .] / the state of crop and animal and fruit / land and clime and country and kingdom'. The *Şemsiyye*, like its *malḥama* models, is structured according to the twelve solar months under their Greek, Syriac and even Turkish names. The day of the week on which the first day of these months falls is accorded great prognosticatory import ('If [it falls] on Sunday the winter will be mild / honey and oil will be plentiful . . .'), bringing with it advisories on meteorological and agricultural outcomes for each of the seven days.[49] Following this, twenty-four or twenty-five celestial omens are listed for each month. Each prognosticatory section follows an identical form. If an eclipse takes place during the month of Tishrīn al-Awwal, for instance, 'the enemies of the king will be weakened'. If, during the following month, a comet appears, 'then for every commander the year will be joyful [*ṣād-kām*]'. Some of these celestial omens are eerily supernatural ('If a human being is seen in the sky . . .', 'If a strange object is seen [flying] in the air . . .').[50]

Ṣāliḥ included several additional sections in his *Şemsiyye*. First, he provided verse comments on the solar months and, following this, detailed descriptions of the Islamic months, omens on the days of their beginning and end, and a listing of events in sacred history taking place during these months. A passage establishes a numerological procedure by which one subtracts the value of the current *Ḥijrī* year from 702 and divides the difference by seven, noting the remainder. This number corresponds to one of seven specific letters of the Arabic alphabet that in turn guide the reader to a table indicating what days of a month of that year are auspicious or ill-omened. Another section uses a gridded table to match the Islamic months to letters of the alphabet, and then the days of the week to appropriate activities (for example, toenails should be cut on Sundays). A section of miscellany details the appropriate times for marriage and sexual intercourse, as well as the prayers that are to be said on those occasions. The book closes with a section on divination (*fāl*) from the Qur'an. 'Let it be known that I have versified the *fāl* in simple Turkish', the author wrote.[51] After performing ablutions, one is to recite several prayers and hold a question in mind. Opening the Qur'an at random, one is to take the first letter of the seventh line on the left-facing page; repeating this seven times, the diviner is then to refer to another table, obtaining from there a composite fortune relating to his or her question. Ṣāliḥ's text ends abruptly: After the *fāl* material for the letter *yā*, the scribe's colophon appears.

The *Şemsiyye* and *Būstān* construct a correspondence between the calendar and celestial omens as predictors, and meteorological and social outcomes as predicted fortune. Hence, it is not clear whether these *malḥama* writings are underpinned by, or themselves justify, any dogmatic philosophical understanding. This style of omen science implies only a non-specific, non-directional connection between the omen and that what is foretold by the omen; this connection functions isolated from the mechanisms of Hellenistic cosmology. The authors expressed their own perception of the great antiquity of this lore by attributing it to the Prophet Daniel and by their continual reference to the Syriac months, much as the tenth-century Ibn al-Waḥshiyya based his *al-Filāḥa al-Nabaṭiyya*, a text on agricultural magic, on the authority of his own Chaldean ancestral rites.[52] Indeed, scholars have speculated that the classical science of omens in general derives from Akkadian and neo-Babylonian religion; the omen sciences are, as it were, records of the intercession of deities who enact their arbitrary preferences over a terrestrial world with which they are fundamentally entangled.[53] The *malḥama* – here detached from its sacral context in the Mesopotamia of deep antiquity, Islamicised and reproducible as verse, prose, or gridded table – turned the calendar and the sky into a device for acquiring knowledge of a sequence of future events. As a system of correspondences based on a body of pre-Islamic lore, the *malḥama* persisted intact because its promise of prognosticatory power was universal and technical, unperturbed by metaphysics across the millennia of its existence.

However, Ṣāliḥ and Aḥmed lived in a post-Ptolemaic setting in which Hellenistic cosmological models were harmonised with Biblical and Qur'anic references to the 'seven spheres' nested within each other.[54] For literate Muslims, such a mechanistic system determined the influence of the solar and lunar cycles on sublunary fates, just as the sun's changes in position across the solar year determine the weather. This dependence of terrestrial events on the outer spheres was often imagined as the intelligence of the heavenly spheres, whose motions define those of the spheres below them, in a sequence ending with earth. Ṣāliḥ and Aḥmed tried to reconcile this with the arbitrary correspondences of the *malḥama*, feeling obliged to embellish it with details from Islamo-Greek cosmology. We can see this in the way in which each solar month is characterised by the rising and setting of a star, implying a dependence of the motion of the sun on that of the outermost sphere of fixed stars.

This is one way, among many others, in which the *Şemsiyye* and the *Būstān* teach us about the eclecticism of Yazıcı Ṣāliḥ's and Aḥmed Bīcān's sources of knowledge on the natural world. Although the bulk of information provided in the *Şemsiyye* and the *Būstān* are derived from one source – Tiflīsī's *Uṣūl al-Malāḥim* – the texts emphasise the heterogeneity of the lore found therein. Aḥmed Bīcān, in his later text, claimed in typical style that the work was based on 'the science of Idrīs [Enoch/Hermes], the discourse of Daniel, the speech of Plato and Luqmān, the utterances of the people of wisdom, the affirmations of the calendar, the prophets' speech and the sages' experience'.[55] This is taken almost *verbatim* from Ṣāliḥ, who also included the authority of one of the standard-bearers of Islamic wisdom traditions, the sixth Shī'ī *imām* Ja'far al-Ṣādiq. Referring to the above sources, Aḥmed said: 'God has revealed (*vaḥy*) to them, or otherwise Gabriel has come and inspired (*ilhām*) them'. Ṣāliḥ asserted: 'God (*Tañrı*) revealed or Gabriel came / in person or "*in a dream as few*"[56] / Or they were inspired otherwise in what they said . . .' The prophetic foundations of the *malḥama* were revelations, such as that of the Holy Book itself; no rational calculations about the positions of the stars and planets along the arcs traced by heavenly spheres went into the writing of *Malḥama* lore. This lore is made available after having been channelled by God through the human gift of prophecy, without which it would have rested silent in the hidden world. It is suggestive that, when in the seventeenth century the Ottoman traveller Evliyā Çelebi likened Ṣāliḥ's *Şemsiyye* to the work of 'the monotheist Pythagoras' (*Fisāgores-i tevḥīdī*),[57] he chose that particular classical sage whose wisdom, in the Islamic imagination, was most related to that of a prophet or seer, as opposed to a philosopher, mathematician, or astronomer.

* * *

In these three writings, Aḥmed Bīcān wove a dense web of semblances between the soul, man, the cosmos and divinity. The hub of all of these is man, distinguished sharply from the rest of nature, from whom these connections are perceived, and for whose sake they are elucidated. In this sense it is not only the *insān 'alemi* doctrine in the *Rūḥu'l-Ervāḥ* that is microcosmic; in the *malḥama*'s esoteric omenology and in the *'Acāib*'s geography, man both represents and embodies nature, analysing it and suffering from it, and man is equally the measure of all things.

In reference to sixteenth-century European science, Michel Foucault has identified that the focal point of this relational map, man as microcosm, had risen during the early modern period to become the prime principle of the ordering of knowledge – 'one half of a celestial atlas'.[58] In a perceptive passage, he has proposed that in this late medieval and early modern epistemology, man-microcosm filled two roles. First, the body and soul of man 'apply the interplay of duplicated resemblances to *all* realms of nature; it provides all investigation with an assurance that everything will find its mirror and macrocosmic justification on another [. . .] scale'.[59] Man is a template and rationale for the rest. Secondly, the macrocosm limits and condenses the potentially infinite interplay of resemblances that intersect in the Man-World, guaranteeing that they are limited by the scope of human perception: 'however immense the distance from microcosm to macrocosm may be, it cannot be infinite; the beings that reside within it may be extremely numerous, but in the end they can be counted [. . .] The similitudes that [. . .] always rest upon one another, can cease their endless flight'.[60] Man, by uniting all of the correspondences between the realms of nature, provides an end-point to this infinite regress.

If man limits the cosmos and makes it intelligible, then perhaps the texts under consideration here each represent epistemological explorations that address this notion of man as microcosmic centre. This is often expressed as a contradiction or uncertainty as to where man stands within the universal scheme – sometimes at the universe's innermost core, other times in its most distant periphery. In the *'Acāib*, Aḥmed wrote that God's throne and each of the archangels are unfathomably large and that, by comparison, the earth and its people are pitifully small; in the *Rūḥ*, man's image is the shape of the cosmos itself. With respect to other animals man is both greater and lesser – 'in his knowledge of truth he resembles angels [. . . ,] in heroism he resembles lions [. . . ,] in his gathering of goods he resembles swine and in his howling to the people of the world he resembles dogs [. . .] and in his contentedness in ignorance he resembles donkeys, and in his rebelliousness Satan'.[61] Even the pragmatic *malḥama*, neutral on the metaphysical structure of man and the universe but eager to find a predictable logic within it, expresses a worry about man's potential to control arbitrary fate and a reverent confidence that prophecy residing in man is a pole around which order can be fixed.

This image recalls the themes recently explored by Gottfried Hagen. Microcosmic man as an organising principle, a finite point in a world of infinite semblances, finds a linguistic expression in the designation of the Sufi saint as *quṭb*, literally 'axis'. In the fifteenth century, the *quṭb* was a real and mythic figure whose hagiographised presence, as Hagen has argued, imparts a system on the chaos of nature. For Aḥmed Bīcān, the 'pole of the world' (*cihānıñ quṭbı*) was his *shaykh* Ḥācı Bayram Velī, who in his holy person bridged the worldly community of earthly seekers, on one side, and the unseen and cosmic realities, on the other. It was in the *quṭb* Hāci Bayram's honour that Aḥmed composed the *'Acāibü'l-maḫlūqāt*, a fact that lays bare the convergence of his mystic vocation, natural history, man and microcosm, and the schemata of the world around him. That is to say, the *insān 'ālemi* experienced in the meditations taught to him by his master Ḥācı Bayram – the universe brought finite into human form – was what Aḥmed aspired to see as delimiting and arranging his world, thus allowing for the pious self to subsist.

Indeed, Aḥmed Bīcān's world called for an organising principle. It certainly seemed that the potential for ethical, pious action, Aḥmed's perennial concern, was restricted by nature and circumstance. The bubonic plague struck Gelibolu and the region at least once a decade. The Ottoman Civil War that had dominated Aḥmed's youth set different geographic and social visions of the Ottoman state against each other. The straits brought the Mediterranean to Aḥmed's doorstep, sometimes in the form of Venetian warships that battled Ottoman ones in front of Gelibolu's harbour. Diplomatic and mercantile encounters in and around Gelibolu brought even non-elite Muslims such as Aḥmed and his brother into contact with travellers from as far afield as France and Central Asia.

The Ottoman borders expanded into new climes, and what had once been the wild lands of the Danubian frontier were now contained by a network of Ottoman vassals. An Ottoman scholastic hierarchy arose in nearby Edirne, Bursa and Istanbul, staffed largely by migrant scholars who brought Ottoman intellectual culture into contact with the fashions of Cairo, Tabriz and Herat. The Ḥanafī jurisprudence of Timurid Khurasan, currents of heterodoxy from the cities of Iran and Anatolia, and local Sufi literature competed inconclusively in Ottoman mosques and *medreses*. New elements of empire crowded into newly conquered Istanbul and, as they did so, aroused both the suspicion and the enthusiasm of the pious. Aḥmed Bīcān's peer and acquaintance Aqşemse'd-dīn served as a spiritual advisor of Sultan Meḥmed II at the time of the conquest, but after a year retired to his rural Anatolian home.

Another profound source of philosophical uncertainty came about when the streams of Islamic academic and Sufi thought encountered the Byzantine legacy. As described in Chapter 3, the possible compatibilities between the two faiths gave rise to what Aḥmed Bīcān and his brother interpreted as a threat of doctrinal disarray. This was not something that bothered Sultan Meḥmed the Conqueror who, based on his diverse and contradictory intellectual and aesthetic interests (which encompassed an antiquarian philhellenism alongside a call to *ġazā*), has been memorably characterised by Julian Raby as 'the sultan of paradox'.[62] Aḥmed Bīcān, a subject of Sultan Meḥmed, thus lived under the rule of paradox – and sought anthropocentric answers to this confusion.

The natural-philosophical studies of Aḥmed Bīcān and his father were not conservative or tradition-bound, but truly exploratory. The devout itinerary across the universe of the *'Acāib*, the macrocosmic philosophy of the *Rūḥ* and the occult *malḥama* of the *Būstān* jointly represent an attitude of eager epistemological experimentation. Each draw from a different ultimate source of knowledge – the first from a mystical-philosophical classification of natural variety, the second from Sufi experience and texts, and the third from esoteric revelation. Concerned with questions rather than systematic answers, they do not present a cohesive structure. Although all three epistemologies can surely be harmonised within a certain system, Aḥmed Bīcān was not a systematiser. In this respect Aḥmed, much like his sultan, accepted some paradox.

In the absence of a more definite way to comprehensively summarise the natural-philosophical outlook of Aḥmed Bīcān, let alone that of fifteenth-century Ottoman writing on nature in general, the words of another fifteenth-century Ottoman are appropriate. The anonymous author of the *Dürr-i Meknūn* ('The Hidden Pearl'), writing around the same time as

Aḥmed, expressed his own faith in the redemptive power of knowledge about nature in times of change: 'Let us recount our knowledge, insofar as the Exalted God [. . .] has given a bit of it to us, so that we may, from it, deduce God's power and majesty – and so that during this meager lifetime passing in these times of discord, we may not miss seeing the world'.[63]

Notes

1. For the roots of Islamicate literature on gemstones, refer to Fuat Sezgin and Mazen Amawi, *Abu l-Rayḥān al-Bīrūnī: K. al-Jamāhir Fī Ma'rifat al-Jawāhir: Texts and Studies* (Frankfurt a. M.: Institute for the History of Arabic-Islamic Science at the Johann Wolfgang Goethe University, 2001).
2. Kutlar, 'Ahmed-i Bican'ın Manzum *Cevahir-Name*'si', pp. 65–66.
3. In a typical verse we read: 'If a person can't sleep every night and day [. . .] and feels no respect among the people / and never finds the presence of his heart's desire / let that man make a seal-ring of lapis / and never let it leave his finger / his respect will grow and his afflictions will be cured'. Ibid. pp. 66–67.
4. *Ş*, fol. 1b.
5. Gottfried Hagen, 'Chaos, Order, Power, Salvation: Heroic Hagiography's Response to the Ottoman Fifteenth Century', *Journal of the Ottoman and Turkish Studies Association* 1, no. 1–2 (2014), pp. 91–109.
6. See Roy P. Mottahedeh, ''Aja'ib in *The Thousand and One Nights*', in *The Thousand and One Nights in Arabic Literature and Society*, ed. Richard G. Hovannisian and Georges Sabagh (Cambridge: Cambridge University Press, 1997), pp. 29–39.
7. Syrinx von Hees, *Enzyklopädie als Spiegel des Weltbildes: Qazwinis Wunder der Schöpfung: Eine Naturkunde des 13. Jahrhunderts* (Wiesbaden: Harrassowitz, 2002).
8. Syrinx von Hees, 'The Astonishing: A Critique and Re-Reading of 'Ağā'ib Literature', *Middle Eastern Literatures* 8, no. 2 (2010), pp. 101–20.
9. Tsvetan Todorov, *The Fantastic: A Structural Approach to a Literary Genre [By] Tzvetan Todorov, translated from the French by Richard Howard* (Cleveland: Press of Case Western Reserve University, 1973).
10. Syrinx von Hees, 'Al-Qazwìnì's *'Ajà'ib Al-Makhlùqàt*: An Encyclopædia of Natural History?' in *Organizing Knowledge: Encyclopaedic Activities in the Pre-Eighteenth Century Islamic World*, ed. Gerhard Endress (Leiden: Brill, 2006), p. 184
11. von Hees, 'The Astonishing', p .112.
12. Ibid. pp. 105–6.
13. Ibid. p. 106.
14. The following discussion is based on Persis Berlekamp, *Wonder, Image, and Cosmos in Medieval Islam* (New Haven: Yale University Press, 2011).

15. Günay Kut, 'Türk Edebiyatında *Acâibü'l-Mahlûkât* Tercümeleri Üzerinde', in *Acâibü'l-mahlûkât*, trans. and ed. Günay Kut (İstanbul: Simurg, 2010), pp. 4–7.
16. Ibid. pp. 7–9.
17. Ahmed Bican, *Acaibü'l-mahlukat*, Süleymaniye Kütüphanesi, Sütlüce Dergahı 108 (Henceforth *AM*).
18. *AM*, fols 1b–6a.
19. *AM*, fol. 2b.
20. Lorraine Daston and Katharine Park, *Wonders and the Order of Nature, 1150–1750* (New York; Cambridge, MA: Zone Books; distributed by MIT Press, 1998).
21. Berlekamp, *Wonder, Image, and Cosmos in Medieval Islam*, p. 23.
22. This mystical reading of Avicenna has been advanced by a long lineage of modern scholars of Sufism, including Henry Corbin and Seyyed Hossein Nasr. However, more recently this has been sharply criticised from a philosophical perspective by Dimitri Gutas. See Dimitri Gutas, 'Avicenna's Eastern ('Oriental') Philosophy: Nature, Contents, Transmission', *Arabic Sciences and Philosophy* 10, no. 2 (2000), pp. 159–80, as well as Dimitri Gutas, 'Intellect Without Limits: The Absence of Mysticism in Avicenna', in *Intellect et Imagination dans la Philosophie Médiévale*, ed. M. Cândida-Pacheco and J. Francisco-Meirinhos (Turnhout: Brepols, 2006), vol. 1, pp. 351–72.
23. Cited in Berlekamp, pp. 40–43.
24. *AM*, fol. 15b.
25. *AM*, fols 19b–20a.
26. *AM*, fols 17b–18b.
27. *AM*, fol. 27a.
28. *AM*, fol. 59a.
29. *AM*, fol. 55a.
30. *AM*, fols 67a–67b.
31. *AM*, fols 57a–57b. Qazwīnī's (and Aḥmed's) choice of using the camel to illustrate the wondrousness of the created world was certainly prompted by verse 88:17 of the Qur'an: 'Do they not consider how the camel was created?'
32. '*Ḥaqq te'ālānıñ nice maḫlūqāt vardır ki ne sen anı bilürsin ve ne ol seni bilürsin. Pes maqṣūd oldur kim kişi kendü 'aczından bilüb Ḥaqq 'aẓāmetine iqrār eyleyüb 'ālemiñ 'acāiblerini görmek yāḫūd işitmek gerekdür*'. *AM*, fols 23b–24a.
33. Until recently believed to survive in only one manuscript in the Österreichische Staatsbibliothek in Vienna, three more copies of the *Ruh* have come to light. In 2014, Siyabend Ebem transcribed and published the text based largely on the recently located *Rūḥu'l-Ervāḥ* in the Egyptian National Library in Cairo (Turki Talat 64/1). See Siyabend Ebem, 'Ahmed Bîcân'a Atfedilen bir Eser'. What follows is based on the *Rūḥu'l-Ervāḥ* in Atatürk Kitağplığı, Nadir Eserler, MS OE 1744 (henceforth *RE*). This passage is found on folio 1b.

34. *RE*, fol. 6b.
35. This microcosmic systematisation of the world against the human being is distinct from but related to the Sufi philosophy of the human body, the subject of a book-length study by Shahzad Bashir. See Shahzad Bashir, *Sufi Bodies: Religion and Society in Medieval Islam* (New York: Columbia University Press, 2011).
36. *RE*, fol. 12b.
37. *RE*, fol. 8b.
38. *RE*, fols 9b–11b.
39. *RE*, fol. 47b.
40. See Dimitri Gutas, *Avicenna and the Aristotelian Tradition: Introduction to Reading Avicenna's Philosophical Works* (Leiden: Brill, 1988). For a study and translation of Avicenna's psychological works by Fazlur Rahman, see Avicenna, *Avicenna's Psychology: An English Translation of Kitāb al-Najāt, Book II, Chapter VI, with Historico-Philosophical Notes and Textual Improvements on the Cairo Edition*, ed. and transl. Fazlur Rahman (Westport: Hyperion Press, 1981).
41. Qur'an 12:53.
42. Qur'an 75:2.
43. Qur'an 89:27–28.
44. For an adequate recent critical edition, see Abdullah Uçman, *Müzekki'n-Nüfus* (İstanbul: İnsan Yayınları, 2013), p. 44. Eşrefoğlu's *Ṭarīqatnāme* has been discussed in Chapter 1.
45. See Ali Ihsan Yurd and Mustafa S Kaçalin, *Akşemseddin, 1390–1459: Hayatı ve Eserleri* (İstanbul: Marmara Üniversitesi, İlâhiyat Vakfı, 1994).
46. Fahd, *La divination arabe*, pp. 408–10. The *Malḥamat Dāniyāl* is not to be confused with either the Greco-Syriac apocalyptic *Visions of Daniel*, discussed in the previous chapter, or the Hebrew Bible's Book of Daniel.
47. A. Fodor, 'Malḥamat Daniyal', in *The Muslim East: Studies in Honor of Julius Germanus*, ed. G. Kaldy-Nagy (Budapest: Eötvös Loránd University, 1974), pp. 85–133.
48. See Çelebioğlu, 'Yazıcı Ṣāliḥ ve Şemsiyye'si', as well as Atilla Batur, 'Yazıcı Ṣāliḥ ve Şemsiyye'si' (unpublished MA thesis, Erciyes Üniversitesi, 1999), pp. 14–15; Sibel Sevinç, *Yazıcı Ṣāliḥ'in Melhamesi (Kitabü'ş-Şemsiyye)* (unpublished MA thesis, Cumhuriyet Üniversitesi, 1999) agrees with this assessment.
49. *Ş*, fols 2b–14a.
50. *Ş*, fols 25a, 27a.
51. *Ş*, fol. 141b.
52. *Ş*, fols 1a–2b. See Jaakko Hämeen-Anttila, *The Last Pagans of Iraq: Ibn Waḥshiyya and His Nabatean Agriculture* (Leiden: Brill, 2006); Ahmad ibn 'Ali ibn Qays al-Kasdani, *L'Agriculture nabatéenne: Traduction en arabe attribuée à Abu Bakr Ahmad b. Àli al-Kasdani connu sous le nom d'Ibn*

Wahsiyya (IV/Xe siècle), trans. Toufic Fahd (Damascus: Institut français de Damas, 1993).

53. F. Rochberg-Halton, 'Elements of the Babylonian Contribution to Hellenistic Astrology', *Journal of the American Oriental Society* 108, no. 1 (1988), pp. 51–62; G. Vajda, 'Quelques Observations Sur la "Malḥamat Dāniyāl"', *Arabica* 23, no. 1 (1976), pp. 84–87.
54. Qur'an 2:29: 'He it is Who created for you all that is in the earth. Then He turned to heaven and fashioned it as seven heavens'.
55. *BH*, fol. 2b.
56. Qur'an 8:43.
57. Evliya Çelebi, *Evliya Çelebi Seyahatnâmesi*, vol. 1, p. 161.
58. Michel Foucault, *The Order of Things: An Archaeology of the Human Sciences* (New York: Pantheon Books, 1971), pp. 30–34.
59. Ibid.
60. Ibid.
61. *AM*, fols 45a–47b.
62. Julian Raby, 'A Sultan of Paradox: Mehmed the Conqueror as a Patron of the Arts', *Oxford Art Journal* 5, no. 1 (1982), pp. 3–8.
63. '*Pes Ḥaqq te'ālā hazretinüñ qudretinden ve 'aẓāmetinden 'ilmümüz irdügi qadar bir mıqdār beyān eyleyelüm tā kim Ḥaqquñ qudretin ve 'aẓāmetin bundan qıyās edesin, bu azacıq 'ömr içinde fitne zamānında cihānı geşt edüb görmege iḫtiyāc olmaya*'. *Dürr-i Meknûn: İnceleme, Çevriyazı, Dizin, Tıpkıbasım*, ed. Ahmet Demirtaş (Istanbul: Akademik Kitaplar, 2009), p. 85. As discussed in this study's introduction, the text has traditionally, and in my view erroneously, been attributed to Aḥmed Bīcān; see Grenier, 'Reassessing the Authorship of the *Dürr-i Meknūn*'.

Conclusion

This study has been an attempt to reconstruct the site of origin of an Ottoman spiritual vernacular. Students of early Ottoman history are challenged by blinding teleologies. The fourteenth and fifteenth centuries progressed within the context of the tensions generated by major social and ideological changes looming in the future: a march towards classical Ottoman Sunnism, an Istanbul-based bureaucracy and its ideological leadership of the Muslims of the eastern Mediterranean. Seen this way, Ottoman institutions and ideas of the fifteenth century are only the seeds from which this classical organism sprouted. This study has attempted to bring the intellectual life and culture of these early centuries out from underneath the shadow of the Age of Süleyman, to envision it as its own whole – in other words, viewing the Ottoman fifteenth century on its own terms, from its own location in space and time, through the eyes of those who experienced it. For this purpose, the Yazıcıoğlus are perhaps not ideal subjects. As anthologists they spent few words on biographical description. While they did not speak much about themselves, they were what they professed to be: keen diagnosticians of the spiritual needs of 'the [common] people of our land'. It is in their assessment of the early Ottoman frontier's ailments and in the medicines that they applied – the volumes of religious sciences that occupied their humble bookshelves – that the humours of the early Ottoman period can be sensed. The spiritual vernacular of Turkish-speaking Ottoman Muslims had other origins and ancestors, to be sure. But the writings of these humble brothers of Gelibolu – a fusion of prophetic narratives, classical religious sciences and mysticism – uncover its roots and define its style.

Scholars of Ottoman society may be disoriented by the apparent absence of the state in the world of the Yazıcıoğlus. For Aḥmed Bīcān and his older brother, the Ottomans were only vague symbols – distant notionally, if not physically – of the advancement of the Turcophone Muslim community into Balkan lands; what actually existed for them was not the 'Ottoman state' but the lords of Gelibolu. Chapter 1 has discussed the family's multi-generational relationship with two members of the *ġāzī* Qaṣṣāboğlu family – first 'Alī, then his son Maḥmūd – and, in between, the *subaşı* İskender whose legacy was secured by the *namāzgāh* that he constructed in Gelibolu. By the middle of the fifteenth century, the family served men such as Aḥmed-i Ḫāṣṣ, who were Ottoman functionaries. These benefactors, increasingly connected to the state, permitted Aḥmed and Meḥmed to study with the intellectual elite of their lands, represented by the nascent Ottoman scholarly community in Edirne and the Bayramī Sufis of Ankara. In their attachments to these '*ġāzī-a'yān*s' and to their teachers of religious sciences, the Yazıcıoğlus were deeply bound to their town of Gelibolu as much as to their community, which they conceived broadly: the Muslims of Rumelia. Their social horizons along this frontier gave them an audience of plebeian new Muslims; their intellectual horizons, expanded by their time in Ankara and Edirne, encompassed the cosmopolitan kinds of Islamic knowledge that could serve this audience and bind them to Islam.

Aḥmed's and Meḥmed's dual inheritance of the Ḥanafī orthodox Edirne curriculum, on one hand, and the Akbarian Sufi heritage of the Bayramīs, on the other, is reflected in their writings in a straightforward manner. Chapter 2 has detailed what kinds of books sat on the bookshelves of the Yazıcıoğlu brothers as they composed their catechistic texts. Here it is possible to see how the intellectual world of the frontier was neither merely a local appearance of a classical canon, nor a 'Turkish' or 'Ottoman' invention cut from whole cloth. Rather, it was a sensitive application of an inherited and very canonical set of texts and ideas to a unique arrangement of local needs. Very little of their library can be said to be unique, or even specifically Ottoman. It was their usage of these texts that was particular.

An Aegean and Rumelian moment conditioned their writing – a society characterised by religious heterogeneity moving under the sign of Ottoman military expansion. This study does not dispute the centrality of the idea of *ġazā*, the complex formulation of borderland confessional awareness that coexisted, as a 'metadoxy',[1] with heterodoxy and inter-confessionality. Chapter 3 has shown that it was a specific environment of conversation about Islam and Christianity that motivated the Yazıcıoğlus' doxologies, a consciousness that the Turcophone Muslim community of Rumelia was both unique and vulnerable. While the brothers' community was sharply ascendant in a political sense, it was constantly in danger of losing its coherence. Ears pressed to the sources of wisdom and law, these provincial pietists were trying to hear, across the distance from the Dardenelles, the messages from the definitional centre of the Islamic community. In the *Envārü'l-'Aşıqīn*, Aḥmed wrote that Adam, cast out of Eden and living on the top of Mount Sarāndīb far from both Heaven and Eve, listened to the clouds as he pined for his lost communication with the divine:

> When Adam stood up, his head would reach up close to the heavens. He would hear the litanies of the angels. Then Adam's beard grew. Before this he was like a young boy. Adam could no longer hear the voices of the angels. He grew quite barbarous. He said, 'O Lord, what has happened to me that I cannot hear the voices of the angels?' The Exalted God said, 'You have debased yourself, you have shamed yourself, and now you cannot hear their words'.[2]

This story may have held power for Thracian Muslims because of their own sense of distance from the linguistic and spiritual heart of Islamic knowledge, hidden behind the Arabic and Persian languages and in the elaborate sciences of scriptural exegesis, law and theosophy. It was the Yazıcıoğlus' duty to interpret these litanies of the angels into the language of living Rumelians, a common Turkish.

This communitarian project aimed to define and promote 'Islam' as such, not any sort of Ottoman Sunnism or Ḥanafi legalism. Faith in a unitary God and in Muḥammad's prophetic mission was considered sufficient. Chapter 4 has outlined the Yazıcıoğlus' abstention from a polemical debate on dogmatics. The Yazıcıoğlus promoted Ibn 'Arabī's doctrines, ignoring their rationalist critics, while appealing to conservative pietists who worried that they were a latter-day innovation. Along another dimension, the Yazıcıoğlus were *not* sensitive to the shadow of Shī'ī heresy, and in fact occasionally drew from Shī'ī lore even as they extolled the Sunnī model of caliphal succession. The Yazıcıoğlus were also relatively non-committal on the question of the apocalypse: the End Times were on the horizon, and the Ottoman sultan would be central in the way in which the apocalypse would play out, but its timing was vague and its outcome uncertain. Indeed, the only certainty was that the faithful would be rewarded with salvation.

It is striking that both Yazıcıoğlu brothers and their father all wrote on natural philosophy; Chapter 5 has explored the meaning of these natural philosophical writings, asking if they might have coalesced not necessarily around some common epistemological ground, but around similar uncertainties and concerns. These 'scientific' writings are all occupied with the role of humans in the universe, using the model of the microcosm conceived in a Sufi way to delimit and order the world. The moral act of human faith and piety gave this world its centre. Like their ecumenical

Islam and their defense of an irenic Sufism, this too was a remedy for the disorder and the social centrifugal forces that threatened the Yazıcıoğlus' precarious community.

* * *

The reader will have to decide whether this book has succeeded in making accessible some fragments of the Yazıcıoğlus' inner life and social world, a piece in the evolution of Ottoman piety and early modern intellectual history. It has, at least, addressed a few questions that puzzle historians of the early Ottoman period. Regarding the role of the state in early Ottoman intellectual formation, this study has argued that, in instances such as the Yazıcıoğlus, the Ottoman house was peripheral, but its venture of European expansion was central. The bounds of Rumelian Muslim non-elite intellectual culture, far from being restricted to 'folk' knowledge, have been shown to extend all the way to Khurasan – but not far beyond a basic canon. The worry about the integrity of Islam amidst widespread ecumenical sentiment demonstrably had a profound effect on Ottoman popular piety. And, in the century prior to the Ottoman-Safavid conflict, the Islam of the frontiers was unsectarian, concerned only with faith and the order it brought.

Each of these lessons may apply to the study of piety in global early modern history in general. The combination of the frontier-centric particularity of early Ottoman pious culture with its fluent participation in a global cultural system – in the case of the Yazıcıoğlus, Ḥanafī religious sciences and Sufism carried by mystics and scholars from Iran, Syria and Egypt – seems to be somewhat characteristic of enduring early modern pieties. It bears similarities with Spain, whose frontier Catholicism swept over the Americas and was encoded in the Counter-Reformation, much like the Yazıcıoğlus' Sunnism was later given the mantle of high faith in the age of Ebū's-Sü'ūd. One must also consider the case of Muscovy, another frontier-state whose pious forms in the early modern period were packaged in texts such as the *Domostroi*[3] and carried far beyond their original context. Finally, it is striking that the state Shī'ism of Safavid Iran was to emerge from a similar milieu of Turcophone pastoralists caught between the edge of the *dār al-islām* and the rising and falling post-Mongol Islamic empires. The Yazıcıoğlus' *Muhammediyye* shares its enduring sacral quality with the poetry of Shāh Ismā'īl, another revered body of Turkish verse, emerging several generations later on the opposite end of the Anatolian plateau; both live to the present, in their respective communities, as expressions of an unmediated piety.

By the same token, I hope that this work has helped to call into question the idea that Ottoman Islam was a uniquely normative or 'central' variant of orthodox Sunnism, master-minded by the pious aims of the sultans. The Yazıcıoğlus cobbled together from medieval non-Turkish sources a popular creed, without the aid of the Ottoman state; the result is a spiritual vernacular melding Ḥanafism and Sufism, a blend that, while enduring, was deeply conditioned by its origins. The characteristics that Ottomanists often praise about that specific imperial culture – with the Ottoman state's strength laying in its potential for organised militarisation and its powerful capacity for bureaucracy – have almost nothing to do with the sensitive fideism of the Yazıcıoğlus, which only temporarily accompanied the priorities of the house of 'Os̱mān. In the sixteenth and seventeenth centuries, the pietism of the Yazıcıoğlus' intellectual heirs, Meḥmed Birgivī and Qāḍīzāde, would instead be voiced as calls to reform against the state.[4] Ottoman Sunnism was one of a number of early modern creeds born to address the needs of frontier populations.

While the Yazıcıoğlus' writings were intended to heal the souls of the believers, these preachers addressing a flock of humble sailors and soldiers also penned their books in order to save their own imperiled souls, so that their writings may be lasting tokens of their lives and call upon the readers to pray for their own salvation. Their books will be measured alongside their souls in the divine Balance that weighs one's virtue in heaven. The Balance, said Aḥmed Bīcān, does not measure material mass, but responds to the ethereal lightness of the soul's substance, wherever it inheres. In this respect, 'the Balance is opposite the balances of this world'. Its plates rise to approach God when something of real value is placed upon it, and they fall when given something as heavy as gold to measure. This study of the Yazıcıoğlus is offered in the hope that scholars of Ottoman and Islamic history and religion might find in it value, as they weigh it in their own Balance.

Notes

1. The term is Kafadar's: 'Maybe the religious history of Anatolian and Balkan Muslims living in the frontier areas of the period from the eleventh to the fifteenth centuries should be conceptualized in part in terms of a 'metadoxy', a state of being beyond doxies, a combination of being doxy-naïve and not being doxy-minded, as well as the absence of a state that was interested in rigorously defining and strictly enforcing an orthodoxy'. Kafadar, *Between Two Worlds*, p. 76.
2. *EA*, fols 30a–30b.
3. Carolyn Pouncy, *The 'Domostroi': Rules for Russian Households in the Time of Ivan the Terrible* (Ithaca: Cornell University Press, 1994).

4. See Madeline C. Zilfi, 'The Kadizadelis: Discordant Revivalism in Seventeenth-Century Istanbul', *Journal of Near Eastern Studies* 45, no. 4 (1986), pp. 251–69; Madeline C. Zilfi, *The Politics of Piety: The Ottoman Ulema in the Postclassical Age (1600–1800)* (Minneapolis: Bibliotheca Islamica, 1988).

Appendix

al-Kisā'ī	Yazıcıoğlu
The first is called Ramaka, beneath which is the Barren Wind, which can be bridled by no fewer than 70,000 angels. With this wind God destroyed the people of 'Ād. The inhabitants of Ramaka are a nation called Muwashshim, upon whom falls everlasting torment and retribution.	The first one's name is Demakad, and there is a barren wind beneath it. God destroyed the tribe of 'Ād with this wind. There is a tribe in it, its name is Tamis, and some of them eat each other.
The second earth is called Khalada, wherein are the implements of torture for the inhabitants of Hell. There dwells a nation called Tamis, whose food is their own flesh and whose drink is their own blood.	The name of the second world is Ḫalada, and to punish its unbelievers there are various implements there. And there is one tribe there named Buşīm, and there is reward and punishment for them.
The third earth is called 'Arqa, wherein dwell mule-like eagles with spear-like tails. On each tail are 360 poisonous tails. On each tail are 360 poisonous quills. Were even one quill placed on the face of the earth, the entire universe would come to an end.	The name of the third world is 'Arq, and there are scorpions there like mules that bite with their tails. If one of the people of this world were to be bitten, the whole world would perish.
The fourth earth is called Ḥaraba, wherein dwell the snakes of Hell, which are as large as mountains [. . .] The inhabitants of this earth are a nation called Jilla, and they have no eyes, hands or feet, but they have wings like bats and die only of old age.	The fourth world's name is Cerebe, and there are snakes there, and there are a people there named Cülhüm. They have wings and fly, but they have no eyes.

The fifth earth is called Maltham, wherein stones of brimstone hang around the necks of infidels [. . .] The inhabitants are a nation called Halja, who are numerous and who eat each other.	The fifth world is called Mülse, and for the heathens there, there is a mountain of brimstone. There are a people there, given the name Mahutat. They eat each other.
The sixth earth is called Sijjīn. Here are the registers of the people of Hell, and their works are vile [. . .] Herein dwells a nation called Qatat, who are shaped like birds and worship God sincerely.	The sixth world is named Siccīn. The deeds of the people of Hell are recorded there. There are a people given the name of Qatat, who conduct worship, taking the form of a bird.
The seventh earth is called ‘Ajiba and is the habitation of Iblis. There dwells a nation called Khasum [. . .] It is they who will be given dominion over God and Magog, who will be destroyed by them.	The seventh world's name is ‘Aj'ba. There is a tribe there named Cüşüm. In the end times, the people of Gog and Magog will come out of there, and subsequently another tribe will come out from under the earth. Gog and Magog will perish and then Satan will be imprisoned.

Bibliography

Manuscripts

Abdurrahman Bistami, 'Dürret Tacü'l-Resail', Süleymaniye Kütüphanesi, Nuruosmaniye 4905.

Alae'd-dīn el-Amasī, *Tarik-i Edeb*, Süleymaniye Kütüphanesi, Laleli 1876.

Aḥmed Bīcān, *Envāru'l-'Aşıqīn*, Süleymaniye Kütüphanesi, Pertev Paşa 229-M.

Aḥmed Bīcān, *Envarü'l-Aşıkin*, Üsküdar Hacı Selim Ağa 467.

Aḥmed Bīcān, *'Acāibü'l-Mahlūqāt*, Süleymaniye Kütüphanesi, Ali Nihat Tarlan 100.

Ahmed Bican, *Acaibü'l-mahlukat,* Süleymaniye Kütüphanesi, Sütlüce Dergahı 108.

Aḥmed Bīcān, *Kitābü'l-Müntehā*, Süleymaniye Kütüphanesi, Kılıç Ali Paşa 630.

Aḥmed Bīcān, *Kitābü'l-Müntehā*, Süleymaniye Kütüphanesi, Hacı Mahmud Efendi 1657.

Aḥmed Bīcān, *Kitābü'l-Müntehā*, Süleymaniye Kütüphanesi, Yazma Bağışlar 7585.

Aḥmed Bīcān, *Rūḥu'l-Ervāḥ*, Atatürk Kitaplığı, Nadir Eserler, OE Yazmalar 1744.

Aḥmed Bīcān, *Rūḥu'l-Ervāḥ*, Cod. N. F. 202, 204, Historische Sammelhandschrift, Österreichische Staatsbibliothek, Vienna.

Aḥmed Bīcān, *Būstānu'l-Haqāiq*, Millet Kütüphanesi, A. E. Şerire 561.

Aḥmed Bīcān, *Cevhernāme*, Süleymaniye Kütüphanesi, Ayasofya 3452.

'Defter-i Esāmī-i Sancaḳ-i Gelibolu (Awā'il Shawwāl 879/February 1475)', Atatürk Kitaplıgı, Cevdet Collection no. 79.

Eşrefoğlu Rumi, *Tarikatname*, Süleymaniye Kütüphanesi, Hacı Mahmud Efendi 4667.

İsmail Hakkı Bursevi, *Şerh ul-Muhammediye el-Müsemma bi-Ferah ür-Ruh*, Süleymaniye Kütüphanesi, Hacı Mahmud Efendi 2241.

János Házi, 'Machumet propheta, vallásán levő egy fő irástúdo doctornac irásából' (Cassan, 1626), Lucian Blaga Central Library, Cluj-Napoca, BMV 1795.

Mehmed Emirzade, 'Majmu'a 1694–1716', Houghton Library, Harvard University, MS Arab 292.
Meḥmed Yazıcıoğlu, *Kitāb-i Muḥammediyye*, Vakıflar Müdürlüğü, 431-A.
Meḥmed Yazıcıoğlu, 'Muhammediye', Lund University Library, Box 3, Jarring Collection 55.
Meḥmed Yazıcıoğlu, *Maghārib al-Zamān*, Süleymaniye Kütüphanesi, Nuruosmaniye 2596.
Meḥmed Yazıcıoğlu, *Sharḥ Fusūs al-Ḥikam*, Süleymaniye Kütüphanesi, Pertev Paşa 293.
'Sırr-ı Canan', Millet Kütüphanesi, Manzum 937.3.
Süleyman b. Davud es-Suvari, *Zehretü'r-riyad*, Süleymaniye Kütüphanesi, Aya Sofya 4329.
'Tapu Tahrir Defteri T. T. 0012', Başbakanlık Arşivi, T. T. 0012.
Yazıcı Sāliḥ, *Şemsiyye*, Süleymaniye Kütüphanesi, Pertevniyal 766.
Yazıcı Sāliḥ, *Şemsiyye,* Turkish Manuscripts Cod. Or. 1448 (2), Leiden University Library.

Published Texts of the Yazıcıoğlus

Batur, Atilla. 'Yazıcı Ṣāliḥ ve Şemsiyye'si'. Unpublished MA thesis. Erciyes Üniversitesi, 1999.
Bican, Ahmed. *Envārü'l-'Āşıqīn = Âsikların Nurları.* Edited by Ahmet Kahraman. İstanbul: Tercüman, 1973.
Bican, Ahmet. *El-Müntehâ: Fusûsu'l-Hikem Üzerine bir Çalışma.* Edited by Ayşe Beyazit. İstanbul: İnsan Yayınları, 2011.
Bican, Ahmed. *Envārü'l-'Āşıqīn.* İstanbul: [n. p.], 1283 [1866–67].
Bican, Ahmed. *Envārü'l-'Āşıqīn.* İstanbul: Matba'a-i 'Osmaniyye, 1301 [1883–84].
Bican, Ahmed. *Anwar al-Ashiqin* (Kazan: [n. p.], 1898).
Çelebioğlu, Âmil, ed. *Muhammediye, I-II.* İstanbul: Millî Eğitim Bakanlığı, 1996.
Yazıcıoğlu, Mehmed. *Kitab-i Muhammediyye.* İstanbul: Bosnavî Hacı Muharrem Efendi'nin Taş Destgâhı, 1280 [1863].
Yazıcıoğlu, Mehmed. *Kitab-i Muhammediyye.* İstanbul: Unknown Imprint, 1283 [1866–67].
Yazıcıoğlu, Mehmed. *Kitab-i Muhammediyye.* İstanbul: Der-i Sa'adet, 1323 [1905–6].
Yazıcıoglu, Mehmed. *Muhammediyye* (İstanbul: Matba'a-i Osmaniyye, 1300 [1882–83].

Other Published Primary Sources

Ahmedi, *İskender-Nāme: İnceleme-Tıpkıbasım.* Edited by İsmail Ünver. Ankara: Türk Dil Kurumu, 1983.
Amiroutzes, George. *El diálogo de la fé con el sultán de los turcos: édición*

crítica. Edited by Óscar de la Cruz Palma. Madrid: Consejo Superior de Investigaciones Científicas, 2000.

'Aşıkpaşazade, *Tevarih-i Âl-i Osman'dan Aşıkpaşazade Tarihi*. Edited by 'Ali Bey. İstanbul: Matba'a-yı Âmire, 1332 [1914].

'Aṭṭār, Farīd al-Dīn. *Farid Ad-Din 'Attār's Memorial of God's Friends: Lives and Sayings of Sufis*. Translated and edited by Paul E. Losensky. New York: Paulist Press, 2009.

Austin, R. W. J. *The Bezels of Wisdom*. New York: Paulist Press, 1980.

Avicenna, *Avicenna's Psychology: An English Translation of Kitāb Al-Najāt, Book II, Chapter VI, with Historico-Philosophical Notes and Textual Improvements on the Cairo Edition*. Translated by Fazlur Rahman. Westport: Hyperion Press, 1981.

Bican, Ahmed. *Dürr-i meknun*. Edited by Necdet Sakaoğlu. İstanbul: Tarih Vakfı Yurt Yayınları, 1999.

Bican, Ahmed. *Dürr-i Meknûn: İnceleme, Çevriyazi, Dizin, Tıpkıbasım*. Edited by Ahmet Demirtaş. İstanbul: Akademik Kitaplar, 2009.

Bican, Ahmed. *Dürr-i Meknun: Kritische Edition mit Kommentar*. Edited by Laban Kaptein. Asch: Selbstverl. Laban Kaptein, 2007.

[Bursalı], Mehmed Tahir. *Osmanlı Müellifleri*. İstanbul: Matba'a-i Amire, 1914.

Bursalı, Mehmet Tahir. *Osmanlı Müellifleri*. Edited by A. Fikri Yavuz and İsmail Özen. İstanbul: Meral Yayınları, 1972.

Bursevi, İsmail Hakkı. *Şerh ul-Muḥammediye el-Müsemma bi-Ferah ür-Ruh*. İstanbul: Elhac Muharrem Efendi Bosnavî Matbaası, 1877.

de Clavijo, Ruy González. *Embajada a Tamorlán: Estudio y edición de un manuscrito del siglo XV*. Edited by Francisco López Estrada. Madrid: Consejo superior de investigaciones científicas, Instituto Nicolás Antonio, 1943.

Cyriac of Ancona. *Later Travels*. Translated by Edward W. Bodnar and Clive Foss. Cambridge, MA: Harvard University Press, 2003.

Eşrefoğlu Rumi. *Tarikatname*. Edited by Esra Keskinkılıç. İstanbul: Gelenek, 2002.

Evliya Çelebi, *Evliya Çelebi Seyahatnâmesi*. Edited by Orhan Şaik Gökyay, Robert Dankoff, Seyit Ali Kahraman, Yücel Dağlı and İsmet Sezgin. İstanbul: Yapı Kredi Yayınları, 1996.

Doukas, *The Decline and Fall of Byzantium to the Ottoman Turks*. Translated by Harry J. Magoulias. Detroit: Wayne State University Press, 1975.

Al-Ghāzāli, Abu Hāmid. *The Niche of Lights = Mishkat al-Anwar*. Translated by David Buchman. Provo: Brigham Young University Press, 1998.

Ibn Hishām, 'Abd al-Malik. *The Life of Muhammad*. Translated by A. Guillaume. London: Oxford University Press, 1955.

İznikî, Kutbe'd-dîn. *Mukaddime*. Edited by Kerime Üstünova. Bursa: T.C. Uludağ Üniversitesi, 2003.

Jāmī, Nūr-ad-Dīn 'Abd-ar-Raḥmān Ibn-Aḥmad. *Naqd an-nuṣūṣ fī šarḥ naqš al-fuṣūṣ*. Edited by William C. Chittick. Tihrān: [n. p.], 1977.

al-Kasdani, Ahmad ibn 'Ali ibn Qays. *L'Agriculture nabatéenne: Traduction en arabe attribuée à Abu Bakr Ahmad b. Àli al-Kasdani connu sous le nom d'Ibn Wahsiyya (IV/Xe siècle)*. Translated by Toufic Fahd. Damascus: Institut français de Damas, 1993.

Kātib Çelebi. *Kitāb Kashf al-Ẓunūn 'an Asāmī al-Kutub wa al-Funūn*. İstanbul: Maṭba'at al-'Ālem, 1892.

al-Kisā'ī, Muḥammad ibn 'Abd Allāh. *The Tales of the Prophets of Al-Kisā'ī*. Translated by Wheeler M. Thackston. Boston: Twayne Publishers, 1978.

Kritovoulos. *History of Mehmed the Conqueror*. Translated by Charles T. Riggs. Princeton: Princeton University Press, 1954.

Latifi. *Tezkiretü'ş-Şu'arâ ve Tabsıratü'n-Nuzamâ: İnceleme, Metin*. Edited by Rıdvan Canım. Ankara: Atatürk Kültür Merkezi Başkanlığı, 2000.

Mecdi Edirneli, Mehmed. *Hadaik üs-Şakaik*. Istanbul: Dar üt-tibaat ül-amire, [n. d.].

Mecdi, Mehmed Efendi. *Ḥadā'iq al-Shaqā'iq*. Edited by Abdülkadir Özcan. İstanbul: Çağrı Yayınları, 1989.

Mihailović, Konstantin. *Memoirs of a Janissary*. Translate by Benjamin Stolz. Ann Arbor: University of Michigan, 1975.

Muḥammad ibn Ismā'īl. *Sahih al-Bukhārī*. Liechtenstein: Thesaurus Islamicus Foundation, 2000.

Muntaner, Ramón. *Cronica Catalana de Ramón Muntaner: Texto Original y Traducción Castellana*. Translated by Antonio de Bofarull. Barcelona: Jaime Jepus, 1860.

Muṣṭafā bin Aḥmed 'Âlî. *Künhü'l-Aḫbār*. İstanbul: Darü't-Tıba'ati'l-amire, 1277.

Nesimi. *The Quatrains of Nesimi, Fourteenth-Century Turkic Hurufi*. Edited by Kathleen R. F. Burrill. The Hague: Mouton, 1972.

Nestor-Iskander. *The Tale of Constantinople: Of its Origin and Capture by the Turks in the Year 1453*. Translated by Walter K. Hanak and Marios Philippides. New Rochelle: A. D. Caratzas, 1998.

Neşri. *Kitâb-ı cihan-nümâ*. Edited by Faik Reşit Unat and Mehmet Altay Köymen. Ankara: Türk Tarih Kurumu Basımevi, 1995.

Oruç Beğ. *Oruç Beğ Tarihi (1288–1502)*. Edited by Necdet Öztürk. İstanbul: Çamlıca, 2007.

Qazwīnī, Zakarīyā ibn Muḥammad. *'Ajā'ib al-makhlūqāt wa gharā'ib al-mawjūdāt*. Edited by Fārūq Sa'd. Bayrūt: Dār al-Āfāq al-Jadīdah, 1973.

al-Qashani, 'Abd al-Razzaq. *A Glossary of Sufi Technical Terms*. Translated by Nabil Safwat and David Pendlebury. London: Octagon Press, 1984.

al-Qušayrī, Muslim Ibn al-Ḥaǧǧāǧ. *Ṣaḥīḥ Muslim*. Liechtenstein: Thesaurus Islamicus Foundation, 2000.

Ṣaghānī, al-Ḥasan ibn Muḥammad. *Mashāriq al-anwār*. Dersaadet [İstanbul]: Matbaa-yı Reşadiye, 1911.

Sarı 'Abdullāh Efendi, *Ṣemeratü'l-fuād fi'l-mebde ve'l-me'ād*. İstanbul: Matba'a-i Amire, 1288 [1871–82].

Sarınay, Yusuf, and Abdullah Sivridağ. *75 Numaralı Gelibolu Livası Mufassal*

Tahrir Defteri (925/1519): Dizin ve Transkripsiyon. Ankara: Başbakanlık Devlet Arşivleri Genel Müdürlüğü, Osmanlı Arşivi Daire Başkanlığı, 2009.

Schiltberger, Johannes. *The Bondage and Travels of Johann Schiltberger, a Native of Bavaria, in Europe, Asia, and Africa, 1396–1427*. Edited by Filip Jakob Bruun, translated by J. Buchan Telfer. London: Hakluyt Society Publications, 1879.

Shahrastānī, Muḥammad ibn ʻAbd al-Karīm. *Muslim Sects and Divisions: The Section on Muslim Sects in Kitāb al-Milal wa 'L-Niḥal*. Translated by A. K. Kazi and J. G. Flynn. London: Kegan Paul International, 1984.

Süleyman Çelebi. *Mevlid: Vesîletü'n-necât*. Edited by Ahmed Ateş. Ankara: Türk Tarih Kurumu Basımevi, 1954.

Süleymān Çelebi. *Mevlid*. Edited by Neclâ Pekolcay. Ankara: Türkiye Diyanet Vakfı, 1993.

Taşköprüzade, Ahmed. *al-Shaqā'iq al-Nuʻmāniyya fī ʻUlamā' al-Dawla al-ʻUthmāniyya*. Edited by Ahmed Subhi Furat. İstanbul: İstanbul Üniversitesi Edebiyat Fakültesi Basımevi, 1985.

al-Tibrīzī, Muḥammad ibn ʻAbd Allāh Khaṭīb. *Mishkāt al-Maṣābīḥ*. Edited by Muḥammad Mahdī Sharīf. Beirut: Dar al-Kutub, 2012.

Tursun Beg. *Târih-i Ebü'l-Feth*. İstanbul: Baha Matbaası, 1977.

Yazıcızâde Ali, *Tevârîh-i Âl-i Selçuk*. Edited by Abdullah Bakır. İstanbul: Çamlica, 2009.

Secondary Literature

Addas, Claude. *Quest for the Red Sulphur: The Life of Ibn Arabi*. Cambridge: Islamic Texts Society, 1993.

Ágoston, Gábor. 'Muslim Cultural Enclaves in Hungary under Ottoman Rule'. *Acta Orientalia Academiae Scientiarum Hungaricae* 45, no. 2/3 (1991): 181–204.

Ahmed, Shahab. 'Mapping the World of a Scholar in Sixth/twelfth Century Bukhāra: Regional Tradition in Medieval Islamic Scholarship as Reflected in a Bibliography'. *Journal of the American Oriental Society* 120, no. 1 (2000): 24–43.

Ahmed, Shahab, and Nenad Filipovic. 'The Sultan's Syllabus: A Curriculum for the Ottoman Imperial Medreses Prescribed in a Fermān of Qānūnī I Süleymān, Dated 973 (1565)'. *Studia Islamica* 98/99 (2004): 183–218.

Akpınar, Cemil, 'Hacı Paşa'. *İslam Ansiklopedisi*.

Alexander, Paul J. 'Medieval Apocalypses as Historical Sources'. *The American Historical Review* 73, no. 4 (1968): 997–1018.

Alexander, Paul Julius. *The Byzantine Apocalyptic Tradition*. Berkeley, Calif.: University of California Press, 1985.

Algar, Hamid. 'The Naqshbandī Order: A Preliminary Survey of Its History and Significance'. *Studia Islamica* 44 (1976): 123–52.

Bibliography

Algar, Hamid. 'Reflections on Ibn 'Arabi in Early Naqshbandî Tradition'. *Journal of the Muhyiddin Ibn 'Arabi Society* 10 (1991): 45–57.

Algar, Hamid. 'Muhammad Parsa', *İslam Ansiklopedisi.*

Allouche, Adel. T*he Origins and Development of the Ottoman-Ṣafavid Conflict (906–962/1500–1555).* Berlin: Klaus Schwarz Verlag, 1983.

Ambros, Edith. 'Yazidji-Oghlu'. *Encyclopaedia of Islam, Second Edition.*

Amir-Moezzi, Mohammad Ali. *The Divine Guide Early Shi'ism: The Sources of Esotericism in Islam.* Albany: State University of New York Press, 1994.

Amoretti, Biancamaria. 'Religion in the Timurid and Safavid Periods'. In *Cambridge History of Iran*, vol. 6, pp. 610–55. Cambridge: Cambridge University Press, 1986.

Anooshahr, Ali. *The Ghazi Sultans and the Frontiers of Islam: A Comparative Study of the Late Medieval and Early Modern Periods.* London: Routledge, 2009.

Antov, Nikolay. *The Ottoman 'Wild West': The Balkan Frontier in the Fifteenth and Sixteenth Centuries* (Cambridge: Cambridge University Press, 2017).

Arnakis, G. G. 'Gregory Palamas among the Turks and Documents of His Captivity as Historical Sources'. *Speculum* 26, no. 1 (1951): 104–18.

Arnakis, G. G. 'Gregory Palamas, the Hiones, and the Fall of Gallipoli'. *Byzantion* 22 (1952): 305–12.

Arnakis, G. G. 'Futuwwa Traditions in the Ottoman Empire: Akhis, Bektashi Dervishes, and Craftsmen'. *Journal of Near Eastern Studies* 12, no. 4 (1953): 232–47.

Atanasova, Kameliya. 'The Sufi as the Axis of the World: Representations of Religious Authority in the Works of Ismail Hakki Bursevi (1653–1725)'. Unpublished doctoral dissertation, University of Pennsylvania, 2016.

Atçıl, Abdurrahman. *Scholars and Sultans in the Early Modern Ottoman Empire.* Cambridge: Cambridge University Press, 2018.

Atçıl, Abdurrahman. 'The Kalam (Rational Theology) Section in the Palace Library Inventory'. In *Treasures of Knowledge: An Inventory of the Ottoman Palace Library (1502/3–503/4).* Edited by Gülru Necipoğlu, Cemal Kafadar and Cornell H. Fleischer, pp. 309–88. Leiden; Boston: Brill, 2019.

Ayverdi, Ekrem Hakkı. *Osmanlı Mi'mârîsinde Çelebi ve II. Sultan Murad Devri, 806–855 (1403–1451): II.* İstanbul: Baha Matbaası, 1972.

Azamat, Nihat. 'Ḥācı Bayram-i Velī'. *İslam Ansiklopedisi.*

Baalbaki, Ramzi. 'al-Saghani'. *Encyclopaedia of Islam, Second Edition.*

Babinger, Franz. 'Von Amurath zu Amurath: Vor- und Nachspiel der Schlacht bei Varna'. *Oriens* 3, no. 2 (1950): 229–265.

Babinger, Franz. *Mehmed the Conqueror and His Time.* Princeton: Princeton University Press, 1978.

Balivet, Michel. *Islam mystique et révolution armée dans les Balkans ottomans: La vie du cheikh Bedreddin, le 'Hallâj des Turcs', 1358/59–1416.* Istanbul: Editions Isis, 1995.

Bashir, Shahzad. *Messianic Hopes and Mystical Visions: The Nūrbakhshīya between Medieval and Modern Islam*. Columbia: University of South Carolina Press, 2003.

Bashir, Shahzad. *Fazlallah Astarabadi and the Hurufis*. Oxford: Oneworld, 2005.

Bashir, Shahzad. *Sufi Bodies: Religion and Society in Medieval Islam*. New York: Columbia University Press, 2011.

Bayraktar, Mehmet. 'Dâvûd-i Kayserî'. *İslam Ansiklopedisi*.

Bayramoğlu, Fuat. *Hacı Bayram-ı Veli: Yaşamı, Soyu, Vakfı*. Ankara: Türk Tarih Kurumu Basımevi, 1983.

Berlekamp, Persis. *Wonder, Image, and Cosmos in Medieval Islam*. New Haven: Yale University Press, 2011.

Binbaş, İlker Evrim. *Intellectual Networks in Timurid Iran: Sharaf Al-Dīn 'Alī Yazdī and the Islamicate Republic of Letters*. New York: Cambridge University Press, 2016.

Birge, John K. *The Bektashi Order of Dervishes*. London: Luzac, 1994.

Bostan, İdris. 'Saruca Paşa'. *İslam Ansiklopedisi*.

Breebart, Deodaat Anne. 'The Development and Structure of the Turkish Futuwa Guilds'. Unpublished doctoral dissertation. Princeton University, 1961.

Brinner, William M. *'Arā'is al-majālis fī qiṣaṣ al-anbiyā' or 'Lives of the Prophets'*. Leiden: Brill, 2002.

Burak, Guy. 'Faith, Law and Empire in the Ottoman "Age of Confessionalization" (Fifteenth–Seventeenth Centuries): The Case of "Renewal of Faith"', *Mediterranean Historical Review* 28, no. 1 (2013), pp. 1–23.

Burak, Guy. *The Second Formation of Islamic Law: The Hanafi School in the Early Modern Ottoman Empire*. New York: Cambridge University Press, 2015.

Büchner, V. F. and Golden, P. B. 'Saksīn'. *Encyclopaedia of Islam, Second Edition*.

Cahen, Claude. *Pre-Ottoman Turkey: A General Survey of the Material and Spiritual Culture and History, c. 1071–1330*. New York: Taplinger, 1968.

Cahen, Claude. 'Sur les traces des premiers akhis'. In *60 Yıldönümü Münasebetiyle Fuad Köprülü Armağanı* (İstanbul: [n. p.], 1953).

Calmard, Jean. 'Les Rituels Shiite et le Pouvoir: L'imposition du Shiism Safavide, eulogies et maledictions canoniques'. In *Études Safavides*. Edited by Jean Clamard, pp. 109–50. Paris-Tehran: Institut Français de Recherche en Iran, 1993.

Chittick, William C. 'The Last Will and Testament of Ibn ᶜArabi's Foremost Disciple and Some Notes on Its Author'. *Sophia Perennis* 4 (1978): 43–58.

Chittick, William C. 'Sadr Al-Din Qunawi on the Oneness of Being'. *International Philosophical Quarterly* 21, no. 2 (1981): 171–84.

Chittick, William C. *The Sufi Path of Knowledge: Ibn Al-ᶜArabi's Metaphysics of Imagination*. Albany: State University of New York Press, 1989.

Chittick, William C. *Faith and Practice of Islam: Three Thirteenth Century Sufi Texts*. Albany: State University of New York Press, 1992.

Chittick, William C. 'Ṣadr Al-Dīn Muḥammad B. Isḥāḳ B. Muḥammad B. Yūnus Al-Ḳūnawī'. *Encyclopaedia of Islam, Second Edition*.

Chodkiewicz, Michel. 'The Diffusion of Ibn 'Arabī's Doctrine', *Journal of the Muhyiddin Ibn 'Arabi Society* 9 (1991): 36.

Chodkiewicz, Michel. *Seal of the Saints: Prophethood and Sainthood in the Doctrine of Ibn 'Arabi*. Cambridge: Islamic Texts Society, 1993.

Clayer, Nathalie. *Mystiques, État et société: Les Halvetis dans l'aire balkanique de la fin du XVe siècle à nos jours*. Leiden: Brill, 1994.

Clayer, Nathalie, Alexandre Popović and Thierry Zarcone. *Melâmis-Bayrâmis: Études sur trois mouvements mystiques musulmans*. Istanbul: Les Editions Isis, 1998.

Cohn, Norman Rufus Colin. *The Pursuit of the Millennium*. London: Secker & Warburg, 1957.

Cook, David. *Studies in Muslim Apocalyptic*. Princeton: Darwin Press, 2002.

Corbin, Henry. *Alone with the Alone: Creative Imagination in the Sūfism of Ibn 'Arabī*. Princeton: Princeton University Press, 1998.

Curry, John. *The Transformation of Muslim Mystical Thought in the Ottoman Empire: The Rise of the Halveti Order, 1350–1750*. Edinburgh: Edinburgh University Press, 2010.

Çelebioğlu, Âmil. 'Yazıcı-Oğlu Mehmed ve Muhammediye'si'. Unpublished doctoral dissertation. Erzurum Atatürk Üniversitesi İslâmî Bilimler Fakültesi, 1971.

Çelebioğlu, Âmil. 'Yazıcı Salih ve Şemsiyye'si'. *Atatürk Üniversitesi İslami İlimler Fakültesi Dergisi* 1 (1976): 171–218.

Çelebioglu, Amil, and Kemal Eraslan. 'Yazıcı-Oğlu'. *İslam Ansiklopedisi*.

Dağlı, Caner K. *The Ringstones of Wisdom: Fuṣūṣ al-Ḥikam* Chicago: Great Books of the Islamic World, distributed by Kazi Publications, 2004.

Danışmend, İsmail Hami. *Osmanlı Devlet Erkânı: Sadr-ı-a'zamlar (Vezir-i-a'zamlar), Şeyh-ül-islâmlar, Kapdan-ı-deryalar, Baş-defterdarlar, Reîs-ül-küttablar*. İstanbul: Türkiye Yayınevi, 1971.

Darling, Linda T. 'Reformulating the Gazi Narrative: When Was the Ottoman State a Gazi State?' *Turcica* 43 (2011): 13–53.

Darling, Linda T. 'The Mediterranean as a Borderland'. *Review of Middle East Studies* 46, no. 1 (2012): 54–63.

Daston, Lorraine, and Katharine Park. *Wonders and the Order of Nature, 1150–1750*. New York; Cambridge, MA: Zone Books; Distributed by the MIT Press, 1998.

Davidson, Herbert A. *Alfarabi, Avicenna, and Averroes on Intellect: Their Cosmologies, Theories of the Active Intellect, and Theories of Human Intellect*. New York: Oxford University Press, 1992.

Dedes, Yorgo. 'Süleyman Çelebi's Mevlid: Text, Performance, and Muslim-Christian Dialogue'. In *Şinasi Tekin'in anısına: Uygurlardan Osmanlıya*, pp. 305–49. İstanbul: Simurg, 2005.

Demir, Remzi, and Mutlu Kılıç. 'Cevahirnameler ve Osmanlılar Dönemi'nde Yazılmış iki Cevhername', *Osmanlı Tarihi Araştırma ve Uygulama Merkezi Dergisi* 14 (2003): 1–64.

Demirel, Hamide. *The Poet Fuzûli: His Works, Study of His Turkish, Persian and Arabic Divans*. Ankara: Ministry of Culture, 1991.

DeWeese, Devin. 'The Eclipse of the Kubravīyah in Central Asia'. *Iranian Studies* 21, no. 1/2 (1988): 45–83.

Döner, Nuran. 'İsmail Hakkı Bursevi'nin Kitab-i Kebir'i ve Bursevi'de Varidat Kültürü'. *Tasavvuf: İlmî ve Akademik Araştırma Dergisi* 6 (2005): 311–34.

Dunietz, Alexandra Whelan. 'Qadi Husayn Maybudi of Yazd: Representative of the Iranian Provincial Elite in the Late Fifteenth Century'. Unpublished doctoral dissertation. University of Chicago, 1990.

Dunietz, Alexandra Whelan. *The Cosmic Perils of Qadi Ḥusayn Maybudi in Fifteenth-Century Iran*. Boston; Leiden: Brill, 2016.

Düzdağ, Mehmet Ertuğrul. *Kanunî Devri Şeyhülislâmı Ebussuud Efendi Fetvaları*. İstanbul: Kapı Yayınları, 2012.

Ebem, Siyabend. 'Ahmed Bîcân'a Atfedilen bir Eser: *Rûhü'l-Ervâh*'. *Türk Dünyası İncelemeleri Dergisi / Journal of Turkish World Studies* 14, no. 1 (2014): 49–74.

Emre, Side. *İbrahim-i Gülşeni (ca 1442–1534): Itinerant Saint and Cairene Ruler*. Unpublished doctoral dissertation. University of Chicago, 2009.

Emre, Side. *Ibrahim-i Gulshani and the Khalwati-Gulshani Order: Power Brokers in Ottoman Egypt*. Leiden: Brill, 2017.

Encyclopaedia of Islam, Second Edition. Edited by P. Bearman, Th. Bianquis, C. E. Bosworth, E. van Donzel and W. P. Heinrichs. Leiden: Brill, 1960–2007.

Endress, Gerhard, and Abdou Filali-Ansary. *Organizing Knowledge: Encyclopaedic Activities in the Pre-Eighteenth Century Islamic World*. Leiden: Brill, 2006.

Erkan, Mustafa. 'Mustafa Darir'. *İslam Ansiklopedisi*.

Ertaylan, İsmail Hikmet. *Türk Edebiyatı Örnekleri: Varaka Ve Gülşâh*. İstanbul: İstanbul Üniversitesi, 1945.

Ertaylan, İsmail Hikmet. *Ahmed-i Dâ'î: Hayatı ve Eserleri*. İstanbul: Üçler Basımevi, 1952.

Erünsal, Ismail E., ed. *XV-XVI. Asır Bayrâmi-Melâmiliği'nin Kaynaklarından Abdurrahman El-Askeri'nin Mir'âtü'l-ısk'i*. Ankara: Türk Tarih Kurumu Basımevi, 2003.

Fahd, Toufic. *La Divination arabe: Études religieuses, sociologiques et folkloriques sur le milieu natif de l'Islam*. Paris: Sindbad, 1987.

Faroqhi, Suraiya. *Der Bektaschi-Orden in Anatolien: Vom späten fünfzehnten Jahrhundert bis 1826*. Vienna: Verlag des Institutes für Orientalistik der Universität Wien, 1981.

Fazlıoğlu, İhsan. 'İlk Dönem Osmanlı İlim ve Kültür Hayatında İhvânu's-Safâ ve Abdurrahmân Bistâmî'. *Divan* 1, no. 2 (1996): 229–40.

Fierro, Maribel. 'Al-Aṣfar'. *Studia Islamica* 77 (1993): 169–81.

Fleischer, Cornell. 'Royal Authority, Dynastic Cyclism, and "Ibn Khaldûnism" in Sixteenth-Century Ottoman Letters'. In *Ibn Khaldun and Islamic Ideology*. Edited by Bruce Lawrence, pp. 46–68. Leiden: Brill, 1984.

Fleischer, Cornell. *Bureaucrat and Intellectual in the Ottoman Empire: The Historian Mustafa Âli (1541–1600)*. Princeton: Princeton University Press, 1986.

Fleischer, Cornell. 'The Lawgiver as Messiah: The Making of the Imperial Image in the Reign of Süleyman'. In *Soliman Le Magnifique et Son Temps, Actes Du Colloque de Paris. Galeries Nationales Du Gran Palais, 7-10 Mars 1990*. Edited by Gilles Veinstein, pp. 159–77. Paris: La Documentation Française, 1992.

Fleischer, Cornell. 'Mahdi and Millennium: Messianic Dimensions in the Development of Ottoman Imperial Ideology'. In *The Great Ottoman-Turkish Civilization, vol. 3: Philosophy, Science and Institutions*. Edited by Kemal Çiçek, pp. 42–54. Ankara: Yeni Türkiye, 2000.

Fleischer, Cornell. 'Seer to the Sultan'. In *Cultural Horizons: A Festschrift in Honor of Talat S. Halman*. Edited by Jayne L. Warner, pp. 290–99. Syracuse: Syracuse University Press; Istanbul: Yapı Kredi Yayınları, 2001.

Fleischer, Cornell. 'Shadow of Shadows: Prophecy and Politics in 1530s Istanbul'. *International Journal of Turkish Studies* 13, no. 1–2 (2007): 51–62.

Fleischer, Cornell. 'Ancient Wisdom and New Science: Prophecies at the Ottoman Court in the Fifteenth and Sixteenth Centuries'. In *Falnama: The Book of Omens*. Edited by Massumeh Farhad and Serpil Bağcı, pp. 232–43, 329–30. London: Thames and Hudson, 2009.

Fodor, A. 'Malhamat Daniyal'. In *The Muslim East: Studies in Honor of Julius Germanus*. Edited by Gyula Kaldy-Nagy, pp. 85–133. Budapest: Eötvös Loránd University, 1974.

Foucault, Michel. *The Order of Things: An Archaeology of the Human Sciences*. New York: Pantheon Books, 1971.

Gardiner, Noah. 'The Occultist Encyclopedism of ᶜAbd al-Rahman al-Bistami'. *Mamluk Studies Review* 20 (2017): 3–38.

Gibb, Elias John Wilkinson. *A History of Ottoman Poetry*. London: Luzac, 1900.

Goldziher, Ignaz. 'Aṣfar'. *Encyclopaedia of Islam, Second Edition.*

Goudarzi, Mohsen. 'Books on Exegesis (*tafsīr*) and Qur'anic Readings (*qirā'āt*): Inspiration, Intellect, and the Interpretation of Scripture in Post-Classical Islam'. In *Treasures of Knowledge: An Inventory of the Ottoman Palace Library (1502/3–1503/4)*. Edited by Gülru Necipoğlu, Cemal Kafadar and Cornell H. Fleischer, pp. 267–308. Leiden; Boston: Brill, 2019.

Gökbilgin, M. Tayyib. *XV.-XVI. Asırlarda Edirne ve Paşa Livâsı: Vakıflar, Mülkler, Mukataalar*. İstanbul: Üçler Basımevi, 1952.

Göktaş, Recep Gürkan. 'On the Hadith Collection of Bayezid II's Library'. In *Treasures of Knowledge: An Inventory of the Ottoman Palace Library (1502/3–1503/4)*. Edited by Gülru Necipoğlu, Cemal Kafadar and Cornell H. Fleischer, pp. 309–40. Leiden; Boston: Brill, 2019.

Gölpinarli, Abdülbâki. *Melâmîlik ve Melâmîler*. İstanbul: Devlet Matbaasi, 1931.

Grenier, Carlos. 'Reassessing the Authorship of the *Dürr-i Meknun*', *Archivum Ottomanicum* 35 (2018): 193–212.

Gunasti, Susan. 'Political Patronage and the Writing of Qurʾān Commentaries among the Ottoman Turks'. *Journal of Islamic Studies* 24, no. 3 (2013): 335–57.

Gutas, Dimitri. *Avicenna and the Aristotelian Tradition: Introduction to Reading Avicenna's Philosophical Works*. Leiden: Brill, 1988.

Gutas, Dimitri. 'Avicenna's Eastern ('Oriental') Philosophy: Nature, Contents, Transmission'. *Arabic Sciences and Philosophy* 10, no. 2 (2000): 159–80.

Gutas, Dimitri. 'Intellect Without Limits: The Absence of Mysticism in Avicenna'. In *Intellect et Imagination dans la Philosophie Médiévale*. Edited by M. Cândida-Pacheco and J. Francisco-Meirinhos, vol. 1, pp. 351–72. Turnhout: Brepols: 2006).

Güngör, Şeyma. 'Maktel-i Hüseyin'. *İslam Ansiklopedisi.*

Hagen, Gottfried. 'Chaos, Order, Power, Salvation: Heroic Hagiography's Response to the Ottoman Fifteenth Century'. *Journal of the Ottoman and Turkish Studies Association* 1, no. 1–2 (2014): 91–109.

Hämeen-Anttila, Jaakko. *The Last Pagans of Iraq: Ibn Waḥshiyya and His Nabatean Agriculture.* Leiden: Brill, 2006.

von Hees, Syrinx. *Enzyklopädie als Spiegel des Weltbildes: Qazwinis Wunder der Schöpfung: Eine Naturkunde des 13. Jahrhunderts*. Wiesbaden: Harrassowitz, 2002.

von Hees, Syrinx. 'Al-Qazwìnì's 'Ajà'ib Al-Makhlùqàt: An Encyclopædia of Natural History?' In *Organizing Knowledge: Encyclopaedic Activities in the Pre-Eighteenth Century Islamic World.* Edited by Gerhard Endress, pp. 171–86. Leiden: Brill, 2006.

von Hees, Syrinx. 'The Astonishing: A Critique and Re-Reading of 'Ağā'ib Literature'. *Middle Eastern Literatures* 8, no. 2 (2010): 101–20.

Heinzelmann, Tobias. *Populäre religiöse Literatur und Buchkultur im Osmanischen Reich: Eine Studie zur Nutzung der Werke der Brüder Yazıcıoğlı*. Würzburg: Ergon-Verlag, 2015.

Helewa, Sami. *Models of Leadership in the Adab Narratives of Joseph, David and Solomon: Lament for the Sacred.* Lanham; Boulder; New York; London: Lexington, 2018.

Hıra, Ayhan. 'Şeyh Bedreddin'in Fıkıhçılığı'. Unpublished doctoral dissertation. Marmara University, 2006.

Hodgson, Marshall G. S. *The Venture of Islam: Conscience and History in a World Civilization, 3 vols*. Chicago: University of Chicago Press, 1974.

Homerin, Th. Emil. 'Ibn Taimiya's Al-Sufiyah Wa'l-Fuqara'. *Arabica* 32 (1985): 219–44.

Imber, Colin. 'A Note on "Christian" Preachers in the Ottoman Empire'. *Journal of Ottoman Studies* 10 (1990): 59–67.

Imber, Colin. *The Ottoman Empire, 1300–1650: The Structure of Power*. New York: Palgrave Macmillan, 2002.

Imber, Colin. *The Crusade of Varna, 1443–45*. Aldershot; Burlington: Ashgate, 2006.

İnalcık, Halil. *Fatih Devri Üzerine Tetkikler ve Vesikalar*. Ankara: Türk Tarih Kurumu, 1954.

İnalcık, Halil. 'Dervish and Sultan: An Analysis of the Otman Baba Vilayetnamesi'. In *Manifestations of Sainthood in Islam*. Edited by Grace Martin Smith and Carl W. Ernst, pp. 209–24. Istanbul: The Isis Press; Gorgias Press, 2011.

İnalcık, Halil. 'Gelibolu', *Encyclopaedia of Islam, Second Edition*.

İslam Ansiklopedisi. Ankara: Türkiye Diyanet Vakfı, 1988–2016.

Ivanyi, Katharina Anna. 'Virtue, Piety, and the Law: A Study of Birgivi Mehmed Efendi's *Al-Tariqa Al-Muhammadiyya*'. Unpublished doctoral dissertation. Princeton University, 2012.

Izutsu, Toshihiko. *Sufism and Taoism: A Study of Key Philosophical Concepts*. Berkeley: Berkeley University Press, 2016.

Kafadar, Cemal. *Between Two Worlds: The Construction of the Ottoman State*. Berkeley: University of California Press, 1996.

Kafadar, Cemal, and Ahmet Karamustafa. 'Books on Sufism, Lives of Saints, Ethics, and Sermons'. In *Treasures of Knowledge: An Inventory of the Ottoman Palace Library (1502/3–1503/4)*. Edited by Gülru Necipoğlu, Cemal Kafadar and Cornell H. Fleischer, pp. 439–507. Leiden; Boston: Brill, 2019.

Kaptein, Laban. *Eindtijd en Antichrist (ad-Daǧǧāl) in de Islam: Eschatologie bij Aḥmed Bīcān*. Leiden: Onderzoekschool CNWS, Rijksuniversiteit Leiden, 1997.

Kaptein, Laban. *Apocalypse and the Antichrist Dajjal in Islam: Ahmed Bijan's Eschatology Revisted*. Asch: privately published, 2011.

Karamustafa, Ahmet T. *God's Unruly Friends: Dervish Groups in the Islamic Later Middle Period, 1200–1550*. Salt Lake City: University of Utah Press, 1994.

Karamustafa, Ahmet T. *Sufism: The Formative Period*. Berkeley: University of California Press, 2007.

Karamustafa, Ahmet T. 'Kaygusuz Abdal: A Medieval Turkish Saint and the Formation of Vernacular Islam in Anatolia'. In *Unity in Diversity: Mysticism, Messianism and the Construction of Religious Authority in Islam*. Edited by Orkhan Mir-Kasimov, pp. 329–42. Leiden: Brill, 2014.

Karataş, Hasan. 'The City as a Historical Actor: The Urbanization and Ottomanization of the Halvetiye Sufi Order by the City of Amasya in the Fifteenth and Sixteenth Centuries'. Unpublished doctoral dissertation. University of California, Berkeley, 2011.

Kastritsis, Dimitris J. *The Sons of Bāyezīd: Empire Building and Representation in the Ottoman Civil War of 1402–1413*. Leiden; Boston: Brill, 2007.

Katz, Marion Holmes. *The Birth of the Prophet Muhammad: Devotional Piety in Sunni Islam*. London; New York: Routledge, 2007.

Kister, M. J. '*Haddithu 'an bani isra'ila wa-la haraja*: A Study of an Early Tradition'. *Israel Oriental Studies* 2 (1972): 215–39.

Kister, M. J. 'The Sīrah Literature'. In *Arabic Literature to the End of the Umayyad Period*. Edited by A. F. L. Beeston, T. M. Johnstone, R. B. Serjeant and G. R. Smith, pp. 352–67. Cambridge: Cambridge University Press, 1983.

Koçak, Aynur. *Ahmet Bîcan'in Eserleri Üzerine bir İnceleme*. İstanbul: Üçdal Neşriyat, 2003.

Korobeinikov, Dimitri. *Byzantium and the Turks in the Thirteenth Century*. Oxford: Oxford University Press, 2014.

Köprülü, Mehmet Fuat. *The Origins of the Ottoman Empire*. Translated by Gary Leiser. Albany: State University of New York Press, 1992.

Köprülü, Mehmet Fuat. *Early Mystics in Turkish Literature*. Edited by Gary Leiser. Translated by Robert Dankoff. London; New York: Routledge, 2006.

Knysh, Alexander D. *Ibn Arabi in the Later Islamic Tradition: The Making of a Polemical Image in Medieval Islam*. Albany: State University of New York Press, 1999.

Krstić, Tijana. *Contested Conversions to Islam: Narratives of Religious Change in the Early Modern Ottoman Empire*. Palo Alto: Stanford University Press, 2011.

Kut, Günay. *Acâibü'l-mahlûkât*. İstanbul: Simurg, 2010.

Kutlar, Fatma. 'Ahmed-i Bican'ın Manzum *Cevahir-name*'si'. *İnsan Bilimleri Araştırmaları* 7 (2002): 59–68.

Kutlar, Fatma. 'Cevher Konulu Eserler: Cevahirnameler ve Diğerleri'. *Prilozi Za Orijentalnu Filoligiju* 56 (2007/6): 77–87.

Lane, Andrew J. *A Traditional Mu'tazilite Qur'an Commentary: The Kashshāf of Jār Allāh al-Zamakhsharī (d. 538/1144)*. Boston; Leiden: Brill, 2006.

Le Gall, Dina. *A Culture of Sufism: Naqshbandīs in the Ottoman World, 1450–1700*. Albany: State University of New York Press, 2005.

Lellouch, Benjamin, and Stéphane Yerasimos, eds. *Les Traditions apocalyptiques au tournant de la chute de Constantinople: Actes de la table ronde d'Istanbul, 13–14 Avril 1996*. Istanbul: Institut français d'études anatoliennes Georges Dumézil; l'Harmattan, 2000.

Levi della Vida, Giorgio. 'The "Bronze Era" in Moslem Spain'. *Journal of the American Oriental Society* 63, no. 3 (1943): 183–91.

Lindner, Rudi Paul. *Nomads and Ottomans in Medieval Anatolia*. Bloomington: Research Institute for Inner Asian Studies, Indiana University, Bloomington, 1983.

Lindner, Rudi Paul. *Explorations in Ottoman Prehistory*. Ann Arbor: University of Michigan Press, 2007.

Lowry, Heath W. *The Nature of the Early Ottoman State*. Albany: State University of New York Press, 2003.

Madelung, Wilfred. 'al-Mahdī'. *Encyclopaedia of Islam, Second Edition*.

Markiewicz, Christopher. *The Crisis of Kingship in Late Medieval Islam: Persian Emigres and the Making of Ottoman Sovereignty*. Cambridge: Cambridge University Press, 2019.

Martin, B. G. 'A Short History of the Khalwati Order of Dervishes', in *Scholars, Saints, and Sufis: Muslim Religious Institutions in the Middle East Since 1500*.

Edited by Nikki R. Keddie, pp. 275–306. Berkeley: University of California Press, 1972.

Masad, Mohammad Ahmad. 'The Medieval Islamic Apocalyptic Tradition: Divination, Prophecy and the End of Time in the 13th Century Eastern Mediterranean'. Unpublished doctoral dissertation. Washington University in St. Louis, 2008.

Mavroudi, Maria. 'Plethon as a Subversive and His Reception in the Islamic World'. In *Power and Subversion in Byzantium*. Edited by D. Angelov and M. Saxby, pp. 177–204. Farnham: Ashgate Variorum, 2013.

Mazzaoui, Michel M. *The Origins of the Ṣafawids: Šī'ism, Ṣūfism, and the Ġulāt*. Wiesbaden: F. Steiner, 1972.

McChesney, Robert. *The Waqf in Central Asia*. Princeton: Princeton University Press, 1991.

McChesney, Robert. 'A Note on the Life and Works of Ibn 'Arabshah'. In *History and Historiography of Post-Mongol Central Asia and the Middle East: Studies in Honor of John E. Woods*, edited by Judith Pfeiffer, Sholeh Quinn and Ernest Tucker, p. 226. Wiesbaden: Harrassowitz, 2006.

McGinn, Bernard. *Visions of the End: Apocalyptic Traditions in the Middle Ages*. New York: Columbia University Press, 1979.

Mélikoff, Irène. *Le Destan d'Umur Pacha: Düsturname-i Enveri*. Paris: Presses Universitaires de France, 1954.

Mélikoff, Irène. *Hadji Bektach: Un mythe et ses avatars: Genèse et évolution du soufisme populaire en turquie*. Leiden: Brill, 1998.

Mélikoff, Irène. 'D̲j̲amāl al-Dīn Aḳsarayī'. *Encyclopaedia of Islam, Second Edition*.

Mengüç, Murat Cem. 'Histories of Bayezid I, Historians of Bayezid II: Rethinking Late-Fifteenth-Century Ottoman Historiography', *Bulletin of the School of Oriental and African Studies* 76, no. 3 (2013): 373–89.

Melvin-Koushki, Matthew S. 'The Quest for a Universal Science: The Occult Philosophy of Sa'in Al-Din Turka Isfahani (1369–1432) and Intellectual Millenarianism in Early Timurid Iran'. Unpublished doctoral dissertation. Yale University, 2012.

Ménage, V. L. 'Bīd̲j̲ān'. *Encyclopaedia of Islam, Second Edition*.

Minorsky, Vladimir. 'Jihān-Shāh Qara-Qoyunlu and His Poetry (Turkmenica, 9)'. *Bulletin of the School of Oriental and African Studies* 16, no. 2 (1954): 271–97.

Mir-Kasimov, Orkhan. *Words of Power: Ḥurūfī teachings between Shi'ism and Sufism in Medieval Islam: The Original Doctrine of Faḍl Allāh Astarābādī*. London: I. B. Tauris, in association with the Institute of Ismaili Studies, 2015.

Moin, A. Azfar. *The Millennial Sovereign: Sacred Kingship and Sainthood in Islam*. New York: Columbia University Press, 2012.

Molé, Marijan. 'Les Kubrawiya entre Sunnisme et Shi'isme'. *Revue des Études Islamiques* 29 (1961): 61–142.

Molé, Marijan. 'Profession de foi de deux Kubrawis: 'Alī Hamadānī et Muhammad Nūrbakhsh'. *Bulletin d'Études Orientales* 17 (1961/62): 133–204.

Monfasani, John. 'Review: *Jorge Ameruzes de Trebisonda, El Diálogo de La Fe Con El Sultán de Los Turcos*, Ed. and Trans. (into Spanish) Oscar de La Cruz Palma'. *Speculum* 79, no. 4 (2004): 1024–25.

Monfasani, John. *George Amiroutzes, the Philosopher and his Tractates*. Leuven; Walpole: Peeters, 2011.

Mottahedeh, Roy P. ''Aja'ib in The Thousand and One Nights'. In *The Thousand and One Nights in Arabic Literature and Society*. Edited by Richard G. Hovannisian and Georges Sabagh, pp. 29–39. Cambridge: Cambridge University Press, 1997.

Nasr, Seyyed Hossein. *Three Muslim Sages: Avicenna, Suhrawardī, Ibn 'Arabī.* Cambridge, MA: Harvard University Press, 1964.

Nasr, Seyyed Hossein. *An Introduction to Islamic Cosmological Doctrines: Conceptions of Nature and Methods Used for Its Study by the Ikhwān Al-Ṣafā', Al-Bīrūni, and Ibn Sīnā*. Revised ed. London: Thames and Hudson, 1978.

Nasr, Seyyed Hossein. 'Theoretical Gnosis and Doctrinal Sufism and Their Significance Today'. *Transcendent Philosophy* 6 (2005): 1–36.

Nassiri, Giv. 'Turco-Persian Civilization and the Role of Scholars' Travel and Migration in Its Elaboration and Continuity'. Unpublished doctoral dissertation. University of California, Berkeley, 2002.

Necipoğlu, Gülru, Cemal Kafadar and Cornell H. Fleischer, eds. *Treasures of Knowledge: An Inventory of the Ottoman Palace Library (1502/3–1503/4)* Leiden; Boston: Brill, 2019.

Ocak, Ahmet Yaşar. *Osmanlı İmparatorluğunda Marjinal Sufilik: Kalenderiler, XIV–XVII. Yüzyıllar*. Ankara: Türk Tarih Kurumu Basımevi, 1992.

Ocak, Ahmet Yaşar. *Zındıklar ve Mülhidler yahut Dairenin Dışına Çikanlar: 15.–17. Yüzyıllar*. İstanbul: Türkiye Ekonomik ve Toplumsal Tarih Vakfı, 1999.

Ocak, Ahmet Yaşar. *Osmanlı Toplumunda Tasavvuf ve Sufiler: Kaynaklar, Doktrin, Ayin ve Erkan, Tarikatlar, Edebiyat, Mimari, Güzel Sanatlar, Modernizm*. Ankara: Türk Tarih Kurumu, 2005.

Öden, Zerrin Günal. *Karası Beyliği*. Ankara: Türk Tarih Kurumu Basımevi, 1999.

Ökten, Ertuğrul. 'Jami: His Biography and Intellectual Influence in Herat'. Unpublished doctoral dissertation. University of Chicago, 2007.

Ökten, Ertuğrul. 'Scholars and Mobility: A Preliminary Assessment from the Perspective of al-Shaqāyiq al-Nu'māniyya'. *Journal of Ottoman Studies* 41 (2013): 55–70.

Öngören, Reşat. *Tarihte bir Aydın Tarikatı: Zeynîler*. İstanbul: İnsan Yayınları, 2003.

Öz, Mustafa. 'Cemaleddin Aksarayi'. *İslam Ansiklopedisi.*

Özçelik, Kenan. 'Yusuf-i Meddah ve *Maktel-i Hüseyn*: İnceleme-Metin-Sözlük'. Unpublished MA thesis. Ankara Üniversitesi, 2008.

Özervarlı, M. Sait. 'Ottoman Perceptions of Al-Ghazālī's Works and Discussions on His Historical Role in Its Late Period'. In *Islam and Rationality: The Impact of al-Ghazālī. Papers Collected on His 900th Anniversary*. Edited by Frank Griffel, vol. 2, pp. 253–82. Leiden: Brill, 2016.

Peacock, A. C. S. *Islam, Literature and Society in Mongol Anatolia*, 2019. Cambridge: Cambridge University Press, 2019.

Peacock, A. C. S., and Sara Nur Yıldız, eds. *Literature and Intellectual Life in 14th–15th Century Anatolia.* Würzburg: Ergon Verlag, 2016.

Peacock, A. C. S., Bruno de Nicola and Sara Nur Yıldız. *Islam and Christianity in Medieval Anatolia.* Surrey; Burlington: Ashgate Publishing Company, 2015.

Pfeiffer, Judith. 'Confessional Ambiguity vs. Confessional Polarization: Politics and the Negotiation of Religious Boundaries in the Ilkhanate'. *In Politics, Patronage, and the Transmission of Knowledge in 13th–15th Century Tabriz.* Edited by Judith Pfeiffer, pp. 129–68. Leiden: Brill, 2014.

Pfeiffer, Judith. 'Mevlevi-Bektashi Rivalries and the Islamisation of Public Space in Late Seljuq Anatolia'. In *Islam and Christianity in Medieval Anatolia.* Edited by A. C. S. Peacock, Bruno de Nicola and Sara Nur Yıldız, pp. 309–27. Burlington: Ashgate, 2015.

Pouncy, Carolyn. *The 'Domostroi': Rules for Russian Households in the Time of Ivan the Terrible.* Ithaca: Cornell University Press, 1994.

Pregill, Michael. '*Israiliyyat*, Myth and Pseudepigraphy: Wahb b. Munabbih and the Early Islamic Versions of the Fall of Adam and Eve'. *Jerusalem Studies in Arabic and Islam* 34 (2008): 215–84.

Raby, Julian. 'A Sultan of Paradox: Mehmed the Conqueror as a Patron of the Arts'. *Oxford Art Journal* 5, no. 1 (1982): 3–8.

Rahman, Fazlur. *Islam.* Chicago: University of Chicago Press, 1979.

Rahman, Fazlur. *Major Themes of the Qur'an.* Chicago: University of Chicago Press, 2009.

Repp, Richard. *The Müfti of Istanbul: A Study in the Development of the Ottoman Learned Hierarchy.* London: Ithaca: Published by Ithaca Press for the Board of the Faculty of Oriental Studies, Oxford University, 1986.

Rifat, Ahmet. *Luğat-i Tarihiyye ve Coğrafiyye.* İstanbul: Mahmut Bey Matbaası, 1881.

Rochberg-Halton, F. 'Elements of the Babylonian Contribution to Hellenistic Astrology'. *Journal of the American Oriental Society* 108, no. 1 (1988): 51–62.

Ryder, Judith R. *The Career and Writings of Demetrius Kydones: A Study of Fourteenth-Century Byzantine Politics, Religion and Society.* Leiden; Boston: Brill, 2010.

Schamiloglu, Uli. 'The Rise of the Ottoman Empire: The Black Death in Medieval Anatolia and Its Impact on Turkish Civilization'. In *Views From the Edge: Essays in Honor of Richard W. Bulliet.* Edited by Neguin Yavari, Lawrence G. Potter and Jean-Marc Oppenheim, pp. 255–79. New York: Columbia University Press, 2004.

Setton, Kenneth M., ed. *A History of the Crusades.* Philadelphia: University of Pennsylvania Press, 1955.

Setton, Kenneth M. *Western Hostility to Islam and Prophecies of Turkish Doom.* Philadelphia: American Philosophical Society, 1992.

Sevinç, Sibel. 'Yazıcı Ṣāliḥ'in Melhamesi (*Kitabü'ş-Şemsiyye*)'. Unpublished MA thesis. Cumhuriyet Üniversitesi, 1999.

Sezgin, Fuat, and Mazen Amawi. *Abu L-Rayḥān al-Bīrūnī: K. al-Jamāhir Fī Ma'rifat al-Jawāhir: Texts and Studies*. Frankfurt a. M.: Institute for the History of Arabic-Islamic Science at the Johann Wolfgang Goethe University, 2001.

Sezgin, İbrahim. 'Gelibolu Kazasının Sosyal ve Ekonomik Tarihi'. Unpublished doctoral dissertation. Marmara Üniversitesi, 1998.

Shukurov, Rustam. *The Byzantine Turks, 1204–1461*. Leiden: Brill, 2016.

Siniossoglou, Niketas. *Radical Platonism in Byzantium: Illumination and Utopia in Gemistos Plethon.* Cambridge; New York: Cambridge University Press, 2011.

Smith, Grace Martin. *Varqa ve Gülşâh: A Fourteenth Century Anatolian Turkish Mesnevi (Translation, Glossary and Introduction*). Leiden: Brill, 1976.

Starr, Joshua, *The Jews in the Byzantine Empire, 641-1204.* New York: B. Franklin, 1970.

Subtelny, Maria Eva. 'A Timurid Educational and Charitable Foundation: The Ikhlāṣiyya Complex of ᶜAlī Shīr Navāʾī in 15th-Century Herat and Its Endowment'. *Journal of the American Oriental Society* 111, no. 1 (1991): 38–61.

Subtelny, Maria Eva, and Anas B. Khalidov. 'The Curriculum of Islamic Higher Learning in Timurid Iran in the Light of the Sunni Revival under Shāh-Rukh'. *Journal of the American Oriental Society* 115, no. 2 (1995): 210–36.

Şahin, Haşim, 'Somuncu Baba'. *DİA2* v. 37, pp. 377-378.

Şahin, Kaya. 'Constantinople and the End Time: The Ottoman Conquest as a Portent of the Last Hour'. *Journal of Early Modern History* 14, no. 4 (2010): 317–54.

Şahin, Kaya. *Empire and Power in the Reign of Süleyman: Narrating the Sixteenth-Century Ottoman World.* New York: Cambridge University Press, 2013.

Taeschner, Franz. 'Beiträge zur Geschichte der Achis in Anatolien', *Islamica* 4/1 (1929): 1–47.

Taneri, Aydın. *Osmanlı İmparatorluğu'nun Kuruluş Döneminde Vezir-i a'zamlık, 1299–1453*. Ankara: Ankara Üniversitesi Dil ve Tarih-Coğrafya Fakültesi, 1974.

Taşkömür, Himmet. 'Books on Islamic Jurisprudence, Schools of Law, and biographies of Imams from the Hanafi School'. In *Treasures of Knowledge: An Inventory of the Ottoman Palace Library (1502/3–1503/4).* Edited by Gülru Necipoğlu, Cemal Kafadar and Cornell H. Fleischer, pp. 389–422. Leiden; Boston: Brill, 2019.

Terzioğlu, Derin. 'Sufis in the Age of State-Building and Confessionalization'. In *The Ottoman World.* Edited by Christine Woodhead. Milton Park: Abingdon 2012.

Terzioğlu, Derin. 'How to Conceptualize Ottoman Sunnitization'. *Turcica* 44, (2012/13): 301–38.
Terzioğlu, Derin. 'Where *'İlmihal* Meets Catechism: Islamic Manuals of Religious Instruction in the Ottoman Empire in the Age of Confessionalization'. *Past & Present* 220, no. 1 (2013): 79–114.
Todd, Richard. *The Sufi Doctrine of Man: Ṣadr Al-Dīn Al-Qūnawī's Metaphysical Anthropology*. Leiden: Brill, 2014.
Todorov, Tsvetan. *The Fantastic: A Structural Approach to a Literary Genre [By] Tzvetan Todorov. Translated from the French by Richard Howard.* Cleveland: Press of Case Western Reserve University, 1973.
Togan, A. Z. W. *Ibn Faḍlān's Reisebericht*. Abhandlungen für die Kunde des Morgenlandes, xxiv/3. Leipzig, 1938.
Trapp, Erich. *Manuel II. Palaiologos: Dialoge mit einem 'Perser'*. Wien: Österreichische Akademie der Wissenschaften, Kommission für Byzantinistik, Institut für Byzantinistik der Universität Wien; in Kommission bei H. Böhlau's Nachf., Graz, 1966.
Uçman, Abdullah. *Müzekki'n-Nüfus*. İstanbul: İnsan Yayınları, 2013.
Uğur, Abdullah. 'Yazıcıoğlu Ahmed Bican Efendi ve *Envarü'l-Aşıkin* Adlı Eseri (İnceleme-Metin)'. Unpublished doctoral dissertation. Marmara Üniversitesi, 2019.
Uğur, Abdullah. *Yazıcıoğlu Aḥmed Bīcān and his Envārü'l-'Aşıḳīn* (Cambridge: Department of Near Eastern Languages and Civilizations, Harvard University, 2019).
Uslu, Zeynep Oktay. 'The Şathiyye of Yunus Emre and Kaygusuz Abdal: The Creation of a Vernacular Islamic Tradition in Turkish'. *Turcica* 50 (2019), pp. 9–46.
Usluer, Fatih. *Hurufilik: İlk Elden Kaynaklarla Doğuşundan İtibaren*. İstanbul: Kabalcı Yayınevi, 2009.
Uzunçarşılı, İsmail Hakki. *Osmanlı Tarihi.* Ankara: Türk Tarih Kurumu, 1947.
Uzunçarşılı, İsmail Hakki. *Osmanlı Devletinin Merkez ve Bahriye Teşkilatı.* Ankara: Türk Tarih Kurumu, 1948.
Uzunçarşılı, İsmail Hakki. *Osmanli Devletinin İlmiye Teskilâti.* Ankara: Türk Tarih Kurumu Basimevi, 1965.
Vajda, G. 'Quelques observations sur la "Malḥamat Dāniyāl"'. *Arabica* 23, no. 1 (1976): 84–87.
Varlık, Nükhet. *Plague and Empire in the Early Modern Mediterranean World: The Ottoman Experience, 1347–1600.* New York: Cambridge University Press, 2015.
Vauchez, André. *Sainthood in the Later Middle Ages.* New York: Cambridge University Press, 1997.
Vryonis, Speros. *The Decline of Medieval Hellenism in Asia Minor and the Process of Islamization from the Eleventh through the Fifteenth Century.* Berkeley: University of California Press, 1971.

Wansbrough, John E. *The Sectarian Milieu: Content and Composition of Islamic Salvation History*. Oxford; New York: Oxford University Press, 1978.

Wittek, Paul. *Das Fürstentum Mentesche: Studie zur Geschichte Westkleinasiens im 13.-15. Jh.* Istanbul: Universum-Druckerei, 1934.

Wittek, Paul. *The Rise of the Ottoman Empire*. London: The Royal Asiatic Society, 1938.

Wittek, Paul. 'Yazi̊ji̊oghlu 'Alī on the Christian Turks of the Dobruja'. *Bulletin of the School of Oriental and African Studies* 14, no. 3 (1952): 639–68.

Woodhouse, C. M. *George Gemistos Plethon: The Last of the Hellenes*. Oxford: Clarendon Press, 1986.

Woods, John E. *The Aqquyunlu: Clan, Confederation, Empire*. Salt Lake City: University of Utah Press, 1999.

Yaşaroğlu, M. Kamil. 'Mûsâ İznikî'. *İslam Ansiklopedisi.*

Yazıcı, Tahsin. 'Fetihten Sonra İstanbul'da İlk Halveti Şeyhleri: Çelebi Muhammed Cemaleddin, Sümbül Sinan ve Merkez Efendi'. *İstanbul Enstitüsü Dergisi* 2 (1956): 87–113.

Yerasimos, Stéphane, *La Fondation de Constantinople et de Sainte-Sophie dans les traditions turques: Légendes d'empire*. Istanbul; Paris: Institut français d'études anatoliennes; Librairie d'Amérique et d'Orient, J. Maisonneuve, 1990.

Yıldırım, Rıza. 'Turcomans Between Two Empires'. Unpublished doctoral dissertation. Bilkent University, 2008.

Yıldız, Sara Nur. 'From Cairo to Ayasuluk: Haci Paşa and the Transmission of Islamic Learning to Western Anatolia in the Late Fourteenth Century'. *Journal of Islamic Studies* 25, no. 3 (2014): 263–97.

Yıldız, Sara Nur. 'A Hanafi Law Manual in the Vernacular: Devletoğlu Yūsuf Balıḳesrī's Turkish Verse Adaptation of the Hidāya-Wiqāya Textual Tradition for the Ottoman Sultan Murad II (824/1424)', *Bulletin of the School of Oriental and African Studies* 80, no. 2 (2017): 283–304.

Yılmaz, Hüseyin. *Caliphate Redefined: The Mystical Turn in Ottoman Political Thought.* Princeton: Princeton University Press, 2019.

Yurd, A. İhsan. *Fatih Sultan Mehmed Hanın Hocası, Şeyh Akşemseddin: Hayatı ve Eserleri*. İstanbul: Yurd, 1972.

Yurd, Ali Ihsan, and Mustafa S. Kaçalin. *Akşemseddin, 1390–1459: Hayatı ve Eserleri.* İstanbul: Marmara Üniversitesi, Ilâhiyat Vakfı, 1994.

Yurdagür, Metin. 'Bergamalı İbrahim'. *İslam Ansiklopedisi.*

Yürekli, Zeynep. *Architecture and Hagiography in the Ottoman Empire the Politics of Bektashi Shrines in the Classical Age.* Farnham; Burlington: Ashgate, 2012.

Zachariadou, Elisabeth A. 'Manuel II Palaeologos on the Strife between Bāyezīd I and Ḳāḍī Burhān Al-Dīn Aḥmad'. *Bulletin of the School of Oriental and African Studies* 43, no. 3 (1980): 471–81.

Zachariadou, Elisabeth A. *Trade and Crusade: Venetian Crete and the Emirates of Menteshe and Aydin (1300–1415).* Venice: Istituto ellenico di studi bizantini e postbizantini di Venezia per tutti i paesi del mondo, 1983.

Zachariadou, Elisabeth A. *Romania and the Turks, c.1300–c.1500*. London: Variorum Reprints, 1985.

Zachariadou, Elisabeth A., ed. *The Ottoman Emirate (1300–1389): Halcyon Days in Crete 1 : A Symposium Held in Rethymnon 11–13 January 1991*. Rethymnon: Crete University Press, 1993.

Zadeh, Travis E. *Mapping Frontiers across Medieval Islam: Geography, Translation, and the 'Abbasid Empire*. London; New York: I. B. Tauris, 2011.

Zarcone, Thierry. *The Qâdiriyya Order*. İstanbul: Simurg, 2000.

Zilfi, Madeline C. 'The Kadizadelis: Discordant Revivalism in Seventeenth-Century Istanbul'. *Journal of Near Eastern Studies* 45, no. 4 (1986): 251–69.

Zilfi, Madeline C. *The Politics of Piety: The Ottoman Ulema in the Post-Classical Age (1600–1800)*. Minneapolis: Bibliotheca Islamica, 1988.

Index

'Abdullāh b. Mubārak, 153
'Abdullāh b. 'Umar, 89
'Abdurraḥmān b. 'Awf, 157
al-Abharī, Athīr ad-dīn, 184
Abraham, 111, 119, 139, 192
Abū al-Fidā, 83
Abū Bakr, 156–7
Abū Ḥurayra, 89
Abū-Layth, 96n34
Abū 'Ubayda b. al-Jarrāh, 157
'Ād tribe, 119
Adam, 8, 76, 119, 208
  and Ibn 'Arabī, 139, 140
  and *malḥama* tradition, 196
  and Shī'ism, 158
al-'Adawiyya, Rābi'a, 153
Adelard of Bath, 187
Adrianople *see* Edirne
Afterlife, 125–7
aḥādīth, 85, 90, 91, 146, 188
Ahmad, Shahab, 93
Aḥmed, Rükne'd-dīn, 185
Aḥmed-i Dā'ī, 83
Aḥmed-i Ḫāṣṣ, 32, 33, 57–8, 61, 64, 207
'Āisha, 89
'Ajā'ib (wonder) genre, 183–91
'Ajamī, Fakhr al-dīn, 47, 48
al-'Ajamī, Ḥabīb, 153
'Ajamī, Sayyid 'Alī, 47
Akhlāṭī, Shaykh Ḥusayn, 62, 92
Aksarayī, Ḥamīdu'd-dīn *see* Ṣomuncu Baba
Alexander cycle, 183, 190–1
Alexander, Paul J., 162, 169–70
Alexander the Great, 15, 24
'Alī b. 'Abdu'r-raḥmān, 185
'Alī Baba, Emīr, 100
'Alī ibn Abu Ṭālib, 89, 148, 156–7, 160, 125
Amadeo VI of Savoy, 106
A'māq cycle, 162, 166–9, 170
el-Amasī, 'Alāe'd-dīn
  Ṭarīq-i Edeb ('The Path of Propriety'), 117
Ambros, Edith, 16
Amiroutzes, George
  De fide uel Philosophus, 112–13
Amoretti, Biancamaria, 156, 158
Amorium, 168–9
Anatolia, 1, 5, 9, 10
  and frontier, 104–5
  and Islam, 90–1
  and sources, 19, 20
  and Sufism, 50–2, 61, 65
Andalusia, 152
Andronikos II, Emperor, 104
Andronikos IV, Emperor, 107
angels, 76, 89–90, 119, 124–5
  and death, 126–7
  and 'Man-World', 192–3, 194
animals, 189–90
Ankara, 8, 10, 34–5, 52, 70n62
  and battle of (1402), 39
  and Sufism, 53
al-Anṣārī al-Harawī, Abū Ismā'īl 'Abdullāh
  Manāzil al-Sā'irīn, 155

Index

anthropocentrism, 113–14, 192
apocalypticism, 24, 161–71, 193–4, 195, 208
Aqbıyıq, 54
Aqqoyunlu, 141–2
al-Aqsarayī, Cemālu'd-dīn Muḥammed, 84, 85
Aqşemse'd-dīn, 13, 33, 148–9, 154, 195
  Menāqıb, 54
  al-Risālat al-nūriyya, 53, 55, 174n29
Aquinas, Thomas, 187
Arabic language, 90
Arberry, A. J., 138
Ardabīlī, Khvāje 'Alī, 50
Ardabīlī, Ṣafī al-dīn, 50
Aristotle, 187
  De Anima, 194
Arnakis, George, 106
Asen, Andronikos, 105
'Āşıq Çelebi, 56
'Āşıq Paşa, 55
'Aşıqpaşazade, 106
el-'Askerī, 'Abdurraḥmān
  Mir'ātü'l-'ışq, 50, 51, 53
Astarābādī, Fażlullāh, 10, 18
astrology *see* cosmology
Atçıl, Abdurrahman, 19
'Aṭṭār, Farīd al-dīn, 55, 125, 152–3
al-'Atūfī, Khayr al-din, 20, 93
Austin, R. J. W., 139
Avicenna, 146, 184, 185, 203n22
Aydınoğulları, 105
Azerbaijan, 10, 141–3
'Azrā'īl (Angel of Death), 89, 126

Bacon, Francis, 187
al-Baghawī, Abū Muḥammad, 81–2, 85, 89
  Anwār al-Tanzīl, 93
  Maṣābīh al-Sunna, 45, 93, 98n55
al-Baghdādī, Junayd, 148, 153
Balivet, Michel, 51
Balkans, 1, 6, 9–10, 21, 30, 39
  and Blond People, 169–70
  and Civil War, 102
Bashir, Shahzad, 18
al-Başrī, Ḥasan, 153
Batur, Atila, 35
al-Bayḍāwī, Qadi, 92
  Anwār al-Tanzīl, 83–4
  Ṭawāli' al-Anwār min Maṭāli' al-Anẓār, 97n36
Bāyezīd (dervish), 5
Bāyezīd I, Sultan, 1
Bāyezīd II, Sultan, 10, 19–20, 93
Bayqara, Sulṭān-Ḥusayn, 156
Bayram Velī, Ḥācı, 6, 8, 10, 13, 33
  and Anatolia, 50–2, 65
  and Ankara, 34
  and Bisṭāmī, 62
  and oral knowledge, 86–7
  and *quṭb*, 200
  and *shaykh*s, 153
Bayramiyye, 148–9, 152, 154, 207
Bayramoğlu, Fuat, 51
Bayraqlı Baba, 100
Bedre'd-dīn Simavī, eyẖ, 47, 48–9, 51, 102, 114
  Menāqibāame, 10
  Vāridāt, 69n54
beehives, 188
beglik culture, 20
Bektaşiyye, 54, 156, 176n59
Berlekamp, Persis, 184–5
Bethlen, Gábor, 130
bewilderment (*ḥayret*), 187
Beyazit, Ayşe, 16
Bidlīsī, Idrīs, 18
Binbaş, İlker Evrim, 10, 18, 62
Birgivī, Meḥmed
  al-Tariqa al-Muhammediyya, 96n34
Bisṭāmī, 'Abdurraḥmān, 49, 92, 94
  Kitāb Durrat Tāj al-Rasā'il wa Ghurrat Minhaj al-Waṣā'il, 10, 62
Bisṭāmī, Bāyazīd, 148, 153
Blond People (*Banū al-Aṣfar*), 167–70, 178n96
Boccaccio, Giovanni, 125
borderland *see* frontiers
Brue, Joseph, 16
Bukhara, 91
al-Bukhārī, Muḥammad al-Ḥanafī, 92
  al-Fatāwā al-Ẓāhiriyya, 86
Bursa, 2, 31–2
Bursevī, Ismā'īl Ḥaqqı, 39, 46, 49, 69n54, 93

Būstānu'l-Ḥaqāiq (Yazīcīoğlu, Aḥmed), 3, 8, 9, 13, 61
and *malḥama* tradition, 196, 197, 198
Byzantines, 104, 108, 131n21, 166–70, 201

Cairo, 49
calendar, 188–9, 196–8
caliphate, 156–7
Çandarlı family, 134n60
Catalan Grand Company, 104–5, 109
Çelebioğlu, Âmil, 16, 22, 32, 35, 66n2
and Qaṣṣāboğlu Maḥmūd, 44
and Zayn al-'Arab, 45
Central Asia, 90, 143
Cevher Ḫatun, 37, 38
Chalcedonians, 121
charity, 76, 124
Christianity, 1, 2, 7, 8
and apocalypticism, 166–70
and Gelibolu, 108, 109–10
and Islam, 23, 102–3, 110–14, 207–8
and legal rulings, 122–3
and wonder, 187
see also Jesus Christ
Çirmen, 37, 38
Civil War, 39–40
Clavijo, Ruy Gonzáles de, 107–8, 126
Cohn, Norman
Pursuit of the Millennium, 161
confessionalisation, 19, 101, 102
Constantinople, 6, 30, 126, 185
and Conquest, 60, 166–71
Cook, David
Studies in Muslim Apocalyptic, 162–3, 164, 166
cosmology, 2, 76, 180–2, 184, 192–3, 196–9
Creation, 3, 8, 165, 174n29, 180
Cruz Palma, Óscar de la, 113
Cüneyd, 108
Curry, John, 19
Cyriaco of Ancona, 109

Dābbat al-Arḍ (Beast of the Earth), 162, 164
Dajjāl, 162, 163, 164, 165, 170
Daniel, 196, 197
Dardanelles, 1, 4, 42–3, 59, 100, 106
Ḍarīr, Mustafa
Sīretü'n-nebīy, 80
Darling, Linda, 104
Daston, Lorraine, 187
death, 125–7
Dedes, Yorgos, 111, 118
Demetrios Leontarios, 108
Dervīş Bāyezīd, 44–5, 61, 65, 68n39
Dhū al-Qarnayn, 76
Dimetoka, 106
divination (*fāl*), 197
Doukas, 108, 114, 126
Dürr-i Meknūn ('The Hidden Pearl'), 62, 121, 163–5, 201–2

Edirne, 1, 2, 8, 31–2
and population, 106
and scholars, 46–8
and Süleymān, 39
and Yazıcıoğlus, 207
Egypt, 9–10, 49, 90, 92
elites, 41, 64–5, 115–16
Emre, Yūnus, 17, 19
Envārü'l-'Āşıqīn (Yazīcīoğlu, Aḥmed), 2–3
and classification, 75–6
and composition, 88–90
and *fetvās*, 122–3
and *'ilm-i ḥāl* genre, 117–18
and Islam, 123–5
and patterns, 90–4
and prophet stories, 118–22
and Shī'ism, 158
and sources, 73, 74–5, 76–88
and warfare, 128
Enverī
Düstūrnāme, 105, 126
Eraslan, Kemal, 16
esoteric revelation, 196–9, 201
ethics, 182–91
Evliyā Çelebi, 56, 63, 73, 93, 199

fantastic, 189
al-Faryābī, Maḥmūd, 91
fasting, 76, 117, 124
Fāṭima, 94, 158, 160
Fazlıoğlu, İhsan, 10, 62

Fenarī, Molla Şemsü'd-dīn Meḥmed Şāh, 9, 62, 165–6, 192
Miṣbāḥ al-Uns, 90, 141
Ta'līq 'alā Awā'il al-Kashshāf, 84
Fenarī family, 48, 49
fetāvā (legal rulings), 77, 86, 122–3
Filipovic, Nenad, 93
fiqh (legal theory), 77
Firdawsī, 31
fish, 188, 190–1
'Five Presences', 146
Fleischer, Cornell, 17, 163
Flemming, Barbara, 17
Fodor, A., 196
Foucault, Michel, 199
frontiers, 103–4, 127–9
Fuḍayl b. 'Iyāḍ, 153
Fużūlī
Hadīqat al-Sü'edā, 159

Gabriel (angel), 78, 87–8, 89, 119, 120, 192
Gallipoli *see* Gelibolu
Ġavsī Aḥmed Dede, 56
ġazā (frontier fighting), 7, 42, 57, 101–3, 127–9, 130n6
ġāzī, 33–43, 64, 101–2, 129–30, 207
Gelibolu (Gallipoli), 1, 2, 4–5, 7
and Aḥmed-i Ḫāṣṣ, 57–8
and bubonic plague, 126
and community, 114–15
and holy wars, 104–8
and intellectual culture, 74
and İskender b. Hācı Paşa, 42–3
and Kadıköyü, 39–40
and landscape, 100
and religion, 108–10
and Ṣaruca Beg, 38
and sources, 13
and traders, 200
and warfare, 128
and Yazıcıoğlu brothers, 20–1, 22, 29, 207
al-Ghazālī, Abū Hāmid, 86, 89, 93, 148, 184
Iḥyā 'Ulūm al-Dīn ('Revival of the Religious Sciences'), 77, 87, 90, 115, 117–18, 134n59
al-Ghulām, 'Uqbat, 153
Gibb, E. J. W., 16, 34
Gīlanī, 'Abd al-Qādir, 55
Gīlānī, Ibrāhīm Zāḥid, 153–4
Göktaş, Recep Gürkan, 93
Gölpınarlı, Abdulbaki, 18
Goudarzi, Mohsen, 93
Greeks, 109
Gülşehrī
Manṭıqu't-Ṭayr, 125
Gülşenī, Ibrāhīm-i, 141–2
Gürani, Molla, 48, 62

Ḥācı Paşa of Germiyan, 42, 92, 97n36
al-Haddād, Abū Ḥafs, 154
ḥadīth, 5, 75, 76–8, 93, 124
and *Envārü'l-'Āşıqīn*, 89
and sources, 81–6
and warfare, 129
see also *aḥādīth*
Hagen, Gottfried, 182, 200
Hajj, 63–4, 124
Ḫalīfe Çelebi, 84
Ḫalīl, Ḥāfiz, 10, 114
Ḫalīl Paşa, 105
Ḫalvetiyye, 10, 19, 54, 142, 152, 153–4
Hammer-Purgstall, Joseph von, 16
Ḥanafism, 47, 48, 61, 90–3, 210
Haravī, Ḥaydar, 10, 13, 46–7, 61, 65
and Bedre'd-dīn Simavī, 48, 49
and Taftazānī, 84
Ḥasan, 158, 159
Házi, János, 130
heaven, 76
Hees, Syrinx von, 183–4
Heinzelmann, Tobias, 17–18
Hell, 193
Ḥıżr Dede, 54
Hodgson, Marshall, 21, 113
holy wars, 101–2, 104–7
Huart, Clement, 138–9
Hūd, 119
Ḫüdāyī, 'Azīz Meḥmed, 49
Hungary, 130, 170
Ḥurūfism, 18
Ḥusayn, 88, 158, 159
Ḫüsrev, Molla, 48, 84

Ibn ʿAbbās, 89
Ibn al-ʿArabī, 6, 11, 55, 86, 208
Fuṣūṣ al-Ḥikam ('The Bezels of Wisdom'), 79, 137–51
and metaphysics, 192, 194
and mystics, 93
and 'the Perfect Man', 113
and Syria, 90
and Sufism, 152
Ibn ʿArabshāh, Shihāb al-Dīn, 82–3
Ibn Baṭṭūṭa, 160
Ibn Ḥajar al-ʿAsqalānī, 83
Ibn Ḥanbal, Aḥmad, 153
Ibn Hishām, 80, 81, 118
Ibn Isḥāq, 118
Sīrat al-Nābīy, 80
Ibn Kathīr
al-Bidāya wa al-Nihāya, 78
Ibn Sīnā, 184–5, 187, 194
Ibn Ṭaymiyya, 143
al-Ṣūfiyya wa al-Fuqarā, 147
Ibn al-Waḥshiyya
al-Filāḥa an-Nabaṭiyya, 197
Ibrāhīm b. Adham, 153
ijāza documents, 92
Ikhwān al-Ṣafā, 10, 62
ʿilm-i ḥāl genre, 76, 116–18
'immutable essences' (*aʿyān-i sābite*), 146
India, 90
al-insān al-kāmil ('the Perfect Man'), 181, 192
Iran, 10, 90, 91–2, 209
and Ibn al-ʿArabī, 142, 143
Iraq, 90
ʿIrāqī, 55
İskender b. Hācı Paşa, 32, 33, 34–7, 41–3, 61, 64
and *namāzgāh*, 207
Islam, 1–2, 9–10, 123–5
and Anatolia, 20, 90–1
and apocalypticism, 162–3, 166–9
and Christianity, 7, 23, 102–3, 110–14, 207–8
and community identity, 114–15
and dogmatics, 137–8
and elites, 115–16
and *fetvās*, 122–3
and *ġazā*, 101
and Gelibolu, 4–5, 108–10
and Ibn al-ʿArabī, 138–44
and morality, 182
and Ottomans, 209–10
and salvation, 118
and vernacular, 21–2
and Yazıcıoğlus, 5–6
see also Shīʿism; Sufism; Sunnī Islam
Ismāʿīl, Shāh, 155, 209
'Israelite lore' (*isrāʾīliyyāt*), 77–9
Isrāfīl (angel), 89
Istanbul *see* Constaninople
Italians, 109; *see also* Venice
Ivan Alexander of Bulgaria, Tsar, 106
İz, Fahir, 16
İzniqī, Mūsā, 83
İzniqī, Qutbu'd-dīn
Muqaddime, 76, 116–18, 124–5

Jacob, 192
Jacobites, 121
Jāmī, ʿAbdu'r-raḥmān, 142
Jandī, Muʿayyad al-Dīn, 55, 140–1
Sharḥ Fuṣūṣ, 144–5, 146
Jesus Christ, 110, 111–12, 116, 118–21
and apocalypticism, 162, 163, 164, 165
jewels, 3, 180
jihād, 124, 128
Jihānshāh, 156
jinn, 189
John V Palaiologos, Emperor, 105, 106, 107
John VI Kantakouzenos, Emperor, 100, 105
Joseph, 149–50, 192
Joshua, 188
Judaism, 77–8, 113
Jurjānī, Sayyid Sharīf, 9, 47–9, 69n49, 84, 92, 148
and al-Zamakhsharī, 93

Kaʿb al-Aḥbār, 77–8, 89
Kadıköyü, 39–40
Kafadar, Cemal, 127
Between Two Worlds, 101–2
Kāfiyajī, 92
Kahraman, Ahmet, 16

kalām (rational theology), 85, 143, 146, 149
Kallipolis *see* Gelibolu
Kaptein, Laban, 15, 17
Apocalypse and the Antichrist Dajjāl in Islam, 163–4, 165
Karaman, 6, 54
Karamustafa, Ahmet, 19, 154
Karataş, Hasan, 19
Karbalā, 159–60, 161
al-Kashgharī', Maḥmūd
Dīwān lughāt al-Turk, 87
Kāshifī, Ḥusayn Vā'iẓ
Majālis-i Va'ẓ, 87
Rawḍat al-Shuhadā, 159
Kātib Çelebi, 14, 47, 87
Kaygusuz, Abdāl, 19, 160
Khalidov, Anas, 92
Khurasan, 9, 90, 91–3, 142, 154
Khvāfī, Ḥaydar Haravī, 5, 46, 92
al-Khwāfī, Bishr, 153
al-Kisā'ī, Muḥammad ibn 'Abdullāh, 79, 96n19, 118, 119–20
Kitābü'l-Müntehā ('The Utmost') (Yazīcīoğlu, Aḥmed), 3, 4, 12, 8–9, 60–1, 137, 138
and Hajj, 63–4
and Shī'ism, 156–7
and Sufism, 151
and warfare, 128
Knysh, Alexander, 143
Konstantin the Philosopher, 39
Köprülü, Fuad, 18, 102
Kosovo, 6, 60
Kritovoulos, 126
Krsti , Tijana, 19, 124
Kubraviyya, 156
al-Kūfī, Jihād, 153
Kut, Günay, 185
Kutlar, Fatma, 16
Kydones, Demetrius, 108
De Non Redenda Gallipoli, 106–7

Lane, Andrew, 83
Lapseki, 100, 110
Laṭīfī, 111–12
Tezkire, 7
Le Gall, Dina, 19
legal texts (*fetāvā*), 77, 86, 122–3
Lindner, Rudi, 102
Lowry, Heath, 102
Luqmān, 76

Ma'azoğlu Hasan, Beypazarılı
Cenadil Qal'esi, 160
McGinn, Bernard
Visions of the End, 161–2
Madanī, Abu Hāzim, 153
madhhab, 91, 92
Madyan tribe, 120
Maghārib al-Zamān (Yazīcīoğlu, Meḥmed), 2–3, 8, 11
and classification, 75–6
and completion, 58–9
and Islam, 123–5
and patterns, 90–4
and prophet stories, 118–22
and sources, 74–5, 76–88
maghāriba (Westerners), 152
maghāzī ('battles') texts, 80
Magnus, Albertus, 187
Mahdī, 160, 163, 164, 170
Maḥmūd Paşa, 112, 116
Makkī, Abū Ṭālib, 148
Malāmatiyya, 152
Malāmiyya, 154
malḥama (omen science) tradition, 33, 196–9
Malḥamat Dāniyāl ('The Omens of Daniel'), 196
Mālik b. Dīnār, 153
Malkara, 56–7
Mamluks *see* Egypt
'Man-World' ('World of Man') (*insān 'ālemi*), 192–4, 199–200
Manuel II Palaiologos, Emperor, 108, 127
Dialogues with a Persian, 51, 110–11
maqtals, 159–60
al-Marghīnānī, Burhān al-dīn, 92
al-Hidāya, 93, 97n43, 98n55
al-Marghinānī, Niẓām al-Dīn
Jawāhir al-Fiqh, 86, 122
Markiewicz, Christopher, 18
Marv, 90
Masad, Mohammad, 162
mashāriqa (Easterners), 152

Māturīdī, 47, 143, 145, 146, 147
Mecca, 119
Meddāḥ, Yūsuf-i
  Maqtel-i Hüseyn, 159
Medina, 119
medreses, 9, 84, 93
Meḥmed, ʿĀlim, 150–1
Meḥmed Beg, 105
Meḥmed I, Sultan, 4, 82–3
Meḥmed II, Sultan, 6, 30, 43, 56
  and apocalypticism, 168, 169, 170–1
  and patron of arts, 201
  and religion, 113
Mélikoff, Irène, 18
Melvin-Koushki, Matthew, 18
Ménage, Victor, 16
Mevleviyye, 152
Michael (angel), 89
Michael IX, Emperor, 105
microcosm, 191–5, 200
Mihailović, Konstantin, 112, 116, 127
Mir-Kasimov, Orkhan, 18
mirabilia tradition, 183
al-Miṣrī, Dhū al-Nūn, 153
Mongols, 20
months of the year, 188–9, 196–8
morality, 182, 185, 188
Morea, 6
Moses, 119, 188
Muḥammad (Prophet), 8, 76, 79–81
  and Jesus, 110, 111–12, 116, 118–20
Muḥammad b. Wasiʿ, 153
Muḥammediyye (Yazīcīoğlu, Meḥmed), 2, 5, 8, 12, 39
  and Blond People, 178n96
  and classification, 75–6
  and composition, 59
  and Islam, 123–5
  and patterns, 90–4
  and prophet stories, 118–22
  and Shīʿism, 158–9
  and sources, 73–5, 76–88
Muhanna, Elias, 183
Munkar, 124
Muntaner, Ramón
  Crónica, 105
Müntehā see *Kitābü'l-Müntehā*
Murād I, Sultan, 37, 38, 106, 107
Murād II, Sultan, 6, 30, 36–7, 51–2, 56–7
  and Aḥmed-i Ḫāṣṣ, 58
  and Gelibolu, 108–9
  and Sufism, 54
  and Varna, 102
Mūsā Çelebi, 39, 49
Musannifek, 48, 84
Muscovy, 209
Muslims *see* Islam
Muṣṭafā ʿĀlī
  Künhü'l-Aḫbār, 34
Muṣṭafā, Düzme, 108

Nakīr, 124
Naqshbandiyya, 19, 142, 152
natural philosophy, 24, 181–3, 185, 188, 201, 208–9
Nehcü'l-Ferādis ('The Clear Path to Heaven'), 125–6
Nesīmī, Seyyid, 54
Neşri, 127
Nestor-Iskander
  Tale of the Taking of Tsargrad, 170
Nestorians, 120–1
Niʿmatullāh, Shāh, 10
Nishapur, 90, 91
Niẓāmī, 31
Noah, 119
Nūrbakhsh, Sayyid, 10
Nūrbakhshīs, 18

Ocak, Ahmet Yaşar, 19, 49, 114
Oktay Uslu, Zeynep, 19
omens, 196–8
Orḫān, Sultan, 56, 100, 141
Oruç Beg, 126
Ottomans, 29–30, 134n60
  and administrators, 55–8
  and borderlands, 5
  and Civil War, 39–40
  and conquests, 1–2, 6–7
  and elites, 41, 64–5
  and expansion, 200–1
  and Islam, 209–10
  and navy, 37–8
  and palace library, 19–20
  and politics, 31–2

and warfare, 101–2, 127–9
and Yazıcıoğlus, 206–9

Palamas, Gregory, 110, 127
Paradise, 193
Park, Katharine, 187
Pārsā, Muḥammad, 142
Peacock, A. C. S., 19, 20, 124–5, 160
people of wisdom (*ehl-i ḥikmet*), 187
'Perfect Man', 181, 192
piety, 5, 18–19, 73–4, 209
pilgrimage, 117; *see also* Hajj
plague, 125–6, 200
plants, 189–90
Plato, 187
Plethon, Gemistos, 111
'popular religion', 21–2
prayer, 76, 117, 124
preaching manuals (*va'ẓ*), 77, 87
prophet stories, 75, 76, 77–9, 118–22
and Ibn al-'Arabī, 139–40, 149–50
and 'Man-World', 192
Pythagoras, 199

Qādīkhān, Fakhru'd-in Hasan, 92
Fatāwā, 86, 122
Qādiriyya, 54–5
Qara Memi Celebi, 56
al-Qaranī, Uways, 153
Qāshānī, 'Abd al-Razzāq, 141
Istilāḥāt al-Ṣūfiyya, 151
Sharḥ Manāzil, 155
al-Qāsim Bābur, Abū, 156
Qaṣṣāboğlu 'Alī, 7–8, 32, 35–8, 40–1, 64, 207
and Gelibolu, 107
Qassāboğlu Maḥmūd Paşa, 32–3, 43–4, 56–7, 61, 64, 207
and Gelibolu, 100
al-Qassār, Ḥamdūn, 154
Qayṣerī, Dāvūd-i, 141, 192
al-Qazwīnī, Abū Zakariyā, 8
'Ajā'ib al-Makhlūqāt wa Gharā'ib al-Mawjūdāt ('The Wonders of Creation and the Oddities of Existing Things'), 3, 181, 183–4, 185–7, 188, 189
qiṣaṣ al-anbiyā see prophet stories

Qūj, 192
al-Qūnawī, Ṣadr al-dīn, 55, 192
Miftāḥ Ghayb al-Jam' wa Tafsīlihi, 140–1
Naqsh al-Fuṣūṣ, 142, 146
Qur'an, 5, 76–7, 194–5
Ṣūrat al-Mā'ida, 121
quṭb, 200

Raby, Julian, 201
rāfıẓīs, 157–8
Ramadan, 124
Rawshanī, Dede 'Umar, 141–3
al-Rāzī, Fakhr al-Dīn, 89, 92, 124, 148
Mafātīḥ al-Ghayb, 84–5, 93
Repp, Richard, 19
Resurrection, 4, 76, 86
revelation, 196–9, 201
Rif'at, Aḥmed
Luğat-i Tarihiyye ve Coğrafiye, 71n84
Risāletü'l-İslām, 124, 125
Rum, 54
Rumelia, 2, 5, 19, 33–43; *see also* Gelibolu
Rūmī, Eşrefoğlu, 10, 54–5
Müzekkī'n-Nüfūs ('Purifier of Souls'), 195
Ṭarīqatnāme, 52–3
Rūmī, Jalālu'd-dīn, 20, 55
Rūmī, Muṣliḥu'd-dīn Hocazāde, 48

'sacred words' (*qudsī kelīmeler*), 86
Sa'd b. Abī Waqqās, 157
al-Ṣādiq, Ja'far, 148, 153, 198
Ṣafaviyya, 54, 152, 153–4, 155–6
al-Saghānī, Raḍīy al-Dīn Ḥasan, 89
al-Mashāriq al-Anwār, 85, 91, 93, 98n55
Şahin, Kaya, 15, 17
'Constantinople and the End Time', 164–5, 171
Sa'īd b. Zayd, 157
al-Sakhāwī, 170
Ṣāliḥ (prophet), 78–9
salvation, 118, 123, 135n67
Samarqand, 9, 90, 92
al-Ṣamarqandī, Abū-Layth, 82–3, 86, 89, 92, 96n34
al-Saqaṭī, Sariy, 153

al-Saqsīnī, Sulaymān ibn Dawūd (al-Sūwarī) , 89–90, 94
  Zahrat al-Riyāḍ, 87–8, 158
Ṣarı ʿAbdullāh
  Semerātü'l-Fuād, 34
Ṣaruca Beg, 33, 37–40, 61, 64, 107
Saruḫan, 106
al-Ṣayyād, 162
Şāzī of Kastamonu
  Destān-i Maqtel-i Hüseyn, 159, 160
Schamiloglu, Uli, 125–6
Schiltberger, Johannes, 107, 108
self-effacement, 66n1
Seljuqs, 20, 90–1, 104
Semerāt, 51–2
Şemsiyye ('Solar [poem]') (Yazıcıoğlu, Ṣāliḥ) , 2, 3, 7–8, 11, 35–7
  and cosmology, 180–1
  and *malḥama* tradition, 196–7, 198–9
sense perception (*naẓar*), 187, 188
sevāb (divine compensation), 124
Şeyḫī of Kütahya, 33, 53–4
Shāfiʿī, Imām, 153
Shāfiʿī jurisprudence, 9–10
Shāhrukh, 9, 92
Shaqīq, Abū ʿAlī, 153
sharʿīa, 93
*shaykh*s, 151–4
Shīʿism, 23, 87–8, 155–61, 208, 209
Shuʿayb, 120, 150
Sigismund of Hungary, King, 107
Signs of the Hour, 162, 164, 165, 166, 168
Sikkīnī, Dede ʿÖmer, 53, 154
Simavī, Bedre'd-dīn, 92
Sinān Paşa, 100
sīra sources, 79–81, 118
Siraj al-Qulūb, 125
Sirhindī, Aḥmad, 142
Solomon, 119, 121
Ṣomuncu Baba, 10, 50–1, 54
soul, 194–5
Spain, 152, 209
Subtelny, Maria Eva, 92
Sufism, 3, 6, 10, 18–19, 60, 210
  and Anatolia, 50–2, 61, 65
  and Bayramiyye, 148–9
  and bewilderment, 187, 188
  and community, 151–5
  and Dervīş Bāyezīd, 45
  and hierarchies, 32
  and Ibn Ṭaymiyya, 147
  and mysticism, 195
  and philosophy of man, 192
  and *ṭarīqa*, 52–5
  and 'the Perfect Man', 113–14
  see also Naqshbandiyya
al-Ṣufyānī, 162
Suhrawardī, Shihābu'd-dīn, 55
Şükrullāh, 127
Süleymān, Sultan, 64, 93, 106
Süleymān Çelebi, 39, 49
  Mevlīd, 80, 111–12, 118, 120
  Veṣīletü'n-necāt ('The Path of Safety'), 125–6
Sunnī Islam, 6, 19, 23, 73–4, 93, 155–61
Ṣūrat al-Fātiḥa, 89
Syria, 9–10, 90, 92, 166–7

al-Ṭabarī, 135n77
al-Tabrīzī, Walī al-Dīn Muḥammad
  Mishkāt al-Maṣābīḥ, 82
Taeschner, Franz, 16
tafsīr, 77, 81–6, 89
Taftazānī, Saʿd al-dīn, 9, 47, 48, 69n49, 92, 93
  Ḥāshiya al-Kashshāf, 84
  and Ibn al-ʿArabī, 145, 146
  Risāla fī waḥdat al-wujūd, 143–4
Tahir, Bursalı Meḥmed, 56
  ʿOsmanlı Mü'ellifleri, 39
taḥrīr, 109
al-Ṭāʾī, Dāvūd, 153
Ṭalḥa, 157
ṭarīqa, 52–5
Taşköprüzāde
  al-Shaqāʾiq al-Nuʿmāniyya, 92
Terzi Ṣaruca Paşa, 100
Terzioğlu, Derin, 19, 116–17
al-Thaʿlabī, Abū Isḥāq Aḥmad
  Arāʾis al-Majālis fī Qiṣaṣ al-Anbiyā, 78–9
Thamūd, 78–9
Thawrī, Ṣufyān, 153
thought (*fikr*), 187, 188
Thrace, 7, 13, 22, 32, 104–5; *see also* Gelibolu

Index

al-Tiflīsī, Abū al-Fażl Ḥubaysh
Uṣūl al-Malāḥim ('The Principles of Omenology'), 33, 196, 198
time, 188–9, 196–8
Tīmūr, 1, 9, 30
Timurids, 18, 29, 155–6
Todorov, Tzvetan, 183
Togan, Zeki Velidi, 87
Transoxania, 9, 91–2
Treasures of Knowledge: An Inventory of the Ottoman Palace Library (1502/3–1503/4) (Necipoğlu/Kafadar/Fleischer), 19–20
Trebizond, 112
Tribe of Israel, 188–9
Turka, Sa'īn al-dīn, 10, 18, 94, 142
Turkish language, 7–8
Turks, 104–5, 106, 109
Turner, Frederick Jackson
The Frontier in American History, 103
Tus, 90
Ṭūsī, Molla Naṣīr al-Dīn, 47, 48, 86, 88, 91
Twelver Shī'ism, 156

Uğur, Abdullah, 18
'ulamā, 5
'Umar, 156–7
Umur b. Demirtaş, 83
Umūr Beg, 105
Unity of Existence, 145, 146, 147–8
Usluer, Faith, 18
'Uthmān, 156–7
Uzjandī, Jalāl al-dīn Khujandī, 144–5
Uzunçarşılı, İsmail Hakkı, 19, 34–5, 42

vafq (magic squares), 185
Valī, Shāh Ni'matullāh, 142
Varna, 6, 8, 60, 102, 170
and Battle of, 54, 136n93
Venice, 4, 7, 100, 108, 131n18, 169
visionary 'states' (*aḥvāl*), 191–2
Visions of Daniel, 167, 169–70
Vladislav of Hungary, King, 136n93, 170

Wahb ibn Munabbih, 77–8
Wansbrough, John, 118, 135n67
warfare, 101–2, 127–9; *see also* holy wars
wisdom, 187
Wittek, Paul
Rise of the Ottoman Empire, 101, 102
wonder (*'ajab*), 183–91
wujūdī, 146, 147, 148, 149

Yazdī, Sharaf al-dīn 'Alī, 18, 94
Yazıcıoğlu, Aḥmed Bīcān, 3–8
'Acāibü'l-Maḫlūqāt, 8, 12, 182, 183–91, 200
and apocalypticism, 163–71
and Bayram Velī, 50, 52
and biography, 30–1
Cevhāhīrnāme ('Jewel-book'), 3, 9, 13, 61, 180
and community identity, 114–15
and confessionalisation, 101, 102
and cosmology, 181–3
and death, 125–7
and *Dürr-i Meknūn* ('The Hidden Pearl'), 13–17
and Gelibolu, 20–1, 29, 30
and hierarchies, 31–2
and Ibn al-'Arabī, 138–9, 144–51
and intellectual community, 32–3
and Islam, 23–4, 115–16
and later years, 60–1
and natural philosophy, 201
and Ottomans, 206–9
and patronage, 65
and popular religion, 21–2
and Qaṣṣāboğlu Maḥmūd, 43–4
Rūḥu'l-Ervāḥ ('The Spirit of Spirits'), 3, 9, 12–13, 181, 182, 191–5
and Shī'ism, 155–61
and sources, 22–3
and Sufism, 10–11, 151–5
and warfare, 127–9
see also *Būstānu'l-Ḥaqā'iq*; *Envārü'l-'Āşıqīn*; *Kitābü'l-Müntehā* ('The Utmost')
Yazıcıoğlu, Meḥmed, 3–8, 34, 39, 55–6
and apocalypticism, 163–71
and Bayram Velī, 50, 52
and biography, 30–1
and community identity, 114–15
and confessionalisation, 101, 102
and death, 60, 125–7

Yazıcıoğlu, Meḥmed *(cont.)*
and Dervīş Bāyezīd, 44–5
and Edirne, 46–8, 49
and Gelibolu, 20–1, 29, 30
and hierarchies, 31–2
and Ibn al-ʻArabī, 144–51
and intellectual community, 32–3
and Islam, 23–4, 115–16
and Ottomans, 206–9
and patronage, 65
and popular religion, 21–2
and Qaṣṣāboğlu family, 43–4, 57
and seclusion, 58–9, 100
Sharḥ Fuṣūṣu'l-Ḥikam ('Commentary on *Fuṣūṣ al-Ḥikam*'), 3, 12, 59, 137–8
and Shīʻism, 155–61
and sources, 22–3
and Sufism, 10–11
and travels, 62–3
and warfare, 127–9
and Zayn al-ʻArab, 45–6
see also *Maghārib al-Zamān*; *Muḥammediyye*
Yazıcıoğlu, Ṣaliḥ, 3–4, 33–43, 54, 61, 107
and Gelibolu, 29, 30
and hierarchies, 31–2
and patronage, 65
see also *Şemsiyye*
Yazıcıoğlu ʻAlī
Tevārīḫ-i Āl-i Selcūq, 36–7
Yerasimos, Stéphane, 15, 16–17, 121
Yıldız, Sara Nur, 19
Yılmaz, Hüseyin, 18

al-Zamakhsharī, Abū al-Qāsim Maḥmūd, 86, 92
al-Kashshāf, 83–4, 93, 98n55
Zayn al-ʻArab al-Nakhchivānī al-Miṣri, 5, 45–6, 91, 93
Sharḥ Maṣābīḥ al-Sunna, 82
Zbornik Popa Dragolia, 169–70
zekāt (almsgiving), 124
Zeyniyye, 54
Zeyrek, Molla, 54, 62
zikr (verbal remembrance), 124
Zubayr, 157

EU representative:
Easy Access System Europe
Mustamäe tee 50, 10621 Tallinn, Estonia
Gpsr.requests@easproject.com

www.ingramcontent.com/pod-product-compliance
Lightning Source LLC
Chambersburg PA
CBHW051114230426
43667CB00014B/2581
* 9 7 8 1 4 7 4 4 6 2 2 8 0 *